Kaua'i

Hanalei &
the North Shore
p136

Waimea Canyon &
the Westside
p206

Lihu'e
p82

...th Shore
79

Contents

PLAN YOUR TRIP

ON THE ROAD

MARK BOSTER /GETTY IMAGES ©

PRINCEVILLE P152

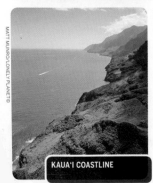

MATT MUNRO/LONELY PLANET ©

KAUA'I COASTLINE

ALEXANDER HOWARD/LONELY PLANET ©

Contents

KALAHEO P203

SPECIAL
FEATURES

Welcome to Kaua'i

Emerald mountains, weeping waterfalls, red-rock canyons, jaw-dropping beaches, clear seas and big waves. Kaua'i's natural gifts are unparalleled in Hawaii, the USA, the world.

Outdoor Adventure

With an astonishing list of outdoor adventures, Kaua'i will puncture your resort bubble. Here you can soar over and settle into tropical valleys in a helicopter, zip through treetops on a cable, navigate narrow single tracks to the shoulders of a sleeping giant or down deep into a grand canyon. You can paddle a sacred river or motor into sea caves, wander isolated beaches, drop in and get barrelled on a point break, or drift with sea turtles in coves saturated in that perfect blue. Each new experience merges unforgettably with the island's majesty.

Feel the Mana

The island inspires inward explorations too. On Kaua'i, the mana (spiritual essence) of the *'aina* (land) is palpable, because the values of the ancient Hawaiians are alive and well and rooted in a holistic understanding of the natural world. You will encounter this in simple ways, such as when someone gives you directions *mauka* (inland) or *makai* (seaward), or in a passing shaka (Hawaii hand greeting sign) when you yield on a one-lane bridge. Hawaiian culture is built on moderation, balance, fairness and unity, producing a gentle pace of life, strong families and legendary hospitality.

Island Way of Life

You can't help admiring the way that Kaua'i has preserved itself in the face of the 21st century. Here, no town surpasses 10,000 people. By law, no building is taller than a coconut tree, and it is impossible to circumnavigate the coast by car. When a multimillion-dollar ferry arrived to begin service to neighboring islands, Kaua'i residents, concerned over environmental and other issues, blocked its path. It never returned. Visitors do, however. That doesn't mean Kaua'i lacks challenges. There continue to be conflicts on the Westside over the dominance of big agriculture, but on the whole the island projects harmony.

Locally Grown

A 'locals only' ethos that flowered from surf culture and permeated the Hawaiian Islands influences social, political and commercial life on Kaua'i too. Happily, of late it also has influenced chefs, supermarkets and restaurants island-wide. Anywhere you eat on Kaua'i, from the fast food of Bubba's Burgers (p164) to JO2 (p119), the latest restaurant from renowned chef Jean Marie Josselin, you are likely to be feasting on sustainably grown meat and vegetables cultivated on the island by local farmers, or fish caught by local anglers just offshore. That freshness brings flavor you'll love, and it nourishes the local economy too.

Why I Love Kaua'i

by Adam Skolnick, Writer

It's the near perfect climate. No, it's the double rainbows and the warm blue seas that can carry a humpback whale's song on invisible underwater currents for upward of five miles. Scratch that, it's the Technicolor sunsets best enjoyed beer in hand. Or maybe it's the more subtle vibration of ease. On Kaua'i, the pace of life, the fun-loving locals, the plentiful, unrestricted parking (no, but seriously) and the pure nature offer the ability to access modern life from a harmonious perch. Which produces in most adult humans something approaching inner peace.

For more about our writers, see p288

Above: Na Pali Coast Wilderness State Park (p177)

Kaua'i

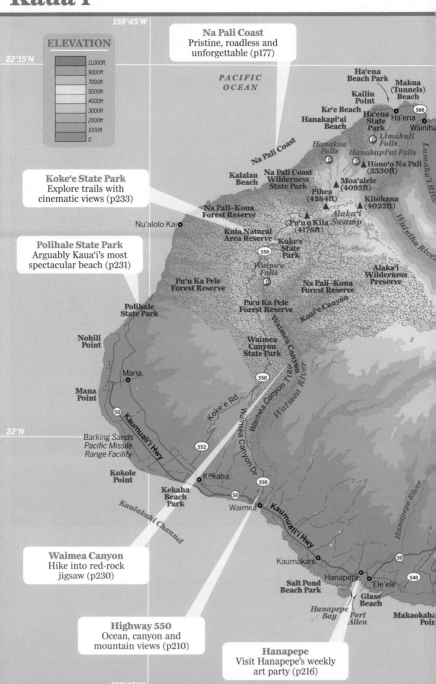

ELEVATION

11,000ft
9000ft
7000ft
5000ft
4000ft
3000ft
2000ft
1000ft
0

Na Pali Coast
Pristine, roadless and unforgettable (p177)

Koke'e State Park
Explore trails with cinematic views (p233)

Polihale State Park
Arguably Kaua'i's most spectacular beach (p231)

Waimea Canyon
Hike into red-rock jigsaw (p230)

Highway 550
Ocean, canyon and mountain views (p210)

Hanapepe
Visit Hanapepe's weekly art party (p216)

159°45'W

22°15'N

22°N

159°45'W

PACIFIC OCEAN

Ha'ena Beach Park
Makua (Tunnels) Beach
Kailiu Point
Ke'e Beach
Ha'ena State Park
Ha'ena
Wainiha
Hanakapi'ai Beach
Limahuli Falls
Na Pali Coast
Hanakoa Falls
Hanakapi'ai Falls
Hono'o Na Pali (3330ft)
Lumahai River
Wainiha River
Kalalau Beach
Na Pali Coast Wilderness State Park
Moa'alele (4095ft)
Kilohana (4022ft)
Pihea (4284ft)
Alaka'i Swamp
Na Pali–Kona Forest Reserve
Pu'u o Kila (4176ft)
Koke'e State Park
Alaka'i Wilderness Preserve
Nu'alolo Kai
Knia Natural Area Reserve
550
Waipo'o Falls
Na Pali–Kona Forest Reserve
Koai'a Canyon
Pu'u Ka Pele Forest Reserve
Polihale State Park
Pu'u Ka Pele Forest Reserve
Nohili Point
Waimea Canyon State Park
550
Mana
Mana Point
50
Kaumuali'i Hwy
Koke'e Rd
Waimea Canyon Trail
Waimea Canyon
Waimea River
Barking Sands Pacific Missile Range Facility
552
Kokole Point
Kekaha
550
Waimea Canyon Dr
Kekaha Beach Park
Waimea
550
50
Kaumuali'i Hwy
Kaulakahi Channel
Hanapepe River
Kaumakani
50
Hanapepe
Ele'ele
540
Salt Pond Beach Park
Glass Beach
Hanapepe Bay
Port Allen
Makaokaha'i Point

N 0 ——— 10 km
0 ——— 5 miles

159°30'W
159°15'W

22°15'N

Hanalei Bay
Surf, stroll, sunbathe, repeat (p159)

Princeville
Take a helicopter tour of Kaua'i (p152)

Kilauea Point National Wildlife Refuge

Kauapea (Secrets) Beach

Kilauea Point

Hanalei
Hunt vintage art and fashion (p158)

Pali Ke Kua (Hideaways) Beach

'Anini Beach Park

...maha'i ...each

Princeville

Kalihiwai Bay

Kahili (Rock Quarry) Beach

Kepuhi Point

Larsen's Beach

Kuhio Hwy

Kalihiwai

Kalihiwai Beach

Hanalei Bay

Hanalei

Kilauea

Moloa'a Beach

Hanalei National Wildlife Refuge

56

Ko'olau Rd

'Aliomanu Beach

.t Mamalahoa (3745ft)

Kalihiwai River

Hanalei River

Moloa'a Forest Reserve

Kealia Forest Reserve

Kalalea Mountain

Anahola Beach Park

Halelea Forest Reserve

Anahola

56

'Ahihi Point

Paliku (Donkey) Beach

Makaleha Mountains

Moalepe Stream

Mt Wai'ale'ale (5148ft)

Kapukaiki (849ft)

Kealia

Kealia Beach

Opaeka'a Stream

Nounou Mtn (Sleeping Giant) (1241ft)

Kapa'a

Kapa'a Beach Park

Mt Kawaikini (5243ft)

Wailua River (North Fork)

581

Waipouli

56

Alakukui Point

Kaholalele Falls

Opaeka'a Falls

580

Wailua

Wailua Bay

Wailua River (South Fork)

Wailua River State Park

Lydgate Beach Park

Mt Kahili (3089ft)

Wailua Falls

583

Wailua River
Paddle Kaua'i's most sacred river (p107)

22°N

Kuhio Hwy

Hanama'ulu

Hanama'ulu Bay

56

Lihu'e
Wander laid-back, local Lihu'e (p82)

Puhi

50

Lihu'e

Kaumuali'i Hwy

Kipu Falls

Kalapaki Beach

Nawiliwili Bay

Maha'ulepu Heritage Trail
Cliffs, blowholes, pristine beaches (p180)

Lawa'i

50

Omao

Waita Reservoir

520

Kalaheo

530

Koloa

Kawelikoa Point

Ha'ula Beach

Kawailoa Bay

Maha'ulepu Coast

Spouting Horn Beach Park

Po'ipu Beach Park

Po'ipu

Maha'ulepu Beach

Shipwreck Beach

Makahuena Point

Ka'ie'ie waho Channel

Po'ipu
Kaua'i's sun-drenched beach town (p189)

Tropical Botanical Gardens
The magnificent island landscape decoded (p194)

Po'ipu Beach Park
An underwater universe awaits (p192)

159°15'W

Kaua'i's
Top 15

Na Pali Coast

1 The sight of the primordial Na Pali Coast (p49) rising out of the sea, with its knife-edge pinnacles and alluring valleys, is a gripping backdrop for any adventurer attracted to the sea or trail. For high-octane thrills, zip around sea caves in a Zodiac, seek out your inner Iron Man on a 12-hour, 17-mile sea kayak journey or hump a pack along the Kalalau Trail. Prefer more luxury? Sail comfortably aboard a steady catamaran. Mai tai included.

Waimea Canyon

2 Absorb the grand vistas from roadside lookouts and wilderness trails in Waimea Canyon (p230). Nicknamed the Grand Canyon of the Pacific by Mark Twain when he visited all those many moons ago, this red-rock jigsaw looks the part. In the wet season the walls and ledges grow green and the rocks weep with waterfalls. Adventurers take note. You can hike down to the canyon floor and camp there too. But whoever goes down must hike up!

Hanalei Bay

3 Kaua'i's pre-eminent horseshoe bay is the ultimate destination for many travelers. Surf gods such as the late Andy Irons and legendary Laird Hamilton built their reps on its half-dozen surf breaks. But even if you aren't here for waves, the beach, with its wide sweep of cream-colored sand and magnificent jade mountain views, will entice you into long walks along the shore, and longer naps in the shade. Black Pot Beach Park (Hanalei Pier; p159)

Koke'e State Park

4 The combination of Koke'e State Park's (p233) Nu'alolo Trail, Nu'alolo Cliffs Trail and Awa'awapuhi Trail is enough to satisfy the most adventurous trailblazer. Those strenuous climbs with hair-raising drops on both sides promise breathtaking views. There's also a long boardwalk through the Alaka'i Swamp, a misty primordial bog and bird-watcher's paradise at the very top of the mountains. If you follow it to the end, you'll have walked 15 miles and reached Mt Wai'ale'ale, the wettest place on earth. Alaka'i Swamp Trail (p235)

Kayaking the Wailua River

5 Once home to ancient Hawaiian royalty, the state's only fully navigable river (p113) still holds the mystique and allure that has drawn generations up these sacred waters. Encounter heiau (ancient stone temples), come ashore for a short trek to a 'secret' waterfall, swim, then dry out in the sun. Though experienced kayakers may opt to go it alone, several companies offer guided tours that reveal the river's unique history. No experience required. Kids can come too.

Po'ipu

6 Perhaps a bit too planned and manicured for some, sunny Po'ipu (p189) is the heart of South Shore and plenty beautiful and wild too. Its beaches and bays are ideal for small children and beginning snorkelers, its surf breaks a bit less crowded, and dive sites unmatched. Shopping and dining can likewise be wonderful, and the sunsets absolutely glorious. Po'ipu Beach Park (p192)

Polihale State Park

7 A spiritual beach – that, in essence, is Polihale (p231). Ancient Hawaiians thought so, and nothing has changed. The broad and sprawling sands, the vast Pacific and the nearby, mighty Na Pali cliffs together spell eternity. There are a number of great beaches on Kaua'i, but none inspire reflection in quite the same way, making this the perfect spot to relax and reflect after a lengthy hike or a busy trip. Suitably, it's at the end of a long, bumpy dirt road.

Hankering for Art in Hanapepe

8 Every Friday is Art Night in the historic Westside town of Hanapepe (p219), when galleries open late and the main street is awash with people hankering for art and a good time. This Old West looka-like is worth a trip on any day; just make sure you stop by Angela Headley Fine Art & Island Art Gallery (p217) for some of the best art Hawaii has to offer, and Japanese Grandma (p221) for top-shelf sushi.

Flying Kaua'i

9 Seeing Kaua'i from the air (p74) is a singular experience that may just define your trip. In fact, it's the only way to see much of the island, the majority of which is privately owned. If you really want to get up close and personal, opt for a helicopter tour, where you can fly much lower and can hover. It's a thrilling experience, one you might want to have at all costs (and it will cost you).

National Tropical Botanical Gardens

10 You don't need a green thumb to enjoy the Garden Island's spectacular National Tropical Botanical Gardens (p194). At its flagship Allerton Garden in Po'ipu, you'll find one man's Shangri La – landscape art that manages to improve on Mother Nature. The vast and unmanicured McBryde Garden provides contrast next door. Then there's the North Shore's Limahuli Garden, nestled mid-valley in Ha'ena's dramatic topography.
Allerton Garden (p189)

Shopping Spree in Hanalei

11 Quirky mixed-media sculpture, refined oil paintings, high-end beach fashion, masks and spears carved by Asmat warriors, the cutest bikinis and the most luscious lotions – designed and crafted on the island – and some spectacular vintage mid-century heirlooms can all be found in the storefronts and boutiques lined up in a hedgerow along Kuhio Hwy in Hanalei (p168). If you're beached out and the trails aren't calling, it's time for some retail therapy.

Snorkeling & Diving the South Shore

12 The South Shore is a wonderland of underwater sights. Here are lava caves and ledges home to resident monk seals, and napping turtles and sharks, and rock reefs home to all manner of tropical fish. If you're lucky, you may meet a passing spinner dolphin pod or hear whale song in the wintertime. Beginner snorkelers should hit Po'ipu Beach Park (p192). Advanced freedivers enjoy Koloa Landing (p195). Scuba divers should call Seasport Divers (p118). All will amaze. Honu (green sea turtle; p261)

Highway 550

13 The island's signature scenic drive (p210), this long ascent takes you from one end of Waimea Canyon to another. And yet you're only halfway there. Next comes Koke'e State Park, whose lookouts are the stuff of postcards, never mind numerous Hollywood films. Along the way you can stretch your legs with a number of short hikes, enough to whet your appetite for legendary trails and enviable photo ops. Waimea Canyon (p230)

Maha'ulepu Heritage Trail

14 This stunning trail (p180) takes you from the popular, more manicured, beaches of Po'ipu onto a far wilder stretch of coast, full of secluded coves, snorkeling reefs, blow holes and dramatic sea cliffs. Experienced South Shore surfers and kite surfers can be seen carving the shallow reef break offshore. It's a 4-mile PhD in geology, too, culminating in the fascinating Makauwahi Sinkhole (p193), where you enter the *Land of the Lost*. Don't worry, you'll find your way back – if you must.

Lihu'e

15 Lihu'e (p83) is easy to overlook. To many it's a drive-through commercial corridor, a place to land, scoop up a rental car and zoom away. But tucked away in amid its throwback downtown are laid-back attractions – including a terrific museum, local eateries, and neighborhoods punctuated by mid-century residential architecture. If you want to experience all the island has to offer, a stroll through Lihu'e is mandatory. Hula dancers at a Lihu'e festival (p92)

Need to Know

For more information, see Survival Guide (p267)

Currency
US dollar ($)

Language
English, Hawaiian

Visas
Rules for US entry keep changing. Confirm current visa and passport requirements for your country at the US Department of State website (www.travel.state.gov).

Money
ATMs are available in all major towns. Visa and MasterCard are widely accepted. American Express and Discover hit or miss.

Mobile Phones
Cell reception good except in remote locations. Only tri- or quad-band models work in the USA.

Time
Hawaiian Standard Time (GMT/UTC minus 10 hours)

When to Go

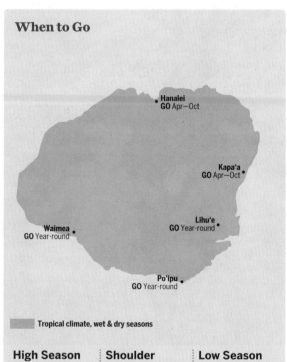

Tropical climate, wet & dry seasons

High Season
(Jun–Sep)

➡ Accommodation prices skew high.

➡ Beaches are busy with families.

➡ North Shore seas are calm.

Shoulder
(Dec–Mar)

➡ Surf is way up on the North Shore and Westside.

➡ Whales arrive and are visible from the land and sea.

➡ Prices are highest around the holidays.

Low Season
(Apr–May, Oct–Nov)

➡ Crowds thin, prices drop.

➡ Festivals abound across the island.

➡ Beaches are empty even though the weather is often perfect.

Useful Websites

Lonely Planet (lonelyplanet.com/usa/hawaii/kauai) Destination information, hotel bookings, traveler forum and more.

Kauai Surfrider (https://kauai.surfrider.org) Insights on the state of Kaua'i's waters and the chance to volunteer with local riders to clean up beaches.

The Garden Island (www.thegardenisland.com) Pick up a copy or read online for details on events and local politics.

Kauai Explorer (www.kauaiexplorer.com) Great site for ocean reports, trail information and beach tips.

County of Kaua'i (www.kauai.gov/HoloHolo2020) Explore the progress of the HoloHolo 2020 initiative. A blend of sustainability, transportation, social and infrastructure programs.

Important Numbers

Hawaii's area code (☎808) is optional for local calls and compulsory when calling between islands. Dial 1 before toll-free or long-distance calls, including to Canada (for which international rates apply).

USA's country code	☎1
International access code	☎011
Operator	☎1
Emergency (ambulance, fire & police)	☎911
Directory assistance	☎411

Exchange Rates

Australia	A$1	$0.74
Canada	C$1	$0.73
Europe	€1	$1.11
Japan	¥100	$0.89
New Zealand	NZ$1	$0.69
UK	UK£1	$1.29

For current exchange rates, see www.xe.com.

Daily Costs

Budget: Less than $150

➡ B&B or inn within a town: $70–100

➡ Grocery shopping and farmers markets: $20–40

➡ Kaua'i Bus: $4–8

Midrange: $150–300

➡ Hotel room, condo or B&B: $100–275

➡ Meals at midrange restaurants: $30–50

➡ Rental car: $40–50

Top End: More than $300

➡ Hotel, resort or vacation rental: from $275

➡ Fine dining with three-course meals: from $40

➡ Diving, golf, spa, helicopter tour, sunset cruises: from $200

➡ Rental car: $50–70

Opening Hours

Standard opening hours year-round are as follows:

Banks 8:30am–4pm Monday to Friday, some to 6pm Friday, and 9am–noon or 1pm Saturday

Bars & Clubs to midnight daily, some to 2am Thursday to Saturday

Businesses 8:30am–4:30pm Monday to Friday, some post offices 9am–noon Saturday

Restaurants breakfast 6–10am, lunch 11:30am–2:30pm, dinner 5–9:30pm

Shops 9am–5pm Monday to Saturday, some also noon-5pm Sunday

Arriving in Kaua'i

Lihu'e Airport Car-rental companies located at airport; almost all visitors to Kaua'i rent cars from these agencies. Kaua'i Bus (p274) makes limited runs from airport ($2). Taxis usually run during the day; plan ahead if arriving at night. Taxis can be found curbside outside the baggage-claim area. Average fares from Lihu'e Airport include Kapa'a ($25), Lihu'e ($10), Po'ipu ($40–50) and Princeville ($89–119). There is no uber in Kaua'i, and taxis can be hard to get and expensive. In almost all cases, you are better off renting a car. For families or groups, it may be more economical to book an airport shuttle with **Speedi Shuttle** (p277).

For much more on **getting around**, see p20.

Accommodations

Types of Accommodations

Vacation Rentals

➡ There are a ton of vacation homes for rent on Kaua'i. These range from simple plantation-style cottages to five-bed affairs fit for a king.

➡ Some have great views of the ocean while others are inland.

➡ Like condos, they are rented for longer periods of three to seven days. Cleaning fees often apply.

➡ Negotiate the price.

➡ Vacation rentals offer privacy, a kitchen (or kitchenette) and your own parking space, so you don't have to do the resort marathon. They can also be a real money saver, as you don't have to eat out all the time. There is typically a separate cleaning fee. Make sure you know who to call if there is a problem, as many vacation rentals have nonresident owners.

➡ The best online sources for vacation rentals are Vacation Rentals By Owner (www.vrbo.com) and Craigslist (http://honolulu.craigslist.org/kau/). FlipKey (www.flipkey.com) contains both agency and private listings, as well as helpful reviews.

➡ On paper, tourist accommodations on Kaua'i are only allowed in designated areas, such as Po'ipu, Princeville and Kapa'a. You don't need to be worried about this unless there's a crackdown. If the situation changes, government-approved rentals have a Transit Vacation Rental (TVR) number.

Camping

At all public campgrounds on Kaua'i, camping permits must be obtained and paid for in advance; they are *not* issued in person at campgrounds. Book as far ahead as possible for popular campgrounds, such as the Na Pali Coast.

State park campgrounds can be found in Na Pali Coast State Wilderness Park, Koke'e State Park and Polihale State Park. Permits are required; obtain them up to a year in advance from the Division of State Parks (p227), online or in person. Fees cost $18 to $30 per campsite per night (or $20 per person per night on the Na Pali Coast); maximum-stay limits of three to five nights at each campground are enforced.

For remote backcountry camping on the Westside, the Division of Forestry & Wildlife (p227) issues permits for four campgrounds in Waimea Canyon, three campgrounds (Sugi Grove, Kawaikoi and Waikoali) in and around Koke'e State Park, and the Wai'alae Cabin campground near the Alaka'i Wilderness Preserve. Camping fees are the same as for state parks; maximum-stay limits also apply.

Of the seven county parks with campgrounds, the most pleasant are Ha'ena Beach Park, Black Pot Beach Park (Hanalei Pier) and 'Anini Beach Park on the North Shore, and Salt Pond Beach Park on the Westside. Campgrounds are subject to regular weekly closures (exact days vary by campground).

County camping permits cost $3 per night per nonresident adult camper (children under 18 years are free) and are issued by mail (at least one month in advance) or in person at the Division of Parks & Recreation (p100). Permits can also be obtained in person at four satellite locations: **Hanapepe Neighborhood Center** (☑808-335-3731; www.kauai.gov; 4451 Pu'olo Rd; ☺7:45-4:30pm Mon-Tue & Thu-Sun); **Kalaheo Neighborhood Center** (☑808-332-9770; 480 Papalina Rd; ☺noon-4pm Mon-Fri); **Kapa'a Neighborhood Center**

(☎808-822-1931; www.kauai.gov; 4491 Kou St; ☺7:45am-4:30pm Mon-Fri); and **Kilauea Neighborhood Center** (☎808-828-1421; 2460 Keneke St; ☺8am-noon Mon-Fri). For mail-in permits, only cashier's checks or money orders are accepted for payment, not cash. Do not camp on private property.

Many of the state parks also have cabins. Kind of like camping, because they are so rustic. Kauai Camper Rental (p277) rents VW Westfalia's and camp gear.

Grand Hyatt Kauai Resort & Spa

Booking Accommodations

Lonely Planet (lonelyplanet.com/usa/kaua'i/hotels) Recommendations and bookings.

Parrish Collection Kaua'i (www.parrishkauai.com) Good collection of house and condo rentals.

Po'ipu Beach Resort Association (www.poipubeach.org/places-to-stay/condominium-resorts) Overview of South Shore rental options.

Kaua'i Vacation Rentals (www.kauaivacationrentals.com) Condo rental listings across the island.

Top Choices

Best Hotels & Resorts

St Regis Princeville, Princeville (d from $609; www.stregisprinceville.com)

Grand Hyatt Kauai Resort & Spa, Po'ipu (r/ste $440/2100; www.grandhyattkauai.com)

Waimea Plantation Cottages, Waimea (studio $149, 1-bed $179-239, 2-bed $239-299, 3-bed $299-359, 4-bed $509; www.waimeaplantation.com)

Best B&Bs & Inns

Kaua'i Country Inn, Kapa'a (ste incl breakfast from $149; www.kauaicountryinn.com)

Kaua'i Banyan Inn, Kalaheo (ste incl breakfast $155-230; www.kauaibanyan.com)

Anahata Spa & Sanctuary, Kilauea (r from $145, without bathroom from $80; www.tajjure.net/anahata-spiritual-spa)

North Country Farms, Kilauea (d $160; www.northcountryfarms.com)

Best Vacation Rentals

Parrish Collection Kaua'i, Princeville (www.parrishkauai.com)

Hanalei Dolphin Cottages, Hanalei (2-bedroom cottage $260; www.hanaleicottages.com)

Hale Ohana, Kekaha (3-bedroom house $475; www.kekahaoceansidekauai.com)

Best on a Budget

Green Acres Cottages, Kilauea (d $75-90; www.greenacrescottages.com)

Rosewood, Wailua (r with shared bath $75-125, room with private bath $155, private cottage $155; www.rosewoodkauai.com)

'Ili Noho Kai O Anahola, Anahola (r with shared bath incl breakfast $100; ☎808-821-0179; anahola@kauai.net)

Koke'e State Park Cabins, Koke'e State Park (cabin incl taxes $115; www.westkauailodging.com)

Getting Around Kaua'i

How to Get Around

➡ **Car Rental** Recommended unless on a very tight budget. Well-maintained highway provides access to most of the island. Free parking widely available.

➡ **Bus** Goes through all major towns; limited runs, especially on weekends.

➡ **Bike** Good option if staying in one town. In general, if on the Eastside or North Shore expect some rain.

➡ **Taxi** Flag-fall fee is $3, plus 30¢ per additional 0.1 miles or up to 45 seconds of waiting. Plan on calling for a taxi. (There is no uber in Kaua'i.)

➡ **Resort Shuttle** Complimentary; run regularly within most major resort areas.

Traveling by Car

Car Hire

➡ Renting a car often costs more on Kaua'i than on the other major Hawaiian Islands. Normally, a rock-bottom economy car from a major rental company will cost you $200 per week, with rates doubling during the peak periods. Rental rates will generally include unlimited mileage.

➡ To minimize costs, comparison shop; differences of 50% between suppliers are not unheard of.

➡ Another strategy for cost saving is to use a purely local rental agency. These mom-and-pop firms, which generally operate from home, rent used vehicles that may be 10 years old, but can be had for $20 to $25 per day.

➡ For motorcycle rentals, the go-to place is **Kaua'i Harley-Davidson** (p277), which has

RESOURCES

Automobile Associations

For 24-hour emergency roadside assistance, free maps and discounts on car rentals and accommodations, Hawaii is served by the **American Automobile Association** (AAA; ☐808-593-2221, from Neighbor Islands 800-736-2886; www. hawaii.aaa.com; 1130 N Nimitz Hwy, Honolulu; ⊙9am-5pm Mon-Fri, to 2pm Sat), from its office in Honolulu.

AAA has reciprocal agreements with automobile associations in other countries, so bring your membership card from home.

a 20-bike fleet in Puhi, just outside Lihu'e. For mopeds, try **Kauai Car & Scooter Rental** (p277).

➡ If you want a 4WD for getting to some of the sights, rates average $70 to $120 per day (before taxes and fees). Agencies prohibit driving off-road, meaning that if you get stuck they'll slap a penalty on you.

No Car?

Bus

The county's **Kaua'i Bus** (☑808-246-8110; www.kauai. gov/Bus; 3220 Ho'olako St, Lihu'e; one-way fare adult/senior & child 7-18yr $2/1) stops approximately hourly on weekdays in towns along major highways, with limited services on Saturdays, Sundays and holidays. Routes run island-wide, but don't reach the Na Pali Coast Wilderness,

Waimea Canyon or Koke'e State Parks. Schedules are available online. Check the website for where to buy monthly passes ($40).

Buses are air-conditioned and equipped with bicycle racks and wheelchair ramps. A few caveats: drivers don't give change; surfboards (except for boogie boards), oversized backpacks and luggage aren't allowed on board; stops are marked but might be hard to spot; and schedules do not include a map.

Bicycle

Cycling all the way around the island isn't much fun, due to heavy traffic and narrow road shoulders. But it's a convenient way of getting around beach resorts, and the Eastside has a recreational paved bicycle path running through Kapa'a. Bicycles are rented in Waipouli, Kapa'a, Po'ipu and Hanalei. The best

bike ride on the island is down the winding road of Waimea Canyon.

Tourist resort areas and specialty bicycle shops rent beach cruisers, hybrid models and occasionally high-end road and mountain bikes. Rental rates average $20 to $40 per day (easily double that for high-tech road or mountain bikes). Bikeshare Hawaii (www.bikesharehawaii.org) stations may be coming to the island soon.

Generally, bicycles are required to follow the same rules of the road as cars. Bicycles are prohibited on freeways and sidewalks. State law requires all cyclists under the age of 16 to wear helmets. For more bicycling information, including downloadable cycling maps, search the website of the Hawaii Department of Transportation (http://hidot.hawaii.gov/highways/).

DRIVING FAST FACTS

➡ Stay alert for one-lane-bridge crossings. Whenever there's no sign on one-lane stretches, downhill traffic must yield to uphill traffic.

➡ In-town driving is courteous and rather leisurely. Don't honk (unless a crash is imminent), don't tailgate and let faster cars pass.

➡ Mopeds should be driven in single file at a maximum speed of 30mph.

Road Distances (miles)

	Lihu'e	Kapa'a	Hanalei	Po'ipu
Kapa'a	11			
Hanalei	31	24		
Po'ipu	14	23	44	
Waimea	24	33	56	19

What's New

Labyrinth at Momilani Kai

Set on a gorgeous rocky headland, this memorial labyrinth connects you with a mana (spiritual essence) that moves you as much as the spectacular blowholes, waves and vistas. (p191)

JO2

Chef Jean Marie Josselin, a Wolfgang Puck contemporary, is back with his best kitchen yet. His menu heavily relies on local ingredients to which he adds a subtle flare. The result is all-natural cuisine suitable to anyone – even those of us with allergies to gluten or nuts – without losing the magic that makes his food world class. (p119)

Hunter Gatherer

Owned by a yoga-loving surfer, world traveler and interior designer who stocks clothes, books, art and homewares that ooze style and soul. This is one of those shops where you walk in and can't leave without buying at least one thing and probably a lot more. (p149)

Bangkok Happy Bowl

South Shore nightlife got a much-needed life infusion when this Thai kitchen opened and launched its karaoke night. Drop in and pay homage to Bowie, Prince and George M at Po'ipu's best new nightspot. (p202)

Olivine Beach

It's as if a Hamptons fashion boutique dropped from the sky and landed in down-to-earth Wailua. Further evidence of the creeping sophistication of the Eastside. (p117)

Japanese Grandma

Everybody is talking about the Westside's best sushi joint. (p221)

Hanalei Bread Company

Hanalei's choice breakfast spot, with good coffee, fresh baked bread, pastries and terrific sandwiches. (p164)

Kiko

Our favorite new gift shop on the island is tucked away from the rest of the Old Town Kapa'a main drag and is definitely worth finding. (p129)

Hike Kaua'i Adventures

The best bespoke hiking experiences available on the island. You'll go places you'd never find on your own. (p234)

Adventure Fit Kauai

One of Kaua'i's best athletes leads guests on bespoke training and stand up paddle surfing sessions, and offers hiking and mountain biking tours too. (p111)

Eating House 1849

Roy Yamaguchi's new shingle in Po'ipu is a modern classic with spectacular sunset views. (p199)

Street Burger

If you enjoy a good burger and craft beers, don't miss Wailua's most popular new grill. (p114)

For more recommendations and reviews, see lonelyplanet.com/usa/hawaii/kauai

If You Like...

Hiking

Kaua'i's trails lace lush mountains and fertile valleys. They plummet deep into a red-rock grand canyon, and trace the cliff's ledge of a roadless coastline.

Kalalau Trail Kaua'i's most popular and beautiful trail leads hikers along the unforgettable Na Pali Coast. (p138)

Waimea Canyon Trail Plummet into the Grand Canyon of the Pacific where the views are always spectacular. (p233)

Nounou Mountain Trail A shorter adventure, the eastside's natural gifts are revealed from the pinnacle. (p104)

Nu'alolo Trail Singletrack descends along the shoulders of narrow cliffs that loom over virgin beaches. (p208)

Alaka'i Swamp Trail It takes some doing to get here, but this boardwalk trail penetrates an otherworldly ecosystem. (p235)

Okolehao Trail The best way to break a sweat and get a bird's-eye view of Hanalei Bay. (p139)

Kuilau Ridge & Moalepe Trails A wonderful exploration of Waimea's fertile highlands blessed with keyhole views onto Mt Wai'ale'ale. (p104)

Maha'ulepu Heritage Trail Running east from Po'ipu, this trail navigates cliffs and ledges to reach stunning, isolated beaches. (p180)

Beaches

When it comes to finding that ideal stretch of sand, Kaua'i presents an embarrassment of riches. Whether you crave the all-natural and pristine or something more family friendly, if you need waves or value placid, sheltered coves, this island is a living example of the paradox of choice. Thankfully, with time, you can explore them all.

Lumaha'i Beach If you fancy a romantic stroll, or ideal beach-run terrain, this blonde beauty delivers. (p173)

Ha'ena Beach Park Reefs alive and teeming, ample sand space, on-duty lifeguards and bathrooms, too. (p174)

Ke'e Beach The beach at the end of the road delivers the very best North Shore sunsets. (p176)

Wa'ioli Beach Park A local surf spot with shredding waveriders, volleyball courts and lifeguards. Street parking. (p159)

Black Pot Beach Park Waves are ideal for beginners and groms at this family beach with a (tasty) burrito truck in the parking lot. (p159)

Kealia Beach Park Backed by rising mountains, this is the Eastside's sunbathing and bodyboarding destination of choice. (p123)

Lydgate Beach Park An unmatched playground, bathrooms and lifeguards, and photogenic piles of driftwood on the windswept tide line. (p108)

Po'ipu Beach Park Sheltered lagoons ideal for children, stunning sunsets, frequent sightings of napping monk seals. (p192)

Polihale State Park Where the Na Pali Coast begins on the Westside, the beach is long, blonde, raw and spectacular. (p231)

Kauapea (Secrets) Beach A wide ribbon of white sand runs along stunning cliffs all the way to Kilauea Point. (p145)

Water Sports

You've explored the land, you've chilled on the beach, now it's time to get your aquatic adventure on. From boating to paddling, diving to surfing, Kaua'i offers a multitude of ways to be wet and happy.

Hanalei Bay A half-dozen surf breaks to ride, with varying degrees of difficulty. (p159)

Na Pali Kayak This 12-hour, 17-mile paddle is a test of

endurance and a blast of mind-boggling beauty. (p163)

Bali Hai Tours Ditch the stable catamaran and feel the swells on a Na Pali Zodiac tour. (p163)

Kayak Hanalei Rent a kayak or SUP and paddle the serene Hanalei River. (p162)

Island Sails Kaua'i Learn to navigate a Polynesian sailing canoe on Hanalei Bay. (p153)

Wailua River State Park Paddle up Kaua'i's most sacred river to secret falls on your watercraft of choice. (p113)

Ni'ihau A sunken extinct crater off the island of Ni'ihau offers Kaua'i's most pristine scuba diving. (p45)

Scuba dive the South Shore Kaua'i's South Shore offers clear water, sharks and rays, and stunning macro life. (p195)

Maha'ulepu Beach There are no reliable kite-surfing outfitters on the island, but if you have gear, launch here. (p193)

Local Food

Whether you're an 'eat local' foodie obsessive or not, you will be eating local on Kaua'i, an island with dozens of organic farms, grass-fed beef aplenty and a fishing fleet plying the waters offshore. The results are found in kitchens across the island, from the fast, affordable and convenient, to those that pamper and plate with elegance. Here are the best spots to delve into the local food scene.

JO2 Chef Jean-Marie Josselin's newest and finest kitchen relies heavily on the farmers and fishermen he's collaborated with for decades. (p119)

Waipa Farmers Market Local chefs and farmers collide at

Top: Hiking on the North Shore (p138)
Bottom: Sunset on Kaua'i

this small North Shore farmers market, one of the best on island. (p164)

Ho'opulapula Haraguchi Rice Mill & Taro Farm Tours Explore a working taro farm and get to know the crop that sustained the Hawaiian people for centuries. (p163)

Bubba's Burgers A counterintuitive addition to this list, until you find out that its burgers are made from 100% Kaua'i grass-fed beef. (p164)

North Country Farms Sleep on the grounds of a working organic farm. A basket of home-grown goods will help stock your cottage kitchen. (p19)

Garden Island Chocolate Tour its Kilauea cacao fields and taste the sweetness on a farm-and-factory tour. (p148)

Hānai Market The name and ownership is new, but this market's commitment to selling local produce and beef remains. (p126)

Koloa Fish Market The best fish market on the island offers plate lunches, a selection of *poke* and excellent seared tuna. (p185)

BaraAcuda Tapas & Wine One of the island's best kitchens, it sources most ingredients from local farmers. (p167)

Kauai Juice Co Kaua'i's favorite juice bar synthesizes local produce into addictive juices, smoothies and hot sauce. (p149)

Arts & Antiques

This beautiful island is dotted with a range of art galleries and vintage treasure boxes where all manner of collectibles is on offer. Think anything from found 1950s Japanese buoys, to mid-century glassware and lanterns, to wonderful photography, sculpture and oil paintings to antique woodwork and religious iconography from lands near and far. Nearly every town on the island has something special waiting to be found.

Pagoda A gracious husband-and-wife team run the very best antique shop on the island. (p117)

Yellowfish Trading Company Our favorite shop in Hanalei has too many mid-century treasures to count. (p168)

Hunter Gatherer An expertly curated boutique with a wide range of stunning merchandise. You'll want it all. (p149)

Hanapepe's Art Night Every Friday night, Hanapepe's shops and art galleries keep their doors open late. (p219)

Fish Eye The best photography gallery on Kaua'i has branches in Princeville and Po'ipu. (p157)

Aloha Images The oldest art gallery on the island, with the most renowned artist roster. (p129)

Lotus Gallery A Southeast Asian art gallery at its finest. The best stuff comes from Myanmar. (p150)

Havaiki Traditional, hand-crafted island art, some of it of museum quality. (p169)

Kiko Repurposed materials, a mindfully curated book table, driftwood sculpture. (p129)

Month by Month

January

As the mercury dips a bit and the holidays float into the rearview, Kaua'i experiences a mild tourist exodus and hotel prices drop, even as humpback whales continue to dazzle.

☆ Art Night in Hanapepe

Hanapepe's deservedly popular weekly Art Night is held every Friday of the year. Galleries and shops keep their doors open late, food vendors descend and there is music in the air. It's the best time and place to experience this historic little town. (p219)

☆ Kapa'a Art Walk

On the first Saturday of every month from 5pm to 8pm, Old Town Kapa'a celebrates and showcases island artists and artisans during the Kapa'a Art Walk. Expect live music, food trucks and a block party atmosphere. (p125)

☆ Princeville Night Market

The first monthly Princeville Night Market offers original art and handicrafts, tasty snacks, locally roasted coffee and live music. It's held on the second Sunday of every month. (p155)

February

Winter means nights cool enough to cuddle up, big surf, and whales still blowing offshore. Hotels and restaurants book up well in advance of Valentine's Day. Presidents' Weekend brings a tourist influx too.

☆ Waimea Town Celebration

The Westside comes alive during the annual Waimea Town Celebration in mid-February. There's lei-making and hula-dancing competitions, food, craft and game booths, a beer garden, a canoe race and a *paniolo* (Hawaiian cowboy) rodeo. It's the perfect time for a family visit. (p226)

☆ E Pili Kakou i Ho'okahi Lahui

Featuring instruction from some of Hawaii's top *kumu hula* (teachers of hula), the E Pili Kakou i Ho'okahi Lahui is a two-day retreat held in late February.

March

High surf season winds down on the North Shore, though wind and rain can still taunt and bring heavy swells. Mainland's spring break baits families to Kaua'i's beaches en masse.

☆ Prince Kuhio Celebration

The two-week long Prince Kuhio Celebration honors Prince Jonah Kuhio Kalaniana'ole, known for his efforts to revitalize Native Hawaiian culture during his lifetime. Events include hula, an outrigger canoe race, an international spearfishing tournament and a rodeo, as well as Hawaiian spiritual ceremonies. (p197)

✿ Garden Isle Artsian Fair

The first instalment of the thrice-annual Garden Isle Artisan Fair brings out artisans and their handicrafts, live Hawaiian music and local food. (p125)

May

May is a wonderful time to experience Kaua'i as tourist season hits a short lull in advance of the busy summer season. North Shore waters are more serene and the weather is often perfect.

✿ May Day Lei Contest & Fair

Simple strings of plumeria (frangipani) are mere child's play next to the floral masterpieces entered in Lihu'e's annual May Day Lei Contest. (p92)

✿ Banana Poka Round-Up

Part invasive eradication effort, part handicraft fair, folks gather in gorgeous Koke'e State Park to remove the South American banana poka vine, which they weave into baskets. Come for live music, a rooster-crowing contest and the 'Pedal to the Meadow' bicycle race. (p235)

June

Summer is here, the beaches are packed and the north and west shores are placid as can be. It's a great time to swim, snorkel and dive on Kaua'i.

Top: Hawaiian leis (p258)
Bottom: Art Night (p219), Hanapepe

✕ Taste of Hawaii

Known as the 'Ultimate Brunch Sunday,' Wailua's Taste of Hawaii is a casual affair showcasing 40 chefs from around Hawaii holding down gourmet food booths and serving endless samples. Ample live music too. (p113)

July

High surf rolls onto the South Shore, while the whole island generally sees consistent sunshine. Summertime is sweet on the Garden Island.

✱ Fourth of July Concert in the Sky

Enjoy island food, live entertainment and the grand finale fireworks at the Fourth of July Concert in the Sky at Vidinha Stadium. (p92)

✱ Koloa Plantation Days

Koloa Plantation Days is a family-friendly, nine-day fair celebrating the history of the South Shore with a parade, *paniolo* (Hawaiian cowboy) rodeo, traditional Hawaiian games, Polynesian dancing and plenty of 'talk story' about old times. (p185)

August

Summer crowds are at their most populous, but there's plenty of ocean and beach space and lots of parties, too.

✱ Kaua'i Sand Festival

Sand castles, sand castles, who doesn't love sand castles? You'll be clicking and posting like a school kid when you behold these magnificent sculptures on Hanalei Bay. (p164)

✕ Music & Mango Festival

A late-summer celebration of locally harvested food (yes, the mango looms large) and live music on the nonprofit Waipa Foundation's farmlands on the outskirts of Hanalei. (p164)

✱ Garden Isle Artisan Fair

The second edition of the thrice-annual artisan fair blooms in Old Town Kapa'a. (p125)

☆ Heiva I Kaua'i Ia Orana Tahiti

Imagine dance troupes from as far away as Tahiti and Japan joining mainland US and local Hawaiian dancers for a Tahitian dancing and drumming competition at Kapa'a Beach Park. Yeah, best to plan your schedule accordingly. (p125)

✱ Kaua'i County Farm Bureau Fair

An old-fashioned county fair blooms at Vidinha Stadium in late August. Think: carnival rides and games, livestock shows, a petting zoo, hula performances and lots of local food. (p92)

September

Summer crowds dissipate and ideal weather

conditions usually prevail. When they don't, double rainbows will cheer you up.

☆ Kaua'i Composers Contest & Concert

Encouraging the island's up-and-coming talent to show their skills, the Kaua'i Composers Contest & Concert is held at Kaua'i Community College Performing Arts Center. (p92)

🏃 Kauai Marathon

A popular road race on the South Shore, the Kauai Marathon also features a short-course half marathon. Locals pack the streets to cheer on (or heckle) their (suffering) friends.

☆ Kaua'i Mokihana Festival Hula Competition

Three days of serious hula competitions are staged at the Aqua Kauai Beach Resort. If you've been wanting to watch dancers perform without the luau kitsch, this is your best option. (p92)

October

The best month in the year to travel almost anywhere, and especially here. The weather is lovely, crowds are thin on the ground and hotel prices drop significantly.

✕ Coconut Festival

The two-day Coconut Festival held at Kapa'a Beach Park in early October offers entertainment, exhibits, games, contests and cooking demonstrations all revolving around the *coco.* Live music and hula dancing too. (p125)

🎆 Fall Festival

For 16 years the Kauai Christian Academy has hosted a Fall Festival fundraiser featuring local food and art vendors, a huge silent auction, live music, carnival games, a corn maze, as well as pony and hay rides. (p148)

🍴 Kaua'i Chocolate & Coffee Festival

A spin-off from a popular Honolulu event, the Hanapepe-based Kaua'i Chocolate & Coffee Festival offers tastings, demonstrations, live entertainment and farm tours. (p219)

☆ Eo e Emalani I Alaka'i

A one-day outdoor dance festival at Koke'e Museum commemorating Queen Emma's 1871 journey to Alaka'i Swamp. The festival includes a royal procession, hula dancing, live music and more. (p235)

November

High surf arrives in the north and west, and heavy (or shall we say heavier) rain marks the 'unofficial' start of winter.

☆ Hawaiian Slack Key Guitar Festival

Watch masters of the Hawaiian slack key guitar (*ki-ho'alu*) blend styles (and strings) for this free event at the Aqua Kauai Beach Resort. (p92)

☆ Homegrown Music Festival

Fun, funky and always rocking, the Homegrown Music Festival has taken over Princeville's Church of the Pacific for a weekend each of the past 16 years, and is among the island's best parties. (p155)

🎆 Garden Isle Artisan Fair

The third instalment of Kapa'a's notable artisan fair. (p125)

🍴 Garden Island Range & Food Festival

The Garden Island Range & Food Festival spotlights local chefs, as well as the farmers and ranchers who provide them with Kaua'i-grown ingredients. (p92)

December

Humpback whales have arrived and are ready to reveal themselves to the holiday crowds. Hold your breath, dive down and listen to their song.

🍴 Kalo Festival

Enjoy demonstrations on growing taro and pounding poi, traditional Hawaiian games for kids, local food vendors and live music at the Kalo Festival in Waipa. (p164)

🎆 Lights on Rice Parade

Illluminated floats deliver the Christmas spirit to Rice St in downtown Lihu'e on the first Friday evening of December. Ideal for families. (p94)

Po'ipu Beach Park (p19

Itineraries

Whether you're seeking lazy afternoons or active adventures on the Garden Island, compact Kaua'i will win you over with its heavenly beaches, marvellous trails and excellent dining scene.

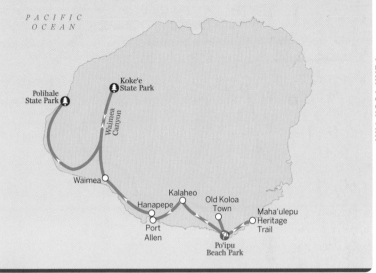

4 DAYS Po'ipu Beach Park to Koke'e State Park

The South Shore and Westside of Kaua'i are known for having a more stable climate (translation: much less rain), and that's just where the appeal begins. Exquisite beaches, great food, stunning sunsets, a blast of local flavor and magnificent trails await.

Start your first day in **Kalaheo** among the locals at bustling Kalaheo Café & Coffee Co, before joining an early tour of the magnificent Allerton Garden. If you surf, paddle out to the wave out front, otherwise hit **Po'ipu Beach Park**. That beach fronts two sheltered lagoons ideal for kids and beginning snorkelers. The next one over, Brennecke's Beach, offers access to a wonderful outside reef accessible only to experienced ocean swimmers and freedivers. On the other flank is a consistent reef break ideal for surfers (mind your manners), and smaller waves for beginners. You'll find parking, bathrooms, picnic shelters and lifeguards here, and in winter you'll see breaching humpbacks offshore. Did we mention the sunsets are world class? Welcome to vacation base camp. When you've had enough, head to **Old Koloa Town** to enjoy tasty Italian food and the island's best cocktails at La Spezia.

On day two, stretch those morning legs on the **Maha'ulepu Heritage Trail**, a most wild and scenic coastal hike. At lunch, head back to Koloa and hit Koloa Fish Market (bring cash) and walk it off with an extended browse of area shops. Drop by Po'ipu Beach Park for another sunset, then stroll the Kukui'ula until you find a dining room that meets your needs. Eating House 1849 is an excellent choice.

On day three head west. Join a Na Pali catamaran tour out of **Port Allen** before strolling **Hanapepe** town. Friday night is Art Night. Tuck in at Japanese Grandma.

It's your last day, so pack a picnic at Ishihara Market in **Waimea**, then drive onto Hwy 550, stopping at all the viewpoints as the road rises past **Waimea Canyon** and into **Koke'e State Park**. Then venture onto the Awa'awapuhi Trail with views overlooking the stunning Na Pali Coast. Wash it down with a final sunset at the end of the road in **Polihale State Park**.

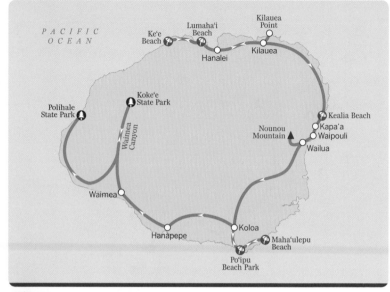

8 DAYS Dream Week

You have one week to explore, taste and experience the best of the Garden Island. Ready, set... go!

Check into Anahata Spa & Sanctuary in **Kilauea** and make your way into **Hanalei**. Park near Hanalei Beach Park, take a dip and stroll the sand, then hit luscious **Lumahaʻi Beach** for sunset. Grab a casual dinner and drinks at nearby Tahiti Nui. After a morning surf lesson on Hanalaei Bay, head to primordial Limahuli Garden, then hike the Kalalau Trail from **Keʻe Beach** to Hanakapiʻai Beach. Catch a Technicolor sunset on Keʻe Beach, then take the slow drive back to Hanalei for dinner at BarAcuda. Wake up in time for a yoga class at Metamorphose, then visit the lighthouse at **Kilauea Point** before spending the rest of the day at Kauapea (Secrets) Beach or Kahili (Rock Quarry) Beach. Dine at Palate in Kilauea.

On day four check into Fern Grotto Inn or Rosewood Kauaʻi in **Wailua**, then paddle the Wailua River. Book dinner at the wonderful JO2 in **Waipouli**. The following morning, breakfast at Java Kai in **Kapaʻa**, then ride the bike path to **Kealia Beach**. That evening hit Kintaro in Wailua for local Japanese or sample the burgers and craft beers at Street Burger. Wake up with a hike to the top of **Nounou Mountain**, then pack up and drive to **Koloa**, pick up lunch at the fish market and spend the day at **Poʻipu Beach Park**. Check into your short-term rental in Poʻipu. Wake up and go scuba diving with Seasport Divers if you're certified; otherwise, hit the Mahaʻulepu Heritage Trail and spend the morning at rugged and beautiful **Mahaʻulepu Beach**. Land in **Hanapepe** by early evening for a bit of gallery hopping, especially if it's Friday Art Night. Dine at Japanese Grandma.

Day eight is all about the trails. Stop at Ishihara Market in **Waimea** to pack a picnic at its deli, then drive Hwy 550, past all manner of viewpoints as the road rises to the rim of **Waimea Canyon**. Venture into **Kokeʻe State Park** and onto Awaʻawapuhi Trail with views overlooking the Kalalau Valley and the stunning Na Pali Coast, before driving on toward the western end of the road where you'll enjoy a final Kauaʻi sunset in **Polihale State Park**.

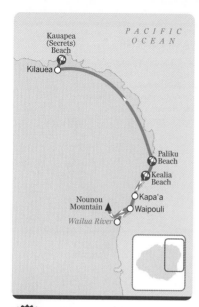

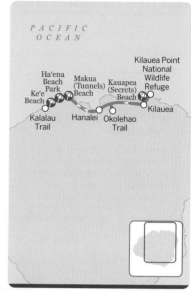

② DAYS Wailua to Kilauea

From one of the state's most sacred rivers to one of the island's most spectacular beaches, with all kinds of beauty and flavor in between.

Start your day with a serene paddle up the **Wailua River**. Whether you choose to join a tour group or blaze your own wake, you will either hop in a kayak or rent an SUP board, glimpse heiau (ancient stone temples) and explore a hidden waterfall. Next fuel up with coffee and breakfast at Java Kai, a **Kapa'a** classic. When you're ready to keep moving, rent a bike and cruise the 5-mile Ke Ala Hele Makalae path. It stretches from the south end of Kapa'a Beach Park to **Paliku Beach**, 5 miles away. Grab a nap at **Kealia Beach**, then spend the rest of the afternoon and early evening exploring the shops in Old Town Kapa'a. At night book a table in **Waipouli** at the wonderful JO2 for an exquisite dinner.

The next morning, climb **Nounou Mountain** then grab some Tiki Tacos in Waipouli and hit one of Kilauea's sublime beaches. We suggest **Kauapea (Secrets) Beach**. Take a quick dip, plant your body in the sand, repeat as necessary. Dine at Palate in **Kilauea**.

③ DAYS Kilauea to Na Pali Coast State Park

Explore the North Shore from Kilauea Point to the mythic end of the road.

Wake up in **Kilauea** with coffee at Kilauea Bakery, a local staple, and a yoga class at Metamorphose. Then drive to **Kilauea Point National Wildlife Refuge** and check out the stately lighthouse. Back in Kilauea, grab lunch at Kilauea Fish Market, have a browse at Hunter Gatherer then hit **Kauapea (Secrets) Beach**. Rinse off and hit the shops and galleries of **Hanalei**, enjoy an exquisite dinner at BarAcuda, and then step over to Tahiti Nui for drinks and laughs until the music stops.

You'll need another hike to get your blood flowing again, so after coffee and a bite at Hanalei Bread Co, and a strategic snack stockpile at Harvest Market, hit the **Okolehao Trail** for a steep, quick one or drive to the end of the road and get a taste of the **Kalalau Trail**. Next hit **Ha'ena Beach Park** or, if you surf, **Makua (Tunnels) Beach** for another well-spent, lazy afternoon. Wake up in time to drive to the end of the road for a **Ke'e Beach** sunset, then hit the sushi bar at Dolphin Restaurant for dinner in dear, sweet Hanalei.

ALAKA'I SWAMP

Bogs, carnivorous plants, wetlands, watersheds and a boardwalk running over all of the above: welcome to the watery wonderland that is the primal Alaka'i Swamp. (p233)

NU'ALOLO KAI: A LAST PARADISE?

This truly ends-of-the-earth, Ancient Hawaiian settlement impresses with its commitment to indigenous history and current affairs. Also: it can be damned fun getting out here. (p216)

Kailiu Point   Ha'ena

Ha'ena   Wainiha
Ha'ena State Park

Hono'o Na Pali

Na Pali Coast
Na Pali Coast Wilderness State Park

Moa'alele (4095ft)   ▲ (3330ft)

Pihea (4284ft)   Kilohana (4022ft)

Lumaha'i River

Wainiha River

Na Pali–Kona Forest Reserve

ALAKA'I SWAMP

Pu'u o Kila (4176ft)

NU'ALOLO KAI

Kuia Natural Area Reserve

Koke'e State Park

Alaka'i Wilderness Preserve

Pu'u Ka Pele Forest Reserve

Na Pali–Kona Forest Reserve

POLIHALE STATE PARK

Nohili Point

Waimea Canyon State Park

Waimea Canyon

○ Mana

Pu'u Ka Pele Forest Reserve

Mana Point

Barking Sands Pacific Missile Range Facility

Waimea River

Kokole Point   Kekaha ○

Kaulakahi Channel

Waimea ○

Hanapepe River

Kalaheo ○

POLIHALE STATE PARK

One of the longest and widest beaches in Hawaii, Polihale isn't just a pretty sweep of sand; according to local lore, it's the spot where Hawaiian souls depart to the afterworld. (p231)

Kaumakani ○

Hanapepe ○   ○ Ele'ele

Makaokahai Point

KALIHIWAI VALLEY

The North Shore is already almost too beautiful for words, but in this isolated valley, which ends at a gorgeous beach, you'll enjoy its charms far from the tourist trail. (p149)

PALIKU (DONKEY) BEACH

This lovely beach isn't the best for swimming, but after putting in the work to get here, you'll appreciate its pretty views and windswept seclusion. (p124)

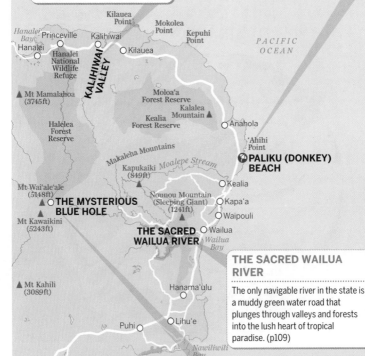

THE SACRED WAILUA RIVER

The only navigable river in the state is a muddy green water road that plunges through valleys and forests into the lush heart of tropical paradise. (p109)

THE MYSTERIOUS BLUE HOLE

This ruggedly beautiful pond, fed by a stream and a waterfall, sits in the shadow of Mt Wai'ale'ale, amid a stunning -and secluded - junglescape you'll have to work to reach. (p117)

MAKAUWAHI SINKHOLE

Descend into this cave complex, a dark and mysterious world that feels an ocean away from sunny Kaua'i, to find one of the richest fossil sites in the islands. (p193)

Poke (cubed raw fish mixed with assorted condiments

Eat & Drink Like a Local

Kaua'i likes to keep it simple. Whether you're savoring four-star Hawaii Regional cuisine or sampling that curious Spam *musubi* (rice ball), you'll find a fascinating fusion of flavors – from Polynesian staples such as taro, banana and coconut to Japanese teriyaki, Chinese noodles and Hawaiian *kalua* (earth oven) pig. The real spoils go to those willing to hunt down the best fish markets, indie bakeries and farmers markets.

ZARZAMORA/SHUTTERSTOCK ©

Regional Treats

Don't miss these local Kaua'i specialties:

Homemade taro chips from Taro Ko Chips Factory (p219).

Steaming noodle soups and *manapuas* (dough rolls stuffed with steamed pork) at Hamura Saimin (p95).

Spam *musubi* and homemade *manju* (Japanese sweet-bean-filled pastry) at Pono Market (p125).

Bentō lunch box from Ishihara Market (p226).

Poke rolls (in rice paper) from Duke's (p96).

The varied sizzling options at Eating House 1849 (p199).

→ The primary starch in Hawaii is sticky, medium-grain white rice. Jasmine rice is tolerated with Thai food, but flaky rice is considered haole (Caucasian) food (and Uncle Ben's is considered inedible).

→ The top condiment is soy sauce (ubiquitously called by its Japanese name, *shōyu*), which combines well with sharp Asian flavors, such as ginger, green onion and garlic.

→ Meat, chicken or fish is often integral to a dish. For quick, cheap eating, locals devour anything tasty, from Portuguese sausage to hamburger steak to corned beef. But the dinner-table highlight is always seafood, especially succulent, freshly caught ahi (tuna).

→ Nonlocal classics (such as pizza and bagels) are usually disappointing. Also bear in mind that 'barbecue' typically means teriyaki-marinated.

→ While Kaua'i's top restaurants can hold their own among statewide peers, you generally won't find the cutting-edge culinary creativity that you'd find on O'ahu and even on Maui or the Big Island.

Two excellent resources on Hawaii cuisine are Edible Hawaiian Islands (www.edible hawaiianislands.com), which covers the gamut, and Hawaii Seafood (www.hawaii -seafood.org), which is all about just that.

Drinks

Cafe culture has taken root on Kaua'i, with baristas brewing espresso at deli counters, indie hangouts and, of course, Starbucks. Local old-timers balk at paying $3-plus for coffee, but today's youth are eager converts to lattes and cappuccinos. You can learn about coffee production at the Kauai Coffee Company (p212).

While fresh fruit is plentiful at farmers markets, fresh fruit juice tends to be pricey and sold mainly at health-food markets and roadside fruit stands, such as the Coconut Cup, which makes tropical smoothies to order. An offshoot of the smoothie is the frosty, an icy dessert with the texture of ice cream, made by puréeing frozen fruit in a food processor. Try it at Banana Joe's Fruitstand (p148). Forgo the supermarket cartons and cans, which tend to be sugary drinks.

Unique to Hawaii are two fruit-juice 'tonics' nowadays marketed mainly to tourists: *'awa* (kava), a mild sedative, and *noni* (Indian mulberry), which some consider to be a cure-all. Both fruits are

Food Experiences

The Island Diet

The island diet is more than just a meal. It's a window on the island itself. But defining it is no simple matter. It's multiethnic, yet distinct from classic fusion cooking. It's got a full-fledged highbrow cuisine, yet its iconic dishes are lowbrow local *grinds* (akin to street food). The only way to understand the island diet is to partake of its pleasures. We describe the major cuisine categories below, all of which have the following elements in common:

Top: Luau performance
Bottom: Shaved ice

pungent (if not repulsive) in smell and taste, so they are typically mixed with other juices.

Among alcoholic beverages, beer is the local drink of choice. Wine is gaining in popularity among the upper-income classes, and all top-end restaurants offer a decent selection. There are a few breweries worth checking out too, such as Kauai Island Brewery & Grill (p216) in Port Allen and Kauai Beer Company (p96) in Lihu'e.

Luau

In ancient Hawaii, a luau commemorated auspicious occasions, such as births, war victories or successful harvests. Today only commercial luau offer the elaborate Hawaiian feast and hula dancing that folks expect to experience. A $75 to $100 ticket buys you a highly choreographed Polynesian dance show and an all-you-can-eat buffet of luau standards – usually toned down for the Western palate – such as poi, *kalua* pig, steamed mahimahi, teriyaki chicken and *haupia* (coconut pudding). The food isn't great...but somehow the whole slightly kitsch, totally over-the-top luau experience should make it to all but the most cynical of tourist itineraries. It's something you only have to do once.

RUSS BISHOP/ALAMY STOCK PHOTO ©

Stop off at the Kauai Coffee Company (p212)

PLAN YOUR TRIP EAT & DRINK LIKE A LOCAL

For the most impressive show, Kilohana Plantation's Luau Kalamaku (p96) offers a compelling theatrical production and professional-caliber dancers. The long-running luau at Smith's Tropical Paradise (p109) is a family affair and, while touristy, the multicultural performances with dancers of all ages have their appeal. Both the Grand Hyatt (p202) and Sheraton (p202) offer beachside luaus in Po'ipu.

If you want to save some bucks, you can sit beachside and watch the show with a bottle of wine...but remember, by paying for the show, your money goes to local performers and local waiters, and is an important part of the local economy.

Private luau celebrations, typically for weddings or first birthdays, are often large banquet-hall gatherings. The menu might be more daring – perhaps including raw *'a'ama* (black crab) and *'opihi* (edible limpet) – and the entertainment more low-key. No fire eaters.

Vegetarians & Vegans

Although locals love their sashimi and Spam, vegetarians and vegans won't go hungry on Kaua'i. A handful of restaurants

---

THE YEAR IN FOOD

Now that agri-tourism and gourmet cuisine are trendy, food festivals are garnering much attention. The Hanalei Taro Festival, a biennial event (even-numbered years), features poi-pounding and taro-cooking contests. More extravagant is Taste of Hawaii (p113), a line-up-and-sample extravaganza dubbed the 'ultimate Sunday brunch.'

Many public festivals and events offer family-friendly outdoor food booths, serving much more than standard concession grub. The Waimea Town Celebration (p226), Koloa Plantation Days Celebration (p185), Coconut Festival (p125) and Kaua'i County Farm Bureau Fair (p92) showcase not only local culture but also local food, from shave ice to plate lunches.

Banana Joe's Fruitstand (p148), Kilauea

cater to vegetarian, vegan, fish-only or health-conscious diets. Notable venues include Postcards Café (p167), Kaua'i Pasta (p119) and Kalaheo Café & Coffee Co (p205), which focus on vegetarian and fish dishes. The high-end Hawaii Regional cuisine menus always have vegetarian options. Asian eateries offer varied tofu and veggie options, but beware of meat- or fish-based broths.

The Other Pink Meat

Simply put, locals love Spam. Yes, *that* Spam. It's a local comfort food, typically eaten sliced and sautéed to a light crispiness in sweetened *shōyu*. Expect to see Hormel's iconic canned ham product served with eggs for breakfast or as a *loco moco* option. It's especially enjoyed as Spam *musubi* (rice ball topped with fried Spam and wrapped with dried seaweed, or *nori*) – folks of all stripes savor this only-in-Hawaii creation that's culturally somewhat akin to an easy, satisfying PB&J sandwich.

The affinity for Spam arose during the plantation era, when canned meat was cheap and easy to prepare for *bentō* (box) lunches. In Hawaii, unlike on the mainland, there's no stigma to eating Spam. If you acquire a taste for it, plan a trip to Honolulu for the annual Waikiki Spam Jam (www.spamjamhawaii.com) and go wild in your own kitchen with *Hawai'i Cooks with SPAM: Local Recipes Featuring Our Favorite Canned Meat,* written by prolific cookbook author Muriel Miura.

Habits & Customs

In most households, home cooking is integral to daily life, perhaps owing to the slower pace, backyard gardens and obsession with food. Meals are held early and on the dot: typically 6am breakfast, noon lunch and 6pm dinner. At home, locals rarely (perhaps never) serve formal sitdown meals with individual courses. Even when entertaining, meals are typically

Noodle dishes, Hamura Saimin (p95), Lihu'e

Hawaiian seafood has some typical crowd-pleasers, plus a few unknown standouts that you'll want to try.

➡ ahi – served seared, grilled, raw... it's a top on everything

➡ aku – this tuna is smaller and has a more robust flavor

➡ akule – bigeye scad with a sweet oily flavor like mackarel

➡ hapu'upu'u – say that five times fast; noted for its delicate white meat

➡ hebi – a mild-flavored billfish

➡ kajiki – Pacific blue marlin

➡ mahimahi – delicious and everywhere

➡ monchong – medium flavor with a high fat content

➡ onaga – ruby snapper

➡ ono – local word for wahoo; can be a bit rubbery

➡ opah – moonfish...a top with local chefs

➡ 'opakapaka – crimson snapper served in filets

➡ shutome – swordfish

➡ tombo – albacore tuna

➡ ulua – jack crevalle

served in a potluck style, often as a spread of unrelated dishes.

If you're invited to a local home, show up on time and bring dessert. Remove your shoes at the door. And don't be surprised if you're forced to take home a plate or two of leftovers.

Except at top resort restaurants, the island dress code means that T-shirts and flip-flops are ubiquitous. The local, older generation tends toward neat and modest attire.

Kaua'i restaurants typically open and close early; late-night dining is virtually nonexistent. In general, locals tip slightly less than mainlanders do, but still up to 20% for good service and at least 15% for the basics.

In top restaurants, you may consider a reservation – otherwise you are generally good to go. Takeaway picnic lunches are an excellent option for lunches. Many hotels, condos and vacation rentals have barbecues, making grilling out and catering your own Hawaiian feasts easier than you'd think.

There's not a lot of nightlife in Kaua'i. Most places close early, with a few exceptions in the bigger tourist centers.

Diving & Snorkeling

While Kaua'i waters cannot quite compare to the calm, clear waters off the Big Island's Kona Coast, diving is still excellent. South Shore waters see the most diving activity, both from shore and dive boats, as the swell isn't quite as strong here most of the year. In the summer when South Shore surf picks up, the North Shore offers wonderful conditions. Translation: there's always somewhere beautiful to dive on Kaua'i. Whether or not you dive, don't leave the island without donning a mask or you'll be missing something. Diverse and spectacular marine life – including plenty of turtles – hugs the shore here.

Diving & Snorkeling Tips

➡ Have a dive medical before you leave your home country – local dive operators may not always ask about medical conditions that are incompatible with diving.

➡ Ensure your travel medical kit contains treatment for coral cuts and tropical ear infections, as well as the standard problems.

➡ For members, **Divers Alert Network** (DAN; ☑ emergency hotline 919-684-9111, info 800-446-2671; www.diversalertnetwork.org; annual membership from $35) gives advice on diving emergencies, insurance, decompression services, illness and injury.

➡ It may be a worthwhile investment to bring or buy your own high-quality mask, if you plan on snorkeling more than once or twice.

➡ As a rule, snorkel early – morning conditions are often best, and if everyone else is sleeping, they won't be crowding the water and kicking up sand to mar visibility.

➡ Don't touch any coral, which are living organisms; watch your fins to avoid stirring up sand; and finally, don't feed the fish.

Diving

South Shore & Eastside

Thanks to mostly smooth conditions which nurture ample visibility beneath the surface, the South Shore is Kaua'i's scuba mecca. For nine months a year, it's the only place to dive, which is why it's the base of operations for all the island's dive shops, and with a dozen sites within a short boat ride from Kukui'ula Small Boat Harbor (p192), there's plenty of variety to keep you coming back. The best part – the proximity of the harbor to the dive shops and the dive sites to the harbor – means it takes less than half a day to suck two tanks dry, unless you are lucky enough to be heading to Ni'ihau (p45). In that case, three tanks are a must.

Koloa Landing (p195) is the best shore dive on the island, and with a maximum depth of 45ft most beginners will do at least one tank here. You'll see frog fish, leaf and devil scorpion fish, and dragon moray eels with orange horns peeking out of rocks sprouting with new corals. You're likely to see turtles too. Koloa Landing is also where Freedive Kauai (p152) drops a line and leads students down to the ocean floor on a single breath. Often they move a bit offshore, away from the reef that the scuba divers enjoy, to get a bit more depth. Beginners will hit 66ft; intermediate students may hit 100ft on a single breath. In the summer they bring students to 'Anini Beach Park (p152) on the North Shore.

Stone House, another terrific beginner's dive, is a finger of lava jutting from the sand ranging from 35ft to 65ft beneath the surface. Big schools of domino damsels and pinnette butterfly fish are common and look like floating walls of color. There are some octopi hiding in the lava rocks here too.

Nukumoi Point (p195) is a turtle-cleaning station stretching from 25ft to 55ft and is another great beginner's dive and ideal if you want to dance with turtles. There are some lovely nudibranch and tiger cowrie shells here, and in winter you'll hear whale song almost the entire dive. If you're really lucky, you just might be visited by a pod of spinner dolphins. You can almost see the reef. Look for where the waves break outside from the Po'ipu Beach Park lifeguard tower.

Sheraton Caverns (p195), a series of collapsed lava tubes home to giant, 100-year-old sea turtles who nap on the lava rock shelves for up to four hours at a time, is considered the best beginner's dive on the island because the visibility is so dependable and you can find a little bit of everything, including octopus, eels, adorable fingernail-sized harlequin shrimp and white-tip sharks. Maximum depth here is 65ft.

Turtle Bluffs (p196) looks like an underwater version of the cliffs you'd find above water at Salt Pond Beach Park (p217). They plummet from 55ft to 85ft and feature big sand caves where sharks are often napping or staking out prey. Lobster, crabs and big bait balls are also common.

Picture a lava rock structure carved by water and time into a series of bowls, and you've got **Fish Bowl**, where big schools of blue stripe snapper and yellow goat fish can lure apex predators. In summer 2016, Seasport Divers (p195) spent quality time with a 15ft tiger shark here. Depth ranges from 35ft to 75ft and visibility and water color are almost always marvelous.

General Store (p195) is another dependable dive site with good visibility even when most sites are murky. It's centered around an 1892 (mostly decomposed) shipwreck. But nearby lava rock formations are punched with shadowy swim throughs where (harmless) sharks often lurk, and some big moray eels too.

Closest to the boat dock, **Harbor Ledges** isn't deep but is a wonderful night dive. Turtles and sharks are common, and reports of dolphins are too numerous to count.

Advanced scuba divers have plenty of terrain to explore off the South Shore. Set between Brennecke's Beach and the Hyatt, **Zac's Pocket**, a ledge that runs from north to south, has arguably the best living coral reef on Kaua'i (not including Ni'ihau). Conditions can be temperamental thanks to swirling currents that often blow divers off the reef – so it's a rare treat to be able to dive here, but if you are so lucky you may glimpse Galapagos, white-tip and grey sharks, manta rays, and humpback whales in winter. The reef stretches from 80ft to 120ft and it's a drift dive.

Another deep dive suitable for advanced-level folks is **Brennecke's Ledge**, a rock outcrop growing with pristine black coral and a depth between 65ft and 85ft. On the branches you can see rare long-nose hawkfish, sponge crabs and the odd manta ray. You'll hear whales in season, and may even see them down there.

Ice Box (p195), a horseshoe-shaped reef with boulders on either end, is another of the deeper sites (65ft to 85ft) but suitable for intermediate divers. It's patrolled by white-tip reef sharks and octopus, lobsters, bigger morays and occasional rays.

The Eastside has one notable dive site. **Ahukini Landing**, a Lihu'e shore dive for all levels when conditions are calm, contains ordnance from WWII and is often home to rays, octopi and lobster. Occasional humpbacks cruise by in winter, though the water is usually too rough for beginners and visibility is hit and miss. Depth ranges from 10ft to 65ft.

North & West Shores

If you happen to arrive on the island in summer, some of the South Shore sites may be murky and hard to access. Thankfully that's perfect timing to explore the often inaccessible north and west shores.

ADAM HESTER/GETTY IMAGES ©

Top: Soldierfish

Bottom: Snorkeling off the Kaua'i coast

The only scuba dive on the North Shore, Tunnels (p175) is a reef made up of lava tubes on the inside and outside of the barrier reef that produces epic surf nine months a year. It's a shore dive, with swim throughs aplenty, common sightings of spotted eagle rays and monk seals, frequent white-tip reef sharks and occasional Galapagos sharks. Depth ranges from 5ft to 65ft. Though there is current, beginners are welcome.

A huge fissure in the Na Pali Coast, between Polihale and Miloli'i, **Mana Crack** is an advanced-level drift dive with phenomenal visibility ranging in depth from 60ft to 120ft and set more than a mile offshore. Expect sharks, rays, eels and much more.

Undoubtedly the very best diving around Kaua'i can be found on **Ni'ihau**, that small island visible offshore and off-limits to visitors. This is the best place to dive with monk seals and sandbar sharks, and trip itineraries almost always include three dives. **Lehua Rock** is the star of the scene. Picture an underwater, extinct volcanic crater with walls dropping down to between 200ft to 400ft on either side. You'll need good breath control to explore the walls, though there is easier diving inside the crater too. Here you may be fortunate enough to swim with wild dolphin pods and watch manta rays soar among massive schools of tropical fish.

A labyrinth of archways home to ghost shrimp, moray eels, frog fish, octopi and sponge crabs, **Ni'ihau Caves** is another favorite. The big feature here is **TV Cave**. Large and square just like your grandpa's television, some divers spend up to 30 minutes exploring that one cave alone. **Neon Cave** is another stunner. It's home to a resident monk seal and is often graced by the presence of huge manta rays. Maximum depth in the caves is 70ft.

Snorkeling
Around the Garden Island

OK, so scuba and freediving aren't for you; still, don't leave Kaua'i without having snorkeled. It's a wonderful entrée into a completely different, beautiful world. Almost anyone can do it and it's dirt cheap. Rental equipment is freely available, but if you're passing through Lihu'e, you can buy some for under $10 at big-box chain stores.

The South Shore has the most snorkeling locations around Po'ipu. The twin lagoons in front of Po'ipu Beach Park (p192) offer terrific entry-level snorkeling. You're likely to see turtles and bunches of tropical fish. The same goes for the beach in front of the Sheraton. If you can make it past the break off Brennecke's Beach (p192), however, the rocks that tumble to the sea from shore on either side offer much better visibility, and there's much more life. Think: turtles, baby reef sharks and tons of fish. Further offshore, Nukumoi Point (p195) beckons, but that's a serious swim and should only be attempted by extremely strong open-water swimmers. If that's you, make sure to check in with the lifeguards before you take off. Koloa Landing (p195) is the best of the bunch on the South Shore. In each and every case, never go it alone.

If you're on the Westside, go to Salt Pond Beach Park (p217), with its shallow waters. On the Eastside, choose Lydgate Beach Park (p108), which has a protected lagoon perfect for kids. On the North Shore, head to 'Anini Beach Park (p152) year round; in summer hit Ke'e Beach (p176) or Makua (Tunnels) Beach (p175). The latter can often be spectacular, but are off-limits to snorkelers when the surf's up. Snorkeling is also a key part of most Na Pali Coast (p177) boat tours.

Kaua'i: Diving & Snorkeling

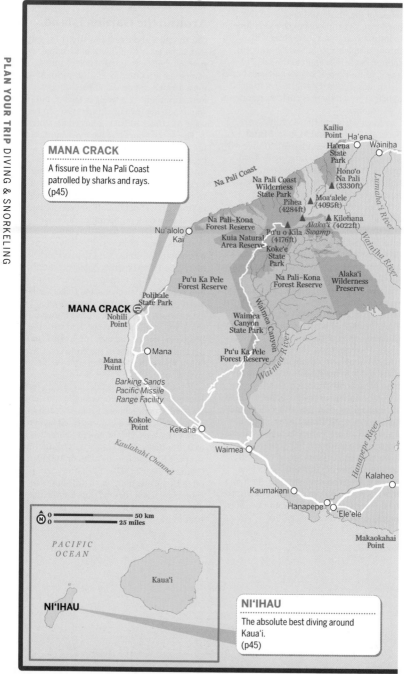

MANA CRACK

A fissure in the Na Pali Coast patrolled by sharks and rays. (p45)

NI'IHAU

The absolute best diving around Kaua'i. (p45)

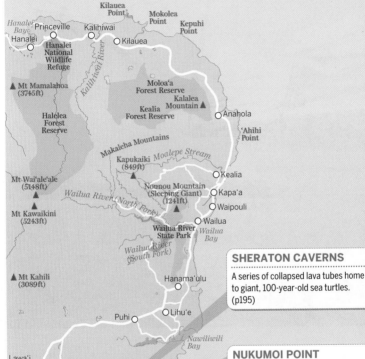

N

0 ———— 10 km
0 ———— 5 miles

PACIFIC
OCEAN

Hanalei Bay Princeville Kalihiwai
Hanalei
Kilauea
Point

Mokolea
Point Kepuhi
Point

Kilauea

Hanalei
National
Wildlife
Refuge

▲ Mt Mamalahoa
(3745ft)

Moloa'a
Forest Reserve
Kalalea ▲
Mountain
Anahola

Halelea
Forest
Reserve

Kealia
Forest Reserve

'Ahihi
Point

Makaleha Mountains

Kapukaiki
(849ft)
▲

Moalepe Stream

▲ Mt Wai'ale'ale
(5148ft)

Wailua River (North Fork)

Nounou Mountain
(Sleeping Giant)
(1241ft)
▲

Kealia

Kapa'a

Waipouli

▲ Mt Kawaikini
(5243ft)

Wailua

Wailua River
State Park *Wailua
Bay*

*Wailua River
(South Fork)*

▲ Mt Kahili
(3089ft)

Hanama'ulu

SHERATON CAVERNS

A series of collapsed lava tubes home
to giant, 100-year-old sea turtles.
(p195)

Puhi Lihu'e

*Nawiliwili
Bay*

Lawa'i
Omao

*Waita
Reservoir*

Koloa

Kawelikoa
Point
*Kaneailoa
Bay*

Maha'ulepu Coast

NUKUMOI POINT

A turtle cleaning station stretching
from 25ft to 55ft.
(p195)

**KOLOA
LANDING**
**SHERATON
CAVERNS** Po'ipu **ZAC'S
POCKET**
**NUKUMOI
POINT**

Ka'ie'ie Waho Channel

KOLOA LANDING

The best shore dive on the island,
ideal for beginners.
(p195)

ZAC'S POCKET

The best coral reef on Kaua'i lives on
this deepwater ledge.
(p43)

Boating off the Na Pali Coast

Plan Your Trip
On the Water

Tucked into Kaua'i's 90 miles of coastline are more than 60 beaches. You need not drive far to find another (and yet another) gorgeous strand. North Shore and Westside beaches are most hazardous during winter (November through March) thanks to big surf, when South Shore and Eastside beaches are relatively calm. The pattern reverses in summer. Before plunging in, click to Kaua'i Explorer (www.kauaiexplorer.com), a Hanalei-based resource on beaches, ocean safety, marine life, ecotourism and much more.

Lifeguard-Protected Beaches

Lifeguard staffing is subject to change, so check with Hawaii Beach Safety (www.hawaiibeachsafety.com) online to confirm that the following beaches still have lifeguards:

➡ **Anahola Beach Park** (p131)
➡ **Ha'ena Beach Park** (p174)
➡ **Black Pot Beach Park (Hanalei Pier)** (p159)
➡ **Hanalei Beach Park** (p159)
➡ **Wai'oli (Pine Trees) Beach Park** (p159)
➡ **Kealia Beach Park** (p123)
➡ **Kekaha Beach Park** (p230)
➡ **Lydgate Beach Park** (p108)
➡ **Po'ipu Beach Park** (p192)
➡ **Salt Pond Beach Park** (p217)

Na Pali Coast Sea Tours

Glimpsing the Na Pali Coast by sea is an unforgettable experience. Primordial valleys of green not only beckon you to explore, but also to head back in time. Depending on your craft, you can paddle, snorkel, venture into sea caves or just kick back with a tropical drink, luxuriating in one of the world's great views. Assuming you can stomach the wave action, there's really no question of whether you should experience this Kaua'i highlight – the only question is how. Here's some help with sorting through the complexities.

Boat Tours

You have three types to choose from: catamarans (powered or sail), rafts (either Zodiacs or rigid-hulled inflatable boats; RIBs) or kayaks.

Catamarans are the cushiest, offering smoother rides, ample shade, restrooms and crowd-pleasing amenities, like on-board water slides and unlimited food and beverages. Some are equipped with sails (and actually use them), while others are entirely motorized. If you've only sailed monohulls before, this is a far more stable and roomy experience.

Rafts are the thrill-seeker's choice, bouncing along the water, entering caves (in mellower weather) and making beach landings, but most lack any shade, restrooms or comfy seating, so they're not for everyone (bad backs beware). The best rafts are RIBs, with hard bottoms that allow smoother rides (sit in back for less jostling but potentially more sea spray). The largest may include a canopy and even a toilet.

Kayaks are for people who want a work-out with their Na Pali Coast tour. They're of the sit-on-top variety, with seat backs and pedal rudders. You don't need to be a triathlete or kayaking expert to use one, but you should be in top physical condition, as kayak tours can last 12 hours and you'll be paddling 17 miles.

Departure Point

You can access the Na Pali Coast from the North Shore or from Westside. If you're visiting in the summer months, the North Shore – whether Hanalei or 'Anini – is definitely preferable, and the only option for kayaks, which paddle 17 miles from Ha'ena Beach Park to Polihale State Park. Kayak trips are organized by two outfitters in Hanalei.

Boat trips from Westside have to cover a lot of extra water before they reach the Na Pali Coast. As a result, they only get to see half the coastline. But in the winter months when waves are brutal on the North Shore, those tours stop running, leaving you no other choice. Westside tours depart from Port Allen Harbor. However, winter weather still takes its toll, preventing landings at Nu'alolo Kai and limiting snorkeling opportunities.

Preparations

Book Na Pali Coast boat or kayak tours as early in your trip as possible (ideally before you arrive), as high surf or foul weather may cause cancellations. If you are prone to seasickness – a very real issue – inquire about sea conditions, take medication ahead of time and opt for the catamaran. Morning trips generally see the calmest seas.

Kayaking
River

With seven rivers, including the only navigable one statewide, river kayaking is all the rage on Kaua'i. A Wailua River tour, which includes a dip at a 130ft waterfall, is the classic. Due to the river's popularity, the county strictly regulates its use (eg no tours on Sundays). Most outfitters are located in Wailua, Hanalei and Lihu'e.

If you're seeking a solitary nature experience, you should visit Kaua'i's other rivers, smaller but perhaps more charming and leisurely. Hanalei River and Kalihiwai Stream are highly recommended. A handful of kayak tours navigate the Hule'ia River, which passes through the off-limits Hule'ia National Wildlife Refuge.

Sea

Sea kayaking off Kaua'i should be done on tour because of rough surf. Beginners can learn in Po'ipu and Hanalei, while the fit and ambitious can challenge themselves on the grueling 17-mile Na Pali journey, possible only in summer. If you are indeed experienced, in summer it's possible to rent kayaks and camping gear for a Na Pali paddle under your own steam.

Ocean Safety

The Hawaiian Islands don't have a continental shelf. Consequently, the ocean doesn't roll up gently to their doorstep: it strikes hard. This creates swimming conditions that are altogether different than those on the mainland. The ocean has a devastating power here, producing dangerous rip currents, rogue waves and

Kayaking along the Na Pali Coast

undertows. For most visitors, the following warning applies: *you cannot think of swimming in Hawaii the way you think of swimming back home.* This is particularly true of Kaua'i, which has the highest per capita drowning rate of all of the main Hawaiian Islands. About seven tourists drown here each year. In 2016 there were 11 drownings through to November, or one a month.

To protect yourself, heed the basic warnings:

➡ Never turn your back on the ocean.

➡ Never swim alone. If you're an inexperienced swimmer, swim only at lifeguarded beaches. At beaches without lifeguards, swim only if (and where) locals are doing so.

➡ Observe the surf for a while before entering. Look for recurring sets of waves, currents and other swimmers.

➡ Observe the wind. Windy conditions increase ocean chop.

➡ Don't walk on coastal rocks, where an unexpected wave can sweep you out. It's easy to misjudge the 'safe zone.'

➡ Don't assume that water conditions are consistent in all regions.

Stand up paddle surfing (SUP)

There is, of course, no reason why you can't have a great time swimming on Kaua'i. Just use your head, and if that little voice is warning you about something, listen to it. In Hawaii there is a saying: 'When in doubt, don't go out.' These are words to stay alive by. For current information and more advice, read the ocean report and safety tips at Hawaii Beach Safety (http://hawaiibeach safety.com) and Kaua'i Explorer (www. kauaiexplorer.com).

Stand Up Paddle Surfing

In the 1960s, Waikiki watermen developed stand up paddle surfing (SUP) when teaching groups of beginning surfers. Standing on their boards, using a paddle to propel themselves, they could easily view their surroundings. In the early 2000s, SUP emerged as a global sport when big-name pros, including and especially local boy, Laird Hamilton, started doing it as a substitute when waves were flat or when they wanted to catch especially big surf outside the main lineup. Companies that provide rentals and lessons have cropped up by beaches and rivers island-wide, including at Lihu'e's Kalapaki Beach, near Wailua on the Eastside, around Po'ipu on the South Shore and in Hanalei on the North Shore.

Swimming

You can find protected swimming lagoons year-round at Lydgate Beach Park and Salt Pond Beach Park. Elsewhere, swimming is a seasonal sport. On the North Shore, swimming is lovely in summer, when waters are glassy at Hanalei Bay and Ke'e Beach. In winter, when giant swells pound the North Shore, head to the South Shore, especially Po'ipu Beach Park.

Lap swimmers who need lanes and walls can take advantage of the Olympic-sized YMCA pool in Lihu'e.

Humpback whale

Whale Watching

Each winter about 10,000 North Pacific humpback whales migrate to the shallow coastal waters off the Hawaiian Islands to breed, calve and nurse. Whale-watching boat tours are a hot-ticket item, especially during the peak migration season (January through March). Although it can't compete with the sheer number of whales spotted off Maui or the Big Island, Kaua'i still sees plenty of migratory whales, with some of its North Shore waters protected by the **Hawaiian Islands Humpback Whale National Marine Sanctuary** (www. hawaiihumpbackwhale.noaa.gov). Whale-watching boat tours depart mainly from Port Allen Harbor on the Westside. But if you park yourself on the Princeville cliffs, Kilauea Point (p144) or at Po'ipu Beach Park (p192) on any winter's day, you are likely to see whales spouting and breaching all day long.

Surfing at sunset, Po'ipu Beach Park (p192)

Plan Your Trip

Surfing

People have been riding the waves of Kaua'i for over 500 years, and there are an estimated 300 surf breaks surrounding the island. From a few decent beginner spots – especially along the South Shore – to powerful waves, tubes and reef breaks that are better suited to practiced experts, there is something for everyone on Kaua'i.

Surf Beaches & Breaks

Given the steepness of the waves, short boarders and big gun riders will find more versatility on Kaua'i's waves. Long boards still make their way into the lineup, especially when the waves aren't quite so big. You can also ride stand-up paddle boards, boogie boards or just head out for bodyboarding sessions. Bringing your own board can be expensive. Consider renting or buying locally (then reselling upon departure).

Water temperatures range from 78°F to 82°F (26°C to 28°C), and most people just ride with board shorts and a rash-guard. If you get cold easily, you may consider a light wetsuit in winter.

Surfline (www.surfline.com) reports current conditions at the island's best-known surf breaks, as does **Surf Forecast** (www.surf-forecast.com) and **Kauai Explorer** (www.kauaiexplorer.com). Alternatively, call the **Surf Hotline** (☑808-241-7873).

North Shore

Hanalei Bay (p158) is the sexus, nexus and plexus of Kaua'i surfing. Here, you will find both reef and point breaks. Head to the south side of the pier to surf the gentle waves at Kiddies if you are just getting your start. The eastern point of the bay has four reef breaks (The Bowl, Flat Rock, Impossibles and Super Impossibles) that can sometimes be connected for one of the longest rides on the islands. A quarter mile east of here, Summers is big with the SUP crowd, while still further east below the cliffs you find Hideaways.

Heading west from Hanalei, you find Waikokos (p159), a gentle left that rarely gets above 4ft. Near here you can find tougher reef breaks at Wiapa, Chicken Wings and Middles (p159).

West of Wainiha (p173), you find the twin guns of Tunnels (p175) and Cannons, sometimes referred to as the Pipeline of Kaua'i.

Near Kilauea (p144), check out Rock Quarry Beach on the eastern edge of town, or head to Kalihiwai Beach west of here for a killer right point break.

South Shore

As a general rule, surf tourism is relegated to the South Shore around Po'ipu (p189). Not such a bad deal as there are some fun waves to be had there. Breaking best in the summer on south swells, spots such as PK's (p196), Acid Drop (p196) and Centers (p196) challenge even advanced surfers. First-timers can get their feet wet at Waiohai (p196) near the Marriott resort, and Donovans (p196) (aka Learners), in front of the Kiahuna. Only bodyboarding and bodysurfing are permitted at Brennecke's Beach (p192) – no stand up surfing.

Po'ipu Beach Park (p192) is crowded but has a really good beginner wave called Lemon Drops, while Shipwreck Beach (p192) and Maha'ulepu Beach (p193) draw only experts.

Westside

Pakalas (Kaumuali'i Hwy), also known as Infinities, near Waimea, is the Westside's hottest break, but it's for locals only and the unprotected western waters mean winter breaks are treacherous.

The Waimea Rivermouth (p225) has dirty water, but fun waves that can be suitable for beginners. For strong waves from Waimea, try Davidson (p230) or Major's Bay (p230).

In Polihale State Park (p231) you get mostly beach breaks, with the takeoff points and rides changing with the winds. On the south end, look for a reef break at Queen's Pond. On the north, hit up the beach peaks or go to Echo's, just at the start of the Na Pali Cliffs (advanced riders only). Boogie boarders have fun here.

SURF LINGO

Hawaii has a wonderful surfing lexicon. A few words you definitely want to know:

aggro – aggressive

Barney – defined in the classic 1987 surf movie *North Shore* as a 'kook in and out of the water,' it means somebody that doesn't know what they are doing

Betty – hot surfer chick

brah – brother or friend

green room – inside of a wave's tube

grom or grommet – younger surfers (who are probably better than you)

howlie – white person or non-Hawaiian

Eastside

Transitional swells happen on the Eastside, where surfers hit Kealia Beach Park (p123) and Lihu'e's Kalapaki Beach (p87), a good spot for the SUP crowd. Eastside swells often break on distant reefs and hence get blown out except during early-morning hours and leeward wind conditions.

On the Eastside, Unreals (p131) breaks at Anahola Bay. It's a consistent right point that can work well on an easterly wind swell, when leeward winds are offshore. Locals rule at Anahola and can be unwelcoming to outsiders.

Surfing lessons in Hanalei (p162)

Learning to Surf

There are dozens of surf schools and surf shops. Classes usually last 60 minutes to a couple hours, with board rental included in the price. Try for small classes to get the most out of the instruction. Surfing lessons and board rentals are available primarily in Hanalei and Po'ipu, as well as at Kalapaki Beach in Lihu'e.

Beginners don't normally require much more than an intro class. Classes generally run from an hour to two. Trust us, you won't be able to paddle after a two-hour session. They include some practice on the beach, then you head to the lineup. Instructors will often push you on to the waves to help you get the hang of it.

Surfing is an intuitive sport. The best way to learn to surf is to just get out there and surf. Start with a few requisite jumps to the top of your board on the beach (á la Point Break), then find a small set of waves to try to ride. The key to catching a wave is power. Paddle as hard as you can, then try to stand up. After you fall, try it again.

Staying safe here means not paddling out for waves that are too big for your abilities. Watch rip currents, know where the channel is, and think about the way the shape of the reef might just affect the shape of your head.

Surfing Etiquette

Just as Hawaiian royalty had certain breaks reserved just for them, so goes it on Kaua'i's surf breaks. Respect locals and local customs or you might end up with a

black eye (and a bad reputation). Tourists are welcome – especially on the South Shore – but deference to local riders is always recommended.

In the water, basic surf etiquette is vital. The person closest to the peak of the wave has the right of way. When somebody is already up and riding, don't take off on the wave in front of them. Don't paddle straight through the lineup. Rather, head out through the channel where the waves aren't breaking and then find your way into the lineup. When you wipe out – and you'll do this plenty – try to keep track of your board.

Also, remember you're a visitor out in the lineup, so don't expect to get every wave that comes your way. There's a definite pecking order and, frankly, as a tourist you're at the bottom. That said, usually if you give a wave, you'll get a wave in return.

As a tourist in Hawaii, there are some places you go and there are some places you don't go. For many local families the beach parks are meeting places where generations gather to celebrate life under the sun. They're tied to these places by a sense of community and culture, and they aren't eager for outsiders to push them out of time-honored surf spots.

WEST OF WAINIHA

Here you'll find the Pipeline of Kaua'i and extreme rides that are simply insane. (p175)

POLIHALE STATE PARK

Super-fun beach breaks that move with the tide and can get downright big if the swell is right. (p231)

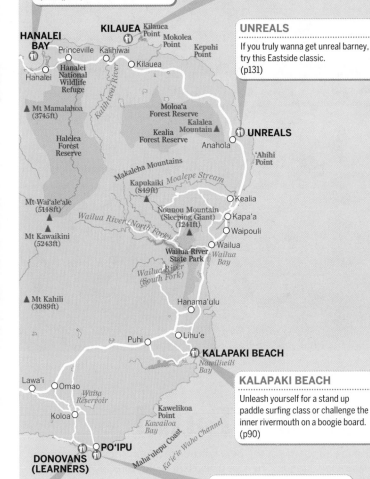

HANALEI BAY

This is it! The most radical, steep, long and tasty waves on the island. Choose from hard-crashing reef breaks and smooth-sailing beach spots. (p159)

KILAUEA

This less-trodden spot has a raucous point break.
(p145)

UNREALS

If you truly wanna get unreal barney, try this Eastside classic.
(p131)

KALAPAKI BEACH

Unleash yourself for a stand up paddle surfing class or challenge the inner rivermouth on a boogie board. (p90)

PO'IPU

Good for beginners – and more friendly to tourists – there are several nice rights in town. (p192)

DONOVANS (LEARNERS)

The top learning wave on Kaua'i, this simple ride takes you right into shore. (p196)

Ziplining in Kaua

Plan Your Trip
On the Land

Kaua'i has some of the best land-born adventures of any of the Hawaiian Islands. The steep, verdant mountains of Waimea Canyon and the Na Pali Coast offer world-class hiking, longer treks and even short family adventures. When you've had your fill, spend a day or two taking on a zipline, heading out for a horseback ride, cruising on backroads on ATV, camping in lost corners of the forest or golfing on drop-dead-gorgeous golf courses.

Ziplining

Ziplines, which first appeared in Costa Rica, are now proliferating across Hawaii. But location matters – and Kaua'i's magnificent forests are hard to beat. This outdoor adventure requires neither skill nor training, but participants must meet minimum age (generally seven years for a tandem ride) and maximum weight restrictions (ballpark no more than 280lb). Some operators offer superman flights (where you fly head first), others include rappelling through waterfalls or ATV tours.

Top outfits include:

➡ **Koloa Zipline** (p185)

➡ **Skyline Eco-Adventures** (p194)

➡ **Just Live** (p90)

➡ **Kaua'i Backcountry Adventures** (p91)

➡ **Princeville Ranch Adventures** (p154)

Camping

Kaua'i offers camping at all levels of roughin' it. Some campgrounds, such as 'Anini Beach Park, are within view of houses; others, such as the campground at Kalalau Beach, are miles from civilization. For camping supplies and rentals, the best rental source is Pedal 'n Paddle (p162) in Hanalei. You can also buy camping gear from some outdoor outfitters, such as Da Life (p100) at Kalapaki Beach and Aloha XCHNG (p205) in Kalaheo, or from chain retailers like Kmart, Walmart and Costco in Lihu'e.

On the North Shore, try Kayak Kaua'i (p162) and Na Pali Kayak (p163) out of Hanalei to get geared up for Na Pali adventures.

Another backcountry option is to stay in the number of rustic cabins located within the state parks and preserves. Whatever you do, make sure you are not camping on private campsites. Everybody loves going to the beach at night – to look at the stars, drink wine, and make out. It's generally fine, but you should check with locals first to make sure you're going to a beach that's cool for tourists.

State Parks

State-park campgrounds can be found at the following parks:

➡ **Na Pali Coast Wilderness State Park** (p177) Camping at Hanakapi'ai and Kalalau Valleys requires an overnight hike.

➡ **Koke'e State Park** (p233) Drive-up and hike-in camping, and a bunch of cabins.

➡ **Waimea Canyon State Park** (p78) Hike-in camping only, and a few cabins worth checking out.

➡ **Polihale State Park** (p231) Beachfront camping.

Permits are required from the Division of State Parks (p227), obtainable either in person in Lihu'e or online at https://camping.ehawaii.gov up to a year in advance. Fees range from $18 to $30 per night (or $20 per person per night on the Na Pali Coast). Maximum-stay limits of three to five nights are enforced.

For backcountry camping on the Westside, the Division of Forestry & Wildlife (p227) issues free permits for four backcountry campgrounds in Waimea Canyon, three campgrounds in and around Koke'e State Park, and the Waialae campground near the Alaka'i Wilderness Preserve. Apply online or in person at the Lihu'e office.

County Parks

The county maintains seven campgrounds on Kaua'i, all of which have bathrooms, cold-water outdoor showers and picnic tables. Moving clockwise around the island, these are the following:

➡ **Ha'ena Beach Park** (p174) (closed 10am Monday to noon Tuesday)

➡ **Black Pot Beach Park (Hanalei Pier)** (p159) (open Friday and Saturday nights only)

➡ **'Anini Beach Park** (p152) (closed 10am Tuesday to noon Wednesday)

➡ **Anahola Beach Park** (p131) (closed 10am Thursday to noon Friday)

➡ **Hanama'ulu Beach Park** (temporarily closed for camping at the time of research)

➡ **Salt Pond Beach Park** (p217) (closed 10am Tuesday to noon Wednesday)

➡ **Lucy Wright Park** (p223) (closed 10am Monday to noon Tuesday)

➡ **Lydgate Park** (p108) (open 7am to 6pm)

The best county campgrounds are the coastal parks at Ha'ena, Hanalei, Salt Pond Beach, and the particularly secluded and idyllic 'Anini Beach. The parks at Lucy Wright, Anahola and Hanama'ulu tend to attract a rougher, shadier crowd and are not recommended for solo or female campers. Each campground is closed one day a week for cleaning and in order to prevent people from permanently squatting there.

Camping permits cost $3 per night per adult camper (children under 18 years free) and are issued in person or by mail (at least one month in advance) by the Division of Parks & Recreation (p100) in Lihu'e. For mail-in permits, only cashier's checks or money orders are accepted for payment.

ATV tours, Kipu Ranch Adventures, Lihu'e

resort fees, golf in the afternoon for the 'twilight' rate. All the courses rent clubs and several require carts. For an afternoon of fun with the kiddos, check out the North Shore's Kauai Mini Golf & Botanical Gardens (p148).

Golf

Kaua'i has only nine golf courses, but there's something for every taste and budget. Pros and experts can try the Makai Golf Club (p154) in Princeville. The best course in Lihu'e is the oceanfront Hōkūala Resort (p89), while the Puakea Golf Course (p90) is no slouch in and of itself. Nearby Wailua Municipal Golf Course (p112) is a cheaper alternative. Po'ipu Bay (p193) and Kiahuna Golf Courses (p194) in Po'ipu are a little more affordable than the northern counterparts. Probably the cheapest course by far is the Kukuiolono Golf Course (p204) on the South Shore near the village of Kalaheo. To save on

Horseback Riding

Vast pastureland from open coastal cliffs to jungly rainforests provides ample terrain for horseback riding. A handful of stables offer tours, mainly for beginners and families. On the South Shore, CJM Country Stables (p195) rides along the Maha'ulepu Coast, while on the North Shore, Princeville Ranch Stables (p153) and Silver Falls Ranch (p147) traverse green pastures, ranch lands, streams and waterfalls. Even though it's hot, it's recommended that you wear long pants to avoid very painful riding sores on your inner thighs and ankles. It's how the cowboys do it!

Camping on the Na Pali Coast (p59)

ATV

Kaua'i has an endless number of dirt tracks, and large expanses of unpopulated private land. This makes it a beckoning playground for an all-terrain vehicle (ATV). If you've never driven one before, don't be cowed by the great big four-wheeled thing; it's a breeze, and loads of fun. Just be prepared to swallow a few bugs and get dirty. Most operations now have traditional four-wheeler ATVs, as well as more modern (and more stables razors and other off-roaders). You have to be 16 years or older to drive, and generally, tours require riders are at least five years old.

Of the few companies that specialize in ATV tours, try **Kipu Ranch Adventures** (☎808-246-9288; www.kiputours.com; Kipu Rd; tours adult/child from $98/45; ☺daily tour hours vary, by reservation only) in Lihu'e or Koloa Zipline and Kaua'i ATV Adventures (p185).

Climbing the Sleeping Giant (p104), Nounou Mountain, Kapa

Plan Your Trip

Hiking & Biking

Kaua'i arguably has some of the best hiking and trekking of all the Hawaiian Islands. For inexperienced hikers or families with small kids, plenty of shorter trails get you closer to the nature, flora and fauna of Kaua'i. Historic trails in some of the older villages will introduce you to a unique history and culture, with interpretive signs and guided routes. Trails can be extended over a few days, with intermittent stops at camps or cabins, and there's loads of variety (from beachfront walks to slippery treks down impossible steep slopes).

Guided Hikes

The Kaua'i chapter of the Sierra Club (p275) leads guided hikes ranging from beach clean-up walks to hardy day-long treks. With a suggested donation of only $5 per person for nonmembers, these outings are an extraordinary bargain. All hikers must sign a liability waiver, and those aged under 18 must be accompanied by an adult. Advance registration may also be required; check the website in advance.

Other guided hike options:

➡ **Kaua'i Nature Tours** (p113) offers hiking tours all over the island. While they are expensive, they include guides who are full of endless tales, scientific facts, and colorful historical and cultural information about the island.

➡ **Hike Kaua'i Adventures** (p234) offers bespoke hiking adventures all over the island with a friendly guide who knows the island backward and forward.

Hiking
Where to Hike

If you don't explore the island on foot, you're missing out on Kaua'i's finest (and free) terrestrial offerings. Hike up mountaintop wet forests, along steep coastal cliffs and down a colossal lava canyon – places you can't get to by car. Trails range from easy walks to precarious treks, catering to all skill levels. For the most variety, head to Waimea Canyon (p78) and Koke'e State Parks (p233). Don't miss the Pihea Trail (p235), which connects to the Alaka'i Swamp Trail, for a look at pristine native forest filled with

singing birds, or trek the Awa'awapuhi Trail (p208) or Nu'alolo Trail (p208) for breathtaking views of the Na Pali cliffs.

Along the Na Pali Coast, the wilderness Kalalau Trail (p138) now attracts anyone with two legs – but only for the first section to Hanakapi'ai Beach. Eastside hikes head inland and upward, such as the Nounou Mountain Trails (p104), which afford sweeping mountain-to-ocean views, and the Kuilau Ridge and Moalepe Trails (p104). In addition to official trails, Kaua'i's vast coastline allows mesmerizing ocean walks, particularly along the cliffs of the Maha'ulepu Heritage Trail (p180) and the endless carpet of sand in remote Polihale State Park (p231). In Lihu'e, an afternoon walk out to the Ninini Point Lighthouse (p88) is a gorgeous way to spend the afternoon.

On the South Shore, the McBryde (p182) and Allerton Gardens (p189) are a great spot to walk with families and friends and take in an afternoon picnic, while on the North Shore, the Limahuli Garden (p174) provides a tropical entrance to Eden and fun hikes through large gardens. Combine your river adventures on the Wailua River (p113) with a hike to a lost waterfall.

Some of the bigger hikes in the state parks will likely be too strenuous for young kids. But your tots will love running through the maze at Lydgate Beach Park (p108), or cruising the boardwalk at Ke Ala Hele Makalae (p127) on the Eastside. The short jaunt to Kilauea Point (p144) is a top spot for birdwatching. The Canyon Trail (p209) in Waimea Canyon State Park is widely considered the best kid-friendly hike on the Westside, as are the short interpretive trails out to the lookouts along the drive.

The villages of Koloa, Waimea and Hanapepe all have signed historical walks.

Hiking Safety on Kaua'i

A lot of people die in Kaua'i hiking out on trails that have been closed, or out to remote beaches that see large waves. Don't be a statistic.

➡ Before you leave, tell somebody where you are going and when you expect to be back.

➡ Take enough water for your entire trip, especially the uphill return journey, and treat any water found along the trails.

➡ Rain is always a factor, especially on the North Shore, at Koke'e State Park and in Waimea Canyon. Trails that are doable in dry weather can become precariously slippery with mud.

NU'ALOLO TRAIL

One of the most challenging trails in Koke'e State Park, this thigh-buster takes you over knife ridges to a towering overlook of the Na Pali Coast. (p208)

KALALAU TRAIL

Is this the best hiking trail in the Pacific? Could be. Enjoy coastal views, verdant cliffs and pristine wilderness along the Na Pali Coast's signature hike. (p138)

CANYON TRAIL

Bring the tots for exploration of Waimea Canyon. They'll love stopping to smell the hibiscus along the way. (p209)

Kailiu Point Ha'ena
Ha'ena Wainiha
State Park

KALALAU TRAIL 🏕

Hono'o
Na Pali
▲ (3330ft)

Na Pali Coast
Na Pali Coast
Wilderness
State Park
Pihea ▲ Moa'alele
(4284ft) (4095ft)

Na Pali–Kona
Forest Reserve ▲ Kilohana
Nu'alolo Kai ○ Kuia Natural Alaka'i (4022ft)
Area Reserve Pu'u o Kila Swamp
(4176ft)

NU'ALOLO TRAIL 🏕 Koke'e
State
Park

Pu'u Ka Pele **CANYON** Na Pali–Kona Alaka'i
Forest Reserve **TRAIL** Forest Reserve Wilderness
Preserve

Polihale
State Park Waimea

Nohili Canyon
Point State Park

Pu'u Ka Pele
Forest Reserve

Mana
Point ○ Mana

Barking Sands
Pacific Missile
Range Facility

Kokole
Point Kekaha ○

Waimea ○

Kaulakahi Channel

Kalaheo

Kaumakani ○

Hanapepe ○ Ele'ele

Makaokahai
Point

Lumaha'i River

Wainiha River

Waimea Canyon

Waimea River

Hanapepe River

N 0 ————— 10 km
   0 ————— 5 miles

KUILAU RIDGE & MOALEPE TRAILS

Take in the beauty and bounty of these tropical trails, thick with ferns and misty views of arching rainbows. (p104)

NOUNOU MOUNTAIN TRAILS

Take in panoramic views of the Eastside from the top of the world. (p104)

Kilauea Point
Mokolea Point
Kepuhi Point

Hanalei Bay
Princeville
Kalihiwai
Hanalei
Kilauea

PACIFIC OCEAN

Hanalei National Wildlife Refuge

Kalihiwai River

▲ Mt Mamalahoa (3745ft)

Moloa'a Forest Reserve
Kalalea Mountain ▲
Kealia Forest Reserve

Halelea Forest Reserve

Anahola

'Ahihi Point

Makaleha Mountains
Kapukaiki (849ft)
Moalepe Stream

Mt Wai'ale'ale (5148ft) ▲

KUILAU RIDGE & MOALEPE TRAILS

Kealia

NOUNOU MOUNTAIN TRAILS

Kapa'a

Waipouli

Mt Kawaikini (5243ft) ▲

Nounou Mountain ▲ (Sleeping Giant) (1241ft)
Wailua

WAILUA RIVER

WAILUA RIVER

Combine a canoe paddle with a hike to a lost waterfall in this emerald paradise. (p104)

LYDGATE BEACH PARK

Hanama'ulu

▲ Mt Kahili (3089ft)

Puhi
Lihu'e

Nawiliwili Bay

LYDGATE BEACH PARK

One of the most accessible paved beach-trails, Lydgate is great for adventures with the whole family. (p108)

Lawa'i
Omao

Waita Reservoir

MAHA'ULEPU HERITAGE TRAIL

Kawelikoa Point

Koloa

Kawailoa Bay

MCBRYDE GARDEN

Po'ipu

Makahuena Point

Maha'ulepu Coast

Ka'ie'ie Waho Channel

MAHA'ULEPU HERITAGE TRAIL

Get away from the tourist crowds to visit lost beaches, blowholes and windswept coastlines. (p180)

MCBRYDE GARDEN

This large botanic garden can be hiked in a few hours, with stops at orchid gardens, spice trails and more. (p194)

➡ Cell phones can be handy, but may lack reception in many remote areas (eg Koke'e State Park, Na Pali Coast).

➡ Pack first-aid supplies and snacks.

➡ Wear appropriate footwear: while Chacos or Tevas are fine for easy coastal walks, bring hiking shoes or boots for major trails.

➡ Flash floods are real threats wherever there are stream or river crossings. Never cross a waterway when it's raining. River fords may quickly rise to impassable levels, preventing you from returning for hours or days.

➡ If possible, hike with a companion.

➡ Don't go off-trail or bushwhack new trails and take care not to cross private property.

➡ Lava terrain is frequently eroded and can be unstable, especially along cliffs.

➡ Never go beyond fenced lookouts.

➡ Note the time of sunset and plan to return well before it's dark. Be aware that daylight will fade inside a canyon long before sundown.

➡ Bring a flashlight just in case.

➡ Most accidents occur not due to a trail's inherent slipperiness or steepness, but because hikers take unnecessary risks. Park and forestry officials have little patience for this, because it requires expensive rescue missions that jeopardize others' safety.

➡ When hiking along the coast, be aware of rising tides, tide tables and frequent large waves. Kaua'i has more drowning deaths than any of the Hawaiian Islands. A lot of people visit beaches that should be off-limits.

Cycling & Mountain Biking

Road Cycling

It's possible to ride along the belt highway in the Westside, South Shore and most of the Eastside, but there are no bike lanes and road shoulders can be narrow or nonexistent. Only experienced cyclists should consider cycling as transportation on Kaua'i.

Once the Eastside's coastal path, Ke Ala Hele Makalae, is completed, cycling from Lihu'e all the way to Anahola will be doable by the masses. For now, the path is used only recreationally in stretches near Lydgate Beach Park and from Kapa'a Beach Park north to Paliku (Donkey)

Mountain biking, Waimea Canyon

Beach. Bear in mind that cyclists share the path with pedestrians.

Cycling the North Shore past Princeville is impossible along the narrow cliffside highway. However, the Westside is a very different story. Cycling downhill on Hwy 550 from Waimea Canyon is so spectacular that it has been turned into a guided tour; book ahead with Outfitters Kauai (p233).

Mountain Biking

If you aren't afraid of mud and puddles, you can go wild on countless dirt roads and a few trails islandwide. The Powerline Trail (p155) is a decent, if potholed and muddy, option – and you can start from either Wailua or Princeville. The dirt roads near Po'ipu, above Maha'ulepu Beach, are flat but nice and dry, and you're less likely to encounter rain showers there. For a solitary ride, your best bets are the hunter roads at Waimea Canyon State Park. For more information contact Na Ala Hele (p272) and Kauai Cycle (p118), an Eastside bike rental and repair shop with a knowledgeable crew.

The road to Waimea Canyon (p210)

Plan Your Trip
Driving

On an impossibly scenic island, it seems superfluous to point out those avenues, roads and highways that earn exceptional status even by Kaua'i's high standards. Especially when the most casual drive to the nearest Big Save is capable of golden reveals – such as, say, a double rainbow over a humble plantation cottage nestled on a lawn. On the Garden Island there are roads to paradise within paradise, places and vistas the hordes might miss on their mad scramble to do and see. Although, to be fair, we've listed obvious winners too. Some of the drives are long, others quick, and each one breathtaking in its own way.

End of the Road – North

Heading north out of Hanalei, **Kuhio Hwy** narrows a bit further and becomes a dreamy ribbon of asphalt that snakes between jungled lava cliffs weeping with waterfalls, and a coastline that's among the most beautiful on earth. Along the way there will be a succession of one-lane bridges, rivers to cross and empty beaches on which to stop and stroll. They'll flick by one after another: first Lumaha'i (p173) then Ha'ena (p174), until you pass the jade Eden that is Limahuli Garden (p174) on the left and enter **Ha'ena State Park**, where you'll meet the end of the road. Time your arrival for just before sundown and the explosion of color you're sure to witness should come with plentiful parking.

Highway 580 (Eastside)

The drive into the Wailua Homesteads along Kuamo'o Rd is among the island's most textured. Starting at the river mouth in Wailua River State Park, you'll pass two heiau and 'Opaeka'a Falls (p109), and wind your way past several trailheads and quiet neighborhoods quilted in farmland surrounded by jade peaks. Rainbows are common and, on drizzly days, the mist only makes it more beautiful. Follow the route all the way to the Keahua Arboretum (p109) at the end of the road.

Koloa, Po'ipu

The various well-trod routes from Hwy 50 into Koloa, from Koloa to Po'ipu, and from the beach through Lawai and back to the highway, may be routine but they are still stunning. The eucalyptus trees that form the Tree Tunnel (p185) along **Maluhia Rd** – the main branch that connects Koloa to the highway – were planted in 1911. The trees are well over 50ft tall and their canopies interconnect. From there you have two options into Po'ipu. The loveliest is the **Koloa Bypass Rd,** and while it skips Koloa town, you're rewarded with views of the old **Koloa Sugar Mill** and the rolling grasslands of Pu'u Hi, which rumbled with volcanic activity, oh about 150,000 years ago. On your way back to Hwy 50 after a day at the beach, consider taking the westerly **Ala Kalanikaumakai** bypass past the Kukui'ula development and through lush **Lawai**.

Halewili Road

Heading west from Kalaheo toward 'Ele'ele, Port Allen and beyond, you have two choices. You can stay with **Hwy 50**, which is rather straight and uneventful – though on Kaua'i there are always mountain views – or you can make a left on **Hwy 540**, aka **Halewili Rd**, past Kauai Coffee Company's (p212) coffee bushes and facilities with gorgeous ocean views beckoning beyond. The road is straight at first but banks right hard, so watch your speed. Now you are parallel to the coast on your way back toward the highway, which you'll rejoin in **'Ele'ele**. This is a quick but worthy detour, and can sometimes be faster than staying on the highway.

ALEKOKO (MENEHUNE) FISHPOND DETOUR OVERLOOK (LIHU'E)

Here's a drive many overlook. Beginning at Kalapaki Beach (p87), head southwest on **Niumalu Rd**, past **Nawiliwli Harbor** where cruise and container ships dock, through tiny **Niumalu** and onto **Hulemalū Rd**. As the road rises you'll enjoy a mountainous landscape, looming and gorgeous until you reach the **Alekoko (Menehune) Fishpond Overlook** (p87). The mountains themselves tell the story of the naughty supernatural prince and princess who were turned to stone and have guarded the fishpond for eternity. You can see them: two knobs jutting from the top of the sheer cliff. Continue on **Old Hulamalū Rd** and more of tranquil rural Kaua'i will unfurl. This is a proper, potholed backroad with sweeping views. Hang a right on **Kipu Rd** and you'll connect to Hwy 50, with access to the Eastside, South Shore and beyond.

Alekoko (Menehune) Fishpond

Waimea Canyon Drive & Koke'e Road

A can't miss (read: obvious) choice, and for good reason. Rising from Waimea (p223), the canyon road (p231) passes multiple overlooks (p231) with majestic views of what Mark Twain once called the Grand Canyon of the Pacific. This jigsaw of red rock, dappled with green in the winter when it's gushing with waterfalls, looks the part too. Soon after, you'll join **Koke'e Rd**, which passes a last canyon lookout (p231) at 3120ft above sea level, before meandering into Koke'e State Park (p233) where you can access multiple trails. On the way back, stay with Koke'e Rd all the way downhill and you'll get a different view before landing in Kekaha (p230), the most westward town on the island.

End of the Road – West

Past the Kekaha cornfields and the **Pacific Missile Range Facility**, **Hwy 50** peters out to a rutted and rough dirt track that branches northwest for 4 miles to Polihale State Park (p231). Your cell coverage may die, and as the red dust rises behind you, and the Na Pali cliffs rise to your right, you may feel like the last people on earth. That's not necessarily a pleasant feeling, but it is exciting, and when the road ends you will be on Kaua'i's wildest, longest and widest stretch of sand. From here the coastline is roadless until those cliffs wind back around to Ke'e Beach (p176) on the North Shore. Make sure you're in a 4WD-capable vehicle with high clearance and a spare tire handy, but don't you dare miss it. If you bring beers (and you should), bring a tent too. Camping (p231) is not only allowed, it's encouraged at Polihale.

Green Kaua'i

The foundation of life for ancient Hawaiians was the philosophy of aloha *'aina* – love, care and respect for the land. Eco-concepts such as 'green' and 'sustainable' weren't catchphrases introduced by foreigners; they were principles already built into the fabric of everyday life, based upon a spiritual relationship with the land. Today those principles and that love are coming full circle on the Garden Island.

Helpful Organizations

➡ **Island Breath** (www.islandbreath.org) Dig deep into local issues with its links to newspaper and independent articles on Kaua'i's hot-button sustainability topics.

➡ **Kauai Explorer** (www.kauaiexplorer.com) While known mainly for its outstanding ocean-safety tips, this refreshingly concise site also contains preservation tips and a handy 'Where to Recycle' guide.

➡ **Malama Kaua'i** (www.malamakauai.org) This Kilauea-based grassroots organization is the island's watchdog, dedicated to protecting the *'aina*'s ecosystems and culture with a biweekly KKCR public-radio show, volunteering opportunities and more.

The Island Goes Green

Truth be known, being 'green' is not easy, especially on an island where staunchness is a positive attribute and change is met with resistance nearly every step of the way. Taking a broad overview of Kaua'i, one can see an isolated island threatened by over-development, traffic, a lack of affordable housing, waste creation, and an extreme reliance on imported fuel and food. However, look closer and what becomes visible are the efforts of a community working together to create and implement realistic future-based alternatives to the unsustainable practices that have taken over.

Voluntourism

While relishing in all the tropical delights Kaua'i has to offer, an hour or two spent volunteering can be satisfying. Listed here are a few volunteering opportunities. When possible, make arrangements in advance.

Hui O Laka (☑808-335-9975; www.kokee.org) Get dirty while working to restore forested areas impacted by overuse or invasive species, or participate in the annual bird count.

Kaua'i Habitat for Humanity (☑808-335-0296; http://kauaihabitat.org/volunteer/) ✿ Help build affordable housing in the island's low-income communities.

Waipa Foundation (p161) Call ahead to sign up or enquire about volunteer opportunities with this nonprofit organization.

Malama Kaua'i (☏808-828-0685; www.
malamakauai.org) Half-day volunteering projects
take place at the community gardens and 'Food
Forest' in Kilauea.

Koke'e Resource Conservation Program
(☏808-335-0045; www.krcp.org) ✎ Accepts
short-term and long-term volunteers and interns
to help with weed-control projects in and around
Koke'e, Waimea Canyon and Na Pali Wilderness
Coast State Parks. It involves strenuous hiking and
use of herbicides. Bunk-bed housing is provided
at the historic Koke'e Civilian Conservation Corps
(CCC) Camp.

National Tropical Botanical Garden
(NTBG; North Shore ☏808-826-1668 ext.
3, South Shore 808-332-7324 ext 232; www.
ntbg.org/donate/volunteer.php) Call or email
in advance to find out about the 'Vacation and
Volunteer' program.

Sierra Club (www.hi.sierraclub.org/kauai)
A pioneer in the environmental movement, this
nonprofit organization's Kaua'i chapter offers
guided outings, such as full-moon hikes, and half-
day volunteer projects cleaning up beaches and
restoring native plants.

Surfrider Foundation (☏808-635-2593;
http://kauai.surfrider.org) Public beach clean-
ups happen regularly, and can always use more
volunteers.

Impact of Tourism

High up on the list of ecological concerns
is tourism, an issue with which Kauaians
have a love-hate relationship. It drives the
economy but also affects the environment
and increases the cost of living.

In the mid-2000s resort and luxury
developments went gangbusters, with over
5000 residential units and 6100 resort
units on the drawing board. The largest
project, Po'ipu's massive Kukui'ula community, is on its way to being another enclave
of wealthy second-home buyers. While
Kukui'ula gets some credit for its Club
Cottages, which were designed to meet
Leadership in Energy and Environmental
Design (LEED) certification standards, its
asking price of almost $3 million is unaf-
fordable for most. Exclusive communities
like this can't help but shift island demo-
graphics away from people who are truly
connected to the land.

Environmentally, the biggest impacts of
tourism are from cruise ships and helicopters. Cruise ships burn diesel fuel, releasing

REDUCE, REUSE, RECYCLE
••••••••••••••••••••••••••••••••••••
Here's a list of convenient island recycling centers:

North Shore (5-3751 Kuhio Hwy)
At the Hanalei Transfer Station,
across from the Prince Golf Course in
Princeville.

Eastside (4900 Kahau Rd) In Kapa'a
at the end of Kahau Rd, behind the
ball field near the bypass road.

Lihu'e (4303 Nawiliwili Rd) At the
back of the Kmart parking lot on the
pavilion side of the store.

Nawiliwili Harbor (3343 Wilcox Rd)
At Reynolds Recycling, just north of
the harbor, at the corner of Kanoa Rd.

South Shore (2100 Ho'one Rd) In
the Brennecke's parking lot opposite
Po'ipu Beach Park.

Port Allen (4469 Waialo Rd) North
of the harbor at 'Ele'ele Shopping
Center.

Westside At Waimea Canyon Park
(4643 Waimea Canyon Dr) and Kekaha Landfill (6900-D Kaumuali'i Hwy).

exhaust fumes equivalent to thousands of
cars into the island's atmosphere. Their
discharge of ballast water and wastes
can pollute the ocean, damage coral reefs
and accidentally release invasive species.
Helicopter tours are popular with visitors,
but some residents and environmental
groups point out that those pleasure flights
contribute to both air and noise pollution. They also diminish the enjoyment of
Kaua'i's natural areas for those who choose
to visit them in low-impact ways, such as
by hiking or kayaking.

On the Ground

When it comes to putting green theory
into practice there are definite steps you
can take as a visitor to reduce further
harm to the *'aina* (land) without forgoing any of its charms. Available as a free
mobile app, the handy Green Kaua'i Map
(www.malamakauai.org) provides a list of
local businesses and organizations with
environmentally, socially and culturally

JOHN ELK/GETTY IMAGES ©

Top: Limahuli Garden (p174)

Bottom: Kaua'i Museum (p88)

responsible practices. Though the list is based on self-identification as being 'green,' it's a good starting point.

Transportation

Given limited bus services and safe bicycle lanes, there's no getting around the fact that you'll probably need a car on Kaua'i. But choosing a small rental car and efficiently planning daily excursions can make a difference. Perhaps pick a couple of home-based accommodations around the island. Then, at each place, keep your sightseeing to within that region. Along with saving on unnecessary fuel costs this will allow you to really plug in to your immediate surroundings, and most likely will result in a richer, more local travel experience.

Consider offsetting the carbon of your flight to the island by buying carbon credits. There is a bunch of companies now doing it and you can even arrange it through most major airlines. Some top offset companies include www.terrapass.com, www.myclimate.org and www.carbonfund.org.

Food & Accommodations

When it comes to eating, where you buy is as important as what you buy. Buying locally grown produce, locally caught fish and locally made cheeses, preserves and baked goods is very easy to do. Wherever you're located on the island there is both a weekly farmers market and a fish market open daily within a 20-minute drive or so. To find unique, homegrown food and drinks made around the island, visit the Kaua'i Made (http://kauaimade.net) website or look for its purple-and-green stickers on products when you're out shopping.

In 2009, Kaua'i County passed a ban on plastic bags at retail shops. Grocery stores and big-box chains now charge a small fee for recyclable paper bags, but bringing a reusable tote bag can earn you lots of points with the environmental karma police. The garbage dumps on Kaua'i are nearly overflowing, so it's always important to minimize your waste production. Try to patronize restaurants and food retailers who use biodegradable utensils, avoid styrofoam and feature local produce, dairy, seafood and meats as ingredients on their menus.

Camping is another way to make your vacation more green. Kaua'i offers state and county park campgrounds by the coast and in inland forests. All require getting advance permits, reservable online or available in person from government offices (most are in Lihu'e), so plan ahead.

Activities

For the price of an ATV or helicopter tour, you could instead get an up-close and personal experience with some of the same terrain on an expert-led hike with Kaua'i Nature Tours. Outrigger-canoe sailing with Kauai Outrigger Adventures or Island Sails Kaua'i in Hanalei, Garden Island Surf School or Kauai Island Experience in Po'ipu, or the Kamokila Hawaiian Village in Wailua, makes for a great time on the water.

Possibly the most Kaua'i-friendly activities you can try are those that teach about Hawaiian history and local culture, such as Limahuli Garden (p174) on the North Shore, the Kaua'i Museum (p88) in Lihu'e and the Eastside's Kaua'i Cultural Center. (p112) Agrotourism is also big on Kaua'i, including with Ho'opulapula Haraguchi Rice Mill & Taro Farm Tours (p163) in Hanalei and the renewable-energy-powered Kauai Coffee Company (p212).

Sustainable Agriculture

Another hot issue on Kaua'i is food security. About 90% of the island's food is imported, despite its natural biodiversity. At any given time there is only enough food on Kaua'i to feed the island for three to seven days.

A growing contingent of small-scale organic farmers argues that island agriculture is no longer viable by the old model of corporate-scale, industrialized monocropping (of pineapples and sugarcane, for example) enabled by chemical fertilizers, pesticides and herbicides. Instead, family farms growing diverse crops – for the table or for sale locally, not only globally – would always be sustainable.

Nobody goes into farming to make money, especially on Kaua'i, where limited resources mean that land, water and labor costs are comparatively high. Huge parcels of agricultural land are occupied by major multinational corporations growing genetically modified (GMO) crops, mainly corn. Minds differ on the risks of genetic modification, but many agree that island crops should benefit residents, not multinational corporations.

Plan Your Trip
Kaua'i by Air

There's nothing like seeing Kaua'i by air. Twisting through verdant tropical valleys, landing at remote waterfalls, hovering inside a volcanic crater and soaring like a bird over gorgeous coastline are all possible. Helicopter tours are by far the most common option: while planes can fly no lower than 1000ft to 1500ft, helicopters are allowed to fly as low as 500ft and can hover.

Top Helicopter Operators

➡ **Island Helicopters** (p91)
➡ **Mauna Loa Helicopters** (p92)
➡ **Jack Harter Helicopters** (p91)
➡ **Blue Hawaiian Helicopters** (p90)
➡ **Sunshine Helicopters** (p154)

Fixed-Wing Scenic Flights

With one exception, there seems to be no point in choosing a fixed-wing aircraft to tour Kaua'i, not when you can take a helicopter right to the cone of Mt Wai'ale'ale and hover there to your heart's content. The exception is an open-cockpit biplane, which flies so slowly it may as well be hovering. The combination of the romance of early aviation, the sheer sensation of the wind and roaring engine, and the emerald tropical island sliding below, not to mention sitting side-by-side in near embrace, makes this many a honeymooner's first choice. In fact, if it were up to passengers, biplanes would probably be as popular as helicopters on Kaua'i, but there's currently only one company that offers these scenic flights: AirVentures Hawaii (p89), based in Lihu'e. The tour leaves from Lihu'e Airport and takes you north past the Wailua River and Kilauea Lighthouse. From there, you travel up the lush Hanalei Valley, continuing over the ridge to see waterfalls and cascading 4000ft cliffs. It then continues north past Hanalei to the Na Pali Coast, wrapping past waterfalls and canyon drops through Waimea Canyon, and back to the South Shore, where you might just spot your hotel. They even give you the cool throwback hat and goggles!

Helicopter Tours

The most popular choice for seeing Kaua'i from the air is to take a helicopter ride. You'll have to decide what kind of aircraft you want to fly in, what kind of tour you want (some land in neat places), and whether you want the doors on or off (some passengers like the visibility, others don't like the exposure to wind and possibly rain). Most helicopter tour companies depart from the airports in Lihu'e.

Trips generally last 60 to 90 minutes, and start at around $289 (make internet reservations ahead of time to save some money). Doors off helicopters are totally the way to go if you are an avid photographer (and suffer little from vertigo). But it's noisy and windy, and maybe just a little bit scary. On a six-seater helicopter, two people may be stuck in the middle. You can request a window, but the captain may move people around for weight balance.

You also get to choose from big window, little window and bubbles (like the ones on *MASH*). The big difference is always visibility and noise. More modern helicopters are quieter and generally have big windows. You always wear earphones so you can talk with fellow passengers and lower the noise, but even the slight reduction in sound can make your trip more pleasant. Then again, some of the older helicopters have that sweet *Magnum P.I.* feel that make for a thrilling ride.

Rain delays do happen, and tours will vary their route based on rain and winds. Make sure to check the weather policy with your operator before booking. Generally 24-hour cancellations are required. Consider booking early during your stay, so you can reschedule later if need be.

What should you bring? Ideally, strap everything down (hats, cameras, iThings etc). It can get a little cold, so bring a jacket and long pants, plus decent shoes in case your tour does a landing.

You always approach a helicopter from the front (never the back). The captain will generally indicate what side you should board on. Put your head down and hold onto your hat (just like they do in the movies).

From Lihu'e, expect to see the Nawili-wili Harbor and the Menehune Fish-pond, Kipu Kai and the Tunnel of Trees, Manawaiopuna Falls in Hanapepe Valley, Olokele Canyon, Waimea Canyon, the Na Pali Coast, North Shore beaches like Ke'e and Hanalei, and Mt Waialeale. While the rips up impossibly steep canyons are an adrenaline junkie's dream, it's really the close proximity to waterfalls – many of which can only be seen from the air – that make these trips amazing.

While the tours follow pretty standardized routes, you can talk with your pilot to customize the tour experience, especially if it's just you and your family or sweetheart taking the flight. This means getting closer – or further away from the ground – making more acrobatic banking turns or going with a more easy-breezy approach, and generally determining the way you fly.

Tours include ongoing narration from the knowledgeable pilots. Yes, you can tip them afterward, but it's not required.

For a really unique trip consider doing a tour to Ni'ihau. The trips can be combined with diving and hunting adventures. **Ni'ihau Helicopters** (☑877-441-3500; www.niihau.us; per person $385) does a flyover of the island and ends with snorkeling, while **Ni'ihau Safaris** (☑877-441-3500; www.niihau.us; per hunter from $1750) includes air transport and the hunting of boar, feral sheep and oryx.

To check any tour company's flight record, consult the National Transport Safety Board (www.ntsb.gov) accident database. Consider all options before making a decision.

Travel with Children

Kaua'i is an amusement park of sorts, just of the more natural variety. Instead of riding roller coasters and eating too much cotton candy, *keiki* (kids) can snorkel amid tropical fish, eat just the right amount of shave ice, zipline in forest canopies and enjoy sandy beaches, with bodyboarding hot spots and shallow, toddler-sized lagoons. As for you, if you came to Kaua'i to recapture a childlike free-spiritedness, those tots you're toting may prove to be an inspiration for letting go and diving into some fun in the sun!

Top Kids Attractions

➡ **Kamokila Hawaiian Village** (p109)
➡ **Kaua'i Museum** (p88)
➡ **Limahuli Garden** (p174)
➡ **Kilohana Plantation** (p86)
➡ **McBryde Garden** (p182)
➡ **Canopy & Zipline Tours** (p185)

Practicalities

Calling Kaua'i 'kid-friendly' would be an understatement; *na keiki* (children) are adored on the Garden Island. There's an explanation for this – cuteness aside. The entire island has a small-town vibe and, as the saying goes, 'we're all in the same canoe.' When it comes down to it, people look out for each other, and each others' kids, because almost everybody else has kids too.

Not much can go wrong on Kaua'i – except in the water. Temperatures never drop below 65°F (18°C), driving distances are relatively short and everyone speaks English. Still, proper planning can be a game changer, especially when traveling with kids. With just a few tidbits of insider information you can minimize costs and maximize adventure.

Finding an appropriate home base is a good first step. Resorts and hotels typically allow children under 18 years to stay for free with their parents and might even provide rollaway beds or cribs. Po'ipu's **Sheraton Kaua'i Resort** (☑808-742-1661, 866-716-8109; www.sheraton-kauai.com; 2440 Ho'onani Rd; r $249-359) and Grand Hyatt Kaua'i Resort & Spa (p181), the **St Regis** (☑808-826-9644, 866-716-8140; www.stregisprinceville.com; 5520 Ka Haku Rd; d from $609) in Princeville and the Marriott (☑800-220-2925; www.marriott.com; 3610 Rice St) in Lihu'e offer professionally supervised 'day camps.' And kids will love playing in the monstro pool areas. Vacation-rental rates often apply only to doubles; kids above a certain age might count as extra guests at a cost of $15 to $25 each per night. B&Bs are generally not as kid-friendly, as they tend to be more intimate and host multiple parties in close proximity.

Most car-rental companies lease child-safety seats (cost per day $10 to $12, or per week $50 to $60), but they're limited so it's best to reserve in advance. Supplies, such as disposable diapers and infant formula, are sold island-wide, but try shopping in Lihu'e and on the Eastside for the best selection and prices. Facilities for diaper changing and breastfeeding are scarce, and doing either in public is frowned upon, so chances are backseat improvisation will be necessary.

Need to Know

➡ **Changing facilities** Sparse; plan for improvisation.

➡ **Highchairs** Ubiquitous.

➡ **Kids' menus** At most restaurants.

➡ **Diapers (Nappies)** Cheapest and best selection in Lihu'e or on the Eastside.

➡ **Strollers** For rent from **Kauai Baby Rentals** (☑808-651-9269, 866-994-8886; www.kauaibabyrentals.com) along with everything else one could need, including cribs, toys and booster seats to name a few.

➡ **Car seats** For rent from car companies; you must reserve in advance or just bring your own.

➡ **Breastfeeding** Generally done discreetly or in private.

➡ **Age limits** While age limits apply to some activities and upscale B&Bs, so do discounts.

➡ **Strong currents on the coasts** Can make for dangerous conditions. Find a well-protected beach.

Food & Drink

Hawaii is a family-oriented and unfussy place, so all restaurants welcome children, many even with *keiki* menus, or you can ask for half portions. Highchairs are usually available, even at Kaua'i's finest resorts.

If restaurant dining is not your family's strong suit, no problem. Eating outdoors is among the simplest and the best of island pleasures. Pack a picnic, stop for smoothies at roadside stands, and order plate lunches or fish wraps at patio counters. Accommodations providing full kitchens are convenient for eat-in-breakfasts, especially if you stock up on exotic fruit at farmers markets. A luau is definitely recommended, as is challenging your kids to eat fresh fish, *poke* (cubed raw fish mixed with *shōyu*, sesame oil, salt, chili pepper, *'inamona* or other condiments), poi (steamed, mashed taro) and other local delicacies.

The food itself should pose little trouble, as Kaua'i grocers stock mainstream national brands, just at around 140% of the cost you're expecting.

Children's Highlights

The **Kauai Youth Directory** (www.kauaiyouthdirectory.com) is an extensive resource for numerous youth and teen activities on the island, with links to recreational, environmental and cultural youth activities that may coincide with your visit.

For valuable tips and interesting anecdotes check out Lonely Planet's *Travel with Children*.

In the Water

With 55 miles of beach coastline, ocean activities are bound to be a part of the agenda. If your child cannot swim or fears the ocean, try one of Kaua'i's gentle 'baby beaches' in Po'ipu or Kapa'a for toddlers. Lydgate Beach Park (p108) is an ideal starter beach for grade-schoolers or anyone who needs well-protected waters. Although not lifeguard-staffed, 'Anini Beach Park's (p152) massive offshore reef creates consistently calm waters ideal for kids.

Snorkeling is generally family-friendly on Kaua'i, exciting for young kids and teens alike, especially in Po'ipu.

Boss Frog (p185) is a great starting point as it rents gear and has a wealth of knowledge and direction to share. Little kids love the float-on-top boogie boards with the windows so you can see below. Otherwise, indulge in a thrilling cruise to snorkel the iconic Na Pali waters. If your kid has never sailed before, a smoother catamaran ride might be safer than a zippy raft adventure. Many Na Pali operators will not take children aged under six. If your kid gets seasick, sit downstairs in the middle of the boat.

Surf lessons are another fun family activity and can be a big hit with teenagers looking to beef up their coolness résumé. Kaua'i's waters are relatively uncrowded, and beginner groups are generally small and personalized. If your child (or you) associates the word 'surf' with iPads and laptops more than set waves and 'hanging 10,' go bodyboarding before trying the real thing as it's much easier to learn and provides that all-important seed of confidence. The best beginner breaks are in Po'ipu and Lihu'e. As with any waterborn activity, you have to be respectful of the waves. Kaua'i has some strong currents. Keep to the shallows and well-protected areas with young ones, and protect from them from sun and dehydration.

On Land

When all fingers and toes are thoroughly wrinkled, there are some land-based activities that are especially geared toward children. At Lydgate Beach Park, you'll find two massive playgrounds with swings, slides, bridges and mysterious nooks and crannies. Na 'Aina Kai Botanical Gardens (p145) includes a special children's area with a wading pond, jungle playground, treehouse and more. Smith's Tropical Paradise (p109) is a family-friendly park where there are no time limits to strolling the island-themed 30-acre grounds. There's a train trip from the Kilohana Plantation (p86) that younger kids will love, as well as occasional crafts, sand-castle building and lei-making courses at the resorts. A kayak adventure up the Wailua River (p113) and ziplining are both usually a hit with teens – many have age and weight limits – as is cruising around the shops of Kapa'a or Hanalei for tropical knickknacks to show off back at school.

Hiking trails abound on Kaua'i, though some are geared more toward the experienced enthusiast. At **Waimea Canyon** (http://hawaiistateparks.org; ⏸) and Koke'e State Parks (p233), you'll find trails ranging from simple nature walks to strenuous treks amid the striking landscape of a gargantuan lava gorge and rugged forestland. Hiking even a couple of hundred feet up the Kalalau Trail (p138) offers unforgettable views.

Other great adventures include horseback riding, or bicycling along the Eastside coastal path.

Bring lots of water and snacks for hikes, plus sun protection.

Regions at a Glance

Sure, Kaua'i is an outdoor adventure destination. Try and deny it and the overwhelming evidence of sensational beaches, big waves, epic diving and snorkeling, and lush mountains laced with miles of hiking trails will beat your case. It stands to reason that each region will have a touch of the outdoor beauty you might expect, yet there's so much more to experience. The locally grown island cuisine veers from delicious to sensational, the farm tours are life-affirming and there's an abundance of tempting art galleries and boutiques. Each specific corner of Kaua'i offers all of that in its own special way. On an island where local roots matter like nowhere else, it makes sense that each region offers something unique enough to keep you moving until you've sampled them all.

Lihu'e

Commercial
Center
Landscape
Food

Workaday Living
Once a sugar town, like all the rest, Lihu'e is now a plain-looking commercial center that grows on you once you step out of your rental car. Downtown can be particularly charming and the museum is a winner.

Hidden Beauty
An attractive beach with a working harbor framed by green hills and an age-old fishpond best seen from the back roads. Lihu'e is a lot more than its drab shopping centers would have you believe.

Funky Kitchens
Aromatic *pho* on the cheap, seafood plate lunches your Hawaiian auntie would love, wood-fired thin-crust pizza and dynamite pie for dessert.

p82

Kapa'a & the Eastside

Food
Art & Architecture
Festivals

Restaurant Row
Here you'll find creative Japanese burger joints, new-school food trucks, age-old steak houses and sushi bars and an all-star chef's newest obsession; this is the best place to eat on island.

Old Town Kapa'a
Where pastel-brushed, clapboard storefronts of Old Town Kapa'a are filled with dreamy modern canvasses and handblown glass sculpture.

Party Time
Coconuts, hula, art, handicrafts, music and more are celebrated in fun-loving, up-for-anything Kapa'a.

p102

Hanalei & the North Shore

Surfing
Shopping
Food & Drink

Hanalei Bay

If you conjured a surf town from stardust, it would be populated by sun-bronzed barefoot, young-at-heart souls who descend on a beautiful blue bay surrounded by mountains weeping with waterfalls and swelling with gentle waves small and large. Welcome to Eden.

Retail Therapy

Hanalei's main drag offers evocative art, sensational mid-century antiques and tasteful fashion. You won't go home empty-handed.

North Shore Nourishment

A bakery for morning coffee and treats. Organic grocer and farmers markets. Wonderful tapas bar with a wine list to match. An all-time classic dive bar. Yes, you shall be fed and watered well here.

p136

Po'ipu & the South Shore

Diving
Beaches
Shopping

Beneath The Surface

Whether you wish to venture below with a tank of air or a single deep breath, this is where you can dive with snoozing sharks and dancing turtles, swim through lava tubes and listen to whale song reverberate in your brain.

Natural Highs

A windswept edge of wild sand, a beach park built for families, a sea beckoning for exploration and mind-blowing sunsets that are hard to match.

Ye Olde Sugar Town

Koloa's quaint, leafy throwback shopping district will take you back in time.

p178

Waimea Canyon & the Westside

Hiking
Camping
Boating

State Park Trails

Three state parks, two of which are in the mountains and laced with the most spectacular trails this side of the Na Pali Coast.

Nature's Lullaby

Pitch your tent deep in a red-rock jigsaw, in an elegant grove of Japanese spruce, or on Kaua'i's longest, wildest and arguably most beautiful beach.

Na Pali Coast

You must see Na Pali from the water. Catamarans, Zodiac and rigid-hull inflatables (RIBs) all disembark from Port Allen and venture on half-day cruises along Kaua'i's roadless coast. Some vessels penetrate sea caves and offload you onto virgin beaches; others serve mai tais.

p206

On the Road

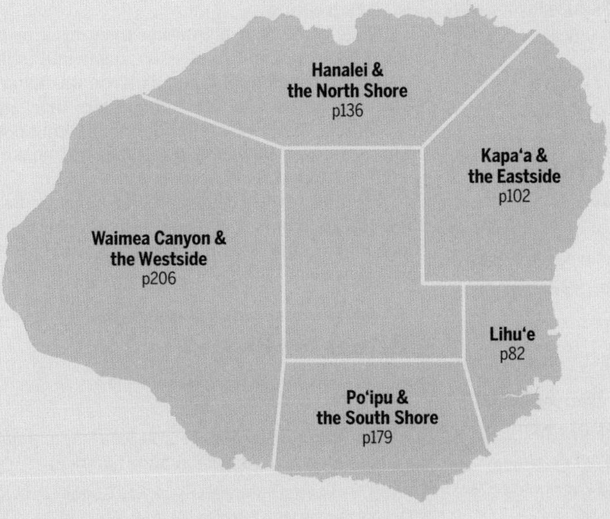

Hanalei &
the North Shore
p136

Kapa'a &
the Eastside
p102

Waimea Canyon &
the Westside
p206

Lihu'e
p82

Po'ipu &
the South Shore
p179

Lihu‘e

☏ 808 / POP 6455

Best Places to Eat

➡ Kaua‘i Community Market (p94)

➡ Hamura Saimin (p95)

➡ Gaylord's (p96)

Best for History

➡ Grove Farm (p86)

➡ Alekoko (Menehune) Fishpond Overlook (p87)

➡ Kilohana Plantation (p86)

➡ Lihu‘e Lutheran Church (p89)

Why Go?

The island's commercial center is strip-mall plain, but there's an abundance of economical eateries and shops along with a down-to-earth, workaday atmosphere that's missing in resort areas. While Kalapaki Beach is a charmer, Lihu‘e is more a place to stock up on supplies after arrival at the airport before heading out on your island adventure.

Lihu‘e arose as a plantation town back in 1849 when sugar was king, and its massive sugar mill (still standing south of town along Kaumuali‘i Hwy) was Kaua‘i's largest. The mill closed in 2000, ending more than a century of operations. It left behind an ethnic melting pot of Asian, European and Hawaiian traditions that make the town what it is today.

Activities tend to center around Kalapaki Beach with a few top golf courses and cool beaches nearby. This is the kickoff point for helicopter tours and a few fun excursions to waterfalls.

When to Go

➡ The weather is always nice here – less rainy than the north and less dry than the south.

➡ Kaua‘i Community Market is on Saturday and Grove Farm tours on Monday, Wednesday and Thursday.

➡ Don't miss the Hawaiian Slack Key Guitar Festival in November and the May Day festivities.

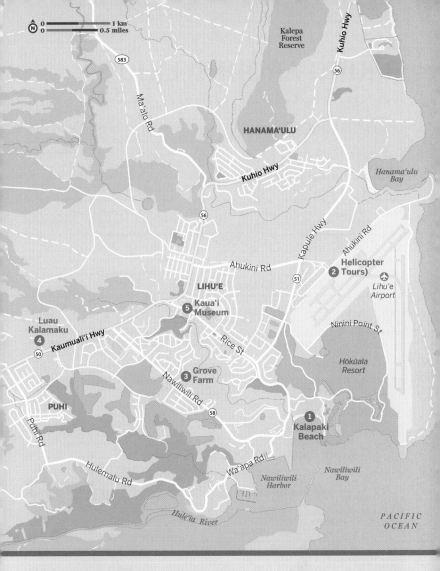

Lihu'e Highlights

❶ Kalapaki Beach (p87) Chilling on this Kaua'i classic melds natural beauty with loads of fun for the whole family.

❷ Helicopter tours (p75) Slicing through canyons on a once-in-a-lifetime flight over the soaring cliffs of the Na Pali Coast, Mt Wai'ale'ale's rain-soaked crater and the 'Grand Canyon of the Pacific.'

❸ Grove Farm (p86) Traveling back in time in this authentically restored 19th-century sugar plantation property is like a large-scale still life.

❹ Luau Kalamaku (p96) Embracing the kitsch at the island's best luau (Hawaiian feast) successfully combines the traditional and the contemporary.

❺ Kaua'i Museum (p88) This treasure trove will teach you all about the unique history of the Garden Island.

HIKING AROUND LIHU'E

LIHU'E'S HIDDEN BEACHES

START DUKE'S
END NININI POINT LIGHTHOUSE
LENGTH TWO TO THREE HOURS; 2 MILES

Take an afternoon off from beach-bumming to hike to Ninini Point lighthouse on this easy hike that can be combined with a picnic lunch. Along the way, expect jets overhead, 360-degree views of Nawiliwili Bay, lost beaches and a few glimpses of an amazing golf course.

Start from **Duke's** (p96) on Kalapaki Beach. Walking east along the oceanwalk you'll find an elevator that takes you up to the lagoons and fairways of **Hōkūala Resort** (p89). Walk along the road toward the ocean wind, following signs for beach access. Look across the fairways and lawns for a glimpse of **Kukui Point Lighthouse** (Map p88), then grab a trail heading down to the water from the beach access signs.

The trail is quite steep, and there are no handrails, so take your time. The first beach you hit is **Running Waters Beach** (p86). If the waters are chill, and the tides are low, there are some incredible tide pools just before the beach. From there, hotfoot your way across lava rocks to **Ninini Beach** (p86). This is a perfect spot for an afternoon picnic, but the waters are normally too rough for anything but wading. From Ninini, another steep trail takes you up onto the golf course. Stay on assigned paths (known as the Shoreline Trail) and make your way toward **Ninini Point Lighthouse** (p88). Head back

PAUL HIGLEY/SHUTTERSTOCK ©

Kalapaki Beach (p87), Lihu'e

The capital of Kaua'i isn't the first outdoors destination most visitors associate with the island, but the treks (and beaches!) in this area are not to be missed.

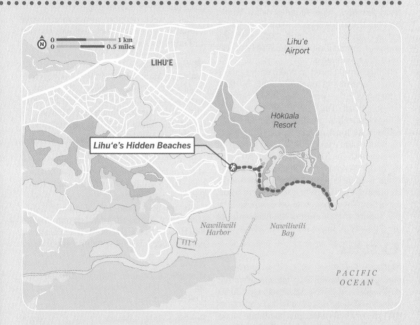

through Hōkūala Resort golf course on the Shoreline Trail to grab the access road for the lighthouse.

If you want to just visit the lighthouse, the road here begins off Kapule Hwy, just over 0.5 miles south of the intersection with Ahukini Rd and marked with two concrete slabs. You'll walk for just over 2 miles, past a guard gate (usually empty)

and Hole 12 of the Hōkūala golf course, most of it rutted dirt road, before you reach the short spur to the lighthouse.

Built in 1906, this lighthouse remains operational. Expect to see a few people living in their cars in the woods out here. Hawaiians still fish, pick 'opihi (edible limpet) and gather limu (edible seaweed) nearby.

History

Lihu'e's modern history is steeped in sugar. In 1849 German settlers established the first local sugarcane plantation, which struggled until the development of irrigation in 1856. Thereafter, profitability grew, attracting entrepreneur George Wilcox from Hanalei, who founded what would become the area's largest plantation, Grove Farm. Lihu'e's sugar mill (still standing south of town along Kaumuali'i Hwy) was once Kaua'i's largest.

Lihu'e's mill closed in 2000, ending more than a century of operation. But by then Lihu'e had already morphed into a very different animal. The Lihu'e you see today is almost entirely a creation of the past half-century. As tourism has replaced the sugar economy, Lihu'e has had the good fortune of hosting both the island's biggest airport, and its major seaport, Nawiliwili Harbor. The result is Kaua'i's second-largest town and its commercial center. When it comes to trade, exporting sugar has now been replaced by the importation of most of the necessities of life – including sugar, if you can believe that.

Sights

★ Grove Farm   HISTORIC SITE
(Map p88; ☑ 808-245-3202; http://grovefarm.org; 4050 Nawiliwili Rd; 2hr tour adult/child 5-12yr $20/10; ⊙ tours 10am & 1pm Mon, Wed & Thu, by reservation only) History buffs adore this plantation museum, but kids may grow restless. Grove Farm once ranked among the most productive sugar companies on Kaua'i. George Wilcox, the Hilo-born son of Protestant missionaries, acquired the farm in 1864. The main house feels suspended in time, with rocking chairs sitting still on a covered porch and untouched books lining the library's shelves. A highlight is making it for the free train ride on the second Thursday of each month.

Call a week or more in advance to join a small-group tour, which includes cookies and mint tea served on the lanai (porch).

★ Wailua Falls   WATERFALL
(Ma'alo Rd) Made famous in the opening credits of *Fantasy Island,* these falls appear at a distance. When they are in full flow and misting the surrounding tropical foliage, it's a fantastic photo op. While officially listed as 80ft, the falls have been repeatedly measured to have a far greater drop. Heed the sign at the top that warns: 'Slippery rocks at top of falls. People have been killed.' Many have fallen while trying to scramble down the steep path beyond.

To get here from Lihu'e, follow Kuhio Hwy (Hwy 56) north. Turn left onto Ma'alo Rd (Hwy 583), which ends at the falls after 4 miles. Expect crowds and difficult parking.

Ninini Beach   BEACH
(Map p88) Accessible from the Hōkūala Resort (p89), this gorgeous beach is perfect for a picnic (but bad for swimming).

Running Waters Beach   BEACH
(Map p88) You don't want to swim here, but the water is sure pretty and there's some

---

GROVE FARM & KILOHANA PLANTATION

There are two Wilcox family homes that you can visit today, both situated on roughly 100-acre estates. Grove Farm Homestead is the original house of George Wilcox, and a beacon of understatement. In contrast, Gaylord Wilcox's home at Kilohana Plantation is a 16,000-sq-ft Tudor mansion, once the most expensive home on Kaua'i.

The homes also occupy opposite ends of the tourism spectrum. **Grove Farm** is utterly authentic, to an astonishing degree. It is as if nothing has changed in decades – because it hasn't. If you want to enter old Hawaii, then this is your first stop, and a fascinating experience.

Kilohana Plantation (Map p88; ☑ 808-245-5608; www.kilohanakauai.com; 3-2087 Kaumuali'i Hwy; admission free, attraction prices vary; ⊙ 10:30am-9pm Mon-Sat, to 3pm Sun) FREE, on the other hand, has largely been created for tourists (the Wilcox estate was never actually a plantation). Part of the original mansion has been turned into a restaurant, **Gaylord's** (p96). The train is not from Hawaii, but Alaska; the tracks were laid by current employees. The enormous luau pavilion was financed by cruise line Norwegian Cruise Line, which deposits hundreds of passengers there every week. The **Koloa Rum Company** (p97) has been recently created from scratch. The end result is more of a well-done theme park than a historic site. Having said that, you can certainly enjoy both of these destinations equally well, it will just be for entirely different reasons.

LIHU'E IN...

One Day

Jump-start your Kaua'i experience with something you will never forget: an early morning flight with **Jurassic Falls Helicopter Tour** (p91) through paradisial valleys with a landing at an awesome waterfall.

Spend the bulk of the day on **Kalapaki Beach**, a classic stretch of Hawaii beach, with water sports galore to choose from. For some easy surfing, try renting a paddleboard from **Kalapaki Beach Surfing** (p90). If you need to stretch your legs, stroll the palatial open-air corridors of the **Kaua'i Marriott**, or walk the breakwater in Nawiliwili Park for a look at the island's main **harbor** (Map p88). Consider lunch at **Duke's Barefoot Bar.**

Get a quick overview of local history on the **Kilohana Plantation Train** as you chug along through the fields and meet the local farm animals – a winner with children. Tickets can be combined with a luau (check-in at 5pm).

Luau Kalamaku (p96) is a cross between a Hawaiian luau and a polished dinner theater. You'll get Lihu'e's best night-time entertainment and a compelling adventure-romance topped off by a mesmerizing fire dance. Be sure to wander the grounds of Kilohana Plantation first, and try a shot of spiced rum at **Koloa Rum Company** (p97).

Two Days

For breakfast try the *loco moco* (two fried eggs, hamburger patty, rice and gravy) at the **Kalapaki Beach Hut** for a bit of regional flavor. Try to get a seat upstairs.

Next check out **Grove Farm Homestead**, the Wilcox family home, which has managed to remain untouched for decades. It doesn't get any more authentic than this.

By now it should be time to sip noodles for lunch at **Hamura Saimin.**

Next explore the tropical mountainsides just outside of town with a super-cool adrenaline-pumped adventure. For fast descents, try the zipline adventure offered by **Just Live** (p90) or hit up **Kaua'i Backcountry Adventures** (p91) for mountain tubing. Top off your afternoon by journeying to **Wailua Falls** for picture-perfect views of this *Fantasy Island* favorite before enjoying an afternoon beer at the **Kauai Beer Company** (p96) or local roasts at **Hā Coffee Bar** (p96).

Cafe Portofino (p96) is one of the finer dining experiences in Lihu'e with a good mix of seafood and Italian dishes, plus excellent sunset patio views over Kalapaki Beach.

For even more adventure, consider grabbing the makings for sunset tapas at the **Kaua'i Community Market**, plus maybe a little bottle of wine, and heading to **Ninini Beach** for a romantic sunset meal. If you plan on staying after sunset, bring a flashlight, as the trail here is rough.

---

good tide pools nearby. Access is by a very steep trail (with no handrails) from the edge of Hōkūala Resort. Follow signs that say beach access.

Alekoko (Menehune) Fishpond Overlook VIEWPOINT
(Map p88; Hulemalu Rd) This roadside overlook offers an oft-photographed vista of the Hule'ia Valley, where the Hule'ia River winds beneath a ring of verdant peaks. The river is walled off at one bend to form a 39-acre *loko wai* (freshwater fishpond). Local legend attributes construction to *menehune,* the 'little people' of Hawaiian mythology. The best time to visit is just before sunset. It's about 0.5 miles west of the entrance to Nawiliwili Harbor.

On the north side of the river lies the 240-acre **Hule'ia National Wildlife Refuge** (Map p88; www.fws.gov/huleia), a breeding ground for endemic waterfowl. The refuge is closed to the public, except for guided kayaking tours.

Kalapaki Beach BEACH
(Map p88; 🖫) This sandy beach and sheltered bay is tucked between a marina and the mountains. It's overlooked by the Marriott resort facing Kalapaki Bay and by an enviable collection of houses atop a rocky ridge to the east. Its easy-access location and versatility make it popular with families. But

Lihu'e Area

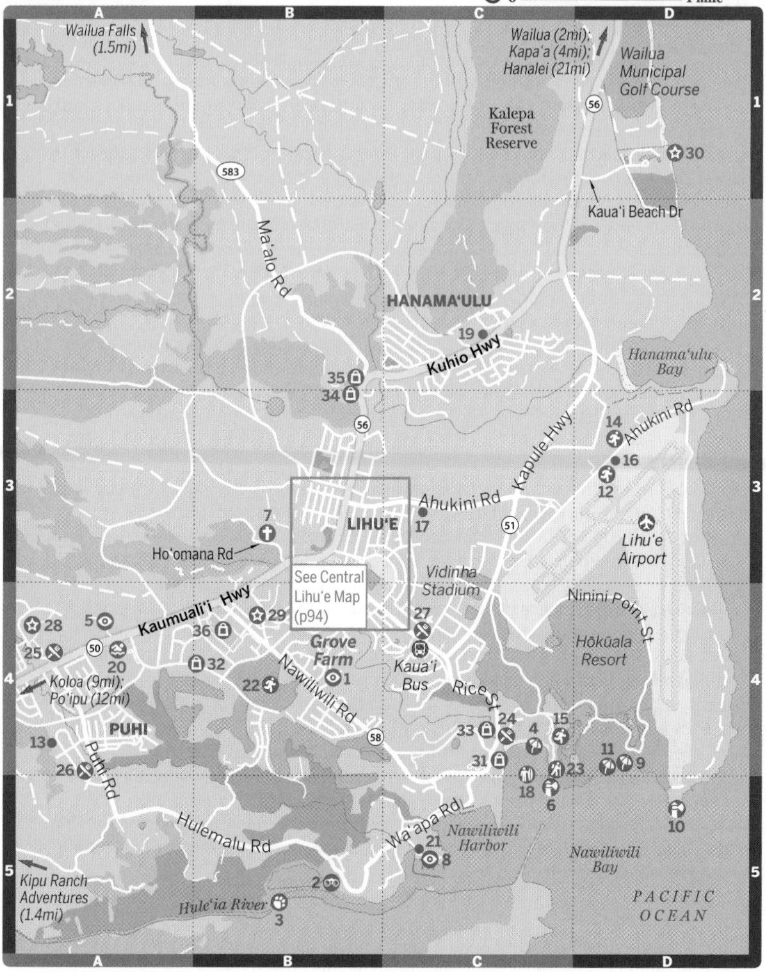

the sandy bottom and river outlet here make for 'dirty water.' Calmer waters toward the east are good for swimming. Swells to the west draw bodyboarders and both novice and intermediate surfers.

Kaua'i Museum MUSEUM

(Map p94; ☎808-245-6931; www.kauaimuseum.org; 4428 Rice St; adult/child $15/free; ⏰10am-5pm Mon-Sat, tours 10:30am Mon-Fri) The island's largest museum is set in two buildings – one of which was built with lava rock in 1960. Come here for a quick grounding in Kaua'i's history and ecology, and in Hawaiian history and culture in general. A smattering of Asian art is also on display. The free guided tour is well worth it.

Ninini Point Lighthouse LIGHTHOUSE

(Map p88) FREE This lighthouse was built in 1906. It's been automated, so alas, no light keeper. You can get here by taking the Ninini Point Trail. By car, take the road through the Hōkūala Resort, turning off near the airstrip to a dirt road headed to the point.

Kaua'i Society of Artists GALLERY

(KSA; Map p88; www.kauaisocietyofartists.org; Kukui Grove Center, 3-2600 Kamauali'i Hwy; ⏰11am-5pm Sat-Thu, to 8pm Fri) FREE Island

Lihu'e Area

artists share gallery space at the mall and exhibit thoughtful works in oils, pencil, watercolor, sculpture materials, mixed media and photography. It's free to browse.

Lihu'e Lutheran Church CHURCH
(Map p88; www.lihuelutheranchurch.com; 4602 Ho'omana Rd; ⊙daily, services 8am & 10:30am Sun) Hawaii's oldest Lutheran church is a quaint clapboard house, with an incongruously slanted floor that resembles a ship's deck and a balcony akin to a captain's bridge. The building is actually a faithful 1983 reconstruction of the 1885 original (built by German immigrants) leveled by Hurricane Iwa. It's located just off Kaumuali'i Hwy (Hwy 50). There are Hawaiian-language classes here most Fridays at 6pm.

 Activities

★ **AirVentures Hawaii** SCENIC FLIGHTS
(Map p88; ☏ 808-651-0679; https://kauaiair tour.com; Lihu'e Airport, 3651 Ahukini Rd; 1hr tours $245; ⊙ tours Mon-Fri, by reservation only) When it comes to fixed-wing aircraft, there's nothing like an open-cockpit biplane. This outfit's gorgeous YMF-5 Super can seat two people up front. Visibility may not be the same as by helicopter, but the roar of the engine and the wind makes for a memorable experience. You'll even get to don an old-fashioned cloth aviator's hat and goggles.

Hōkūala Resort GOLF
(Map p88; ☏ 808-241-6000; www.hokualakauai. com; 3351 Ho'olaule'a Way; green fees incl cart rental $135-205) Designed by Jack Nicklaus, the

HISTORIC TRAINS

Train fans, listen up. Between the late 1880s and early 1900s, Kaua'i relied on railroads for the running of the sugar business. Workers would catch the morning train out to the fields and spend the day moving cars loaded with cut cane to the mills, or moving bags of processed sugar to the nearest ship landing. None of the trains were meant for passenger use. **Grove Farm** owns four of these historic plantation steam locomotives. Three have been restored to full operation, and one is fired up every second Thursday of the month for a short ride.

recently redone 18-hole, par-72 Hōkūala Course has to be one of the most beautiful golf courses in the world. There's plenty of ocean-front holes. Book tee times up to 90 days in advance. Club and shoe rentals available.

Kalapaki Beach Surfing SURFING
(Map p88) It's an easy paddle out of about 50yd to the reef, and there's no pounding shore break to get through. Most go right for a mellow, predictable wave, but there are more aggressive lefts, too. This is one of the most popular stand up paddle surfing (SUP) breaks around thanks to the chill waves. Bodyboarders work the river mouth.

Blue Hawaiian Helicopters SCENIC FLIGHTS
(Map p88; ☑ 800-745-2583, 808-245-5800; www.bluehawaiian.com/kauai/tours; 3651 Ahukini Rd; 55min tours $246) Flies high-end Eco-Star choppers, offering more space, glass and comfort with less noise due to quiet, enclosed tail rotors. Grab a souvenir DVD of your flight for an extra $25.

Kauai Beach Boys WATER SPORTS
(Map p88; ☑ 808-246-6333; 3610 Rice St; 90min surfing or SUP lessons $79, surfboard rental per hr/day $15/35, SUP rental per hr/day $27/70; ☺ 8am-6pm, lesson hours vary) On Kalapaki Beach, this concessionaire rents snorkel gear, kayaks, surfboards and stand up paddle boards at reasonable prices, with 90-minute surfing and SUP lessons given several times daily. Call ahead for sailing lessons or to book a sailboat cruise on the bay.

Shoreline Trail RUNNING
(Map p88; Hōkūala Resort) This running path covers 5 miles and encircles the Hōkūa-

la Resort golf course. It is open to the public, but you should be respectful of golfers. Along the way, you'll pass some incredible golf course holes, and have great views of the ocean, with easy access to Ninini and Running Waters Beach.

Escape Room AMUSEMENT PARK
(Map p94; ☑ 808-635-6957; www.escaperoomkauai.com; 4353 Rice St; escape room sessions per person $20-35; ☺ by reservation) Like a mystery? This escape room sets up clues for you and your team to save the world, find missing scientists or solve the Tiki Lounge mystery. It's a good diversion for families on a rainy day.

Kauai Ohana YMCA SWIMMING
(Map p88; ☑ 808-246-9090; www.ymcaofkauai.org; 4477 Nuhou St; day passes member/nonmember $5/10; ☺ 5:30am-9am & 11am-7pm Mon-Fri, 10am-5:30pm Sat & Sun) Lap swimmers, get your fix at this open-air, Olympic-sized pool. A small weights/cardio workout room is also available, but towels and padlocks for lockers aren't provided. US mainland YMCA members should bring their card from home.

Puakea Golf Course GOLF
(Map p88; ☑ 808-245-8756; www.puakeagolf.com; 4150 Nuhou St; green fees incl cart rental $45-85) The lush cliffs of Mt Ha'upu serve as a backdrop to this Robin Nelson–designed public course. Club rentals are available. Book tee times up to three months ahead. Save big after 3pm.

State of Hawai'i Division of Aquatic Resources FISHING
(Map p94; ☑ 808-274-3344; http://dlnr.hawaii.gov/dar/; 3060 Eiwa St, Room 306) Stop here for fishing information. There is no marine recreational fishing license in Kaua'i. Some places do prohibit fishing. This is also the place to get permits and info on collecting fish for aquariums back home.

☞ Tours

Most 'flightseeing' tours depart from Lihu'e Airport. Book ahead online for major discounts.

★ Just Live ADVENTURE
(Map p88; ☑ 808-482-1295; www.justlive.org; Anchor Cove Shopping Center, 3416 Rice St; zipline tours $79-125; ☺ tours daily, by reservation only) This outfit stands above the rest – literally – by offering Kaua'i's only canopy-based zipping, meaning you never touch ground

after your first zip. The 3½-hour tour includes seven ziplines and four bridge crossings, or there's a scaled-down 'Wikiwiki' zip tour. The 'Eco-Adventure' adds a climbing wall, a 100ft rappelling tower and a heart-stopping monster swing.

Participants must be at least nine years old and weigh between 70lb and 250lb.

Island Helicopters   SCENIC FLIGHTS
(Map p88; ☎808-245-8588, 800-829-8588; www.islandhelicopters.com; 50/75min tours $297/379) Pilots with this long-running helicopter tour company have perfect safety records, and they only fly AStar helicopters, equipped with floor-to-ceiling windows. The 'Jurassic Falls' tour includes an exclusive 25-minute landing at 350ft-high Manawaiopuna Falls, hidden deep in Hanapepe Valley.

Safari Helicopters   SCENIC FLIGHTS
(Map p94; ☎800-326-3356, 808-246-0136; www.safarihelicopters.com; 3225 Akahi St; 60/90min tours $239/304) Flies AStar helicopters on the standard circle-island tour. The longer 'ecotour' includes a 40-minute stop at Robinson Ranch's wildlife refuge overlooking Olokele Canyon.

Kaua'i Backcountry Adventures   ADVENTURE
(Map p88; ☎888-270-0555; www.kauaibackcountry.com; 3-4131 Kuhio Hwy; 3hr tubing/zipline tours incl lunch $105/125; ☺tours hourly 8am-2pm, by reservation only; ⊞) This 3½-hour zipline tour features seven lines, which are elevated as high as 200ft above ground and run as far as 900ft (almost three football fields). Afterward, you can refuel with a picnic lunch at the swimming pond. The family-friendly tubing tour (for ages five and up) floats through an old sugar plantation's ditch-and-tunnel irrigation system. Zipliners must be at least 12 years old and weigh between 100lb and 250lb.

Kauai Plantation Railway   TOURS
(Map p88; ☎808-245-7245; www.kilohanakauai.com; Kilohana Plantation, 3-2087 Kaumuali'i Hwy; 40min train rides adult/child 3-12yr $19/14, 4hr train & walking tours $75/34; ☺hourly departures 10am-2pm, guided tours 9:30am Mon-Fri; ⊞) If you crave a bit of history and agricultural education, hop on this vintage-style train for a scenic 40-minute ride through a working plantation. The four-hour train and walking tour combo will get you into the fields and orchards, where you can pluck tropical fruit straight from the tree and feed the sheep, goats and wild pigs. Luau packages are available.

Captain Don's Sportfishing   FISHING, CRUISE
(Map p88; ☎808-639-3012; http://captaindonsfishing.com; Nawiliwili Small Boat Harbor, 2494 Niumalu Rd; half-/full-day shared charters per person $140/250, 2/4hr private charters for up to 6 passengers from $325/600; ☺by reservation only) One of the many fishing charters departing from Nawiliwili Small Boat Harbor, Captain Don's gives guests creative freedom to design their own trip (fishing, whale-watching, snorkeling, a Na Pali Coast cruise) on the 34ft *June Louise*. Captain Don has decades of experience on Kaua'i's waters.

Island Adventures   ADVENTURE
(Map p88; ☎808-246-6333; www.islandadventureskauai.com; Da Life, 3500 Rice St; tours incl lunch adult/child 6-12yr $180/157; ☺tours 8am Mon-Wed & Sat, 11am Fri, by reservation only) Jump on a 5½-hour tour into Hule'ia National Wildlife Refuge, where you'll paddle 2.5 miles in; hike to two waterfalls on private land; learn how to wet rappel 60ft down the side of a waterfall; and take a lazy swim followed by a picnic lunch.

Jack Harter Helicopters   SCENIC FLIGHTS
(Map p88; ☎808-245-3774, 888-245-2001; www.helicopters-kauai.com; 4231 Ahukini Rd; 60/90min tours $289/434) This pioneering outfit (operating since 1962) offers a standard enclosed, six-passenger AStar or a doors-off, four-passenger Hughes 500 helicopter. Longer doors-on tours are also offered.

LIHU'E FOR CHILDREN

Kalapaki Beach (p87) Set in an idyllic cove overshadowed by a lighthouse, this is a great lounging beach and also good for beginner surfers.

Kauai Plantation Railway Chug along the lines of this vintage train that takes you through historic orchards, gardens and more.

Kaua'i Backcountry Adventures Go for the tubing tour that takes you through a sugar-plantation's aqueducts.

Captain Don's Sportfishing Head out for a day trip to snorkel or whale-watch in the South Shore waters.

Kauai Ohana YMCA The best budget bet for swimming-pool fun.

HOW TO SPEND RAINY DAYS IN LIHU'E

Kaua'i Museum (p88) The best museum on the island offers well-curated exhibits.

Wailua Falls (p86) Kick off your fantasy trip with a visit to these magical falls.

Kilohana Plantation (p86) This tourist trap has a cigar factory, rum tour and plenty of shopping.

Kukui Grove Cinema 4 Escape with B-run movies in this throwback Cineplex.

Clayworks (p100) Indulge your craftsy side with pottery classes.

Outfitters Kauai   ADVENTURE
(Map p88; ☑ 808-742-9667, 888-742-9887; www.outfitterskauai.com; Outfitters Kayak Shack, Nawiliwili Small Boat Harbor, 2494 Niumalu Rd; zipline tours adult/child 7-14yr from $128/118, 5hr SUP tours incl lunch adult/child 12-14yr $128/98; ⊙ by reservation only; ☑) Multiactivity tours at Kipu Ranch just outside town combine tandem ziplines with aerial bridges, hiking, and kayaking the Hule'ia River; the weight limit for zipliners is 250lb. Unique SUP river tours include short hikes, swimming and a motorized canoe ride back upstream. Also consider doing a whale-watching sea kayak or Na Pali Coast kayak.

Aloha Kaua'i Tours   ADVENTURE
(Map p88; ☑ 808-245-6400; www.alohakauaitours.com; 1702 Haleukana St; half-day tours adult/child 5-12yr $80/63) Specializes in 4WD trips on back roads, including a half-day trip (minimum four people, weekdays only) that rumbles through the gate used in filming *Jurassic Park* and ends with a 3-mile round-trip hike to a waterfall pool fed by a stream from mighty Mt Wai'ale'ale. Book at least 24 hours in advance.

Mauna Loa Helicopters   SCENIC FLIGHTS
(Map p88; ☑ 808-652-3148; www.helicopter-tours-kauai.com; Harbor Mall, 3501 Rice St; 1hr tours from $287) Highly qualified pilots don't skimp on full 60-minute private tours for up to three passengers. Small groups allow for more-personalized interaction between pilot and passengers. You can choose to have the doors on or off, and all seats are window seats.

✨ Festivals & Events

For an up-to-date, comprehensive calendar of events, check www.kauaifestivals.com online.

★ **Hawaiian Slack Key Guitar Festival**   MUSIC
(http://slackkeyfestival.com; ⊙ mid-Nov) FREE
This opportunity to see master slack key guitarists is not to be missed. It's usually staged at the Aqua Kaua'i Beach Resort.

May Day Lei Contest   CULTURAL
(www.kauaimuseum.org; ⊙ early May; ☑) Established in 1981, the Kaua'i Museum's annual lei contest brings out legendary floral art, with do-it-yourself workshops, live music and an auction.

Kaua'i Mokihana Festival Hula Competition   CULTURAL, DANCE
(☑ 808-822-2166;   www.maliefoundation.org; ⊙ mid- to late Sep) Three days of serious hula competitions are staged at the Aqua Kaua'i Beach Resort. Both *hula kahiko* (ancient) and *hula 'auana* (modern) styles enchant.

Garden Island Range & Food Festival   FOOD & DRINK
(adult/child $35/18; ⊙ mid-Nov) This annual foodie gathering at Kilohana Plantation spotlights local chefs, as well as the farmers and ranchers who provide their Kaua'i-grown ingredients. Future dates and the location of this festival are subject to change.

Kaua'i County Farm Bureau Fair   FAIR
(www.kauaifarmfair.org; Vidinha Stadium; adult/child $5/2; ⊙ late Aug; ☑) Old-fashioned family fun happens at Vidinha Stadium. The fair brings carnival rides and games, livestock shows, a petting zoo, hula performances and lots of local food.

Kaua'i Composers Contest & Concert   MUSIC
(www.maliefoundation.org/kaua-i-mokihana-festival; ⊙ mid- to late Sep) ✐ The signature event of the Kaua'i Mokihana Festival, this musical competition showcases homegrown musical talent.

Fourth of July Concert in the Sky CULTURAL
(www.kauaihospice.org/kauai-concert-in-the-sky; adult/child $15/7; ⊙ Jul 4; ☑) Enjoy island food, live entertainment and the grand finale fireworks show set to music at Vidinha Stadium.

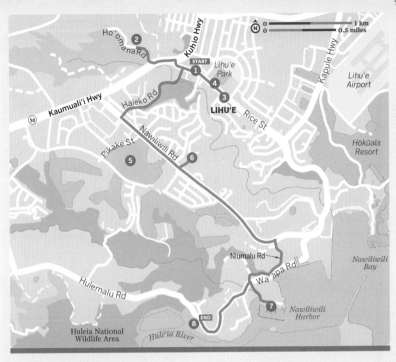

City Walk
Lihu'e Historic Tour

START KAUA'I MUSEUM
END ALEKOKO (MENHUNE) FISHPOND
LENGTH FIVE TO SIX HOURS; 4.5 MILES

Lihu'e is short on sights, but with a little creativity, you can make a fun walking tour that takes you past some of the town's most historic spots. The trip runs over 4.5 miles, so you can either walk or drive.

Start from ❶ **Kaua'i Museum** (p88) in the heart of downtown. It has a free guided tour at 10:30am. Once you are all museumed out, head straight across Kaumuali'i Hwy to ❷ **Lihu'e Lutheran Church** (p89). Originally built in 1885 and reconstructed after Hurricane Iwa, this is a faithful reproduction of the original that was built by German immigrants.

If all that religion gets you thirsty or hungry, return downtown for a cool beer at ❸ **Kauai Beer Company** (p96), where you can and should buy a growler for your evening sunset sips, then get maps and make plans for the rest of the trip at ❹ **Kaua'i Visitors Bureau** (p100).

Grab Haleko Rd heading southwest to Nawiliwili Rd, where you turn seaward and walk for about 0.7 miles past ❺ **Puakea Golf Course** to Grove Farm Rd, then turn left and go a few hundred yards to ❻ **Grove Farm** (p86). You'll need to book a guided tour in advance.

Continue down toward the coast on Nawiliwili Rd, turning west onto Niumalu Rd. Take a little detour here to check out the boats and charter a kayak adventure at ❼ **Nawiliwili Small Boat Harbor** (p87) or continue along the road to the ❽ **Alekoko (Menhune) Fishpond** (p87). The overlook offers huge views of the Hule'ia Valley and the Hule'ia River. The walled-off bend forms the 39-acre *loko wai* (freshwater fishpond), said to have been constructed by the *menehune* (the 'little people' that may have been the first settlers to Kaua'i). This is a perfect sunset spot to enjoy a sip of your authentic Kaua'i microbrew.

Central Lihu'e

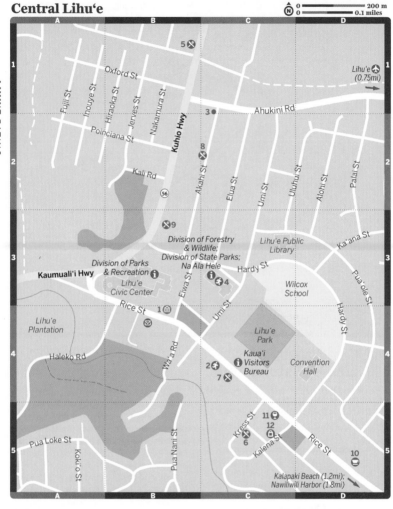

Lights on Rice Parade   PARADE
(http://lightsonrice.org; ⊘ Dec; 🚼) **FREE** A charming parade of illuminated floats takes over Rice St on the first Friday evening of December.

✖ Eating

Eating tends toward local grinds – and who would want to miss that? – but there are a handful of higher-end tourist-focused restaurants near Kalapaki Beach as well.

★ Kaua'i Community Market   MARKET $
(Map p88; ☎ 808-855-5429; www.kauaicommunitymarket.org; Kauai Community College, 3-1901 Kaumuali'i Hwy; ⊘ 9:30am-1pm Sat; 🚗 🚼) 🌿 One of the island's biggest and best farmers markets, in partnership with the Kaua'i County Farm Bureau, brings a bonanza of locally grown, often organic fruits and vegetables: free-range eggs and local dairy cheeses; island-grown coffee and flowers; hand-harvested honey and sea salts; Hawaiian plate lunches and poi; and fresh smoothies, juices, popsicles and baked goods. Don't miss it!

Right Slice   BAKERY $
(Map p88; ☎ 808-212-8320; http://rightslice.com; Puhi Industrial Park, 1543 Haleukana St; pie slices from $5; ⊘ 11am-6pm Mon-Sat) This amazing

Central Lihuʻe

pie vendor graces farmers markets across the island has a commercial bakery. Order an hour ahead for your savory pot pie baked fresh, or swipe a sweet pie – blueberry piña colada, anyone? – by the slice or whole.

Hamura Saimin NOODLES $
(Map p94; ☎808-245-3271; 2956 Kress St; noodles $6-9; ⊙10am-10:30pm Mon-Thu, to midnight Fri & Sat, to 9:30pm Sun;) An island institution, Hamura's is a hole-in-the-wall specializing in homemade saimin (local-style noodle soup). At lunchtime, expect crowds slurping noodles elbow-to-elbow at retro, U-shaped lunch counters. Save room for the other (and much more beloved) specialty, *lilikoʻi* (passion fruit) chiffon pie.

Smiley's Local Grinds HAWAIIAN $
(Map p88; ☎808-245-4772; 4100 Rice St; meals $8-15; ⊙10:30am-1:30pm & 5-8:30pm Mon-Sat) Every workaday island town has its locals' favorite plate-lunch kitchen. 'Mini' plates will leave you stuffed with crispy pork *katsu* (cutlets), Korean-spiced chicken, Hawaiian *kalua* pig or even *laulau* (bundle made of pork or chicken and salted butterfish, wrapped in taro and *ti* leaves and steamed). Contrary to the name, service can be curt.

Kalapaki Beach Hut AMERICAN, HAWAIIAN $
(Map p88; ☎808-246-6330; www.kalapaki beachhut.com; 3474 Rice St; mains $7-10; ⊙7am-8pm;) This rubbah-slippah spot raises the bar for beach-shack cuisine. Order 100% Kauaʻi grass-fed beef burgers with taro fries, catch-of-the-day fish sandwiches or gravylicious *loco moco* (dish of rice, fried egg and hamburger patty topped with gravy or other condiments), with fresh coconuts or shave ice to top it all off.

Pho Kauai VIETNAMESE $
(Map p94; ☎808-245-9858; Rice Shopping Center, 4303 Rice St; mains $7-12; ⊙10am-9pm Mon-Sat) Hidden in a strip mall, this no-frills Vietnamese noodle shop serves steaming bowls of decent *pho* (noodle soup). Choose from meat or vegetable toppings, such as beef brisket, grilled shrimp, snow peas or eggplant.

Fish Express SEAFOOD $
(Map p94; ☎808-245-9918; 3343 Kuhio Hwy; mains $7-12; ⊙10am-6pm Mon-Sat, grill until 3pm) Fish lovers, this is almost a no-brainer. Order chilled deli items, from fresh ahi (yellowfin tuna) *poke* to green seaweed salad, or try a plate lunch of blackened ahi with guava-basil sauce or a gourmet *bentō* (Japanese-style box lunch). Get there early before the best *poke* runs out.

Sweet Marie's Hawaii BAKERY $
(Map p88; ☎808-823-0227; www.sweetmar ieshawaii.com; 3-4251 Kuhio Hwy; items from $2, mains $11-15; ⊙8am-2pm Tue-Sat) A gluten-free bakery operating out of a cute storefront delivers macaroons, cookies, brownies and a host of muffins and cakes, as well as a few breakfast and lunch dishes.

Vim ʻn Vigor HEALTH FOOD $
(Map p94; ☎808-245-9053; 3-3122 Kuhio Hwy; sandwiches around $6; ⊙9am-7pm Mon-Fri, to 5pm Sat;) Stocks healthy snacks, bulk staples and gluten-free and dairy-free products, but not much produce. Vegetarian and vegan sandwiches sell out fast.

Tip Top Cafe LOCAL, DINER $
(Map p94; 3173 Akahi St; mains $6-12; ⊙6:30am-2pm Tue-Sun;) The stark-white building might give you pause, but inside this retro diner teems with locals filling up on good, ol'-fashioned eats. The main draws are its famous banana-macnut pancakes, oxtail soup and *loco moco*.

Times Supermarket SUPERMARKET $
(Map p88; www.timessupermarkets.com; Kukui Grove Center, 3-2600 Kaumualiʻi Hwy; ⊙6am-11pm) Swing by this grocery store, which sells to-go salads, sandwiches, plate lunches and sushi. It has a smoothie bar and a *poke* (cubed raw

fish mixed with *shōyu,* sesame oil, salt, chili pepper, *'inamona* or other condiments) station with 30 varieties made fresh daily.

Duke's
FUSION **$$**

(Map p88; ☎ 808-246-9599; www.dukeskauai.com; Kaua'i Marriott, 3610 Rice St; bar mains $12-20, restaurant mains $28-32; ⊙ restaurant 5-10pm, bar from 11am) You won't find an evening spot more fun and lively than Duke's, which offers a classic view of Kalapaki Beach. The steak-and-seafood menu is none too innovative, but fish tacos served in the downstairs Barefoot Bar are a fave, especially on cheaper 'Taco Tuesdays.' Hula Pie, a mound of macnut (macadamia nut) ice cream in a chocolate-cookie crust, satisfies a touristy crowd. Complimentary valet parking.

Cafe Portofino
ITALIAN **$$$**

(Map p88; ☎ 808-245-2121; http://cafeportofino.com; Kaua'i Marriott, 3610 Rice St; mains $28-50; ⊙ 5-9pm) Overlooking Kalapaki Beach, this is one of the most upscale options in town. The food is less than imaginative, focusing on Italian fare and local catches. Make reservations in advance to get a seat at the edge of the patio.

Gaylord's
HAWAIIAN **$$$**

(Map p88; ☎ 808-245-9593; www.kilohana kauai.com; Kilohana Plantation, 3-2087 Kaumuali'i Hwy; mains lunch $12-18, dinner $21-36, Sun brunch buffet adult/child 5-12yr $30/15; ⊙ 11am-2:30pm & 5-9pm Mon-Sat, 9am-2pm Sun) There is no doubt that the historic Wilcox home at Kilohana Plantation provides a handsome setting, particularly on the verandah. Amid manicured lawns and white tablecloths in an open-air dining room, you can daydream as you fork into a local field greens salad, sesame-seared ahi with tempura avocado or banana-coconut cream pie. Sunday's brunch buffet has a Bloody Mary bar. Make reservations.

Kukui Grove Center
Farmers Market
MARKET

(Map p88; www.kukuigrovecenter.com; Kukui Grove Center, 3-2600 Kaumuali'i Hwy; ⊙ 3pm Mon; ☑ ⃫) ✐ On the garden side of the Kmart parking lot.

Drinking & Nightlife

There are a handful of bars – mostly sports bars – near Kalapaki Beach that cater to the cruise-ship set. The resorts also have bars.

★ Duke's Barefoot Bar
BAR

(Map p88; www.dukeskauai.com; Kaua'i Marriott, 3610 Rice St; ⊙ 11am-11pm) For a convivial, Waikiki-style tropical bar with live music every night, hurry and grab a beachside table before the nonstop evening queue. Happy hour from 4pm to 6pm daily.

Kauai Beer Company
BREWERY

(Map p94; ☎ 808-245-2337; http://kauaibeer.com; 4265 Rice St; ⊙ 3-10pm Tue-Sat) Kaua'i's only microbrewery has a convivial bar downtown, where everyone kicks back with a honeyed IPAloha 2.0, a Lihu'e Lager or a rotating seasonal or nitro-charged brew. Some nights food trucks pull up right outside, while other nights the kitchen is open, serving pub grub (dishes $10 to $14) such as poutine, Bavarian pretzels and taro avocado *poke.*

THE DUKE

When you're kicking back with your tropical drink at **Duke's Barefoot Bar**, you may just wonder – who was Duke anyway?

Duke Paoa Kahinu Mokoe Hulikohola Kahanamoku (1890–1968) is one of Hawaii's most famous sons. In his richly varied life, he was a five-time Olympic medalist in swimming, a Hollywood actor (his film and TV credits include *Mister Roberts*), the sheriff of Honolulu for almost 30 years and the first famous beach boy, as well as being the man credited with spreading surfing to Australia. Duke was also a legitimate hero: in 1925, he used his surfboard to effect the incredible rescue of eight men from a fishing vessel that had capsized in heavy surf off Newport Beach, California; 17 others died. Duke was not really royalty, however, his name notwithstanding. He was named after his father, who was himself named after the Duke of Edinburgh, Scotland. Over the years, however, he earned many honorary titles, such as 'the Father of Surfing.'

For all his successes and international travels, Duke never forgot where he came from. He was always a traditional Hawaiian, speaking the language as much as he could, even preferring a long-board carved from koa wood. When he died of a heart attack in 1968, at the age of 77, his ashes were scattered at sea in front of Waikiki Beach.

Hā Coffee Bar
CAFE

(Map p94; www.hacoffeebar.com; 4180 Rice St; ⊘6:30am-5pm Mon-Sat; 🛜) Coffee hipsterdom has hit Kaua'i at this airy, high-ceilinged cafe, where retro island travel prints and local art hang on the walls. Locally baked maple-cinnamon rolls, focaccia sandwiches, gluten-free treats and teas round out the menu.

☆ Entertainment

High-brow arts and entertainment are lacking. But occasional free concerts and cultural expos make up for it.

★ Luau Kalamaku
LUAU

(Map p88; 🗷877-622-1780; http://luaukalamaku.com; Kilohana Plantation, 3-2087 Kaumuali'i Hwy; adult/child 5-11yr/youth 12-16yr $100/40/60; ⊘5-8:30pm Tue & Fri; 🖐) Skip the same-old commercial luau and catch this dinner theater-in-the-round with a dash of Cirque du Soleil (think lithe dancers, flashy leotards and pyrotechnics) thrown in. The stage play about one family's epic voyage to Hawaii features hula and Tahitian dancing, and showstopping, nail-biting Samoan fire dancing. The buffet dinner is above average, despite the audience size (maximum 1000 people).

Shutters
LIVE MUSIC

(Map p88; Aqua Kaua'i Beach Resort; ⊘5-11pm) Head over to the Kaua'i Beach Resort for live music nightly.

Kaua'i Concert Association
LIVE MUSIC

(🗷808-245-7464; www.kauai-concert.org; tickets from $25) Stages the annual Red Clay Jazz Festivals and classical, jazz and world-music concerts at the **Kaua'i Community College (KCC) Performing Arts Center** (Map p88; 🗷808-245-8311; http://kauai.hawaii.edu/pac/; 3-1901 Kaumuali'i Hwy), where past performers include Berklee College of Music and the Harlem String Quartet.

Kukui Grove Cinema 4
CINEMA

(Map p88; 🗷808-245-5055; www.kukuigrovecinema.com; 4368 Kukui Grove St; tickets $6-9; 🖐) Standard fourplex showing mainstream first-run Hollywood movies.

🛍 Shopping

Lihu'e's biggest mall is the aging, open-air **Kukui Grove Center** (Map p88; 🗷808-245-7784; www.kukuigrovecenter.com; 3-2600 Kaumuali'i Hwy; ⊘9:30am-7pm Mon-Thu & Sat, to 9pm Fri, 10am-6pm Sun; 🛜), home to department stores, sporting-goods and electronics shops, banks and more. Near Nawiliwili Harbor, the busy, low-slung **Anchor Cove Shopping Center** (Map p88; 3416 Rice St) and emptier two-story **Harbor Mall** (Map p88; 🗷808-245-6255; www.harbormall.net; 3501 Rice St) draw mainly tourists from cruise ships and the nearby Marriott.

★ Koloa Rum Company
DRINKS

(Map p88; 🗷808-246-8900; www.koloarum.com; Kilohana Plantation, 3-2087 Kaumuali'i Hwy; ⊘store 9:30am-5pm Mon, Wed & Sat, to 9pm Tue & Fri, to 6:30pm Thu, to 3pm Sun, tasting room 10am-3:30pm Mon, Wed & Sat, to 7:30pm Tue & Fri, to 5pm Thu, to 2pm Sun) Kaua'i's own rum label is a relatively new brand, which means it doesn't have a fine aged rum yet, but its dark and spiced versions win awards. Learn how to mix a classic mai tai during a free rum tasting, starting every 30 minutes daily.

Koa Store
GIFTS & SOUVENIRS

(Map p88; 🗷808-245-4871, 800-838-9264; www.thekoastore.com; 3-3601 Kuhio Hwy; ⊘10am-6pm) 🖊 Other galleries carry high-end masterpieces, but here you'll find more affordable and functional pieces, such as picture frames and jewelry boxes. Many items come in three grades, from the basic straight-grain koa to premium 'curly' koa. All woodcraft are genuine – they're not the cheap fakes sold at tourist traps.

Edith King Wilcox Gift Shop & Bookstore
BOOKS, GIFTS

(Map p94; 🗷808-246-2470; www.kauaimuseum.org; Kaua'i Museum, 4428 Rice St; ⊘10am-5pm Mon-Sat) 🖊 The Kaua'i Museum's gem of a gift shop carries a variety of genuine Hawaiian crafts, such as Ni'ihau shell jewelry, koa woodwork and *lauhala* (a type of traditional Hawaiian leaf weaving) hats, along with collectible contemporary artworks and plenty of Hawaiiana books. Enter the shop, free of charge, through the museum lobby.

BEST PLACES TO SHOP

- Koloa Rum Company
- Koa Store
- Clayworks

JEFF WHYTE/SHUTTERSTOCK ©

1. Wailua Falls (p86)
While officially listed as 80ft, the falls have been repeatedly measured to have a far greater drop.

2. Ninini Point Lighthouse (p88)
Built in 1906, this lighthouse has since been automated.

3. Hamura Saimin (p95)
An island institution, Hamura's is a hugely popular hole-in-the-wall specializing in homemade saimin (local-style noodle soup).

4. Kalapaki Beach (p87)
This sheltered beach's easy-access location and versatility make it a hit with families.

MARK BOSTER/GETTY IMAGES ©

Clayworks
ARTS & CRAFTS

(Map p88; ☑808-246-2529; www.clayworksat kilohana.com; Kilohana Plantation, 3-2087 Kaumuali'i Hwy; ⊙10am-6pm Mon-Fri, 11am-2pm Sat & Sun) A hidden pottery studio and gallery overflows with colorful vases, mugs, bowls and tiles. Potters also offer tutelage at the throwing wheel, and you'll get to take home your *raku*-fired, glazed masterpiece. Call ahead for lessons.

Da Life
SPORTS & OUTDOORS

(Map p88; ☑808-246-6333; www.livedalife.com; 3500 Rice St; ⊙9am-5pm Mon-Fri, 10am-4pm Sat & Sun) This outdoor outfitter and booking agent's retail shop is stuffed with sports gear for all manner of land and sea adventures on Kaua'i. If you forgot to pack it, Da Life probably stocks it.

Kapaia Stitchery
ARTS & CRAFTS

(Map p88; www.kapaia-stitchery.com; 3-3551 Kuhio Hwy; ⊙9am-5pm Mon-Sat) A quilter's heaven, this longtime shop features countless tropical-print cotton fabrics, plus island-made patterns and kits. Stop here also for handmade gifts and apparel, including children's clothing and aloha shirts.

Costco
FOOD

(Map p88; www.costco.com; 4300 Nuhou St; ⊙10am-8:30pm Mon-Fri, 9:30am-6pm Sat, 10am-6pm Sun) This members-only food and goods warehouse is a good spot to stock up if you plan on self-catering.

Longs Drugs
SOUVENIRS, FOOD

(Map p88; ☑808-245-8871; www.cvs.com; Kukui Grove Center, 3-2600 Kaumuali'i Hwy; ⊙7am-10pm) So much more than a drugstore, Longs is an inexpensive place to shop for a wide selection of Hawaii-made products, from children's books to macnuts and crack-seed candy.

Flowers Forever
GIFTS & SOUVENIRS

(Map p94; ☑808-245-4717, 800-646-7579; www. flowersforeverhawaii.com; 2679 Kalena St; ⊙8am-5pm Mon-Thu, to 6pm Fri, to 4pm Sat) Voted 'Best Kaua'i Flower Shop' for 12 years running, Forever Flowers strings together a multitude of flower, maile, *ti*-leaf and more unusual specialty lei. It will ship tropical flowers, plants and lei to the mainland too.

Tropic Isle Music & Gifts
SOUVENIRS, MUSIC

(Map p88; www.tropicislemusic.com; Anchor Cove Shopping Center, 3416 Rice St; ⊙10am-8pm) This tiny shop is crammed with a huge selection of Hawaiiana books, CDs, DVDs, bath and body products, home decor, island-made foodstuffs – you name it. Here you can avoid mistakenly buying mass-produced knockoffs imported from Asia.

ⓘ Information

DANGERS & ANNOYANCES

Getting caught in a riptide is the biggest danger here. The beaches can attract some riffraff after dark.

LGBTIQ TRAVELERS

There are no LGBTIQ specific clubs or services in Lihu'e.

INTERNET ACCESS

There's wi-fi in most hotels and some restaurants.

MEDICAL SERVICES

Lihu'e has the best medical services on the island, with Kaua'i's only major hospital, **Wilcox Memorial Hospital** (p269), with a 24-hour emergency room.

Kaua'i Urgent Care (☑808-245-1532; www. wilcoxhealth.org; 4484 Pahe'e St; ⊙8am-7pm Mon-Fri, to 4pm Sat & Sun) is a walk-in clinic for nonemergencies, and **Longs Drugs** (☑808-245-8871; Kukui Grove Center, 3-2600 Kaumuali'i Hwy; ⊙ store 7am-10pm, pharmacy to 9pm Mon-Fri, to 6pm Sat & Sun) is a full-service pharmacy.

For major emergencies, you may be airlifted to Honolulu.

MONEY

American Savings Bank (☑808-246-8844; www.asbhawaii.com; Kukui Grove Center, 3-2600 Kaumuali'i Hwy) Convenient shopping-mall branch with a 24-hour ATM.

Bank of Hawaii (☑808-245-6761; www.boh. com; 4455 Rice St) Downtown bank with a 24-hour ATM.

OPENING HOURS

Lihu'e works on a standard Monday to Friday work schedule. Expect slightly more regular hours here than on the rest of the island, which is on island time.

POST

Lihu'e Post Office (Map p94; ☑808-245-1628; www.usps.com; 4441 Rice St; ⊙8am-4pm Mon-Fri, 9am-1pm Sat)

TOURISM INFORMATION

Kaua'i Visitors Bureau (Map p94; ☑808-245-3971; www.gohawaii.com/kauai; 4334 Rice St, Suite 101; ⊙8am-4:30pm Mon-Fri) Comprehensive web resources for visitors, with free vacation-planning kits downloadable online. The office staff are helpful.

Division of Parks & Recreation (Map p94; ☑808-241-4463; www.kauai.gov; 4444 Rice St, Suite 105, Lihu'e Civic Center, Lihu'e; ⊙8am-4pm Mon-Fri) For tourist information.

SUPERFERRY NON GRATA

In August 2007, when the Hawaii Superferry sailed toward Nawiliwili Harbor for its first arrival, there was a dramatic stand-off as some 300 Kaua'i protesters blocked its entry. Three-dozen people even swam into the gargantuan ferry's path, shouting, 'Go home, go home!' Ultimately, service to Maui (but not to Kaua'i) was launched in December 2007, but the whole enterprise was indefinitely terminated in March 2009, when the Hawai'i Supreme Court deemed Superferry's environmental impact statement (EIS) invalid.

Why was opposition to the ferry so furious? Actually, the opponents themselves were not 'anti-ferry' but, rather, anti-Superferry. They wanted smaller, passenger-only, publicly owned and slower-moving boats. Their main concerns were nighttime collisions with whales, worsened traffic on Neighbor Islands, the spread of environmental pests and plundering of natural resources by nonresidents. Indeed, during the Superferry's brief run between O'ahu and Maui, some passengers were caught taking home 'opihi (edible limpet), crustaceans, algae, rocks, coral and reef fish.

That said, not all locals were opposed. In fact, many locals (especially O'ahu residents) viewed the Superferry as a convenient way to visit friends and family on Neighbor Islands. They also cited the need for an alternate, fuel-efficient mode of transportation other than airplanes between the islands (though the enormous vessels were actually gas guzzlers).

For a compelling (if overwhelmingly detailed) account, read *The Superferry Chronicles* by Koohan Paik and Jerry Mander, which also analyzes the ferry's ties to US military and commercial interests.

ℹ Getting There & Away

AIR

Lihu'e Airport (LIH; Map p88; ☑808-274-3800; http://hawaii.gov/lih; 3901 Mokulele Loop) Only 2 miles from downtown, this small airport handles all commercial interisland, US mainland and Canada flights.

BOAT

The only commercial passenger vessels docking on Kaua'i at Lihu'e's Nawiliwili Harbor are cruise ships, mainly Norwegian Cruise Line (p277) and Princess Cruises (p277).

ℹ Getting Around

TO/FROM THE AIRPORT

Car rental To pick up rental cars, check in at agency booths outside the baggage-claim area, then catch a complimentary shuttle bus to the agency's parking lot. Or go straight to the rental-car lot, where there may be less of a queue.

Taxi Cabs are infrequently used because most visitors rent cars, but you'll usually find them waiting curbside outside the baggage-claim area. If not, use the courtesy phones to call one.

BUS

Kaua'i Bus (p274) serves Lihu'e with a shuttle that runs hourly from about 6am until 9pm. Stops include Kukui Grove Center, Lihu'e Airport (no large backpacks or luggage allowed), Vidinha Stadium and Wilcox Memorial Hospital. There's also a lunchtime shuttle within central Lihu'e that runs at 15-minute intervals between approximately 10:30am and 2pm.

CAR & MOTORCYCLE

Most businesses have free parking lots for customers. Metered street parking is pretty easy to find.

Kauai Car & Scooter Rental (☑808-245-7177; www.kauaimopedrentals.com; 3148 Oihana St; ⊙8am-5pm) Locally owned agency rents older economy-size island cars from $25 per day, and scooters or mopeds from $35 per day, with additional taxes and fees. Younger drivers (over 21 years) and debit cardholders welcome. Book in advance; free airport pickups available.

Kaua'i Harley-Davidson (☑808-212-9495; www.kauaiharley.com; 3-1878 Kaumuali'i Hwy; ⊙8am-5pm) It'll cost up to $200 per day, plus a $1000 minimum security deposit, but if you want a hog in paradise, you've got one.

TAXI

Kauai Taxi Company (☑808-246-9554; http://kauaitaxico.com) Taxi service. Tours also available.

Akiko's Taxi (☑808-822-7588; www.akikostaxikauai.net; ⊙5am-10pm) Locally owned taxi service.

Kapaʻa & the Eastside

Best Places to Eat

➡ JO2 (p119)

➡ Hukilau Lanai (p115)

➡ Kintaro (p114)

➡ Kenji (p119)

➡ Street Burger (p114)

➡ Tiki Tacos (p119)

Best Outdoors

➡ Wailua River (p109)

➡ Blue Hole (p117)

➡ Nounou Mountain (p104)

➡ Ke Ala Hele Makalae (p127)

Why Go?

If you look past the strip malls and highway traffic, the Eastside fascinates. Its geography runs the gamut, from mountaintop forests to pounding surf and a majestic river. In ancient times, the Wailua River was sacred and Hawaiian royalty lived along its fertile banks. Kapaʻa's historic town center echoes another bygone era of sugar plantations.

Kauaʻi's population is concentrated here. Stretching from Wailua to Kapaʻa, the 'Coconut Coast' has a busy, workaday vibe, as opposed to the swankier resorts of Princeville and Poʻipu. Traffic can grind to a painful halt at any time of day, however. Further north and hidden away from the hubbub is down-home Anahola – a fishing and farming village where Hawaiians make up about half of all residents.

When to Go

➡ Summer (May to September) is the busiest time of year, as the majority of festivals happen in the summertime. The weather is also (usually) dry, which means the homestead trails in the lush interior are often dry and in great condition.

➡ If you aren't bound by school schedules, enjoy the Eastside in October and November when lodging rates are at their lowest, crowds thin on the ground, and yet a couple of intriguing local festivals are on.

➡ Eastside life gets festive around the December holidays. Restaurants are busy and the atmosphere inviting.

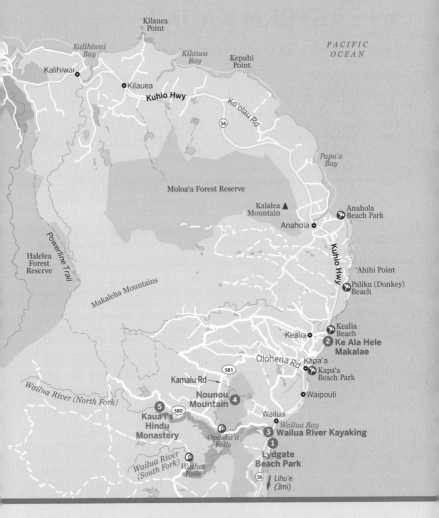

Kapa'a & the Eastside Highlights

① **Lydgate Beach Park** (p108) Exploring playgrounds, sheltered swimming areas and tide-line driftwood piles with the kids.

② **Ke Ala Hele Makalae** (p127) Running, walking or pedaling the 5 miles between Kapa'a Beach Park and Paliku (Donkey) Beach at sunrise.

③ **Wailua River Kayaking** (p113) Feeling the mana (life force) as you paddle the sacred Wailua River into a valley that was the birthplace of kings and the abode of *ali'i* (high royalty).

④ **Nounou Mountain** (p104) Trekking the sweeping river, valley and coastal views of Kaua'i's Eastside from the

'Sleeping Giant' – you'll have to climb as much as 1000ft to earn your photo op.

⑤ **Kaua'i's Hindu Monastery** (p108) Finding serenity in this forest sanctuary – an intricately carved main temple surrounded by bountiful gardens high above the Wailua River.

HIKING, CYCLING & KAYAKING IN EASTERN KAUA'I

HIKING TOUR: NOUNOU MOUNTAIN TRAIL

START KUAMO'O-NOUNOU TRAILHEAD
END NOUNOU EAST TRAILHEAD
LENGTH TWO HOURS; 4 MILES

Climbing the Sleeping Giant is a local's favorite, both for its brevity (it can be done in a couple of hours, which makes it a doable daily workout), the incline that gets the heart pumping and the sweeping views of the Coconut Coast from Anahola to Lihu'e. Although there are **three trails** (Map p114) that converge near the summit, we suggest starting at **Kuamo'o-Nounou Trailhead**. From here it's a slightly more gentle approach through the gorgeous **Norfolk Island pine grove**, with their paper bark and mossy roots, planted in the 1930s by the Civilian Conservation Corps. The drawback is that after rain, the trail can be slick and muddy. Follow it through the pines. The incline is gentle at first but you will soon be huffing and puffing as the trail winds up to the giant's shoulders. Before long you'll converge with the others and pop out on to a plateau, with a much welcome sheltered **picnic area**.

Now atop the giant's chest, only his head prevents you from getting a 360-degree view. There is a trail to the left that leads along a slender ridge to the **true summit**. Signs say that it's off limits, but some take their chances – just know that it is risky and not recommended. If you go for it, take extreme care and be smart. You wouldn't want to be one of those newsy footnotes. You know, the one about the guy who died falling off a cliff while taking a selfie.

Retrace your steps but instead of heading back the way you came, veer right at the fork and head down the exposed **Nounou Mountain East Trail Junction**. It offers sweeping views of the ocean and distant mountains as you switchback down to the **trailhead**. Wear a hat, as the sun can be fierce without the shady pine grove.

Ideally you've dropped a car here. If not, call a taxi or simply start and finish at the same place.

HIKING TOUR: KUILAU RIDGE & MOALEPE TRAILS

START KUAMO'O RD/OLOHENA RD
END KUAMO'O RD/OLOHENA RD
LENGTH HALF DAY; VARIES (8.5 MILES AT THE LONGEST)

The **Kuilau Ridge Trail** (Map p110) is recommended for its sheer beauty: emerald valleys, dewy bushes, thick ferns and glimpses of misty **Mt Wai'ale'ale** in the distance. After 1 mile, you'll reach a grassy clearing with a picnic table. Continue north on descending switchbacks until you meet the mountain-view **Moalepe Trail** (2.25 miles one-way).

Both of these moderate hikes are among the most visually rewarding on Kaua'i. Remember, the trails don't complete a circuit so you must retrace your steps (8.5 miles round-trip). You might want to skip the final mile of the outbound leg, which crosses the treeless pastureland of Wailua Game Management Area.

The Kuilau Ridge Trail starts at a marked trailhead on the right just before Kuamo'o Rd crosses the stream at the Keahua Arboretum, 4 miles above the junction of Kuamo'o Rd and Kamalu Rd. The Moalepe Trail trailhead is at the end of Olohena Rd in the Wailua Homesteads neighborhood.

CYCLING TOUR: EASTSIDE BIKE TRAIL

START KAUAI CYCLE
END JAVA KAI
LENGTH TWO HOURS; 10 MILES

There are other places to rent a pair of wheels, but seeing as though this is a cycling tour you should get yours at **Kauai**

On the east side of Kaua'i, you can trek through jungle, cycle along by the ocean or kayak up the sacred Wailua River, then end up with to-die-for views.

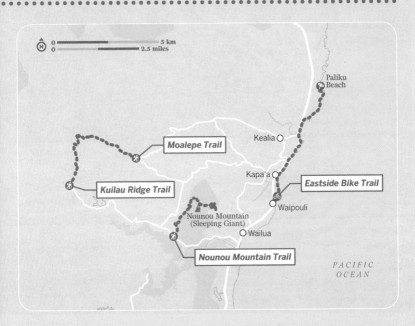

Cycle (p118) in Waipouli, the island's best bike shop. It has a range of equipment offering various degrees of comfort and speed. Grab a multigear bike as there are a few small hills to climb.

Head northeast on Kuhio Hwy. From there, make your first right on Keaka Rd, and a left on Moanakai Rd. With very little traffic you'll be pedaling along the coast without a care in the world. Follow it until you cross the canal on a footbridge, and connect with the Ke Ala Hele Makalae, the island's only dedicated bike path. When the plan for it was hatched, there were grand plans for this path to wrap part way around the whole island, from Lihu'e to Anahola, but this 5-mile stretch is all that has been built, so use it. It is a rather pleasant strip of concrete that follows the contour of the beach, laying flat past **Kapa'a Beach**

Park (p123), then rising slightly higher with the bluffs before dropping down along the stunning **Kealia Beach** (p123), with its shore break perfect for body boarders. The path rises up one more time before its terminus just before Paliku Beach (p124), an isolated cove set between Anahola and Kapa'a, inaccessible to cars.

When you've cooled off in the tides at Paliku or Kealia, hop on your ride and cruise back to Kapa'a. Indulge yourself at **Java Kai** (p128) – with its tasty espresso drinks, smoothies and bagel sandwiches. Afterward walk it off with a long, slow browse among the shops and galleries in Old Town Kapa'a, before returning your trusted steed (ie your rent-a-bike).

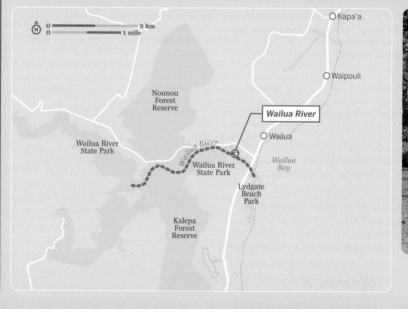

Kapa'a

Waipouli

Nounou
Forest
Reserve

Wailua River

Wailua River
State Park

Wailua River

Wailua

Wailua
Bay

Wailua River
State Park

Lydgate
Beach
Park

Kalepa
Forest
Reserve

N

0   2 km
0   1 mile

KAYAKING TOUR: WAILUA RIVER

START HOLOHOLOKU HEIAU
END HIKINA AKALA HEIAU
LENGTH THREE HOURS; 4 MILES

One of the iconic tours on the island is this pleasant, easily done yet still adventurous paddle up Wailua River. At 20 miles long, it's the longest navigable river flowing in the state of Hawaii.

Begin with a silent prayer at **Holoholoku Heiau** (p109) and don't be afraid to ask for a safe and pleasant journey. If mixing religious beliefs or indulging in prayer isn't your thing, a simple acknowledgment of the local ancestors who built Wailua and this, the oldest temple on the island, won't hurt. From there grab your kayak rental from one of the operations on the Wailua River, steps from the **Wailua River State Park**.

Now its time to paddle upstream. If the wind kicks up or the current feels a bit strong, stay close to the edge of the river and be mindful of boats along the way. Paddle around two bends in the river before your first stop at **Kamokila Hawaiian Village** (p109). Kids will love the traditional Hawaiian-hut reproductions and gardens of guava, mango and banana trees. When you've had your fill, continue upstream for another mile or so and take the north fork in the river. When you reach shore, stash your kayaks and start hiking along a jungle trail for a a little under a mile. It helps to bring amphibious shoes or sandals that strap your feet in securely, as you'll be crossing streams and scrambling over slick rocks. You'll soon reach the 100ft-tall **Uluwehi Falls**. Now's the time to eat that picnic lunch you packed for your journey and sip some water. When you're rested, double back to the river and paddle downstream toward the sea. The current will be at your back, though the wind will likely be in your face. When you reach the dock, return your kayak and follow the river mouth to **Lydgate Beach Park** (p108), where you can pay your respects once more at **Hikina Akala Heiau** (p109). It sits on a small rise overlooking the Coconut Coast.

Top: Wailua River (p109)
Bottom: Kamokila Hawaiian Village (p109), Wailua

❶ Getting There & Away

It's easy to get in and out of this region, where Hwy 50 arcs around the airport in Lihu'e and becomes Kuhio Hwy – the Eastside's main drag, which links Wailua to Waipouli, Kapa'a, Anahola and points north. Kuamoo Rd (Hwy 580) serves the Wailua Homesteads where some of the island's most appealing trails sprout. The Kapa'a Bypass will help you avoid Waipouli–Kapa'a gridlock during rush hour, though traffic can be a drag at anytime here. Most rental-car agencies are clustered around the airport, though Kapa'a has a discount agency.

The county bus system links the region with the south, west and north, and buses are equipped to carry bicycles. Taxis are pretty worthless, however.

Wailua

📶 808 / POP 2300

Wailua has two sides to it. The coast belongs to strip-mall businesses and package tourists, who are packed into oceanfront condos and hotels like happy slices of a pie chart. But if you're after that wild-palm-grove nature magic for which Kaua'i is famous, you can find that here too. Just head to the languid Wailua River or follow hiking trails that wind high into lush forested mountains.

◉ Sights

Take a virtual tour of the **Wailua Heritage Trail** (www.wailuaheritagetrail.org) for an overview of historical sights and natural attractions, with a downloadable map.

★**Kaua'i's Hindu Monastery** HINDU TEMPLE
(Map p110; 📶808-822-3012; www.himalayan academy.com; 107 Kaholalele Rd; ⊙9am-noon, inner gate open after 10:30am) **FREE** Serious pil-

grims and curious sightseers are welcome at this Hindu monastery, set on 70 acres and surrounded by verdant forest above the Wailua River. The property was an old inn, until the monks bought it in 1966. Now it's a blend of organic and botanical gardens, cascading streams, and sacred temples and shrines devoted to Ganesha, Nandi and Shiva.

While visitors can access a limited area on their own, more detailed guided tours are offered for free once a week – call or check the website for details. Modest dress required: no shorts, T-shirts, tank tops or short dresses. If you're not dressed properly, you can borrow sarongs at the entrance.

The **Kadavul Temple** contains a rare single-pointed quartz crystal, a 50-million-year-old, six-sided *shivalingam* (representation of the god Shiva) that weighs 700lb and stands over 3ft tall. In the temple (which visitors may not enter except to attend a 9am daily worship service), monks have performed a *puja* (prayer ritual) every three hours around the clock since the temple was established in 1973. They are currently building another temple at the rear of the property.

★**Lydgate Beach Park** BEACH
(Map p114; www.kamalani.org; ⊙7am-6pm; 🚻) A narrow stretch of blond sand strewn with driftwood can entertain restless kids of all ages, all afternoon. There's generally safe swimming to be found in two pools inside a protected breakwater, and beginner snorkeling too. Other amenities include two big playgrounds, game-sized soccer fields, a paved recreational path, picnic tables and pavilions, restrooms, outdoor showers, drinking water and lifeguards.

To get here, turn *makai* (seaward) on Kuhio Hwy between mile markers 5 and 6. At the park's northern end, multifeatured **Kamalani Playground** is a massive 16,000-sq-ft wooden castle with swings, a volcano slide, mirror mazes, an epic suspension bridge and other kid-pleasing contraptions.

Beware of the open ocean beyond the protected pool – it can be rough and dangerous, with strong currents, huge waves, sharp coral and slippery rocks. When the wind is blowing, kitesurfers put on a tremendous show. Camping is allowed at the south end of the park.

THE SOURCE: MT WAI'ALE'ALE

Nicknamed the Rain Machine, Mt Wai'ale'ale (translated as 'rippling water' or 'overflowing water') averages more than 450in of rainfall annually. With a yearly record of 683in in 1982, it's widely regarded as one of the wettest places on earth. Its steep cliffs cause moist air to rise rapidly and focus rainfall in one area. Believed by ancient Hawaiians to be occupied by the god Kane, it's located in the center of the island, representing Kaua'i's *piko* (navel). It's the source of the Wailua, Hanalei and Waimea Rivers, as well as almost every visible waterfall on the island.

THE SACRED WAILUA RIVER

To ancient Hawaiians, the Wailua River was among the most sacred places across the islands. The river basin, near its mouth, was one of the island's two royal centers (the other was Waimea) and home to the high chiefs. Here you can find the remains of many important heiau (ancient stone temples) and together they now form a national historic landmark.

Long and narrow **Hikina Akala Heiau** (Rising of the Sun Temple; Map p114) sits south of the Wailua River mouth, which is today the north end of Lydgate Beach Park. In its heyday, the temple (built around AD 1300) was aligned directly north to south, but only a few remaining boulders outline its original massive shape. Neighboring **Hauola Pu'uhonua** (meaning 'the place of refuge of the dew of life') is marked by a bronze plaque. Ancient Hawaiian kapu (taboo) breakers were assured safety from persecution if they made it inside.

Believed to be the oldest *luakini* (temple dedicated to the war god Ku, often a place for human sacrifice) on the island, **Holoholoku Heiau** (Map p114) is located a quarter-mile up Kuamo'o Rd on the left. It's believed to be Kaua'i's oldest heiau and a place to pray for good fortune before battle. A trail from here leads uphill to the gnarled headstones of an old Japanese cemetery with sweeping river views. Toward the west, against the flat-backed birthstone marked by a plaque reading **Pohaku Ho'ohanau** (Royal Birthstone), queens gave birth to future royals. Only a male child born here could become king of Kaua'i.

Perched high on a hill overlooking the meandering Wailua River, well-preserved **Poli'ahu Heiau** (Map p114), another *luakini*, is named after the snow goddess Poli'ahu, one of the sisters of the volcano goddess Pele. The heiau is immediately before 'Opaeka-'a Falls Lookout, on the opposite side of the road.

Although Hawaiian heiau were originally imposing stone structures, most now lie in ruins, covered with scrub. But they are still considered powerful vortices of mana (spiritual essence) and should be treated with respect. For a compelling history of the Wailua River's significance to ancient Hawaiians, read Edward Joesting's *Kauai: the Separate Kingdom*.

'Opaeka'a Falls Lookout VIEWPOINT
(Map p114) While not a showstopper, these 150ft-high waterfalls make for an easy roadside stop, less than 2 miles up Kuamo'o Rd. For the best photographs, go in the morning. Don't be tempted to try trailblazing to the base of the falls. These steep cliffs are perilous and have caused fatalities. Cross the road for fantastic photo ops of the Wailua River.

Kamokila Hawaiian Village CULTURAL CENTER
(Map p114; ☏ 808-823-0559; http://villagekauai.com; 5443 Kuamo'o Rd; village admission adult/child 3-12yr $5/3, outrigger canoe tours adult/child $30/20; ☺ 9am-5pm; ⊕) While not a must-see, it's a pleasant diversion, especially for kids. Along the Wailua River, the 4-acre site includes reproductions of traditional Hawaiian structures amid thriving gardens of guava, mango and banana trees. Kamokila also offers canoe rentals and guided **outrigger canoe tours**, leaving hourly, which include paddling, hiking and waterfall swimming.

Turn south from Kuamo'o Rd, opposite 'Opaeka'a Falls. The half-mile road leading to the village is steep and narrow. You can also rent a kayak elsewhere and paddle in.

Smith's Tropical Paradise GARDENS
(Map p114; ☏ 808-821-6895; www.smithskauai.com; adult/child 3-12yr $6/3; ☺ 8:30am-4pm; ⊕) Other gardens might have fancier landscaping, but you can't beat Smith's for value. Take a leisurely stroll along a mile-long loop trail past a serene pond, grassy lawns and island-themed gardens. The setting can seem Disney-esque, with an Easter Island *moai* statue replica, but it's as appealing as it is unpretentious.

Keahua Arboretum PARK
(Map p110) FREE Sitting prettily at the top of Kuamo'o Rd, this arboretum has grassy fields, a gurgling stream and groves of rainbow eucalyptus and other towering trees. Locals come here to picnic and to swim in the freshwater stream and pools, but be aware that the water is infected with leptospira bacteria.

Eastside

Hokualele Rd

15

Kamalomalo'o Pl

10

'Aliomanu Rd

Kuhio Hwy

17

18

12

56

Anahola Stream

Kamane Rd

Anahola Rd

Anahola Poha Rd

13

5

PACIFIC OCEAN

Anahola

0 —————— 500 m
0 —————— 0.25 miles

Kahili
(Rock Quarry)
Beach

Ko'olau Rd

Kuhio Hwy

56

8

Larsen's
Beach Rd

4

*Moloa'a
Beach*

16

Moloa'a Forest Reserve

Kalalea
Mountain

Powerline Trail

Halelea
Forest
Reserve

Makaleha Mountains

O'ohena Rd

581

Kamalu Rd

7 11

Wailua River (North Fork)

2

**Kaua'i's Hindu
Monastery**

580

Nounou Mountain
(Sleeping Giant) ▲
(1241ft)

Opaeka'a
Falls

Wailua

See Wailua Map (p114)

Wailua River (South Fork)

*Wailua
Falls*

14

56

Lihu'e
(2mi)

Eastside

🏃 Activities

Most Eastside hiking trails ascend into Kaua'i's tropical-jungle interior. Expect humidity, red dirt (or mud) and slippery patches after rains.

Adventure Fit Kauai ADVENTURE SPORTS
(☎808-651-4696; https://adventurefitkauai.com; itineraries $100-400) On an island full of fun adventurous athletes, there are few, if any, better than Mariko Strickland Lum. Born and raised Kaua'i, she was a collegiate soccer star on the mainland before returning home and dominating stand up paddle surfing races all over the map. She also customizes adventure and fitness itineraries for guests.

Whether you crave intense morning workouts, a nice long stand up paddle or a hike or mountain bike ride, she's the person to call.

Kauai Water Ski Co WATER SPORTS
(Map p114; ☎808-639-2829, 808-822-3574; www.kauaiwaterskiandsurf.com; Kinipopo Shopping Village, 4-356 Kuhio Hwy; per 30/60min $90/175; ☉9am-5pm Mon-Fri, to noon Sat) Hawaii's only non-ocean water-skiing happens on the Wailua River. Rates are per trip, not per person (maximum number of riders varies by skill level; beginners welcome), and

include water-skiing or wakeboarding equipment and a professional instructor as your driver. Reservations required.

Sacred Waters
SPA
(Map p114; ☑808-651-7144; www.kinipopo village.com/sacred-waters-healing-arts.htm; 4-356 Kuhio Hwy; massages from $105; ⊘by appt) A day spa offering everything from *lomilomi* (traditional Hawaiian massage; literally 'loving hands') and hot stone massage to Ayurvedic body treatment to life coaching. If you don't want to make the trek to her Wailua shop, call and ask for a house call.

Wailua Municipal Golf Course
GOLF
(Map p110; ☑808-241-6666; www.kauai.gov/golf; 3-5350 Kuhio Hwy; nonresident green fees $24-60, club rental $20-35) This 18-hole, par-72 course, designed by former head pro Toyo Shirai, is one of Hawaii's top-ranked municipal golf courses. Plan ahead because morning tee times are sometimes reserved a week in advance. After 2pm, the regular $48 green fee drops by half and it's first-come, first-served. Cart and club rentals available. You'll pay a premium to play on weekends.

Courses

Kaua'i Cultural Center
COURSE
(Map p114; ☑808-651-0682; http://kauaicultural center.com; Coconut Marketplace, 4-484 Kuhio Hwy; 1hr classes from $10; 👪) 🖉 Inside a shopping mall, this tiny community center is run by Leilani Rivera Low, a respected *kumu* hula (hula teacher). Take a beginner's hula, Tahitian dance or ukulele lesson, or learn how to make a *ti*-leaf skirt or flower lei. Call a day ahead to reserve a spot or drop by to ask about walk-in space. Check the website for a schedule of upcoming classes, workshops and events.

Tours

Steelgrass Farm
FOOD & DRINK
(☑808-821-1857; www.steelgrass.org; 5730 Olohena Rd; 3hr tours adult/child under 12yr $75/free; ⊘9am-noon Mon, Wed & Fri; 👪) Learn more about diversified agriculture, cacao growing and the owners' intriguing family history at this working chocolate farm. The farm's other main crops are bamboo and vanilla, but hundreds of tropical species propagate these 8 acres. Advance reservations for tours are required; you'll be given driving directions after booking.

Kayak Wailua
KAYAKING, HIKING
(Map p114; ☑808-822-3388; www.kayak wailua.com; 4565 Haleilio Rd; 4½hr tours $50) This small, family-owned company specializes in Wailua River tours. It keeps its boats and equipment in tip-top shape; shuttles you to the marina launch site; and provides dry bags for your belongings and a nylon cooler for your own food.

CACAO: HAWAII'S NEXT BIG BEAN?

The world's chocolate comes mainly from West Africa, Brazil, Ecuador, Malaysia and Indonesia. But Kaua'i's humid tropical climate and regular rain nurtures the prized cacao bean here, too. It's among the specialty crops that local-agriculture proponents are touting for Hawaii's next generation of farmers. Learn more about diversified agriculture and cacao growing at **Steelgrass Farm**, which offers a unique chocolate-farm tour that includes a tasting of single-estate dark-chocolate bars produced around the world, including those from the Big Island's 'Original Hawaiian Chocolate Factory' and O'ahu's Waialua Estate.

Its other crops are timber bamboo and vanilla, but the 8-acre farm features hundreds of thriving tropical species, which you'll also see on the tour. It's a fantastic introduction if you're curious to see what thrives on Kaua'i, from avocados and citrus to soursop and sapodilla.

The owners, Will and Emily Lydgate, are the great-grandchildren of Kaua'i minister and community leader John Mortimer Lydgate, namesake of **Lydgate Beach Park** (p108). The property was not an inheritance, as 'JM' had no desire to acquire land or profit from the sugar industry. With this thriving example of a 'teaching farm' – meant to experiment with workable crops – the Lydgates are trying to encourage a shift away from the mono-crops and sheer capital outlays of industrial agriculture toward small-scale farming and diversified crops instead. Call ahead if you'd like to visit.

KAYAKING AROUND WAILUA

The 20-mile-long **Wailua River** is fed by two streams originating on Mt Wai'ale'ale. It's the only navigable river across the Hawaiian Islands, and kayaking it has become a visitor must-do. Fortunately, the paddle is a doable 5 miles for all ages.

Tours usually paddle 2 miles up the river's north fork, which leads to a mile-long hike through dense forest to **Uluwehi Falls** (Secret Falls), a 100ft waterfall. The hike crosses a stream and scrambles over rocks and roots, and if muddy it will probably cause some slippin' and slidin'. Wear sturdy, washable, nonslip water-sports sandals.

Most tours last four to five hours, departing in the morning or early afternoon (call ahead for exact check-in times). The maximum group size is 12, with paddlers going out in double kayaks. The pricier tours include lunch, but on budget tours, you can store your own food in coolers or waterproof bags. Bring a hat, sunscreen and insect repellent.

Experienced paddlers might want to rent individual kayaks and go out on their own (for more information on a self-guided tour, see p107). Note that not all tour companies are licensed to rent individual kayaks, and no kayak tours or rentals are allowed on Sundays. Kayaking outfitters are based in Wailua or Kapa'a.

Kayak Kaua'i KAYAKING
(Map p114; 808-826-9844, 888-596-3853; www.kayakkauai.com; Wailua River Marina; double kayak rental per day $85, 4½hr tours $60-85) Reputable island-wide operator offering Wailua River tours and kayak rentals (small surcharge for dry bags and coolers). If you're renting, you'll have to transport the kayak a short distance atop your car.

Ancient River Kayak KAYAKING
(Map p114; 808-826-2505; www.ancientriverkayak.com; 440 Aleka Pl; kayaking tours adult/child $85/65; tours depart 7:15am & 12:45pm Mon-Sat) It rents all kinds of beach gear and runs paddling tours of the Wailua River that include a short hike to and from a 120ft waterfall. Tours depart twice daily, six days a week and include lunch. To ask about gear rental or to book a tour, call or visit the office.

Wailua River Kayaking OUTDOORS
(Map p114; 808-821-1188; https://wailuariverkayaking.com; 169 Wailua Rd; single/double kayak rental $50/85, tours $90;) Located at the boat ramp on the north bank of the Wailua River, this outfit is convenient for individual rentals (no need to transport the kayak), and they offer half-day tours too.

Smith's Motor Boat Service BOATING
(Map p114; 808-821-6892; www.smithskauai.com; Wailua Marina; 80-min tour adult/child $20/10; departures at 9:30am, 11am, 2pm & 3:30pm) If you're curious to see the once-legendary Fern Grotto, this 2-mile flat-bottom-covered boat ride is hokey but homespun. Bear in mind that since heavy rains and rock slides in 2006, visitors can-

not enter the grotto, but must stay on the wooden platform quite a distance from the shallow cave.

Kaua'i Nature Tours HIKING
(808-742-8305, 888-233-8365; www.kauainaturetours.com; tours adult/child 7-12yr from $135/100) For guided hikes, check out geoscientist Chuck Blay's company, which offers a full-day tour – snacks, drinks and transportation included. Guided hikes also hit the North Shore's Na Pali Coast, Po'ipu, and Waimea Canyon and Koke'e State Parks.

Festivals & Events

Taste of Hawaii FOOD & DRINK
(www.tasteofhawaii.com; Jun) On the first Sunday in June, the Rotary Club of Kapa'a hosts the 'Ultimate Sunday Brunch' at Smith's Tropical Paradise (p109), where you can indulge in gourmet samples by 40 chefs from around Hawaii. Dance it off to more than 10 live-music acts. For discounts, buy tickets online in advance.

Eating

Haole Girl Island Sweets BAKERY $
(Map p114; 808-822-2253; www.haolegirlsweets.com; 4-356 Kuhio Hwy; pastries $3-6; 7am-1pm Tue-Sun) Imagine banana bread, quiche with buttery crust, croissants stuffed with goat cheese, spinach and sun-dried tomato, and the world's most decadent sticky buns, all made and sold by a sole proprietor who still gets such a kick out of doing her thing. Come in, smell the warm goodness and munch happily.

Wailua

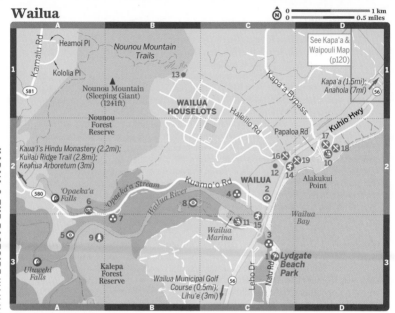

Passion Bakery & Cafe
CAFE $

(Map p114; ☎808-821-0060; www.facebook.com/mcsterioff; 4-356 Kuhio Hwy; mains $8-10; ⊙6am-2pm Mon-Sat) A popular cafe for good coffees and breakfasts that pair feta or vegan sausage with eggs. It also does a tofu scramble and a range of sandwiches. But the freshly baked breads – some of which incorporate taro – are the thing.

Coconut Marketplace
MARKET $

(Map p114; www.coconutmarketplace.com; 4-484 Kuhio Hwy; ⊙8am-noon Tue & Thu) A tiny farmers market is held at this mall on Tuesday and Thursday mornings from 8am until noon. It's in the midst of a major renovation, so there's not much else to see. The work should be done by the end of 2017.

★Kintaro
JAPANESE $$

(Map p114; ☎808-822-3341; 4-370 Kuhio Hwy; small plates $3-15, mains $12-26; ⊙5:30-9:30pm Mon-Sat) Night after night for 33 years, this locals' favorite sushi bar has packed 'em in thanks to thick slices of sashimi and creative rolls that are expertly prepared. The yellowtail sushi and sashimi are especially great. It also has a sprawling cooked-food menu and sizzling teppanyaki service, with chefs showing off at table-side grills. Make reservations.

Caffè Coco
FUSION $$

(Map p114; ☎808-822-7990; www.restauranteur.com/caffecoco; 4-369 Kuhio Hwy; mains $13-21; ⊙11am-2pm Tue-Fri, 5-9pm Tue-Sun; ☝) At this rustic little hideaway, Asian, Middle Eastern and other 'exotic' flavors infuse healthful dishes to delight mindful eaters and gourmets in one stroke. Moroccan-spiced ahi is a standout, served with banana chutney rice and a curried veggie samosa. Seating is in the garden (bring mosquito repellent) and they don't serve beer, wine or booze. Bring your own.

Street Burger
BURGERS $$

(Map p114; ☎808-212-1555; www.streetburgerkauai.com; 4-369 Kuhio Hwy; mains $10-20; ⊙11am-10pm Tue-Sat) The coolest new spot in Wailua has hammered aluminum tabletops, a chalkboard craft-beer menu, and an open grill where gourmet burgers are made. And they are glorious. Choose a Greek burger topped with olive tapenade and feta, an Italian layered with prosciutto, buffalo mozzarella, spinach and marinara sauce, or get serious with a $20 street burger.

The street burger is topped with cured pork belly, a fried egg, arugula, blue cheese and fizzled onions. They make their own veggie patties, and offer six flavors of fries: Parmesan and garlic, pickled peppers and Sriracha, truffle and garlic, herb, chili, and sea salt.

Wailua

Monico's Taqueria MEXICAN $$

(Map p114; ☎ 808-822-4300; http://monicos-taqueria.com; Kinipopo Shopping Village, 4-356 Kuhio Hwy; mains $14-20; ☺ 11am-3pm & 5-9pm Tue-Sun) Everything made by this Oaxaca-born chef tastes fresh and authentic, from stuffed burritos and fish-taco plates to freshly made chips, salsa and sauces. Sip something from the well-stocked tequila bar while you wait.

Kilauea Fish Market SEAFOOD $$

(Map p114; ☎ 808-822-3474; 440 Aleka Pl; mains $10-19; ☺ 11am-8pm Mon-Sat; ☝) Bringing their time-tested skills and recipes down from the original North Shore location, this kitchen makes *broke da mout* (delicious) ahi wraps, fresh *poke* (cubed raw fish mixed with shōyu, sesame oil, salt, chili pepper, 'inamona or other condiments), grilled fish plates, salads with local greens, and more. Get takeout for a picnic on the beach.

Hukilau Lanai HAWAII REGIONAL $$$

(Map p114; ☎ 808-822-0600; www.hukilaukauai.com; Kaua'i Coast Resort at the Beachboy, 520 Aleka Loop; mains $18-32; ☺ 5-9pm Tue-Sun; ☝) Branded by locals as arguably the most consistently great restaurant on the island, seafood is king here, with a half dozen fresh-

catch options, paired with locally grown vegetables and sauced differently every night. It does steaks and chops too and hosts frequent live-music acts. Gluten-free and kids' menus available.

Korean BBQ KOREAN $$$

(Map p114; ☎ 808-823-6744; 4-356 Kuhio Hwy; meals $15-35; ☺ 11am-8:30pm Wed-Sun) Shakespeare once asked, 'What's in a name?' In this case, you know what to expect. Platters of thinly sliced beef and pork, to be grilled with platters of raw vegetables, and devoured with a forkful of kimchi. Lunch and dinner specials available.

BEST WAILUA ON A BUDGET

➡ **Kaua'i's Hindu Monastery** (p108)

➡ **Kuilau Ridge & Moalepe Trails** (p105)

➡ **Nounou Mountain Trails** (p104)

➡ **Wailua Municipal Golf Course** (p112)

➡ **Smith's Tropical Paradise** (p109)

➡ **Self-Guided Wailua River Kayaking** (p107)

🍷 Drinking & Nightlife

Haole Girl Tea Room
TEAHOUSE

(Map p114; ☑808-822-2253; www.haolegirl sweets.com; 4-356 Kuhio Hwy; per person $28.50, à la carte tea per pot $10, pastries per plate $6; ⊙3-8pm Thu & Fri, 2-8pm Sat & Sun) Before this new tearoom opened, the only place on the island for high tea was at the St Regis. Consider this your lower-budget option, and it may be even better. Expect full tea service, a rack of savory croissants, sweet pastries and sticky buns delivered to accompany loose-leaf organic teas brewed in 20oz cast-iron pots.

Trees Lounge
LIVE MUSIC

(Map p114; ☑808-823-0600; www.treesloungekau ai.com; 440 Aleka Pl; ⊙7am-noon & 5pm-12:30am Mon-Sat) On the (very) short list of (semi) reliable island nightspots, it offers fresh oysters on Tuesdays, cheap martinis at happy hour, pub grub such as po'boys and fish skewers, and DJs and live music frequently, as well. Friday is especially popular for a blast of salsa. It has only recently begun serving breakfast, best paired with a Bloody Mary.

Potions
TEAHOUSE

(Map p114; ☑808-634-6477; 4-361 Kuhio Hwy; ⊙11am-8pm Tue-Thu, to 9pm Fri & Sat) All that funky, hippy energy that swirls around Kaua'i has coalesced in this psychedelic Indian kombucha bar where the often sweet fizzy brew is on tap and flavored with dandelion and burdock, chocolate and pepper, ginger and ginseng, chamomile and spearmint. If you're hungry it also does four kinds of vegetarian curries.

Imua Coffee Roasters
CAFE

(Map p114; ☑808-821-1717; www.facebook.com/ imuacoffee; 440 Aleka Pl; ⊙6am-1pm; 🛜) One of several indie coffee roasters to spring up on the island in the past year or two. This one is well located for those on the northern end of the Wailua swirl.

☆ Entertainment

Smith's Garden Luau
LUAU

(Map p114; ☑808-821-6895; www.smithskauai. com; Smith's Tropical Paradise, Wailua Marina; adult $98, child 7-13yr $30, child 3-6yr $19; ⊙4:45pm or 5pm Mon, Wed & Fri; 🚼) It's a Kaua'i institution, attracting droves of tourists yet run with aloha spirit by four generations at the family's riverside gardens. Surprisingly, the highlight is the buffet food, including a roasted pig unearthed from an *imu* (underground oven). The multicultural Polynesian show of Hawaiian hula, Tahitian drum dances and Samoan fire dancing is less exciting.

Coconut Marketplace Hula Show
DANCE, MUSIC

(Map p114; ☑808-822-3641; www.coconutmarket place.com; Coconut Marketplace, 4-484 Kuhio Hwy; ⊙usually 5pm Wed & 1pm Sat; 🚼) **FREE** While touristy, the Coconut Marketplace's free hula show is nevertheless fun and features Leilani Rivera Low and her hula *halau* (school). She's the daughter of famous Coco Palms entertainer Larry Rivera, who occasionally performs Hawaiian music here and talks story at the mall's Kaua'i Cultural Center (p112).

🛍 Shopping

The long-running shopping mall at the northern end of Wailua, Coconut Marketplace (p114), was undergoing a massive renovation at research time. Most stores were vacant and even more demolished and

---

WHATEVER HAPPENED TO COCO PALMS?

Old-timers might recall **Coco Palms Resort** (Map p114) as Hollywood's go-to wedding site during the 1950s and '60s. Built in 1953, it was Kaua'i's first resort, and its romantic lagoons, gardens, thatched cottages, torch-lit paths and coconut groves epitomized tropical paradise. The highest-profile on-screen wedding here was when Elvis Presley wed Joan Blackman in the 1961 film *Blue Hawaii*.

At its height, the Coco Palms was a playground for Hollywood's leading males and their lithe ingenues, and the trendiest mainland couples came here to get hitched. But it was also an Old Hawaii kind of place where guests knew hotel staff on a first-name basis and returned year after year.

In 1992, Hurricane 'Iniki demolished the then-396-room hotel, which sat in benign neglect for years. In early 2006, a new owner announced a $220 million plan to resurrect Coco Palms as a condo-hotel, but plans fell through. By fall 2007, the 18-acre property was back on the market, where it has remained since.

THE MYSTERIOUS BLUE HOLE

How close can you get to Mt Wai'ale'ale by foot? If you can find the Blue Hole, you're there. It's not a 'hole' per se, but a pool fed by a pretty stream and waterfall.

To get here, take Kuamo'o Rd up to Keahua Arboretum. Unless you're driving a 4WD, you should park in the lot and hike in. The unpaved road is head-jarringly rough, and the mud can engulf ordinary cars. Either way, head left on to Wailua Forest Management Rd. After less than 1.5 miles, you'll reach a junction; turn right (a gate blocks the left direction). Go straight for about 2 miles. Along the way, you'll pass an otherworldly forest of false staghorn, guava, eucalyptus and native mamane and ohia trees. The dense foliage introduces you to a rainbow of greens, from deep evergreen to eye-popping chartreuse.

You will then reach a locked yellow gate; it is meant to keep out cars, but the state allows foot traffic (be warned: lots of mud). From here you must slosh about 0.75 miles till you reach the dammed stream, which is the north fork of Wailua River. The stream rises and falls depending on the season and rainfall. Occasionally it is deep enough for kids to swim.

Blue Hole is a quiet, secluded spot, not a tourist destination by a long shot. To avoid getting stuck or lost, hire a guide. You can also hike to the true summit of Mt Wai'ale'ale, by taking the Alaka'i Swamp trail 15 miles from Koke'e State Park to the highest point on the island. Along the way expect to gain nearly 5000ft in elevation. The summit is almost always muddy and wet, with no services. You must be self-sufficient and have some back-country orienteering experience to make it on your own. Bring more food and water than you think necessary.

KAPA'A & THE EASTSIDE WAILUA

ready for a rebuild, though there were a few catch-all shops open for business. The renovation is scheduled to be complete by the end of 2017.

★Pagoda
ANTIQUES

(Map p114; ☑ 808-821-2172; www.pagodakauai. com; 4-369 Kuhio Hwy; ☉ 10am-5:30pm Tue, to 6pm Wed-Fri, to 4pm Sat) A terrific antique treasure chest selling antique Japanese hand-blown glass fishing buoys that continually wash up on Kauai's shore, vintage Japanese kimonos and tea sets, rice sacks and all manner of furniture. The price tag is the first offer, and the owners are often willing to negotiate.

Olivine Beach
FASHION & ACCESSORIES

(Map p114; ☑ 808-742-7222; www.olivinekauai. com; 4-369 Kuhio Hwy; ☉ 10am-6pm Tue-Sat) A high-end fashion boutique that feels dropped in from the Hamptons or Malibu, but looks perfectly at home in Wailua. Owned by a former Donna Karan fashion designer, she stocks Vitamin A bikinis, Stillwater T-shirts, Mother denim and many more high-end labels. There's a great vibe here.

Tiki Boutiki
FASHION & ACCESSORIES

(Map p114; ☑ 808-823-8454; https://tikiboutiki. com; 4-369 Kuhio Hwy; ☉ 10am-6pm Tue-Sat) One of two great women's boutiques set back from the main road. This is a single label store, offering Rachel Pally's colorful, one-size-fits-all bamboo-blend gowns, pants and blouses that flow with simple elegance.

Mint & Sea
CLOTHING

(Map p114; ☑ 808-822-7946; http://instagram. com/mintandseahawaii; 4-369 Kuhio Hwy; ☉ 10am-4pm Mon-Thu, to 6pm Fri & Sat) This fresh-faced, breezy women's boutique is stocked with goodies for women who've outgrown the teenage surfer-chick look. Drapey knit tops, tropical-print shorts, knitted tanks and platform sandals are chic and affordable.

❶ Information

Longs Drugs (☑ 808-822-4918; www.cvs.com; 645 Aleka Loop; ☉ store 7am-10pm daily, pharmacy 8am-9pm Mon-Fri, 9am-5pm Sat & Sun) Pharmacy has an ATM and also sells beach gear, snacks, drinks and souvenirs.

❶ Getting There & Away

Don't look for a town center. Most attractions are scattered along coastal Kuhio Hwy (Hwy 56) or Kuamo'o Rd (Hwy 580) heading *mauka* (inland). Driving north, Kapa'a Bypass runs from just north of the Wailua River to beyond Kapa'a, usually skipping the Waipouli and Kapa'a gridlock.

Waipouli

♪ 808

Waipouli (dark water) and its gentle lagoons once served as a departure point for ancient Hawaiians setting sail for Tahiti and other islands of Polynesia. Nowadays it's less a town than a cluster of restaurants, grocery stores and miscellaneous businesses in strip malls. Which makes it a convenient place to stock up on supplies or, better yet, grab a bite to eat. This is where you'll find Kaua'i's best restaurant.

🏄 Activities

Kayak- and surf-rental outlets in Waipouli are located at a distance from the river and beaches.

Seasport Divers   WATER SPORTS
(Map p120; ♪808-823-9222, 800-685-5889; www.seasportdivers.com; 4-976 Kuhio Hwy; dive trips $90-235; ⊙9am-5pm) Eastside waters are less protected by reefs and choppier due to easterly onshore winds, so diving and snorkeling are limited here. Still, this small branch of a Po'ipu-based outfit rents diving and snorkeling gear, bodyboards and surfboards, and books excellent dive trips – from beach or boat – along the South Shore.

Kauai Yoga on the Beach   YOGA
(♪808-635-6050; www.kauaiyogaonthebeach.com; 4-885 Kuhio Hwy; drop-in classes incl mat rental $20) What could be better than doing your sun salutations on the sand as the sun actually rises (or maybe just a little later in the morning)? Classes are held on the beach in Waipouli, Lihu'e and Po'ipu. Check the website for current schedules and meet-up locations.

Kauai Cycle   CYCLING
(Map p120; ♪808-821-2115; www.kauaicycle.com; 4-934 Kuhio Hwy; per day/week cruiser $20/110, mountain & road bikes $30/165, full suspension mountain bikes $45/250; ⊙9am-6pm Mon-Fri, to 4pm Sat) The best bike shop on the island, Kauai Cycle sells, services and rents cruisers, hybrids, and road and mountain bikes maintained by experienced cyclists. Rental prices include a helmet and lock.

Spa By The Sea   SPA
(Map p120; ♪808-823-1488; http://spabytheseakauai.com; 4-820 Kuhio Hwy; treatments from $140; ⊙9am-6pm) The resident spa at Waipouli Beach Resort (Map p120; ♪808-

822-6000, 800-688-7444; www.outriggerwaipouli.com; 4-820 Kuhio Hwy; studio from $174, 1-/2-bedroom condo from $240/285; ❋@⊗⊛) offers all the treatments: hair, nails, facials, and massages lasting 50 to 80 minutes. Get local with a traditional *lomilomi* massage or a hot stone treatment. Book ahead.

Kauai Photo Tours   PHOTOGRAPHY
(Map p120; ♪808-823-1263; www.hawaiianphotos.net; 4-939 Kuhio Hwy; tours adult/child from $119/89) Part driving, part walking tours of some of Kaua'i's best landscapes with plenty of time scheduled in to capture that perfect shot. Trips last 5½ hours and include a dozen locations on the east and north shores.

Ola Massage   MASSAGE
(Map p120; ♪808-821-1100; http://kauairetreat.com; 4-971 Kuhio Hwy; treatments $45-150; ⊙9am-7pm Mon-Fri, 10am-6pm Sat & Sun) A humble mini-mall massage studio with a range of treatments on the menu. There's reflexology by the half-hour, standard deep-tissue massage by the hour and a *lomilomi* treatment with two therapists.

Golden Lotus Studio   MASSAGE
(Map p120; ♪808-823-9810; www.goldenlotuskauai.org; 4-941 Kuhio Hwy) A massage, dance and yoga studio notable for its affordable student massages available to all comers for just $35. Dance classes and workshops are available throughout the year as well.

Yoga House   YOGA
(Map p120; ♪808-823-9642; www.bikramyogakapaa.com; 4-885 Kuhio Hwy; drop-in classes $20-25) Come find your yogic bliss in this heated studio. Classes are offered daily, so there's plenty of opportunity to get centered. To build some serious prana, get the Out Of Towner special (seven days unlimited for $69). Go online for current schedules.

Snorkel Bob's   SNORKELING, SURFING
(Map p120; ♪808-823-9433; www.snorkelbob.com; 4-734 Kuhio Hwy; rental per week adult/child under 13yr snorkel-set from $25/22, wetsuit/bodyboard from $20/26; ⊙8am-5pm) Beyond the competitive rates, the cool thing about this place is that if you're island-hopping you can rent snorkel gear on Kaua'i and return it on the Big Island, O'ahu or Maui.

🍴 Eating

A couple of fast-food-fusion gems and the island's best chef make Waipouli a great place to eat.

Kenji
FUSION $

(Map p120; ☎808-320-3558; www.kenjiburger.com; 4-788 Kuhio Hwy; mains $8-12; ⊙11am-8pm Mon-Sat) A new-school Japanese fast-food fusion joint spinning up truffle and teriyaki burgers, fried-chicken sandwiches with Sriracha slaw, and a Japanese burrito – the number-one bestseller. More a hand roll than a burrito, it's nori-wrapped rice stuffed with shrimp tempura, crab meat and spicy tuna, drizzled with *unagi* (eel) sauce. More please.

Tiki Tacos
MEXICAN $

(Map p120; ☎808-823-8226; www.facebook.com/tikitacos; Waipouli Complex, 4-961 Kuhio Hwy; mains $6-8; ⊙10am-8:30pm) This laidback place with a reggae soundtrack offers authentic taqueria gravitas right down to the housemade tortillas. Tacos come with chicken, locally caught fish, chorizo, shrimp, Kaua'i-raised lamb, beef or pork, spicy vegetables or tofu, and they're piled high with island-grown cabbage, *queso fresco* (fresh cheese), sour cream and onion. The housemade hot sauces rock.

Pho Kapa'a
VIETNAMESE $

(Map p120; ☎808-823-6868; 4-831 Kuhio Hwy; mains $7-13; ⊙10am-9pm Tue-Sun) A strip-mall Vietnamese noodle shop offering their country's most nourishing export: *pho* (noodle soup with beef broth and rare steak). You can go super-traditional and add tendon and tripe, or ask for chicken, seafood or veggies instead. It also does steamed buns, rice dishes, stir-fried vermicelli noodles and a pork *banh mi.*

Shrimp Station
SEAFOOD $

(Map p120; ☎808-821-0192; 4-985 Kuhio Hwy; dishes $8-14; ⊙11am-8:30pm; 🐾) This offshoot of Waimea's original Shrimp Station serves the same family recipes. With seasonings such as garlic, Cajun and Thai on the shrimp tacos, burgers and plate meals, it's hard to shoot and miss here. Some claim it has the 'Best Coconut Shrimp on the Planet.' Investigate for yourself.

Tropical Dreams
ICE CREAM $

(Map p120; http://tropicaldreamsicecream.com; 4-831 Kuhio Hwy; snacks from $4; ⊙noon-9pm Sun-Thu, to 9:30pm Fri & Sat) A tiny taste of ice-cream heaven, this only-in-Hawaii chain rotates through scores of premium flavors crafted almost entirely from Hawaii-harvested ingredients. It does soft serve as well as old-fashioned scoops. Cash only.

Papaya's Natural Foods
HEALTH FOOD $

(Map p120; ☎808-823-0190; www.papayasnaturalfoods.com; Kauai Village, 4-831 Kuhio Hwy; ⊙8am-8pm Mon-Sat, 10am-5pm Sun, cafe closes 1hr earlier; 🍴) 🌿 Kaua'i's biggest health-food store carries local and organic produce, plus other island specialties such as Kilauea honey and goat cheese. Deli fixings and the salad bar make for a quick, healthy meal, while the cafe grills taro burgers, blends fresh-fruit smoothies and sells shots of Hawaiian *noni* juice (a type of mulberry with smelly yellow fruit used medicinally). It was preparing to move to a bigger location just south from this location at research time.

Shivalik
INDIAN $$

(Map p120; ☎808-821-2333; 4-771 Kuhio Hwy; mains $18-21; ⊙3:30-9:30pm Wed-Mon) Kaua'i's beloved outpost for tandoori cooking and a filling Indian buffet (served every Wednesday and Friday). The tiled interior is dressed up with Indian decor, but it still feels like you're eating in a mall. Nevertheless, locals swear by the food and the terrific mango lassi to wash it down.

Kaua'i Pasta
ITALIAN $$

(Map p120; ☎808-822-7447; www.kauaipasta.com; 4-939b Kuhio Hwy; mains $12-27; ⊙11am-9pm, lounge to midnight Mon-Sat, to 10pm Sun; 🍷) Your ticket to surprisingly good Italian food is this strip-mall bistro. Colorful salads meld peppery arugula, creamy goat cheese and sweet tomatoes. Hot focaccia sandwiches and classic homemade pastas pass muster even with finicky foodies. Gluten-free menu available.

9th Island Sports Bar
PUB FOOD $$

(Map p120; ☎808-822-7773; 4-831 Kuhio Hwy; $11-15; ⊙7am-10pm) They pack a lot of sports bar into a minimall location with four flat-screens strobing surf contests, basketball, baseball and football games. They pour craft beers and serve big breakfasts, plate lunches and a range of burgers and sandwiches – including a popular take on a classic pan cubano made with *kalua* pork, ham and Swiss on sourdough.

★ JO2
FUSION $$$

(Map p120; ☎808-212-1627; www.jotwo.com; 4-971 Kuhio Hwy; dishes $9-35; ⊙5-9pm) Flavors are subtle, fresh, familiar yet inventive at the latest kitchen launched by Wolfgang Puck contemporary, Jean Marie Josselin. His focus is all-natural cuisine crafted from the best seafood and vegetables available on the island.

Kapa'a & Waipouli

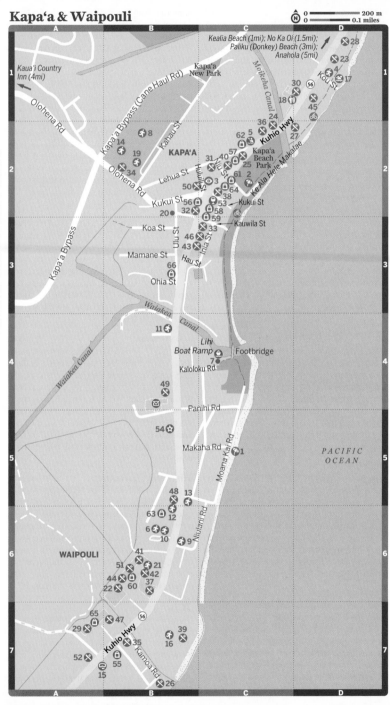

0   200 m
0   0.1 miles

Kealia Beach (1mi); No Ka Oi (1.5mi);
Paliku (Donkey) Beach (3mi);
Anahola (5mi)

Kaua'i Country
Inn (4mi)

Olohena Rd

Kapa'a Bypass (Cane Haul Rd)

Kapa'a
New Park

Moikeha Canal

Kahau St

KAPA'A

Kuhio Hwy

Olohena Rd

Lehua St

Kukui St

Koa St

Mamane St

Hau St

Ohia St

Kukui St

Kauwila St

Ke Ala Hele Makalae

Kapa'a
Beach
Park

Waiakea Canal

Kapa'a Bypass

Waiakea Canal

Lihi
Boat Ramp   Footbridge

Kaloloku Rd

Panihi Rd

Makaha Rd

PACIFIC
OCEAN

Moana Kai Rd

Niulani Rd

WAIPOULI

Kuhio Hwy

Kamoa Rd

Kapa'a & Waipouli

Start with the seafood sampler, which may feature a Korean bibimbap with tuna belly or raw salmon folded over salmon roe and crème fraîche.

Oasis on the Beach　　HAWAII REGIONAL $$$
(Map p120; ☑ 808-822-9332; www.oasiskauai.com; Waipouli Beach Resort & Spa, 4-820 Kuhio Hwy; mains $15-31; ☺ 11:30am-9pm Mon-Sat,

10am-9pm Sun) This is truly on the beach, like the name says, with unmatched ocean views, a romantic atmosphere and sophisticated cuisine featuring local ingredients. It's perfect for sharing elevated fusion dishes or hitting up one of Kaua'i's better happy hours (4pm to 6pm daily).

Bull Shed STEAK **$$$**
(Map p120; ☑808-822-3791; www.bullshed restaurant.com; mains $20-49; ⊙4:30-9:30pm) The Eastside local's steak house serves broiled garlic tenderloin, tender center-cut fillets, and a NY steak topped with blue cheese or garlic butter. It also does ribs, chicken and the house favorite prime rib, which often sells out. Mains come with rice or baked potato and a visit to the salad bar. If the dated interior tells you anything, it's that this spot is old school. It's off the main road, set down a long drive, right on the beach.

Lemongrass Grill FUSION **$$$**
(Map p120; ☑808-822-2288; 4-871 Kuhio Hwy; dishes $8-39; ⊙4-9:30pm) This East Shore institution dishes up solid fusion fare. Think: hoisin charred ribs and fresh fish steamed, seared, or macadamia-nut crusted. It has live music most nights.

Wahoo SEAFOOD **$$$**
(Map p120; ☑808-822-7833; www.wahooogrill. com; 4-733 Kuhio Hwy; mains $14-40) It gets mixed reviews but if you do land here, grab a table on the lanai overlooking a lovely palm grove and order fresh-broiled *ono* (white-fleshed wahoo), *opah* (moonfish), *walu* (sea bass) or ahi. It also sears scallops and grills prime rib, St Louis ribs, and burgers at lunch. It's been around forever.

🍷 Drinking & Nightlife

There are no bars here to speak of, but you can belly up at a fantastic new restaurant with a tasty wine list and creative cocktails, read: JO2; seek out a dark and changeless vinyl dive behind Kaua'i Pasta (p119); order a perfect sunset cocktail on the shore at Oasis; and enjoy a honey wine tasting at Kaua'i's only meadery.

⭐ Entertainment

Outdoor Movies OUTDOOR CINEMA
(Map p120; ☑808-822-4267; www.allsaintskauai. org/movie-nights-on-the-lawn; 4-1065 Kuhio Hwy; ⊙monthly;) **FREE** This Waipouli church hosts monthly double features on its wide lawn. Bring snacks, a blanket and get comfy and enjoy family-friendly entertainment with your brood.

Shopping

Waipouli's two pedestrian shopping malls are **Waipouli Town Center** (Map p120; 4-771 Kuhio Hwy) and **Kaua'i Village** (Map p120; 4-831 Kuhio Hwy).

Nani Moon Meadery & Tasting Room WINE
(Map p120; ☑808-651-2453; www.nanimoon mead.com; 4-939 Kuhio Hwy; tasting flights $8, by the glass $8; ⊙noon-5pm Tue-Sat) 🍷 Nani Moon makes and pours tropical honey wine, which is arguably the oldest alcoholic beverage on earth – humans have been drinking it for 6000 years or more. It crafts a half dozen flavors of mead using only locally sourced ingredients, including tropical fruit and ginger. Most are surprisingly dry, food-forward and 'best enjoyed under moonlight.'

Ambrose's Kapuna Surf Gallery ART
(Map p120; ☑808-822-3926; 770 Kuhio Hwy; ⊙11am-5pm Tue-Sat) Don't miss the chance to meet longtime artist-surfer-philosopher Ambrose Curry. Originally from California, he has lived on Kaua'i since 1968 and is also an artist and board shaper. You will love rambling around his workshop and gallery which are an extension of his whirring mind. He has a fun history of hand planes used by old-time body surfers, and is working most with plywood and resin these days.

Marta's Boat CLOTHING, JEWELRY
(Map p120; ☑808-822-3926; www.martasboat. com; 4-770 Kuhio Hwy; ⊙10am-6pm Mon-Sat) This unique boutique delights 'princesses of all ages' with original block and screen prints on silks and other soft and flowing fabrics, and some funky, fab jewelry. We especially loved her hand-knitted quilts for babies, which would make any new parent smile. A quirky art-love philosophy is at work here.

Moloa'a Bay Coffee DRINK, FOOD
(Map p120; ☑808-821-8100; http://moloaabay coffee.com; 943 Kipuni Way; ⊙8am-noon Mon-Fri) If you've missed sampling this North Shore estate-grown coffee at Kaua'i's top farmers markets, stop by the retail shop on weekday mornings to taste the hand-picked, small-batch roasted brews. Unusually, it also makes flavored teas from dried coffee-fruit husks.

ⓘ Information

There are ATMs inside **Foodland** (Map p120; ☑ 808-822-7271; www.foodland.com; Waipouli Town Center, 4-771 Kuhio Hwy; ⊙ 6am-11pm) in Waipouli Town Center and, just a minute north, inside **Safeway** (Map p120; ☑ 808-822-2464; www.safeway.com; Kaua'i Village, 4-831 Kuhio Hwy; ⊙ store 24hr, pharmacy 8am-8pm Mon-Fri, 9am-6pm Sat & Sun) in the Kaua'i Village shopping center. **Starbucks** offers internet access.

Starbucks (☑ 808-821-1334; www.starbucks.com; Kaua'i Village, 4-831 Kuhio Hwy; ⊙ 5am-9pm).

ⓘ Getting There & Away

Waipouli lies between Wailua and Kapa'a, about 7 miles north of the airport (in Lihu'e).

If you're driving, your only option is the Kuhio Hwy, which can slow to a crawl as it snakes through Old Town Kapa'a.

Kaua'i Bus runs north and south through Waipouli approximately hourly from 6am to 10pm on weekdays (limited weekend service).

This town is oriented toward vehicles and built out with shopping centers set up around huge parking lots. It's no pedestrian paradise.

Kapa'a

☑ 808 / POP 11,000

Kapa'a is the only walkable town on the Eastside, and it has its charms. Although it's not Kaua'i at its most beautiful, sunny Kapa'a has a more down-to-earth disposition than other tourist towns, and its eclectic population of old-timers, fresh transplants, new-age hippies and budget travelers coexists happily. A paved recreational path for cyclists and pedestrians runs along the part-sandy, part-rocky coast, the island's best vantage point for sunrises. Kapa'a's downfall? It sits right along the highway – try walking across the road during rush hour!

⊙ Sights

★**Kealia Beach Park**   BEACH
(Map p110) Blessed with a wild, near-pristine location, a laid-back vibe and easy access via car or the coastal path, scenic Kealia is the Eastside's best beach. Isolated from residential development, the beach begins at mile marker 10 as you head north on the Kuhio Hwy and continues for more than a mile.

The sandy bottom slopes offshore gradually, making it possible to walk out far to catch long rides back. But the pounding barrels can be treacherous and are not recommended for novices; it's a crushing shore break. A breakwater protects the north end, so swimming and snorkeling are occasionally possible there.

Outdoor showers, restrooms, lifeguards, picnic tables and ample parking are available. Natural shade is not, so sunscreen is a must.

Fujii Beach   BEACH
(Baby Beach; Map p120) Nicknamed 'Baby Beach' because an offshore reef creates a shallow, placid pool of water that's perfect for toddlers, it's located in a modest neighborhood that attracts few tourists. This is a real locals' beach. Please be respectful.

Kapa'a Beach Park   BEACH
(Map p120; ☑ pool 808-822-3842; ⊙ park dawn-dusk, pool 7:30am-4:30pm Tue-Fri, 10am-4:30pm Sat, noon-4:30pm Sun; ⊕) From the highway, you'd think that Kapa'a is beachless. But along the coast is a low-key, mile-long ribbon of golden sand. While the whole area is officially a county park called Kapa'a Beach Park, that name is commonly used only for the northern end, where there's a grassy field, picnic tables and a public **swimming pool** (Map p120; ⊙ 7:30am-4:30pm Tue-Fri, from 10am Sat, from noon sun).

The best sandy area is at the south end, informally called Lihi Beach, where you'll find locals hanging out and talking story. Further to the south is Fujii Beach (p123), a locals' spot that's great for kids.

A good starting point for the paved coastal path is the footbridge just north of Lihi Beach. To get there, turn *makai* (seaward) on Panihi Rd from the Kuhio Hwy.

Orchid Alley   GARDENS
(Map p120; ☑ 808-822-0486; 4-1383 Kuhio Hwy; per person $5) Tucked down a little path off the main drag is this darling orchid nursery and butterfly garden. The owners have been here for over 20 years, where they sell orchids they grow themselves and invite guests to tour their netted butterfly garden, just off the main nursery courtyard, swirling with a handful of monarchs and swallowtail butterflies.

🏄 Activities

★**Kapa'a Beach Shop**   WATER SPORTS, CYCLING
(Map p120; ☑ 808-212-8615; www.kapaabeachshop.com; 4-1592 Kuhio Hwy; bike rental per day $10, snorkel-set rental per day/week $7/15; ⊙ 8am-6pm Sun-Fri; ⊕) Located along

KAPA'A & THE EASTSIDE KAPA'A

PALIKU (DONKEY) BEACH

Once unofficially known as a nude spot, Paliku (Donkey) Beach (Map p110) is scenic but rarely swimmable. It's a place where you can escape the cars on the highway and instead amble along on foot, with rocks scattered at the water's edge, windswept ironwood trees and *naupaka* and *'ilima* flowers adding dashes of color.

Summer swells might be manageable, but stay ashore if you're an inexperienced ocean swimmer. From October to May, dangerous rip currents and a powerful shore break take over. Stick to sunbathing or sunrise beach strolls at that time.

The beach is accessible two ways. You can cycle or walk north along Kapa'a's coastal path and turn *makai* (seaward). Or you can drive the Kuhio Hwy to a parking lot with restrooms about halfway between mile markers 11 and 12. Look for the small brown parking and hiking sign.

The beach-access footpath cuts through a 300-acre planned community called **Kealia Kai** (www.kealiakai.com). Public nudity is illegal in Hawaii and the developer has cracked down on folks baring all.

the coastal path, this shop has loads of affordable rental options, including cruiser and hybrid comfort bikes, snorkel sets and other beach gear (chairs, umbrellas and coolers). It also sells scuba, free diving and spearfishing equipment. In fact it is among the better connected spearfishing shops on the island.

Duke's Kayak Adventures KAYAKING
(Map p120; ☑808-639-2834; http://kayaktour kauai.com; 4516 Lehua St; per person $39; ☺tours depart at 7am & 12:15pm Mon-Sat) Offers kayak tours up the Wailua River to Uluwehi Falls. It's the standard Wailua River tour which runs twice daily, six days a week. Book ahead.

Tamba Surf Company SURFING
(Map p120; ☑808-823-6942; www.tamba surfcompany.com; 4-1543 Kuhio Hwy; bodyboard/ surfboard rental per day from $10/25; ☺9am-5pm Mon-Sat) Along with board rentals, this fun, well-branded shop sells hip surf clothing, and new and used boards. Surf fans may recognize the name as seen on the boards, hats and T-shirts of many pro surfers, past and present, who hail from Kaua'i.

Kauai Power Yoga YOGA
(Map p120; ☑808-635-5868; www.kauaipoweryo ga.com; 4-1191 Kuhio Hwy; per class $20, 30 days unlimited $50) Affiliated with Baptiste Power Yoga, a national brand of Vinyasa flow, they offer two to four classes a day within a short walk from Old Town Kapa'a. If you plan on taking more than two classes, buy a month's unlimited pass.

Da Kars of Kauai SCOOTER
(Map p120; ☑808-639-0027; www.scootcoupe hawaii.com; per 1/2hr $30/45; ☺7am-5pm) Fun three-wheel scooters that look like tiny coupes and seat two. They are only good up to 35mph, so you won't be driving them to Hanalei, but you can have them delivered there or anywhere else for another $50. This is one of those concessions that looks a little cheesy and quite fun at the same time.

Coconut Coasters CYCLING
(Map p120; ☑808-822-7368; www.coconut coasters.com; 4-1586 Kuhio Hwy; bike rental per day from $20; ☺9am-6pm Tue-Sat, to 4pm Mon & Sun; ☀) Conveniently located in the heart of Kapa'a town, this outfit rents beach cruisers, road and mountain bikes, tandem bicycles, hybrid comfort bikes, kids' bikes and tow trailers. The shop, which also does repairs, is right by the bike path. It also rents snorkel gear (adult/child $15/12).

Kapa'a New Park TENNIS, SKATING
(Map p120; www.kauai.gov; 4536 Olehana Rd) You'll find free **tennis courts** (Map p120), soccer and baseball fields, and a **skateboarding park** (Map p120) here.

🍴 Courses

Hawaiian Style Fishing FISHING
(Map p120; ☑808-635-7335; www.hawaiianstyle fishing.com; Kalokolu Rd; 4hr trips per person $140, half-/full-day private charter $600/1050) Join gregarious Captain Terry, who shares the catch with you. Shared and private charters (six-passenger maximum) depart from Lihi Boat Ramp at the end of Kaloloku Rd. Book a week or more in advance.

Tours

Wailua Kayak Adventures OUTDOORS
(Map p120; guided tours 808-639-6332, rentals
808-320-0680; www.kauaiwailuakayak.com; 1345
Ulu St; single/double kayak rental per day $30/60,
4½hr tours per couple $90, SUP rental per day $30)
Offers good-value individual kayak and
stand up paddle surfing rentals, but you'll
have to transport your chosen vessel to
Wailua River on top of your car. Rental pick
up available between 8:30am and 10:30am
and returns must be in by 5pm. It also offers affordable guided kayak tours that
include generous snacks at your waterfall
destination.

Festivals & Events

Old Town Kapaʻa comes to life on the first
Saturday of every month, when the shops,
cafes and restaurants stay open late and the
crowds descend from all over for a bit of eating, shopping and people–watching.

★**Coconut Festival** FOOD, CULTURAL
(www.kbakauai.org; Oct;) Celebrate all
things coconut at this free two-day festival
at Kapaʻa Beach Park (p123). Held the first
weekend in early October, it brings coco-
nut-pie-eating contests, a coconut cook-off,
cooking demonstrations, live music, hula
dancing, Polynesian crafts and local food.

Kapaʻa Art Walk ART, CULTURAL
(1st Sat of month) On the first Saturday of
every month from 5pm to 8pm, Old Town
businesses open their doors in celebration,
showcasing island artists, live music and
food. Locals and visitors alike come together in high spirits, and after-parties often
keep going past 9pm. Parking is crowded,
so arrive early or expect to walk into town.
Bring cash.

**Heiva I Kauaʻi Ia
Orana Tahiti** DANCE, CULTURAL
(www.heivaikauai.com; Aug;) In early
August, dance troupes from as far away
as Tahiti, Japan and the US mainland join
groups from around Hawaii at Kapaʻa
Beach Park (p123) for this traditional Tahitian dancing and drumming competition.

Garden Isle Artisan Fair ART, MUSIC
(www.gardenislandarts.org; Mar, Aug & Nov)
Held on various weekends and at various
locations throughout the year, including last
June in Kapaʻa, this fair brings out artisans
and their handicrafts, live Hawaiian music
and local food.

Eating

Roadside restaurants abound, none terrible,
but some terribly touristy. There's a collection of beachside gourmet-food trucks on
the northern end of the Kapaʻa strip.

★**Pono Market** DELI $
(Map p120; 808-822-4581; 4-1300 Kuhio
Hwy; meals $6-14; 6am-6pm Mon-Fri, to 4pm
Sat) Line up for local *grinds* (food) at this
longtime hole-in-the-wall serving generous
plate lunches, homemade sushi rolls, spicy
ahi *poke* rolls, savory seafood delicacies
such as smoked marlin, and traditional
Hawaiian dishes including pork *laulau*
(bundle made of pork or chicken and salt-
ed butterfish, wrapped in taro and ti leaves
and steamed). Bite into a *manju* (cake
filled with sweet bean paste) for dessert. It
serves coffee and scoop ice cream too!

Al Pastor MEXICAN $
(Map p120; 808-652-6953; 4-1620 Kuhio Hwy;
dishes $8-11; 11am-4pm Tue-Sun) The most
popular food truck of the bunch, this is a real-deal, authentic taco truck with fresh fish
tacos and burritos, terrific al pastor and *len-
gua* (beef tongue) tacos, garlic shrimp, and
vegetarian burritos stuffed with beans, rice
and sautéed zucchini, onion and carrots.
USA Today ranked it as a top-25 food truck
in America for a reason.

Scorpacciata PIZZA $
(Map p120; 808-635-5569; www.facebook.
com/scorpacciata-1686288274949394; 4-1306
Kuhio Hwy; pizzas $10-15; 11am-8pm) A per-
manently parked food truck, firing individually sized, thin-crust pizza pies from
local ingredients. Keep it simple with an
authentic margherita, or get adventurous
with the fig and pig, featuring smoked
bacon and fig jam. And don't sleep on the
Parmesan fries.

Paco's MEXICAN $
(Map p120; 808-822-9944; www.pacosta-
coskauai.com; 4-1415 Kuhio Hwy; mains $5-12;
8am-9pm) A family-owned island chain
started by a Mexican-American family who
serve real-deal street tacos and burritos featuring *carne asada, carnitas, chile verde*
and more. It does breakfast all day and
serves menudo on weekends. The ceviche
is good too.

Bubba's Burgers   BURGERS $

(Map p120; www.bubbaburger.com; 4-1421 Kuhio Hwy; mains $4-10; ⊙10:30am-8pm) The Kapa'a edition of the famed Kaua'i burger depot. This one is set in an attractive barn-like building with a wide porch ideal for people-watching to a classic-rock soundtrack. There's plenty of parking too.

Nom Kauai   BURGERS $

(Map p120; ☑808-635-5903; www.facebook.com/nomkauai; 4-1620 Kuhio Hwy; mains $9-13; ⊙8am-4pm Tue-Sat, 9am-2pm Sun) Known for its burgers catered to any time of day. Breakfast burgers and egg sandwiches come in a Belgian waffle bun. A bit later the traditional burgers made from locally sourced grass-fed beef come smothered in buttery mushrooms, blue cheese, bacon or BBQ sauce. It does fried-chicken sandwiches too.

Gopal's Creperie   CRÊPES $

(Map p120; ☑808-635-2164; 4-1620 Kuhio Hwy; crepes $7-12; ⊙8:30am-2pm Tue-Fri, 10am-4pm Sun; ☑) It has a simple mission. To deliver crepes, both savory and sweet, all vegetarian and gluten free, to Kapa'a's hippie masses. It does housemade vegan ice creams and sorbets, and freshly brewed kombucha too.

Kapa'a Farmers Market   MARKET $

(Map p120; www.kauaigrown.org; Kapa'a New Town Park, Kahau Rd & Olohena Rd; ⊙3-5pm Wed; ☑🚻) ⚑ One of the island's biggest and best-attended farmers markets, this weekly outdoor gathering is the spot to pick up local produce such as mangoes, star fruit, ginger and even fresh coconuts. Many of the vendors own organic farms on the North Shore.

Rainbow Living Foods   HEALTH FOOD $

(Map p120; ☑808-821-9759; http://rainbowlivingfood.com; 4-1384 Kuhio Hwy; mains $10-15; ⊙10am-5pm Mon-Fri, to 3pm Sat; ☑) ⚑ Absolutely everything is vegan, organic, raw and both gluten- and dairy-free. Portions can be too limited for the price, but Rainbow's integrity – utilizing local organic farms and serving an abundance of superfoods with inventive preparations – helps justify the expense. The entrance is around back, off Inia St.

Hoku Foods   HEALTH FOOD $

(Map p120; ☑808-821-1500; www.hokufoods.com; 4585 Lehua St; ⊙10am-6pm; ☑) ⚑ This small, back-street, all-natural grocer is ideal for health-conscious types who seek a wide assortment of organic, gluten-free, bulk and raw foods. Stocks locally grown produce, locally sourced fish, and convenient snacks and drinks for hiking or the beach.

Holo Holo Paniolo Grill   BARBECUE $

(Map p120; ☑808-822-4656; 4-1345 Kuhio Hwy; sandwiches $9-10, plates $14-15; ⊙11am-2:30pm Mon, Fri & Sat, 4:30-9:30pm Mon-Sat) The grill smolders with tri tip, chicken, burgers and ribs. Santa Maria–style BBQ emanates from Central California and this is a great opportunity to try it. Order inside and pick a table on the atmospheric patio out front of the historic building. The restaurant is brand new, but the owner has been catering around the island for six years.

Hānai Market   MARKET $

(Map p120; ☑808-822-2228; www.hanaikauai.com; 4-1543 Kuhio Hwy; meals $5-10; ⊙10am-8pm Mon-Sat) One of the many enticing markets on the Kapa'a strip. This one is known for its cooler filled with local, grass-fed beef and fresh fish. It also traffics in ready-made salads and soups and fresh produce, and offers a nice beer and wine selection.

El Rey Del Mar   MEXICAN $

(Map p120; ☑808-353-1717; 4-1638 Kuhio Hwy; dishes $5-9; ⊙7am-7pm) A Mexican seafood truck can be a beautiful thing. It does Ensenada-style fish and shrimp tacos, ceviche tostadas and bulging burritos. There are picnic tables out front.

George's Gyro   GREEK $

(Map p120; 4-1620 Kuhio Hwy; mains $9-15; ⊙11am-9pm Mon-Sat) Good gyro plates made from local fish, organic chicken, lamb or pork, falafel pitas and spanakopita too. Guests rave about this one.

Tege Tege   ICE CREAM $

(Map p120; www.shaveicetegetege.com; 4-1604 Kuhio Hwy; shave ice $7-9; ⊙11:30am-4:30pm) Japanese-style shave ice, topped with sweetness crafted from organic lemon, ginger, coconut, dragon fruit and a dozen other ingredients.

Coconut Cup Juice Bar & Cafe   HEALTH FOOD $

(Map p120; ☑808-823-8630; www.coconutcupjuicebar.com; Hotel Coral Reef, 4-1516 Kuhio Hwy; items $7-13; ⊙8am-5pm; ☑) Almost hidden, this roadside kitchen (slowly) makes big ol' sandwiches, salads and smoothies. Wash down your 'Pineapple Express' veggie wrap or island-style Waldorf salad with a passion-fruit smoothie.

KE ALA HELE MAKALAE
··

The Eastside's **Ke Ala Hele Makalae** (The Path That Goes by the Coast) is a paved shared-use path reserved for pedestrians, cyclists and other nonmotorized modes of transportation. Also known as the Kauai Path (www.kauaipath.org) or Kapa'a Bike Path, it has jump-started locals into daily fitness: walking, running, cycling, rollerblading and, perhaps, forgoing the habit of driving everywhere.

In Kapa'a, the path currently starts at **Lihi Boat Ramp** (Map p120) at the south end of Kapa'a Beach Park and ends just past Paliku (Donkey) Beach at **Ahihi Point**, a 5-mile stretch. The ambitious plan calls for it eventually extending more than 16 miles all the way from Lihu'e's Nawiliwili Harbor to Anahola Beach Park, but those dreams have been in place, with zero progress to show for it, for many years now.

While a loud minority has complained about pouring concrete along the coast, most appreciate the easy access. Sunrise walks are brilliant. And for an added kick, you can head out on a cruiser bike rented in Kapa'a or Waipouli. It would be wonderful to see the path extended sooner rather than later.

Mermaids Cafe
FUSION **$**

(Map p120; ☑ 808-821-2026; www.mermaids kauai.com; 4-1384 Kuhio Hwy; mains $10-15; ☺ 11am-9pm; ✍) 'No shirt, no shoes, no worry' at this walk-up counter that makes humongous burritos and wraps, curry bowls and stir-fry plates. Get the ahi nori wrap with brown rice and wasabi-cream sauce, and you'll return every day thereafter to repeat the experience – maybe adding a coconut-milk Thai ice tea. This is a Kapa'a institution for a reason.

Ono Family Restaurant
DINER **$**

(Map p120; ☑ 808-822-1710; 4-1292 Kuhio Hwy; mains $10-13, shave ice $3.50; ☺ 7am-2pm) A classic diner with big breakfasts, meaty burgers and larger plate lunches built around teriyaki chicken and Portuguese-style pork mains. Grab a cute wooden booth and take in the history and the budget comfort food, or step around the corner to the service window for a blast of the beloved shave ice.

Sukothai
THAI **$$**

(Map p120; ☑ 808-821-1224; 4-1105 Kuhio Hwy; $11-19; ☺ 11am-9pm; ✍) A classic Thai joint with some dishes you don't always see on American menus, such as *pla prig prow* (fish stir-fried with chili paste and cashews), Massaman curry and a *larb* tofu. There are no less than 10 vegetarian dishes on offer and it does all your favorite curries, noodles and rice dishes. Considered the best Thai kitchen on the island.

The Local
GASTRONOMY **$$**

(Map p120; ☑ 808-431-4926; www.thelocal kauai.com; 4-1380 Kuhio Hwy; ☺ 3-9pm Wed-Sun) A farm-to-table gastropub with imaginative dishes like beer-battered tuna belly, spicy buttermilk-fried chicken, starfruit Caprese and lamb empanadas. It does wood-fired pizzas and muddled and mixed cocktails. The bar opens at 3pm. Dinner service begins at 5pm.

Art Cafe Hemingway
CAFE **$$**

(Map p120; ☑ 808-822-2250; www.art-cafe -hemingway.com; 4-1495 Kuhio Hwy; mains $13-23; ☺ 8am-2pm & 6-9pm; 🤖) It does creative omelettes and scrambles for breakfast, veggie curries and beef bourguignon at lunch and dinner, and there is always a quiche du jour. But the desserts – think chocolate samosas and black-pepper soufflé – get most of the local buzz.

Sushi Bushido
JAPANESE **$$**

(Map p120; ☑ 808-822-0664; www.sushi bushido.com; 4504 Kukui St; dishes $5-26; ☺ 4-9pm Mon-Thu, to 9:30pm Fri, 5-9:30pm Sat, 5-9pm Sun) This locals' favorite sushi stop sets up in a funky corner of the Dragon Building. It has pop art on the walls and serves imaginative fusion sushi, such as the yellowtail 'lollipop' roll drizzled with sweet sauce. Prices are high, portions small and waits excruciatingly long, but the social atmosphere and extensive sake list make it a fun night out.

Verde
MEXICAN, FUSION **$$**

(Map p120; ☑ 808-821-1400; www.verdehawaii. com; Kapa'a Shopping Center, 4-1101 Kuhio Hwy; mains $12-16; ☺ 11am-9pm; 🚻) Chef Joshua Stevens' Mexican, New Mexican and California-style cooking might take whatever style of tacos you've been eating back home and put them to shame. Be sure to save room for

THE AIRSPACE ISSUE?

For many, getting a bird's-eye view of the verdant majesty of the Garden Island is a once in a lifetime opportunity. As well, the chance to take a breath from above and witness the island at its finest is worth the discomfort (or thrill) of a soaring chopper and the money the journey requires. But for many on the ground it's an audible thorn in their side.

The Sierra Club and other island advocacy groups have long pushed for limits on the freedom of commercial aircraft to fly over residential neighborhoods and FAA-designated noise-abatement areas. But for now it's a voluntary system. Thus the Sierra Club recommends that passengers ask pilots to avoid sensitive areas, such as the Kalalau Trail, Na Pali Coast valleys and popular beaches. Whether these recommendations are successful remains to be seen, as it's like asking somebody who ordered a banana split to forgo the ice cream and chocolate sauce.

To stop what they call 'disrespectful air tourism,' a group called **StopDAT** (www.stopdat.org) is seeking to pinpoint the best and worst tour companies. As is often the case, one person's pleasure is another person's pain.

Amid all the joy and conflict these tours can bring out is the fact that though locals have their gripes about noise pollution and dangers, most of the tour companies are owned by *other* locals and landing rights (which turn a profit) are leased by some deeply rooted multigenerational Kaua'i families.

the sopaipillas drizzled with honey or the cinnamon-churro fries for dessert. Excellent cocktails.

House of Noodles ASIAN **$$**
(Map p120; ☑ 808-822-2708; 4-1330 Kuhio Hwy; mains $11-17; ☺ 11am-8:30pm) A Thai-Chinese noodle house in a historic building, with a nice range of vegetarian options including stir-fried tofu with bean sprouts, and a vegetarian pad Thai. It also does duck-noodle soup, an udon with chicken, shrimp or pork, and a spicy Thai-noodle soup with the same choices. There's a charming fruit stand out front selling cold coconuts and fresh pineapple for dessert.

Chicken in a Barrel BARBECUE **$$**
(Map p120; ☑ 808-823-0780; http://chickeninabarrel.com; 4-1586 Kuhio Hwy; meals $12-16; ☺ 11am-8:30pm Mon-Sat, to 7pm Sun) A smoky, salty hut a block off the beach, this is the original of its two locations on the island (the other is in Hanalei). It is a barbecue joint, pure and simple, with quarter and half chicken plates, pulled pork, baby-back ribs, and rib and chicken combos, all smothered in their signature sauce.

Kountry Kitchen DINER **$$**
(Map p120; ☑ 808-822-3511; 4-1489 Kuhio Hwy; mains $8-18; ☺ 6am-1:30pm) A good old-fashioned Hawaiian diner, with a bamboo motif on the walls, no-nonsense wait staff and big breakfasts. Consider the Polynesian omelette with kimchi and Portuguese sausage or the grilled fish and eggs. It

also does *kalua*-pig plates, burgers and teriyaki-chicken sandwiches. This way to comfort food.

Happy Snacks THAI **$$**
(Map p120; ☑ 808-212-8145; 4-1609 Kuhio Hwy; mains $11-17; ☺ 9am-6pm) A Thai-Chinese truck serving fish, chicken and beef dishes, wok-tossed in sauces spicy and sweet. It does a range of Thai curries and noodles too.

Sam's Oceanview Restaurant INTERNATIONAL **$$$**
(Map p120; ☑ 808-822-7887; www.samsoceanview.com; 4-1546 Kuhio Hwy; dishes $11-29; ☺ 11am-3pm Thu-Mon, 4-9pm Thu-Mon) Start with ahi *poke* nachos, followed with wild-boar and lamb sausages and Belgian fries, or move on to a flank steak with chimichurri sauce or a vegetarian island curry. California dominates the wine list and the Pacific Ocean dominates the view.

🍷 Drinking & Nightlife

★ **Java Kai** CAFE
(Map p120; ☑ 808-823-6887; www.javakaihawaii.com; 4-1384 Kuhio Hwy; ☺ 6am-7pm; 🛜) 🍴 Always busy, this Kaua'i-based micro-roastery is best for grabbing a cup of joe or a fruit smoothie to go. The muffins, scones, banana bread and coconut-macnut sticky rolls are baked fresh, and the salads are tossed with Kailani Farms greens. Another highlight is the selection of Blair Estate shade-grown organic coffee, grown just a few minutes up the road. If you come early,

avoid the lines and head around back to **Kai Bar** (Map p120; www.javakai.com; ⊘ 7am-11am), in the roastery.

Kauai Juice Co
JUICE BAR

(Map p120; ☎ 808-631-3893; www.kauaijuiceco.com; 4-1384 Kuhio Hwy; ⊘ 8am-5pm Mon-Sat, 9am-4pm Sun) Another foothold in the benevolent Kauai Juice Co empire which pushes addictive green and fruit juices, freshly pressed nut milks and coconut *mana*. 'You must to try the mana!' But everything here is good.

Mariachi's
SPORTS BAR

(Map p120; ☎ 808-822-1612; www.mariachis-hawaii.com; 4-1387 Kuhio Hwy; ⊘ 10am-9pm Mon-Fri, 8am-10pm Sat & Sun) A somewhat less than authentic Mexican joint, but one with a solid tequila selection behind the bamboo mat and wood bar. It's especially popular when big games are on television. Tourists like it for the range of satisfactory but not great burritos, enchiladas, fajitas, tacos and margaritas. We say, skip the recipes and order the good stuff, neat.

Small Town Coffee Co
CAFE

(Map p120; www.smalltowncoffee.com; ⊘ 6am-4pm) This indie coffeehouse brews organic, fair-trade coffee for the hippie-boho crowd, which also enjoys fresh kombucha and chai tea. Good tunes perpetually play from the big red bus in the strip-mall parking lot.

Big Wave Dave's
BAR

(Map p120; ☎ 808-822-3362; 4-1373 Kuhio Hwy; ⊘ 11am-2am Mon-Fri, noon-2am Sat & Sun) A big old stucco barn of a dive bar. Appropriately dark and dank with happy-hour specials from 3pm to 7pm, burgers and chicken wings on the menu, and occasional live music.

Olympic Cafe
BAR

(Map p120; ☎ 808-822-5825; www.olympiccafekauai.com; 4-1354 Kuhio Hwy; ⊘ 6am-9pm Sun-Thu, to 10pm Fri & Sat) Historically, people have long packed this spacious 2nd-floor sports bar to enjoy perched views of the Coconut Coast. With a full bar, copious draft beers and decent island-style bar food, it's been a popular place to grab a drink, especially during happy hour. At research time, however, it was going through renovations with a promise to reopen in 2017.

🛍 Shopping

⭐ Shipwrecked
CLOTHING

(Map p120; http://shipwreckedkauai.com; 4-1384 Kuhio Hwy; ⊘ 9am-5pm) Adjacent to Java Kai, the best clothing shop on the Eastside offers stylish casual and beachwear from mainland-, Australian- and London-based designers like Passenger and Vuori for men, and Joa Brown, Boys and Arrows, and One Teaspoon for women. It has nice threads for kids and local skincare brands too.

⭐ Larry's Music
MUSIC

(Map p120; ☎ 808-652-9999; http://kamoaukulelecompany.com; 4-1310 Kuhio Hwy; ⊘ 11am-4pm Mon-Fri) 🎸 This high-quality uke dealer offers starters for less than $100 and vintage and high-end ukes costing $1000 to $5000. All come with the manufacturer's warranty. Ask about ukuleles and expect a warm and thorough response from the musically talented folks doing the sales. This place is a blast. No wonder they've been around since 1952.

Aloha Images
ART

(Map p120; ☎ 808-821-1382; www.alohaimages.com; 4504 Kukui St; ⊘ 11am-7pm) The oldest art gallery on the island is arguably its best, especially when it comes to highly regarded fine artists – folks such as Steven Valiere, who is local and traffics in fanciful large-format canvases, and Tim Nguyen, who offers surrealist Polynesian scenes with deep soul. Interest-free lay away available.

Kiko
GIFTS & SOUVENIRS

(Map p120; ☎ 808-822-5096; www.kikokauai.com; 4-1316 Kuhio Hwy; ⊘ 10am-6pm) It deals in 'simple goods' including beach and shoulder bags crafted from upcycled rice sacks, saris and plastic bags; a carefully curated book table; some beautiful driftwood fish sculptures; and toys and books for kiddos. It's set back from the street. Enter through an inviting garden.

Kela's Glass Gallery
GLASS

(Map p120; ☎ 808-822-4527; www.glass-art.com; 4-1400 Kuhio Hwy; ⊘ 10am-7pm Mon-Sat, 11:30am-4:30pm Sun) Glowing pendants, glass vases and sculpture, platters and bowls, globes and animals, even waves! The glass comes in many striking colors and forms here at this one of a kind gallery representing dozens of artists and artisans. Even if it's all a bit too much to buy, it's still a fun browse.

a.ell atelier
FASHION & ACCESSORIES

(Map p120; www.aelldesign.com; 4-1320 Kuhio Hwy; ⊘ 10am-6pm Mon-Sat, 11am-6pm Sun) This is the Kaua'i branch of this Portland-based fashion boutique with boho flavor. It offers dresses and gowns of varying elegance, the best of which are under the India Ella label and are made from upcycled Indian saris. It has a rack of cute, Kaua'i-made bikinis and lovely sea-glass jewelry too.

Kauai Store
GIFTS & SOUVENIRS

(Map p120; ☏808-631-6706; www.thekauai store.com; 4-1191 Kuhio Hwy; ☺10am-6pm Mon-Sat) Forgot to buy gifts for the people you claim to love? Drop into this one-stop souvenir shop for Kaua'i-made chocolate, body creams, candles and soaps. There is red sea salt from Hanapepe, and mango-chili sauce from Kauai Juice Co. It also stocks clothing, ceramics, macadamia nuts and much more.

Vicky's Fabrics
ARTS & CRAFTS

(Map p120; ☏808-822-1746; www.vickysfabrics. com; 4-1326 Kuhio Hwy; ☺9am-5pm Mon-Sat) Established in the early 1980s, this simple storefront stocks a wide selection of Hawaiian, Japanese and batik-print fabrics for quilters and crafters. Longtime owner and seamstress Vicky also sells handmade Hawaiian quilts and bags.

Hula Girl
CLOTHING, GIFTS

(Map p120; ☏808-822-1950; www.ilovehulagirl. com; 4-1340 Kuhio Hwy; ☺9am-6pm Mon-Sat, 10am-6pm Sun) This family-run shop is a standout for contemporary Hawaiian clothing and gifts – shirts, dresses, jewelry, souvenirs and more, but also for fabulous reproductions of popular Aloha prints from the 1940s and 1950s. Look for the Avanti label for the best vintage reproductions. You'll pay extra for those, but it's worth it.

Island Hemp & Cotton
CLOTHING

(Map p120; ☏808-821-0225; www.facebook.com/ island-hemp-and-cotton-co-177814715596689; 4-1373 Kuhio Hwy; ☺9:30am-6pm Mon-Sat, 10am-5pm Sun) Firmly and proudly entrenched in the hippie fashion niche, it offers bags, wal-

---

ISLAND INSIGHTS: HULA

The intoxicating, graceful movements of hula dancing have not always been practiced solely by those with two X chromosomes. Prior to Western contact, *kane* (men) performed hula, until early 19th-century Christian missionaries discouraged its practice altogether. Today, a slow-growing revival of *kane* hula has taken shape, with much credit given to local *kumu* (teachers).

---

lets, hats and all manner of flowing garments made from hemp or organic cotton, including a small collection of some very cool, and quite pricey, Johnny Was pieces. Though it has a Kuhio Hwy address, the entrance is on Hululi St.

Whatever
VINTAGE

(Map p120; ☏808-822-1642; 1267 Ulu St; ☺11am-5pm Mon-Sat, noon-4pm Sun) A classic thrift shop cluttered with toss-aways and forget-abouts from the homes, offices and wardrobes of the island. It doesn't look too pretty, but if you're up for a rummage, you may happen upon a treasure. It also has a solid secondhand luggage collection.

Calabash
FASHION & ACCESSORIES

(Map p120; ☏808-482-1856; www.calabash collection.com; 4-1351 Kuhio Hwy; ☺9am-5pm Mon-Sat) A quirky yet upscale gallery of wearable wood and lots of it. Yes, here are wooden belts, caps with flexible wooden bills, and lots of wooden jewelry including all wood watches. Most of the gear is made from Hawaiian favorite, koa wood.

Earth & Sea Gallery
GIFTS & SOUVENIRS

(Map p120; ☏808-821-2831; 4504 Kukui St; ☺10am-8:30pm) A simple but nourishing handicrafts gallery offering wooden bowls, handblown glass, hand-bound journals, sarongs, crystals and more. Even the earnest, inspirational quotes carved into wood resonate without irony here. That in itself is a miracle. Set in the wonderful Dragon building.

Hee Fat General Store
CHILDREN'S CLOTHING

(Map p120; ☏808-823-6169; 4-1354 Kuhio Hwy; ☺10am-6pm) The best goods at this gift and clothing shop are in the kids' section. Think cute T-shirts and onesies featuring critters that live beneath the sea. Oh, and it has fish ashtrays too. It sells popular shave ice around the corner.

Deja Vu Surf
CLOTHING

(Map p120; ☏808-822-4401; www.dejavusurf. com; 4-1419 Kuhio Hwy; ☺9:30am-6pm) A vast air-conditioned emporium of beach and beach-ish gear featuring name brands including Billabong, Da Kine, O'Neill and Volcom. It has a small kids' section and a range of sunglasses, and the most recent GoPros and Skullcandy headphones as well.

Rhiannon's Kauai Spirit
BOOKS

(Map p120; http://rhiannonskauaispirit.com; 4-1378 Kuhio Hwy; ☺11am-6pm Mon-Fri, noon-7pm Sat) A bookstore with a metaphysical lean, which means lots of tarot and goddess cards, incense and candles, crystals, amulets and charms, oh, and books on empowerment, ancient wisdom, and, um, chakras. You know, if you believe in chakras.

Bamboo Works GIFTS & SOUVENIRS
(Map p120; ☑ 808-821-8688; www.bamboo works.com; 4-1396 Kuhio Hwy; ⊙10am-6pm Mon-Sat, 11am-4pm Sun) A gallery of all things bamboo. Think: furniture, lanterns, picture frames and room dividers, and even sunglasses frames, bowls, cutting boards, and, wait for it, surfboards! Heck, they even have socks made out of bamboo.

Leinani FASHION & ACCESSORIES
(Map p120; ☑ 808-821-0000; Lehua St; ⊙10am-6pm) Kind of an odd mix here, but what it has is good quality, including terrific organic-cotton baby swaddles, gorgeous duvets, and an attractive collection of locally made jewelry including black pearls.

❶ Information

First Hawaiian Bank (☑808-822-4966; www. fhb.com; 4-1366 Kuhio Hwy; ⊙8:30am-4pm Mon-Thu, to 6pm Fri) Has a 24-hour ATM.

Kapa'a Post Office (Map p120; ☑808-822-0093; www.usps.com; 4-1101 Kuhio Hwy; ⊙9am-4pm Mon-Fri, to 1pm Sat)

Samuel Mahelona Memorial Hospital (☑808-822-4961; www.smmh.hhsc.org; 4800 Kawaihau Rd) Basic 24-hour emergency care. Serious cases are transferred to Lihu'e's **Wilcox Memorial Hospital** (p269).

❶ Getting There & Away

Kapa'a is 8 miles north of the airport (in Lihu'e).

To avoid the paralyzing crawl to and from Wailua, take the Kapa'a Bypass road.

Kaua'i Bus (p274) runs north and south through Kapa'a approximately hourly from 6am to 10pm on weekdays (limited weekend service).

Old Town Kapa'a is walkable. To get to nearby beaches and some outlying sights, rent a bike from **Kapa'a Beach Shop** (p123) or **Coconut Coasters** (p124).

Family firm **Rent A Car Kauai** (p277) has great customer service, and is a good choice for renting economy-sized cars to 4WD SUVs and pickup trucks. Most vehicles are older models that have racked up a lot of miles. Five-day-minimum rental required; free pickups and drop-offs at Lihu'e Airport.

Anahola
📍 808 / POP 2200

Most travelers don't even stop in sleepy Anahola, a Hawaiian fishing and farming village with rootsy charm and a stunning coastline. Pineapple and sugar plantations once thrived here, but today the area is mainly residential, with subdivisions of Hawaiian homestead lots. The few who spend the night will find rural seclusion among long-time locals.

Grouped together at the side of Kuhio Hwy, just south of mile marker 14, Anahola's diminutive commercial center includes a post office and a convenience store with a fantastic deli.

◉ Sights

★**'Aliomanu Beach** BEACH
(Map p110) Secluded 'Aliomanu Beach is a spot frequented primarily by locals, who pole- and throw-net fish and gather *limu* (edible seaweed). It's a mile-long stretch of beach, with grittier golden sand, a few rocks in the shallows and crystalline water. Wind-swept and rugged in winter, it's serene all summer, and a spectacular stretch of virgin beach all year long.

Hole in the Mountain LANDMARK
(Map p110) Ever since a landslide altered this once-obvious landmark, the *puka* (hole) in Pu'u Konanae has been a mere sliver. From slightly north of mile marker 15 on Hwy 56, look back at the mountain, down to the right of the tallest pinnacle: on sunny days, light shines through a slit in the rock face.

Legend says that the original hole was created when a warrior threw his spear through the mountain, causing the water stored within to gush forth as waterfalls.

Anahola Beach Park BEACH
(Map p110; 🏊) Despite having no sign from the highway, this locals' beach is an easy getaway. Backed by pines and palms, it's blessed with excellent swimming thanks to a wide, sandy bay with a sheltered cove on the south end. At the beach's choppy northern end is the surf break Unreals.

🏃 Activities

Unreals SURFING
(Map p110) On the Eastside, Unreals breaks at Anahola Bay. It's a consistent right point that can work well on an easterly wind swell, when kona (leeward) winds are offshore.

HAWAIIAN HEALING HANDS

In the late 1970s, Angeline Kaihalanaopuna Hopkins Locey moved home to Hawaii after years of living in California. Back in her native land, Angeline, who is three-quarters Native Hawaiian and grew up on O'ahu, experienced a cultural homecoming as well as a geographic one. She embraced Hawaiian healing, studied with *lomilomi kumu* (traditional Hawaiian massage teacher) Margret Machado on the Big Island, and in the mid-1980s established a homestead in Anahola, where she began to share her gift of therapeutic touch with the community. Over the years 'Auntie Angeline' became a local icon, and today her son Michael and granddaughter Malia carry on her legacy.

Angeline's Mu'olaulani (Map p110; ☑ 808-822-3235; www.angelineslomikauai.com; Kamalomalo'o Pl; massage treatments $160; ⊙ 9am-2pm Mon-Fri, by appointment only) is an authentic introduction to Hawaiian healing practices and remains untouristy and frequented by locals. Don't expect plush towels, glossy marble floors or an endless menu of face and nail pampering. A trip to Angeline's is more like visiting a friend's bungalow, with an outdoor shower, wooden-plank deck, massage tables separated by curtains, and simple sarongs for covering up. Treatments include a steam, a sea-salt-clay scrub and a Hawaiian *oli* (chant).

As an expression of *ho'okipa* (hospitality), the Loceys invite guests to stay and sip a drink on the patio after the treatment. The facilities (including showers and sauna) are unisex, but the staff is glad to provide same-sex facilities upon request. Advance reservations are a must; last appointment at noon.

TriHealth Ayurveda Spa SPA
(Map p110; ☑ 808-828-2104; www.trihealth ayurvedaspa.com; Kuhio Hwy; treatments from $150; ⊙ by appointment only) In a simple bungalow just off the highway, you can sample traditional Ayurvedic therapies, practiced by therapists trained both locally and in India. Kudos if you can withstand a full-body (head and all) session in that horizontal steamer.

🍴 Eating

★ Whaler's General Store DELI $
(Map p110; ☑ 808-822-5818; 4-4350 Kuhio Hwy; poke by the pound $8-16; ⊙ 6am-9:30pm) At first it looks like your basic minimart, but hidden among the cold drinks, snacks, flip-flops and sunblock, is a damn good deli with sushi and a range of *poke* by the pound. Flavors include ahi, octopus, shrimp and kimchi, and *pipakaula* – a raw marinated peppery beef. Grab yours to go and grind on the beach.

Anahola Farmers Market MARKET $
(Map p110; Hokualele Rd; meals around $10; ⊙ 10am-2pm Sun) Not so much a traditional farmers market, but a worthy stop for fantastic handicrafts and drums, sterling-silver jewelry, fresh-cut fruit, cold coconuts and tasty wild boar, *huli-huli* (rotisserie-grilled) chicken and sautéed shrimp plate lunches, not to mention fresh-baked

mango bread. There's a warm and welcoming vibe here.

Duane's Ono Char-Burger FAST FOOD $
(Map p110; ☑ 808-822-9181; 4-4350 Kuhio Hwy; burgers $5-8; ⊙ 10am-6pm Mon-Sat, 11am-6pm Sun; 🏠) If you're a fan of In-N-Out and Dairy Queen, you'll go nuts over this drive-in. Try the 'old fashioned' (cheddar, onions and sprouts) or the 'local girl' (Swiss cheese, pineapple and teriyaki sauce). Burgers come slathered in mayo, just FYI. Add a side order of crispy onion rings and a milkshake.

🍷 Drinking & Nightlife

Kalalea Juice Hale JUICE BAR
(Map p110; 4390 Pu'u Hale; drinks $5-8; ⊙ 8am-5pm Tue-Fri, 9am-5pm Sat & Sun) Across from the post office, this juice shack has cold coconuts, raw *noni* juice (a Polynesian elixir), acai bowls, green juice, *liliko'i* (passion fruit) lemonade, and a range of smoothies.

ℹ️ Information

Anahola Post Office (Map p110; ☑ 808-822-4710; www.usps.com; 4-4350 Kuhio Hwy; ⊙ 10am-1:30pm & 2-3:30pm Mon-Fri, 9:30-11:30am Sat).

ℹ️ Getting There & Away

You're either on the bus, which stops in the town center, or you're driving the glorious Kuhio Hwy.

Ko'olau Road

Ko'olau Road is a peaceful, scenic loop drive through rich green pastures dotted with white cattle egrets and bright wildflowers. It makes a nice diversion and it's the way to less-visited beaches (no facilities).

⊙ Sights

★ Moloa'a Beach BEACH

(Map p110; 🚻) This classically curved bay appeared in the pilot for *Gilligan's Island*. There's a shallow protected swimming area good for families at the north end; to the south, the waters are rougher but there's more sand. When the surf's up stay dry, stroll the beach, and enjoy the comingling of aquamarine shallows and deep blues beyond, and birds flitting about the estuary.

Larsen's Beach BEACH

(Map p110) This long, loamy, golden-sand beach, named after L David Larsen (former manager of the Kilauea Sugar Company), is stunning, raw and all-natural, with a scrubby backdrop offering afternoon shade. However, although the aquamarine waters may look inviting, beware of a vicious current that runs along the beach and out through a channel in the reef.

Better to stroll along the waterline and watch the old locals collecting seaweed and *tako* (octopus) from the tide pools. To get here, turn on to Ko'olau Rd from whichever end (ie where it intersects either Kuhio Hwy or Moloa'a Rd); go just over a mile then turn toward the ocean on a dirt road (it should be signposted) and take the immediate left. It's about a mile to the parking area and then a five-minute walk downhill to the beach.

✕ Eating

Moloa'a Sunrise Juice Bar CAFE $

(Map p110; ☏ 808-822-1441; www.moloaa sunrisejuicebar.com; 6011 Ko'olau Rd; items $3-11; ⊙ 7:30am-5pm Mon-Sat, 8am-4pm Sun; 🚻) A roadside shack that sells fresh tropical fruit and tasty smoothies, healthful multi-grain-bread sandwiches, fish tacos, garden salads and addictive chocolate-chip and macadamia-nut cookies. Satisfying if not sensational, it's still an affordable and convenient stop.

❶ Getting There & Away

Kaua'i Bus does not serve the beaches here. To explore the region properly, you'll need your own wheels.

Ko'olau Rd connects with the Kuhio Hwy about 0.5 miles north of mile marker 16 and again just south of mile marker 20.

CHASE CLAUSEN/SHUTTERSTOCK ©

DAVE FIMBRES PHOTOGRAPHY/GETTY IMAGES ©

1. Wailua Falls (p86)

These falls make for a great photo op when they are in full flow and misting against the backdrop of surrounding tropical foliage.

2. Hanalei Bay (p159)

The smooth, buttery scallop of Hanalei Bay is one of the world's great beaches.

3. Shipwreck Beach (p192)

Great for invigorating walks along the half-mile crescent of golden sand. It's best to avoid the water here unless you are an advanced surfer, bodyboarder or bodysurfer.

4. Dolphins (p261)

With their acrobatic spiraling leaps, Hawaiian spinner dolphins are intuitive and curious creatures.

Hanalei &
the North Shore

Why Go?

Forget Eden. The North Shore's quilted green slopes and valleys are the picture of fertility. Somewhere between Hanalei Valley and the 'end of the road,' the seemingly untouched landscape makes it easy to imagine what life must have been like for ancient Hawaiians. Swim through the turquoise sea, bite into juicy fresh-picked wild guava or nap away the afternoon on warm, sugary sand. With the nearest traffic light almost 20 miles away, the North Shore runs on 'island time.' To be sure, this sleepy little enclave is a treasure: it's the island within the island.

Best Places to Eat

➡ BarAcuda Tapas
& Wine (p167)

➡ Hanalei Dolphin
Restaurant
& Sushi Lounge (p167)

➡ Tahiti Nui (p168)

➡ Sushigirl Kauai (p174)

➡ Kilauea Fish
Market (p149)

When to Go

➡ Summer (May to September) is best for families as it typically offers the least rain and serene seas, which makes the beaches safe and ocean swimming and snorkeling possible across the region. Trails are in great condition then too.

➡ Wave riders, however, would do well to come in winter (November to April) when the many beach and reef breaks here are blessed with continuous action.

➡ For the best deals on lodging and for the thinnest crowds on the ground, plan your trip for May, October or November (prior to the Thanksgiving holiday).

➡ August is great for soaking up island culture and connecting with locals at the many festivals.

Best North Shore Sunsets

➡ Ke'e Beach (p176)

➡ Hanalei Pavilion
Beach Park (p159)

➡ 'Anini Beach Park (p152)

➡ St Regis Bar
terrace (p157)

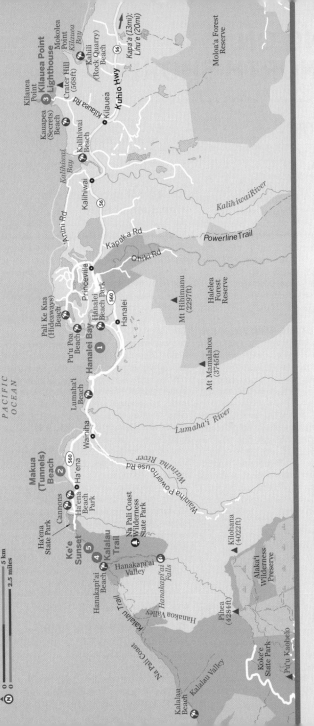

Hanalei & the North Shore Highlights

1 Hanalei Bay (p159)
Strolling 2 miles of golden sand washed with frothy surf may feel like heaven, but it's just Hanalei.

2 Makua (Tunnels) Beach (p175) Sunbathing before and after exploring the underwater caverns and lava tubes or surfing the outer reef is mandatory.

3 Kilauea Point Lighthouse (p144) Drinking in panoramic views of the North Shore – and all its varied wildlife – from the doorstep of its early 20th-century lighthouse.

4 Kalalau Trail (p104) Hiking these 11 cliff-hugging miles along the Na Pali Coast is the most popular overnight trek in the state, and for good reason.

5 Ke'e Sunset (p176) Driving to the end of the road and taking in a superlative sunset is an island rite of passage. Bring mosquito repellent.

HIKING ON THE NORTH SHORE

KALALAU TRAIL

START KE'E BEACH
END KE'E BEACH
LENGTH TWO DAYS; 22 MILES

Winding along *nā pali* (literally, 'the cliffs') offers glimpses of Kaua'i's most pristine valleys, with deep, riveting pleats. It's also the best way to connect directly with the elements, though keep in mind that the trek – if you opt to complete the full 22-mile round-trip – is a steep, rough hike with some dangerous, eroded sections.

The hike's three segments are Ke'e Beach to Hanakapi'ai Beach, Hanakapi'ai Beach to Hanakapi'ai Falls and Hanakapi'ai Beach to Kalalau Valley. There are hunters who can do the entire trail in and out in one day, but most people will either opt for a day hike to Hanakapi'ai Beach or Hanakapi'ai Falls, or will bring camping gear for an overnight backpack all the way to Kalalau Valley.

Take safety concerns seriously. In winter, trails can become rivers, streams can become impassable and the beaches will disappear in high surf. Give thought before heading out on a rainy day and always use extreme caution when swimming at the beaches, especially Hanakapi'ai Beach, where numerous people have drowned over the years.

☆ Ke'e Beach to Hanakapi'ai Beach

It shouldn't take more than an hour to complete this 2-mile trek (4 miles if done as a round-trip day hike) beginning at **Ke'e Beach**. It's a perfect mini-Na Pali experience that passes through small hanging valleys and over trickling streams. When it rises up on the ridge, it offers panoramic views down the entire coast. You'll end this hike at white-sand **Hanakapi'ai Beach**, at the bottom of Hanakapi'ai Valley.

Never turn your back on the ocean here, especially near the river mouth, and don't let the kids play in the shallows out of reach. Swimming at this beach is both dangerous and prohibited.

☆ Hanakapi'ai Beach to Hanakapi'ai Falls

Take this spur trail that branches off the Kalalau Trail to visit the falls and double back to Ke'e for an 8-mile day hike. Otherwise, it can simply be a side attraction on your way to Kalalau Valley.

The trail parallels Hanakapi'ai Stream up the valley for 2 miles. You'll see the remains of age-old taro fields and step through wild guava groves before the canyon narrows, framed by mossy rock walls. The trail ascends gradually and repeatedly crosses the stream. Be particularly careful of your footing on the rocky upper part of the trail, where some of the rocks are covered with slick algae – worse than walking on ice. When it rains, flash floods are likely in this narrow valley, so hike only in fair weather. The steady but not steep incline leads to the spectacular **Hanakapi'ai Falls**. Here falling water tumbles 300ft into a wide pool that's gentle enough for swimming. Directly under the falls, the cascading water forces you back from the rock face – a warning from nature, as falling rocks are common. The setting is idyllic, though not very sunny near the falls because of the massive cliff before you and the narrow canyon behind. Still, it's worth a dip in the refreshing swimming hole. Start early from Ke'e and you'll arrive here before the hordes. Otherwise, you'll have (a lot of) company.

☆ Hanakapi'ai Beach to Kalalau Valley

Going past Hanakapi'ai Beach means you've got 9 miles left and that you've committed to the whole 22-mile round-trip hike. **Hanakoa Valley** is almost halfway and

The rain-lashed, impossibly lush North Shore of Kaua'i feels like a corner of Eden that bobbed away to the Pacific. This tropical dreamscape is ripe for exploration – lace up those boots!

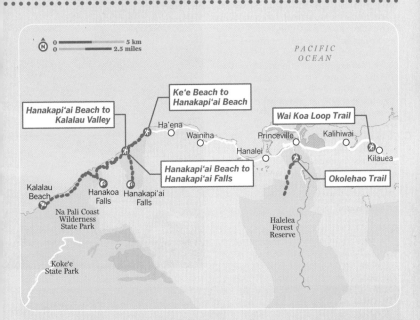

is a rest stop or campground for hikers – depending on how you choose to break up the trail. If you plan on seeing Hanakapi'ai Falls, this makes a good stopping point for your first night. It's also the turnoff for the 0.6-mile round-trip trail to Hanakoa Falls: a worthy stopover, but there's no swimming allowed.

Past Hanakoa the trail gets noticeably drier and more exposed and the blue Pacific lapping the base of the cliff taunts that much more. Hiking poles are helpful along the entire trail, but especially here, along the rocky ledges. Near the end, the trail takes you across the front of Kalalau Valley, where you'll feel dwarfed by 1000ft lava-rock cliffs before proceeding to the campsites on **Kalalau Beach**, just west of the valley.

Kalalau Valley feels a lot like Eden – one populated with hikers and hippies. If you're a good swimmer, consider paying your respects to the ancestors at Honopu

Beach as well. Only attempt to swim during summer.

Book your campsite well in advance; a couple of days should unwind you rather well, then retrace your steps to **Ke'e Beach**. If you time it right and the weather gods conspire in your favor, the journey will end with a magical sunset.

OKOLEHAO TRAIL

START BY THE END OF OHIKI ROAD
END LOOKOUT ABOVE HANALEI
LENGTH HALF-DAY; 2.5-MILE ROUND-TRIP

This steep 2.5-mile round-trip trail affords panoramic views of Hanalei's taro fields, the start of the Na Pali Coast and, on a clear day, Kilauea Lighthouse. It's rumored to be named for 'moonshine,' referring to distilled liquor made from the roots of *ti* plants. The visual spoils are worth the sweaty climb through the forest.

Coming from Hanalei, veer right immediately before Hanalei Bridge, between the river and the taro fields. Go down the road (Ohiki Rd, although it can be tough to spot signs), about 0.5 miles to a parking area on the left. The trail starts across the road.

The first half-mile is a quad burner, which means few other hikers on what is a fairly quiet hike (except for your heavy breathing). After the initial vista at the power-line tower, the trail continues gradually upward through a blend of wild guava, silk oak, eucalyptus and koa trees, offering photo opportunities galore before ending 1200ft above the slow shuffle of Hanalei, at a lookout with a bench waiting for you to settle in and watch the lines roll toward Pine Trees, Middles, Waikokos and Chicken Wings beaches. Bring plenty of water. To go further onto the manta wing twin peaks requires the use of 30 ropes and a lot of dexterity, time and another 1000ft in elevation gain. It's only for advanced hikers and can be dangerous. It's a full-day, 4.6-mile round-trip.

FOMINAYAPHOTO/SHUTTERSTOCK ©

Hanakapi'ai Falls (p138)

JOHN SARTIN/SHUTTERSTOCK ©

Hanalei Valley

WAI KOA LOOP TRAIL

START ANAINA HOU COMMUNITY PARK
END ANAINA HOU COMMUNITY PARK
LENGTH THREE HOURS; 5 MILES

This mostly flat, 5-mile loop trail leads through the greater Namahana Plantation property, starting from Anaina Hou Community Park (also home to Kauai Mini Golf). Along the way you'll traverse a stream and walk through stands of mahogany, fruit orchards, past signs explaining the plantation's history, and you'll see horses, pigs and gorgeous mountain vistas.

Hike for free or rent a mountain bike ($25 for up to six hours). It's terrific terrain for a trail run too. Hikers must sign a waiver, available at the on-site Namahana Cafe, before hitting the trail.

ROAD TRIP >
KUHIO HIGHWAY

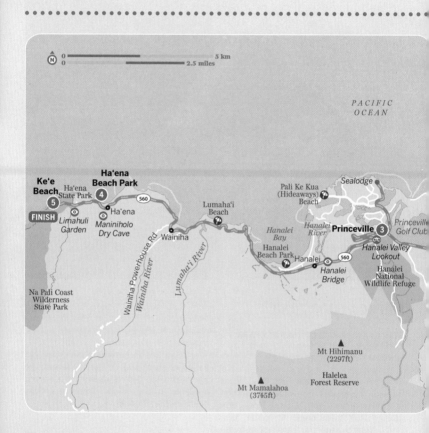

❶ Kilauea Point National Wildlife Refuge

Begin the day's drive at **Kilauea Point National Wildlife Refuge** (p144), where the plentiful bird life, the swirling sea and the historic **Kilauea Lighthouse** (p144) can't be missed. Look left and you'll see gorgeous **Kauapea (Secrets) Beach** (p145) beckoning.

The Drive > Head south along Kilauea Rd, toward Kilauea town.

❷ Kilauea

On the way to **Kilauea** town, stop to browse at **Hunter Gatherer** (p149) and **Lotus Gallery** (p150). When you get to Kilauea, stroll through the cemetery and check out the stunning stained glass at **Christ Memorial Episcopal Church** (p145).

The Drive > From Kilauea, head west along Kuhio Hwy, toward Princeville. If you feel like diverting for a dip at Kauapea (Secrets) Beach, turn right on Kauapea Rd and make a right at the first intersection. Park and follow the trail downhill to the beach.

Start Kilauea Point National Wildlife Refuge

End Keʻe Beach

Length four hours; 17 miles

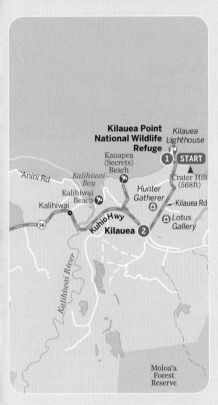

Kilauea Point National Wildlife Refuge

Kilauea Lighthouse

Kauapea (Secrets) Beach

'Anini Rd

Kalihiwai Bay

Kalihiwai Beach

Kalihiwai

Crater Hill (568ft)

Hunter Gatherer

Kilauea Rd

Kuhio Hwy

56

Kilauea

Lotus Gallery

Kalihiwai River

Moloaʻa Forest Reserve

❸ Princeville

As you descend toward the magical arched bridge that spans the Kalihiwai Valley, the tabletop Albezia trees punctuate a magnificent jade landscape. Oh, yes, you're on the North Shore now. Eight miles later you'll have arrived in Princeville, a manicured development on the bluffs. Pass the Princeville Center and drive on to the weathered shingled cottages of **Sealodge** (www.hestara.com; 3700 Kamehameha Rd; 1-/2-bedroom condo from $95/150), where the sea views are unbroken with whales that spout and breach all winter long. Before leaving Princeville, stop at the **Hanalei Valley Lookout** (p153), where the Hanalei National Wildlife Refuge unfurls in full view.

The Drive > Follow the highway downhill, pausing for traffic at the one-lane Hanalei Bridge. Buzz through Hanalei, stopping at Lumahaʻi Beach for a stroll before grabbing a takeaway bite at Sushigirl Kauai in tiny Wainiha, if you're feeling peckish. Keep rolling west on Kuhio Hwy.

❹ Haʻena Beach Park

Stop at **Haʻena Beach Park** (p174) for lunch and make sure to walk to the back wall of the spooky cool **Maniniholo Dry Cave** (p175) across the street.

The Drive > Keep motoring as the narrow road winds along an increasingly breathtaking coastline, the black cliffs dripping with life. Pull into Limahuli Garden to check out the region's beautiful botany before continuing along the Kuhio Hwy to Keʻe Beach.

❺ Keʻe Beach

Walk the 0.75 mile self-guided loop trail, then drive into misty Haʻena State Park where you can explore a pair of **Wet Caves** (p177), the sacred **Kaulu Paoa Heiau** (p176) and beautiful **Keʻe Beach** (p176); the official end of the Kuhio Hwy.

History

With its remote location and epic landscapes, Hanalei Valley has always moved in a natural tempo. Realizing they were blessed with such fecund land, its earliest residents grew large amounts of *mai'a* (bananas), *'ulu* (breadfruit), *'uala* (sweet potatoes), *niu* (coconuts), and *kalo* (taro). Ancient Polynesians considered taro to be their direct ancestor and their 'staff of life.' As time passed, numerous other agricultural ventures took shape, including the growing of tobacco, coffee, rice, sugarcane, cotton and a variety of fruits like pineapples, tamarinds and even oranges and peaches. As with the rest of the Hawaiian Islands, the plantation era on Kaua'i brought Japanese, Chinese, Filipino and Portuguese immigrants to help work the fields, resulting in its present-day multiethnic population.

When Hawaiian kings came to visit the valley, residents practiced the ancient custom of *ho'okupu* (gift giving) by bringing offerings such as fruits, vegetables, fish and pigs for their royalty. Though Hanalei has always carried a reputation of strong aloha, as recently as the 1970s the social temperature and lawlessness of these parts was something akin to the 'Wild West.' With the influx of mainland hippies seeking a tropical utopia, international surfers pining for an endless summer and the lot of them on the lookout for anything but responsibility, growing pains were unavoidable for this haven.

Since the mid-20th century – many thanks to Hollywood's cameras – Hanalei and the surrounding North Shore's peaks, valleys and coastline have gained celebrity status, which also explains the recent influx of celebrity residents.

❶ Getting There & Away

There are only two reliable ways to reach the region: by public transport (ie county bus, airport shuttle), or under your own steam. On Kaua'i a rental car gives you the most flexibility, with most agencies in and around the airport. Taxis are expensive and hard to wrangle.

Kaua'i Bus (p274) Offers hourly service in and out of Hanalei from points south.

North Shore Shuttle (☑808-826-7019; www. kauai.gov/NorthShoreShuttle; one way $4) Public transport serving destinations north of Hanalei.

Kilauea

☑808 / POP 2800

For many visitors, this former 19th-century sugar-plantation town is a quick stop to gas up, grab lunch and take a few photos. Perhaps they're a little too hasty. Kaua'i's northernmost point offers lush vegetation, a wildlife refuge surrounding a century-old lighthouse, sustainable farms, peaceful accommodations and arguably the island's best beach.

◉ Sights

Kilauea Point National Wildlife Refuge
WILDLIFE RESERVE

(☑808-828-1413; www.fws.gov/kilaueapoint; Kilauea Rd; adult/child under 16yr $5/free; ⊙10am-4pm Tue-Sat, closed federal holidays) 🌿 This refuge claims sweeping views from atop the sea cliffs, where you'll also find a 1913 lighthouse. You can occasionally glimpse breaching whales in winter and spinner dolphins year-round offshore. Red-footed boobies, Pacific golden plovers, red-tailed and white-tailed tropic birds and Laysan albatrosses are among the birds spotted here, along with the nene, an endangered Hawaiian goose.

It's a short walk to the lighthouse and along the way there is terrific signage describing the wildlife – some of which are or were recently endangered. The docents are helpful and the small museum offers free binoculars if you care to scan the horizon for whales and the skies for albatross. You'll also spy Moku'ae'ae Island, which is teeming with more protected wildlife. To get here, turn seaward onto Kolo Rd, then take a left onto Kilauea (Lighthouse) Rd and follow it for about 2 miles through town to the end. On Wednesday and Saturday, tours of the lighthouse are available hourly. The first tour is 10:30am and the last at 2:30pm.

Kilauea Lighthouse
LIGHTHOUSE

Built in 1913 and decommissioned in 1976, Kilauea Lighthouse has been known to save aircraft from certain doom. It was shut down during WWII, so the island would not attract attention of would-be Japanese bombers. Tours to the top floor are offered hourly on Wednesday and Saturday. The first tour is at 10:30am and the last at 2:30pm. It was added to the national registry of historic places in 1979.

HANALEI BAY & THE NORTH SHORE IN...

Two Days

Get your bearings with sweeping views from the northernmost point of the island. **Kilauea Point and Lighthouse** doubles as a National Wildlife Refuge and sanctuary for Hawaii seabirds.

Browse the great **Hunter Gatherer** (p149), drop into a **Metamorphose** (p147) yoga class and enjoy a fresh fish wrap at the casual **Kilauea Fish Market** (p149).

Cruise the ribbon road north through Hanalei past several one-way bridges. In Ha'ena, hit **Makua (Tunnels) Beach** (p175), where reef-snorkeling and swimming opportunities abound in the summertime.

Cap off your day with a sunset at **Ke'e Beach** (p176) at the end of the road then double back to Hanalei for a divine wine-splashed dinner at **BarAcuda** (p167).

On day two get your blood pumping with the steep, short climb up **Okolehao Trail** (p159), then grab a coffee and pastry in town at **Hanalei Bread Company** (p164) before renting a kayak or SUP and paddling up the **Hanalei River**.

Decompress as the sunlight fades with a beach walk on idyllic **Lumaha'i Beach** (p173) or let the kids play in the shallows with lifeguards present at **Hanalei Beach Park** (p159). Then drop the kids at home with the grandparents and belly up to the bar at **Tahiti Nui** (p168) for (surprisingly good) dinner and (many) drinks.

Four Days

Rise on day three, make like a local and have coffee at **Kilauea Bakery** (p149), then take a long walk along the sand at **Kauapea (Secrets) Beach** if it's summertime go for a swim. In the afternoon go for a horseback ride on **Princeville Ranch Stables** (p153), before finishing the day with gourmet nibbles and wonderful wines at **Palate** (p149).

The next morning, grab a coffee at **Lei Petite Bakery** (p156), peep at the view from **Hanalei Valley Lookout** (p153), then head down valley and up the road to magical **Limahuli Garden** (p174).

On the way back take a peek inside **Maniniholo Dry Cave** (p175), across the street from glorious **Ha'ena Beach Park** (p174), which is worth some quiet time. Unless, of course, you have a surf lesson booked in Hanalei. They say all it takes is one wave and you're hooked.

Wind down by walking the Hanalei strip, ducking into fun clothing boutiques at art galleries, and then landing at the **Hanalei Dolphin** (p167) for an exquisite sushi dinner. Then it's right back to **Tahiti Nui** (p168), because this is Hanalei and that's where the mellifluous Hawaiian tunes draw a kinetic crowd (especially on weekends).

Christ Memorial Episcopal Church CHURCH (www.christmemorialkauai.org; 2509 Kolo Rd; ☺ services 9am Sun) A stunning historic stone church and cemetery, dating from 1924. Sunday services are held in the humble yet divine chapel, glowing with marvelous stained glass restored in 1968. Mossy tomb stones are spread beneath the palms on all sides of the church.

Na 'Aina Kai Botanical Gardens & Sculpture Park GARDENS (📞 808-828-0525; http://naainakai.org; 4101 Wailapa Rd; tours $35-85; ☺ tours 9am, 9:30am & 1pm Tue-Thu, 9am Fri; 🚼) In a somewhat over-the-top approach, this husband-and-wife operation pays tribute to Hawaiian culture on 240 acres of botanical gardens. Also on the grounds are a beach, a bird-watching marsh and a forest of exotic hardwood trees. Tour reservations are mandatory.

To get here, turn right onto Wailapa Rd, between Miles 21 and 22 on the Kuhio Hwy, and look for signs.

🏊 Beaches

As all of Kilauea is perched several hundred feet above the ocean, reaching its beaches takes a bit of effort, but rest assured that effort will be rewarded. Car break-ins are common, so don't leave any valuables behind.

★**Kauapea (Secrets) Beach** BEACH (Kauapea Rd) Obviously a 'secret' no longer, these powdery white sands extend along massive cliffs for more than a mile, wrapping around two rock reefs, all the way to Kilauea

North Shore

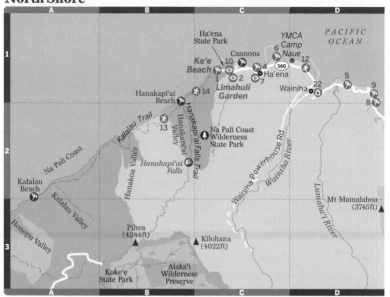

North Shore

Point. There's a sandy ocean floor and sea-shells galore, with crystal-clear seas that are the domain of bait balls and dolphin pods.

Alas, the swimming isn't always safe, thanks to a massive shore break, with frequent close-outs and strong currents that flow along the entirety of the beach. Swimming is especially hazardous during big swells (common in winter), which is why it's popular for surfing. This is a local spot,

so mind your manners. Nudists also dig it, although technically they're breaking the law.

If you can handle such, ahem, sights, don't mind dirt roads or steep trails, adore virginal beaches and savor sunsets, you'll think Secrets is absolutely magical. However, if the swells are even a little bit big or rough, do not go out into knee-high water and don't clamber on the rocky outcrops, as people have drowned here.

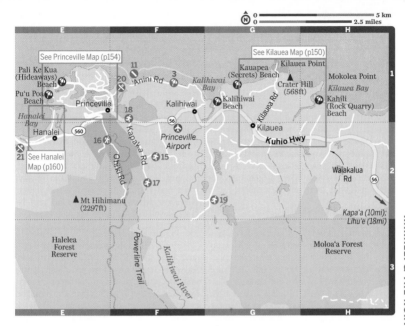

Turn *makai* (seaward) at Kalihiwai Rd (about 0.5 miles north of the gas station) and take a right on the first dirt road just after the initial bend. Drive toward the end of the road, park and find the steep trail down through wild plum trees to the beach.

Kahili (Rock Quarry) Beach   BEACH

This scenic, rugged stretch of beach is tucked away between two vegetated cliffs where Kilauea Stream meets the ocean. There's no protective barrier reef, so when surf's up, waves pound. Calm summer days are best for swimming, but beware the rip current from the stream's outflow.

Public access is via Wailapa Rd, which begins at the Kuhio Hwy midway between Miles 21 and 22. Follow Wailapa Rd north for less than 0.5 miles, then turn left onto the unmarked dirt road (4WD recommended) beginning at a bright-yellow water valve. If you don't have a 4WD, park about 0.5 miles up from the beach and walk down.

Activities

Though there are options for the activity-oriented traveler in Kilauea, the nexus of North Shore action takes place in the heart of Hanalei Bay, only 8 miles away.

★ Metamorphose Yoga Studio   YOGA

(☑ 808-828-6292; http://metamorphoseyoga. com; Kilauea Plantation Center, 4720 Kilauea Rd; drop-in class $18, 5-class pass $75) This studio nestled in the heart of Kilauea is our favorite on Kaua'i. The bright, cheery environs are a direct reflection of the owner and locally beloved teacher, Carolyn Dumeyer. Classes are mostly in the flowing Vinyasa style, though restorative classes are offered too. If you've never dangled from a wall, this is the place to try it! Go online for current schedules and bring extra coin, as the lobby shop is beyond enticing.

North Shore Charters   SNORKELING

(☑ 808-828-1379; http://kauainorthshorecharters. com; 4270g Kilauea Rd; per person $149) The booking office for half-day, sightseeing snorkeling tours aboard a 27ft, rigid-hull inflatable boat. Navigate sea caves and visit pristine bays to snorkel and swim along the spectacular Na Pali Coast. Maximum 14 guests onboard.

Silver Falls Ranch   HORSEBACK RIDING

(☑ 808-828-6718; www.silverfallsranch.com; Kamo'okoa Rd; rides $99-139; ⊙ by appointment only; ⊛) To go for a swim in one of Kalihiwai Valley's waterfalls, take a jaunt on horseback at animal-friendly Silver Falls Ranch, where the 90-minute to three-hour guided tours venture into the island's lush northern interior. Private rides are available too.

Kauai Mini Golf & Botanical Gardens GOLF
(☑ 808-828-2118; http://anainahou.org; 5-2723 Kuhio Hwy; adult/student 11-17yr/child 5-10yr/child under 5yr $19/$15/$11/free; ☺ 8am-8pm, last entry 7pm; 🚻) Part mini-golf, part botanical gardens, this is one environmentally educational round of putt-putt. Winding past Native Hawaiian, Polynesian, plantation-era and East Asian plants, each hole offers a firsthand experience of exquisite flora. It gets busy on weekends, when there may be a wait.

Garden Island Chocolate FOOD
(☑ 808-634-6812; www.gardenislandchocolate.com; adult/child 4-12yr/child 3yr & under $65/29/free; ☺ 9:30am-12:30pm Mon, Wed & Fri; 🚻) A cacao farm that also produces fine gourmet chocolate right here on the North Shore, offering three-hour tours of its farm and chocolate factory three days a week. Includes an extensive tasting of over 20 different types of its chocolate – dark, light, spiced, truffled and creamed.

Pineapple Yoga YOGA
(☑ 808-652-9009; www.pineappleyoga.com; 2518 Kolo Rd; drop-in class/weekly pass $20/90; ☺ usually 7:30-9:30am Mon-Sat) Mysore-style Ashtanga yoga links the breath with 'moving meditation' to create heat throughout the body and sweat (lots of sweat) that detoxifies muscles and organs. The studio is in the parish house of Christ Memorial Church.

🎊 Festivals & Events

Fall Festival CARNIVAL
(https://kauaifestivals.com/festival/fall-festival/2016-10-28; Kauai Christian Academy, 4000 Kilauea Rd; ☺ late Oct; 🚻) **FREE** For 16 years the Kauai Christian Academy has hosted this fundraiser featuring local food and art vendors, a huge silent auction, live music, carnival games, a corn maze and pony and hay rides. Bring the groms!

🍴 Eating

There are no award-winning kitchens here, but the venerable fish market is still doing work and there's an intriguing new wine bar in town with a tasteful menu. We like the new burrito truck too.

Julio's Beach Burritos MEXICAN $
(☑ 808-634-3218; www.facebook.com/julios. beachburritos; mains $6-13; ☺ 11am-3pm Wed-

Sun) A taco truck set on the property of the Kauai Christian Academy, with picnic tables and umbrellas where you can enjoy nachos, tacos, quesadillas and burritos filled with beef machaca, chile colorado, fresh-caught ahi (yellowfin tuna) or mixed veggies.

Namahana Farmers Markets MARKET $
(☑ 808-828-2118; http://anainahou.org; Anaina Hou Community Park, 5-2723 Kuhio Hwy; ☺ 4pm-dusk Mon, 9am-1pm Sat; 🚻) Two of Kilauea's three weekly farmers markets pop up by the mini-golf course. Stop and shop for fresh goat's cheese and sourdough bread, poi bagels, fresh pasta and Kaua'i-grown fruits and veggies. It often has live music. There are swings and a playground here for kids, as well as a half pipe for skaters too.

Banana Joe's Fruitstand MARKET $
(☑ 808-828-1092; www.bananajoekauai.com; 5-2719 Kuhio Hwy; items $5-8; ☺ 9:30am-5:30pm Mon-Sat; 🚻) Inside this tin-roofed shack they're making pineapple-banana frosties (dairy-free) that are worth pulling over for. Have you heard of *atemoya* or *mamey sapote*? Here's your chance to try these exotic fruits.

Fehring Family Farm ICE CREAM $
(www.fehringfamilyfarm.com; 4320 Wailapa Rd; snacks $4-6; ☺ 10am-4pm) An organic farm with a little stand out front selling fruit, cold coconuts, smoothies, lemonade and some terrific frozen goodies. Think organic popsicles and sorbet made from soursop, coconut, mango, dragonfruit and other tropical crops grown on its 7.6 acres.

Namahana Cafe CAFE $
(☑ 808-828-2118; http://anainahou.org; espresso drinks $2-7, dishes $4-10; ☺ 8am-7pm) You'll find this cafe near the first hole on the mini-golf course, in a lovely garden setting. Even locals descend for good organic coffee, breakfast burritos and waffles. It also does taro burgers and a range of other dishes at good prices.

Kilauea Sunshine Market MARKET $
(Kilauea Neighborhood Center, 2460 Keneke St; ☺ 4:30-6:30pm Thu; ☑) It's a modest market with a friendly hippie vibe. A dozen or so local, mostly organic farmers show up to sell mangoes, papaya, cucumbers, tomatoes, salad greens, fresh coconuts and more.

Healthy Hut Market & Cafe HEALTH FOOD $
(☑ 808-828-6626; www.healthyhutkauai.com; 4480 Ho'okui Rd; ☺ 7:30am-9pm; ☑) All of the gluten-free, dairy-free and all-natural groceries, snacks and supplies you'll need,

and some you'll just want for your high-end, healthy lifestyle. Much of the produce this place carries is grown on Kaua'i. Thumbs up for the juice and smoothie bar, and organic coffee and espresso drinks.

Kilauea Fish Market SEAFOOD **$$**
(☏808-828-6244; Kilauea Plantation Center, 4270 Kilauea Rd; mains $10-18; ⊙11am-8pm Mon-Sat) Serves healthy versions of over-the-counter plate lunches such as fresh *ono* (white-fleshed wahoo) or Korean BBQ chicken, mahimahi (white-fleshed fish also called 'dolphin') tacos and tasty ahi wraps. It's around back of the Kilauea Plantation Center and has outdoor picnic tables. Bring your own beer or wine and be prepared to wait.

Bistro HAWAIIAN **$$**
(☏808-828-0480; www.lighthousebistro.com; Kong Lung Center, 2484 Keneke St; mains lunch $10-20, dinner $17-36; ⊙noon-2:30pm & 5:30-9pm) The tasteful, shabby-chic, refurbished plantation cottage ambience works; the wine list is terrific and it does burgers, fish sandwiches, salads, seafood and other carnivorous mains, but not equally well. Our favorite dish in the house? Fish rockets (seared ahi wrapped in lumpia dough, fried with *furikake* – Japanese rice seasoning – and served with wasabi aioli). Live music happens some nights.

**Kilauea Bakery
& Pau Hana Pizza** BAKERY **$$**
(☏808-828-2020; www.kilaueabakery.com; Kong Lung Center, 2484 Keneke St; snacks & drinks from $3, pizzas $16-33; ⊙6am-9pm, pizza from 10:30am; 🖥) This bakery is Kilauea's go-to comfort food and social hub and has an impressive array of hearty soups, baked goods and pizzas (try the 'Billie Holliday' with smoked *ono* and gorgonzola), although not everything is satisfying. That said, the espresso and chai tea are brewed fresh and the people-watching is superb. Don't expect smiles from the harried staff.

🍷 Drinking & Nightlife

★**Kauai Juice Co** JUICE BAR
(☏808-631-5529; www.kauaijuiceco.com; 4270 Kilauea Rd; ⊙8am-5pm Mon-Sat) A link in a healthy, happy chain that reaches across the island, Kauai Juice Co offers 17 types of juice combinations, hand-pressed nut milks, protein shakes, kombucha on tap, kimchi, and a coconut mana butter that can

OFF THE BEATEN TRACK
KALIHIWAI VALLEY
Sandwiched between Kilauea and 'Anini, Kalihiwai ('Water's Edge' in Hawaiian) is a hidden treasure that's easy to miss. If you find it, **Kalihiwai Beach** is ideal for sunbathing, sandcastle building and, swells permitting, swimming, though bodyboarding and surfing along the cliff on the eastern shore are the more common activities here.

Kalihiwai Rd once passed Kalihiwai Beach and connected with the highway at two points. A 1957 tsunami washed out the old Kalihiwai Bridge and it was never rebuilt. Today there are two Kalihiwai Rds, one on each side of the river. To get here, take the easternmost Kalihiwai Rd, about 0.5 miles northwest of Kilauea's gas station.

be spread on toast or stirred into coffee and may just blow your mind. Ninety per cent of its ingredients are locally sourced and you can return the glass bottles for a 10¢ discount off the next one.

Palate WINE BAR
(☏808-212-1974; www.palatewinebar.net; 2474 Keneke St; ⊙5-10pm) A good-eating, great-drinking wine bar with a one-man open kitchen (mains $15 to $19) that produces creative flat breads (including some with a macadamia-nut pesto sauce), open-faced sandwiches, entrée salads, cheese and charcuterie plates, and some scrumptious desserts. It offers free wine tastings from 5pm to 6pm on Sundays.

🛍 Shopping

At the intersection of Kilauea (Lighthouse) Rd and Keneke St, the **Kilauea Plantation Center**, a historic lava-stone complex, sits catty-corner to **Kong Lung Center** (2484 Keneke St), another merchant block. And where there are two, soon there shall be three. In September 2016, construction began on the new **Kilauea Lighthouse Village** (www.kilaualighthousevillage.com; Kilauea Rd).

★**Hunter Gatherer** HOMEWARES
(☏808-828-1388; 4270 Kilauea Rd; ⊙11am-7pm Mon-Sat) The most unique shop on the island, this gift shop and gallery is the home base for a local interior designer who sells a range of personally hand-selected goods.

Kilauea

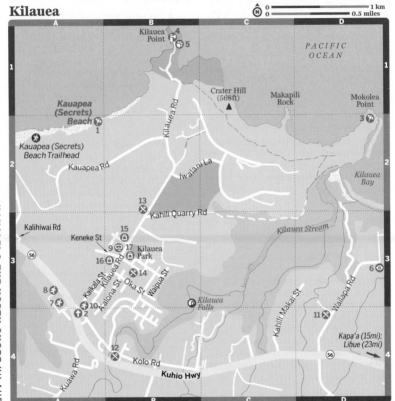

The result is an eclectic blend of clothing, books, art, bath and beauty products, and home furnishings that work perfectly together. Even a brief browse feels good in these environs. We especially liked his global collection of basketry, quilts and masks, and the Pendleton brand towels with Native American prints designed in collaboration with native designers.

Lotus Gallery
ANTIQUES

(☏ 808-828-9898; www.jeweloflthelotus.com; Kong Lung Center, 2484 Keneke St; ☺10am-5pm) With Lotus ponds singing out front, one of two art and antiquities galleries on the North Shore with serious chops. Here you'll find hand-carved jade, 19th-century teak Mandalay Buddhas papered in gold leaf, a Quan Yin sculpture chiseled from quartz, and plenty of black pearls too. It's owned by an experienced appraiser and gemologist who has cultivated sources in Southeast Asia from the 1970s. Don't miss it.

Banana Patch Studio
GIFTS & SOUVENIRS

(☏ 808-828-6522; www.bananapatchstudio.com; Kong Lung Center, 2484 Keneke St; ☺9am-5pm Mon-Sat, 10am-4pm Sun) This Kilauea outpost of the Hanapepe original (p221) is an artist-owned gallery selling ceramic tiles and dishware, almost all of which are designed by the owner and painted by her Hanapepe artisan crew. The lei-makers' painting is a best seller and those wooden postcards are very cool. Ninety per cent of the stock is Hawaiian made.

Shared Blessings Thrift Shop
VINTAGE

(www.christmemorialkauai.org; 2509 Kolo Rd; ☺2-5pm Tue, Thu & Fri, 9:30am-12:30pm Wed, 9:30am-3pm Sat, closed Sun & Mon) A true rummage. This church-run thrift shop, set in the 1925 Parish Hall across the street from the chapel, benefits their food pantry and offers everything from late-model espresso makers and juicers to vintage clothes, linens, hats and used books. It even has surfboards for sale.

Kilauea

HANALEI & THE NORTH SHORE KILAUEA

Coconut Style   CLOTHING
(⏩808-828-6899; www.coconutstyle.com; Kong Lung Center, 2484 Keneke St; ⏰10am-5:30pm Mon-Sat, from 10:30am Sun) A nice blast of color, Coconut Style traffics in all things aloha. From shirts and robes to mumus, duvee covers and more.

Palate Market   WINE
(⏩808-212-1974; www.palatewinebar.net/market; 2474 Keneke St; ⏰10:30am-10:30pm Mon-Sat, from noon Sun) A well-curated liquor store adjacent to the wine bar with the same name. It offers small-batch spirits and good deals on great wines.

Oskar's Boutique   CLOTHING
(⏩808-828-6858; www.oskarsboutique.com; Kilauea Plantation Center, 4270b Kilauea Rd; ⏰10:30am-6pm Mon-Fri, from noon Sat; ♿) ✐ Unique, island-inspired casual and beachwear for men, women and children, including pieces created by local designer MachineMachine. The blouses, beach bags and jewellery are especially good. Check the sales rack out front for deals.

Island Soap & Candle Works   GIFTS & SOUVENIRS
(⏩808-828-1955; www.islandsoap.com; Kong Lung Center, 2484 Keneke St; ⏰9am-8pm) ✐ Though there are several such shops on Kaua'i, at this one the soap is made in-house.

Botanical lotions, body butters, bath oils and creamy shampoos and conditioners will make your friends back home envious. Also notable for its commitment to solar power, forest-friendly packaging and sustainably harvested palm oil.

Cake   CLOTHING
(⏩808-828-6412; Kong Lung Center, 2484 Keneke St; ⏰10am-6pm) A shop within a shop, this sweet women's-wear boutique, adjacent to Kong Lung Trading Co, offers lingerie and blouses, camo cut-offs, sun hats and some terrific if simple jewellery.

Kong Lung Trading Co.   ARTS, CLOTHING
(⏩808-828-1822; www.konglung.com; Kong Lung Center, 2484 Keneke St; ⏰10am-6pm Mon-Sat, from 11am Sun) An Asian-inspired art and clothing boutique selling a wide array of artful tchotchkes (trinkets), silken clothing and all-natural children's clothes, books and toys, set in a beautifully restored stone building dating from 1892.

❶ Getting There & Away

Kilauea is 24 miles north of Lihu'e Airport, where most car-rental agencies are clustered. You'll need wheels to base here. Follow Kuhio Hwy north from Wailua and Kapa'a and you'll find Kilauea Rd. The intersection has a traffic light and a gas station. The town is also accessible by **Kaua'i Bus** (p274), but the sights are scattered here, so bus travel is difficult if you expect to see it all.

North Shore Cab (☏ 808-639-7829; www. northshorecab.com)

'Anini

☏ 808

A beloved beach destination for locals who spend entire weekends here camping, fishing, diving or just 'beaching' it.

⊙ Sights

'Anini Beach Park   BEACH

('Anini Rd; ⌖) Not the island's best-looking beach, but gusty 'Anini is one of Kaua'i's best spots for windsurfing and kiteboarding. It's just as popular for snorkeling and swimming, too. It's making a good fit for families as it's protected by one of the longest and widest fringing reefs in Hawaii. At its widest point, the reef extends more than 1600ft offshore.

Lying less than 3 miles from the Kuhio Hwy, the park is unofficially divided into dayuse, camping and windsurfing areas. Facilities include restrooms, outdoor showers, drinking water, picnic pavilions and BBQ grills. Note that the shallows do bottom out at low tide, so timing your snorkel is key, or you may have to step awkwardly around exposed coral and sea urchins on your way in.

The best part of the bay is at the very end of the beach where it abuts a gorgeous 100ft tall lava cliff. That's where the cleanest, clearest water and best snorkeling is found. It makes for good SUP terrain too. Weekends draw crowds; weekdays are low-key.

🏃 Activities

★ Freedive Kauai   DIVING

(☏ 808-212-7043; www.freedivekauai.com; Discover Freediving $100, Open Water certification $350) The only freediving school on the island is owned by Kaua'i's own Michelle Marsh and her partner, Josh Meneley. They offer fourhour Discover Freediving and three-day, AIDA-certified Open Water courses, off 'Anini Beach or Koloa Landing. Under their watch, even novices plummet to 66ft (20m) on a single breath. Michelle is one of America's best women in the sport of competitive freediving.

Josh and Michelle are trained instructors certified by the governing body of competitive freediving. The four-hour course offers a glimpse of the techniques required for safe underwater exploration without a tank. During the three-day training you will learn the relaxation techniques that can extend the length of your breath hold, as well as finning and equilization techniques required to move through the water in a relaxed, oxygen-efficient manner along a line that extends vertically toward the sea floor. You'll be surprised what you can do. Beginners usually hold their breath for over two minutes and swim to 66ft (20m) after the three days. Intermediate students can eclipse three minutes and 100ft, but that's only possible during the winter training available off Koloa Landing on the South Shore.

Na Pali Sea Breeze   SNORKELING, CRUISE

(☏ 808-828-1285; www.napaliseabreezetours.com; charter per person $85-195) The only tour leaving out of 'Anini aims for a personable experience. The pre-trip rendezvous location is usually at the captain's house (except during winter, when departures are from Lihu'e's Nawiliwili Harbor). Ocean conditions permitting, sea-cave exploration is a highlight, along with an hour of snorkeling and lunch. Inquire about whale-watching and fishing charters.

Windsurf Kaua'i   WINDSURFING

(☏ 808-828-6838; www.windsurf-kauai.com; 'Anini Beach Park; 2hr lessons $125; ☉ by appointment only) Learn what it's like to glide on water with Celeste Harvel. With 30 years of windsurfing experience, she guarantees you'll be sailing in your first lesson. Lessons are by appointment only, usually at 10am and 1pm Monday to Saturday.

❶ Getting There & Away

'Anini demands you have your own transport as the bus doesn't make it here. To find it, cross Kalihiwai Bridge, go up the hill and turn right onto (the second) Kalihiwai Rd, bearing left onto 'Anini Rd soon thereafter. The beach park comes up after several bends along the ocean.

Princeville

☏ 808 / POP 2200

Princeville (dubbed 'Haolewood') is a methodically landscaped resort community that is about as carefully controlled and protected as a film set – which it sometimes actually is. Comprising high-end resorts, manicured golf courses and a mixture of cookie-cutter residences, vacation rentals and even some working-class condo complexes, what Princeville lacks in personality it makes up for in convenience.

History

Princeville traces its roots to Robert Wyllie, a Scottish doctor who became foreign minister to King Kamehameha IV. In 1853 Wyllie aquired land for a sugar plantation in Hanalei. When the king and his wife, Queen Emma, came to visit in 1860, Wyllie named his plantation and the surrounding lands Princeville to honor their two-year-old son, Prince Albert, who died only two years later. The plantation later became a cattle ranch.

◉ Sights

Hanalei Valley Lookout　　　　VIEWPOINT

Take in views of farmland that's been cultivated for more than 1000 years, including broad brushstrokes of valley, river and taro. Today it's protected as the Hanalei National Wildlife Refuge. Park opposite Princeville Center and take care to watch for pedestrians when pulling out onto the busy highway.

☂ Beaches

★ Pali Ke Kua (Hideaways) Beach　　BEACH

Hideaways is a cove notched in the cliffs with a short strand of golden sand and turquoise shallows. It's an ideal snorkel and swim spot (when it's calm), with a teeming reef just off the beach. Be wise and don't get caught out when the tide comes in.

Park at the tiny, always-crowded lot past the St Regis resort gatehouse, where a path between two fences leads to a steep rope-assisted scramble down to the beach. A path to the left of the gatehouse takes you to Pu'u Poa Beach. Although public, it sits below and adjacent to the St Regis resort and serves as its on-campus beach.

Honu Cove　　　　　　　　　　BEACH

Beloved by locals but best visited only on calm days, this secret cove awaits at the end of Kamehameha Rd. At the bottom of the trail, stay left along the cliffs and you'll find a beach with good snorkeling and green sea turtles. Come at high tide.

To find it, take the first right past the Westin, follow it all the way to the end and keep left. From the parking area, you'll see a trail that hugs the cliffs.

Pu'u Poa Beach　　　　　　　　BEACH

Although public, this beach sits below and adjacent to the St Regis resort and serves as its on-campus beach.

🏃 Activities

★ Island Sails Kaua'i　　　　　BOATING

(☑ 808-212-6053; www.islandsailskauai.com; Pu'u Poa Beach; 90min cruises adult/child from $99/60; ⊙ by reservation only) Whether snorkeling in the morning, cruising in the afternoon or catching a sunset, this is your chance to ride in a traditional Polynesian sailing canoe. The red-painted *Ku'upa'aloa* pulls right on the beach in front of the St Regis Princeville resort.

★ Princeville Ranch Stables　　HORSEBACK RIDING

(☑ 808-826-7669; http://princevilleranch.com; Kuhio Hwy at Kapaka St; tours $119-149; ⊙ Mon-Sat, by appointment only; 🚻) Offering a beautiful ride, even for beginners, the pleasant 3½-hour trip to Kalihiwai Falls includes picnicking and a swim. Find the stables between Miles 26 and 27 on the Kuhio Hwy. Wear jeans and bring sunblock and insect repellent. Minimum age for riders is eight to 10 years old depending upon the trip; maximum weight limits vary.

Halele'a Spa　　　　　　　　　　SPA

(☑ 808-826-9644; www.stregisprinceville.com; St Regis Princeville, 5520 Ka Haku Rd; treatments from $165; ⊙ 9am-7pm, by appointment only) Translated as 'house of joy,' this 11,000-sq-ft palatial escape offers massages, replete with couples and VIP treatment rooms. The interior incorporates native Hawaiian woods and

---

QUEEN'S BATH

This deadly spot – formed by a sharp lava-rock shelf – has pools that provide a natural and rather inviting-looking swimming hole. Often hit by powerful waves, it's notorious for pulling visitors out to sea, which happens annually. Though the surf at times splashes softly, what many visitors don't realize is that waves come in sets, meaning that a 15-minute flat period could be followed by a 15ft wave that seemingly comes out of nowhere. People die here every year, most commonly by walking along the ledge used to access the pool. For safety, we recommend staying away.

Princeville

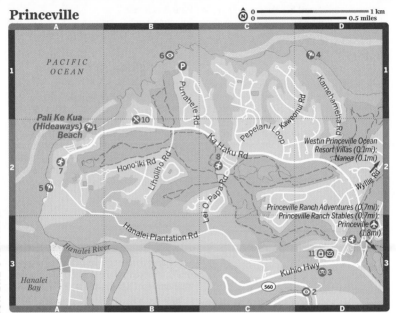

natural fibers, and treatments are based upon a foundation of traditional Hawaiian medicine, which utilizes botanical and ocean resources, such as taro, clay and seaweed. Spa treatments include complimentary fitness-center access.

Princeville Ranch Adventures   ADVENTURE
(☑808-826-7669; http://princevilleranch.com; Kuhio Hwy at Kapaka St; tours $99-169; ☺by reservation only; ⊞) This family-oriented enterprise can bring out your adventurous side, whether it's for a waterfall hike, a zipline ride, a horseback cattle drive, or a kayak tour to a secluded swimming hole. Age and weight requirements vary. Reservations required.

Makai Golf Club   GOLF
(☑808-826-1912; www.makaigolf.com; 4080 Lei O Papa Rd; green fees incl car rental from $149, 9-hole round from $55) Princeville's golf club offers 27 holes designed by Robert Trent Jones Jr. The newly renovated 18-hole **Makai Course** is championship rated and runs out to the magnificent coastline. That's the main draw, and its website's booking engine offers best available rates any given day. The **Woods Course** is a gentle nine-hole course with a flat green fee. Club and shoe rentals available.

Tennis at the Makai Club   TENNIS
(☑808-826-1912; www.makaigolf.com; 4080 Lei O Papa Rd; 90min court rental per person $15, min $30; ⊞) Gorgeous outdoor hard courts host lessons offered daily by the local pro, and also pickup games, though you can book out courts for private play too. Call up to a week in advance for reservations. Racket rental available.

Sunshine Helicopters   SCENIC FLIGHTS
(☑808-270-3999, 866-501-7738; www.sunshinehelicopters.com; 45min tours $249-324) Departing from Princeville airport, Sunshine Helicopters offers convenience if you're on the North Shore. Flights buzz along the Na Pali Coast and over Waimea Canyon. First-class seating with extra leg room next to the pilot costs extra.

Prince Albert Park   PLAYGROUND
(4304 Emmalani Dr; ☺7am-7pm; ⊞) A gorgeous stretch of green with jungle gyms for *keiki*, and a backstop for baseball if your kids need a place to ramble and romp off beach.

Pilates Plus   HEALTH & FITNESS
(☑808-652-7551; www.pilatespluskauaiwc.com; Princeville Center, 5-4280 Kuhio Hwy; class/private session $15/55) A full-service Pilates gym, with affordable mat classes and pricier private and

Princeville

duet sessions using the Reformer. Call for class times or to schedule an appointment.

Princeville Yoga YOGA
(☑ 808-826-6688; www.princevilleyogakauai. com; Princeville Center, 5-4280 Kuhio Hwy; drop-in classes $20, 5-class pass $75) In Bikram style, a skilled team of yogis lead classes for any and all willing to practice in a room heated to between 95°F (35°C) and 100°F (38°C). Mat ($1) and towel ($2) rentals available. Go online for current class schedules.

Mana Yoga YOGA
(☑ 808-652-3823; www.manayoga.com; 3812 Ahonui Pl; classes $20, 4-class pass $60; ◌ usually 8:30-10am Mon & Wed) Michaelle Edwards has created her own version of yoga that may straighten even the most unruly of spines. Combining massage and yoga, it heals with natural poses rather than those better suited to contortionists.

Powerline Trail MOUNTAIN BIKING
Measuring more than 11 miles each way, this mountain bike ride presents challenging steep climbs, deep ruts and even deeper puddles (bike-tire deep) before finishing near Wailua's Keahua Arboretum (p109). The scenery doesn't measure up to the sheer audacious wild beauty of other island trails, however. The trail starts about 2 miles down Kepaka St, the road to Princeville Stables.

Look for the Na Ala Hele trailhead sign just past an obvious water tank, where the road turns to red dirt.

Festivals & Events

Homegrown Music Festival MUSIC
(www.facebook.com/homegrownmusicfestival kauai; Church of the Pacific, 5-4280 Kuhio Hwy; tickets per day/weekend $25/40, children 14yr & under free; ◌ late Nov) A funky, rocking music festival held in mid-November and featuring established and emerging, local and international rock and reggae artists. It's held on the grounds of the Church of the Pacific and is among the island's best parties.

Princeville Night Market ART
(Princeville Center, 5-4280 Kuhio Hwy; ◌ 4-8pm 2nd Sun of month) Everything from locally roasted coffee to stationary to handicrafts to original art is on available from the tented stalls set up around Princeville Center. You'll find live music and tasty bites here too.

✗ Eating

North Shore

General Store & Café AMERICAN $
(☑ 808-826-1122; Princeville Center, 5-4280 Kuhio Hwy; burritos & burgers $5-8, pizzas $12-21; ◌ 6am-8pm Mon-Fri, 7am-8pm Sat, 7am-6pm Sun) A greasy-spoon mini-mart that's also a coffee bar serving up bagel sandwiches, legendary breakfast burritos, grass-fed Prince-

ville beef burgers and popular pizzas. It also sells locally made hot sauce and packages of local grass-fed beef. Congratulations, you may have found the best eating gas station mini-mart in the US of A.

Federico's FreshMex Cuisine   MEXICAN $

(☑ 808-826-7177;   http://federicoskauai.com; Princeville Center, 5-4280 Kuhio Hwy; mains $5-12; ☺ 9am-8pm Mon-Sat; 🍴) Your standard strip-mall Mexican joint, but with relatively reasonable prices for above-average ceviche tostadas and chipotle fish tacos, among other enticing options. It does Mexican breakfasts too.

Lei Petite Bakery & Coffee Shop   CAFE $

(☑ 808-826-7277;   Princeville Center, 5-4280 Kuhio Hwy; items $2-8; ☺ 6:30am-4pm Mon-Sat, 7am-1pm Sun; 🍵) Princeville's prime people-watching can be found at this caffeine filling station dishing up açai bowls, fruit scones and tasty breakfast sandwiches. Expect long lines in the morning.

Sandwich Isle   DELI $

(☑ 808-827-8272; Princeville Center, 5-4280 Kuhio Hwy; sandwiches $10-13) A little deli window in the corner of the Princeville Center with a few dedicated tables on the deck. It does an 'Italian Job' sub with salami, mortadella, pepperoni, pickled peppers and provolone; a 'Philly' with roast beef, muenster cheese and horseradish aioli; and a 'New Yorker' which pairs pastrami with aged white cheddar.

Lappert's Hawaii   ICE CREAM $

(www.lappertshawaii.com;   Princeville Center, 5-4280 Kuhio Hwy; ☺ 10am-9pm; 🍴) The comforting smell of waffle cones beckons, as do scoops of sweet island flavors such as Kaua'i pie (Kona coffee ice cream with coconut flakes and macadamia nuts).

Foodland   SUPERMARKET $

(☑ 808-826-9880; www.foodland.com; Princeville Center, 5-4280 Kuhio Hwy; ☺ 6am-11pm) The North Shore's biggest supermarket has an abundance of fruits and vegetables, freshly prepared sushi and some damn good *poke*, wine and beer.

★ Kaua'i Grill   HAWAIIAN $$$

(☑ 808-826-2250;   www.kauaigrill.com; St Regis Princeville, 5520 Ka Haku Rd; mains $45-89; ☺ 5:30-9:30pm Tue-Sat) Kaua'i Grill is where the cuisine is sophisticated and the views extend for miles. Pan-seared black cod with Malaysian chili sauce and sautéed Kona lobster are the stars, while tarragon-braised octopus and kampachi sashimi play well-crafted supporting roles. Wine pairings encouraged. Vegetarian and gluten-free menus available. Advance reservations essential.

Nanea   HAWAIIAN $$$

(☑ 800-827-8808;   www.westinprinceville.com; Westin Princeville Ocean Resort Villas, 3838 Wylie Rd; mains lunch $17-19, dinner $25-45; ☺ 7-10:30am, 11am-2:30pm & 5:30-9:30pm Mon-Sat, 8:30am-12:30pm & 5:30-9:30pm Sun; 🍴) 🍃 Nanea's Hawaii fusion dishes are elegant, but not always quite worth the price tag. The menu integrates locally caught seafood, island-grown greens, goat's cheese, honey and beef. Lunch is the better value. Reservations recommended.

Hideaways Pizza Pub   PIZZA $$$

(☑ 808-378-4187;   www.hideawayspizzapub.com; 5300 Ka Haku Rd; mains $16-35, pizzas $13-33; ☺ 5-10pm) On the Pali Ke Kua property in the clubhouse-office building, you can go old school with a Hawaiian-style or straight pepperoni pizza, or new school with a Greek pizza featuring artichokes, kalamata olives, a creamy cucumber sauce and feta cheese. It also does pastas, a ginger-crusted ahi and a cherry pepper-pork tenderloin.

Tiki Iniki Bar & Restaurant   AMERICAN $$$

(☑ 808-431-4242;   www.tikiiniki.com; Princeville Center, 5-4280 Kuhio Hwy; mains lunch $12-17, dinner $16-32; ☺ 11:30am-midnight; 🍴) With a faux thatched roof and memorabilia from the long-gone Coco Palms Resort, this place nails the retro Hawaiiana vibe. It's the kind of tourist trap more suited to sipping tropical cocktails like mai tais or the 'Hanalei Sling' than eating, although there are burgers, wraps, seafood, pasta and salads on the menu. It also serves later than anywhere else in Princeville. Dinner reservations advised.

Lotus   THAI

(☑ 808-826-9999; Princeville Center, 5-4280 Kuhio Hwy; ☺ 11am-9pm) A Thai and Chinese takeout joint offering pan-seared *mahimahi* (white-fleshed fish also called 'dolphin'), cashew chicken, steamed bok choy with tofu, a spicy basil and eggplant dish, and all the Thai curries, noodles and Chinese stir fries you might desire.

⬤ Drinking & Nightlife

While most restaurants in Princeville have bar stools and bottles, the more social scene can be found down the hill in Hanalei.

HANALEI NATIONAL WILDLIFE REFUGE

Anywhere west of Kilauea will set you on a path ever more pristine the further you go. Following Kalihiwai, you'll catch your first glimpses of even more vast Eden-esque landscapes. Rolling hills abound as you pass through Princeville, where you'll spot the Hanalei Valley Lookout, across from the Princeville Center. It's arguably the best vantage point for the Hanalei National Wildlife Refuge.

One of the largest rivers in the state, the Hanalei River has nurtured its crops since the first *kanaka maoli* (Native Hawaiians) began cultivating taro in its fertile valley fields. Other crops have come and gone. In the mid-1800s, rice paddies were planted here to feed the Chinese sugar-plantation laborers. By the 1930s, four rice mills were operating in the Hanalei area. Today, taro again dominates, with only 5% of its original acreage.

The wildlife refuge, established in 1972, is closed to the public. However, from the lookout you might be able to spot the 49 varieties of birds using the habitat, including the valley's endangered native species: *ae'o* (Hawaiian stilt; slender with black back, white chest and long pink legs), *'alae kea* (Hawaiian coot; slate gray with white forehead), *'alae 'ula* (Hawaiian moorhen; dark gray with black head and distinctive red-and-yellow bill) and *koloa maoli* (Hawaiian duck; mottled brown with orange legs and feet).

To get here, turn left onto Ohiki Rd immediately after the Hanalei Bridge. You can enter the refuge only on the **Ho'opulapula Haraguchi Rice Mill Tour** (p163).

★ **St Regis Bar**   LOUNGE
(☑808-826-9644; www.stregisprinceville.com; St Regis Princeville, 5520 Ka Haku Rd; ◷3:30-11pm) Don't let the elegance or the enormous crystal raindrop chandelier intimidate you. The lobby bar is for any and all wanting to take a load off. The vibe is a step more welcoming than the chichi surroundings, so relax and enjoy the ultimate location for a sunset cocktail and unforgettable views of Hanalei Bay. Some nights the scene is drenched in live jazz.

🛍 Shopping

★ **Fish Eye**   PHOTOGRAPHY
(☑808-631-9645; www.fisheyekauai.com; Princeville Center, 5-4280 Kuhio Hwy; ◷10am-6pm) If seascapes and landscapes are your kind of thing, duck into this nature photography wonderland featuring spectacular photo evidence of Kaua'i's natural gifts in full glory.

Magic Dragon   TOYS
(☑808-826-9144; Princeville Center, 5-4280 Kuhio Hwy; ◷9am-6pm) Stuffed toys and kites, board games and playing cards, remote-control choppers and matchbox-style cars; put it all together and you have an incredible stock of toys and one of the more original shops in Princeville. It also has a nice crafts corner where you can stock up on oils, watercolors and acrylics, sketchbooks and paintbrushes.

Walking In Paradise   SHOES
(☑808-827-8100; www.sandaltree.com; Princeville Center, 5-4280 Kuhio Hwy; ◷9am-6pm) If you, your partner or your children need sandals for beach combing, running or hiking shoes, or something a bit more versatile for day or night, the selection here is surprisingly good. It also stocks reusable water bottles (because store-bought water is a damn scam) and those weird gloves for your feet.

Grande's Gems   JEWELLERY
(☑808-827-8057; www.grandesgemshawaii.com; Princeville Center, 5-4280 Kuhio Hwy; ◷10am-6pm) A stunning little jewel box featuring Honolulu-based Denny Wong's wonderful plumeria designs and others inspired by ocean life. It has blue opals and precious stones, including diamond-encrusted rings and earrings. The more affordable silver is on the shelves. The good stuff is in the case.

Princeville Wine Market   WINE
(☑808-826-0040; www.princevillewinemarket. com; Princeville Center, 5-4280 Kuhio Hwy; ◷10am-8pm) Well-curated new- and old-world wines, infused vodkas and high-end spirits of all kinds are on offer at Princeville's best hooch supply. It even has specialty foods like rabbit sausage, if you have a gourmand gene.

Beauty Bar Kauai   COSMETICS
(☑808-826-6264; www.facebook.com/ Beauty-Bar-Kauai-509000185803071; Princeville Center, 5-4280 Kuhio Hwy; ◷10am-6:30pm Mon-Fri, noon-6pm Sat & Sun) A proper cosmetics

bar with an abundance of make-up, perfumes and scrubs, and make-up artists on call. It sells name brands including Smashbox and local labels like Ili, who does a popular coffee body scrub, and Leahlani, which does face scrubs and a perfumed beauty balm. It even makes its own brand of seasalt hair spray.

Azure CLOTHING
(☑ 808-826-4433; Princeville Center, 5-4280 Kuhio Hwy; ☺ 10am-6:30pm) The most polished clothing shop in Princeville Center, though still rather conservative compared to those in Hanalei. It sells golf and aloha shirts, a range of dresses, jewellery and knick-knacks for the house.

Island Soap & Candle Works GIFTS & SOUVENIRS
(☑ 808-827-8111; www.islandsoap.com; Princeville Center, 5-4280 Kuhio Hwy; ☺ 10am-6pm) The Princeville shingle of the famed Kilauea shop (p151). It does handmade soaps and candles, body lotions and more. It's small but has plenty of smell good here.

Princeville Center MALL
(☑ 808-826-9497; www.princevillecenter.com; 5-4280 Kuhio Hwy) If you're staying in Princeville, you'll inevitably wind up at this assortment of island and luxury lifestyle shops. There's live local entertainment in the food court from 6pm to 8pm nightly and during some days too.

Live A Little CLOTHING
(☑ 808-826-7077; Princeville Center, 5-4280 Kuhio Hwy; ☺ 11am-8pm) A hit-and-miss beachy boutique with mostly average souvenir tees, aloha shirts and sundresses, but it does have some nice earrings, sarongs and polarized sunglasses.

ℹ Information

MONEY

Bank of Hawaii (☑ 808-826-6551; Princeville Center, 5-4280 Kuhio Hwy; ☺ 8:30am-4pm Mon-Thu, to 6pm Fri)

First Hawaiian Bank (☑ 808-826-1560; www.fhb.com; Princeville Center, 5-4280 Kuhio Hwy; ☺ 8:30am-4pm Mon-Thu, to 6pm Fri)

POST

Princeville Mail Service Center (☑ 808-826-7331; Princeville Center, 5-4280 Kuhio Hwy; per 20min $5; ☺ 9am-5pm Mon-Fri)

Princeville Post Office (☑ 808-828-1721; www.usps.com; Princeville Center, 5-4280

Kuhio Hwy; ☺ 10:30am-2:30pm Mon-Fri, to noon Sat)

ℹ Getting There & Away

Princeville is great for walking, running or bicycle cruising. The one main arterial road (Ka Haku Rd) runs through the middle with an adjacent paved recreational path.

The **Kaua'i Bus** (p274) between Lihu'e and Hanalei stops near Princeville Center on the Kuhio Hwy approximately hourly on weekdays (limited weekend service).

ℹ Getting Around

Chevron gas station (Princeville Center, 5-4280 Kuhio Hwy; ☺ usually 6am-10pm Mon-Sat, to 9pm Sun) is the last fuel option before the end of the road.

Hanalei
☑ 808 / POP 500

There are precious few towns with the majestic natural beauty and barefoot soul of Hanalei. The bay is the thing, of course. Its half-dozen surf breaks are legendary, partly because local surf gods such as the late Andy Irons cut their teeth here. Even if you aren't here for the waves, the beach will demand your attention with its wide sweep of cream-colored sand and magnificent jade mountain views.

So will the pint-sized town where you may take a yoga class, snack on sushi, shop for chic beach gear, vintage treasures and stunning art, or duck into a world-class dive bar. Sure, Hanalei has more than its share of adults with Peter Pan syndrome, and you'll see as many men in their sixties waxing their surfboards as you will groms with 'guns' (big-wave surfboards). Which begs the query: why grow up at all when you can grow old in Hanalei?

◉ Sights

Wai'oli Mission House HISTORIC BUILDING
(☺ guided tours 9am-3pm Tue, Thu & Sat) Guided tours of the historic Wai'oli Mission House are currently available for walk-in visitors (no reservations). Check the Grove Farm website (http://grovefarm.org) for details. When you arrive, ring the big bell behind the chimney and a guide will emerge to show you around.

Wai'oli Hui'ia Church CHURCH
(☑ 808-826-6253; www.hanaleichurch.org; 5-5393 Kuhio Hwy) A popular site for quaint church weddings, the original Wai'oli Hui'ia Church

was built by Hanalei's first missionaries, William and Mary Alexander, who arrived in 1834 in a double-hulled canoe. Today the church, hall and mission house remain in the middle of town, set on a huge manicured lawn with a beautiful mountain backdrop.

The green American Gothic–style wooden church that passersby can see today was donated in 1912 by three sons of Abner Wilcox, another island missionary. The doors remain open during the day, and visitors are welcome. A 19th-century Bible printed in Hawaiian is displayed on top of the old organ. The church choir sings hymns in Hawaiian at the 10am Sunday service.

Guided tours of the historic mission house are currently available for walk-in visitors (no reservations) between 9am and 3pm on Tuesdays, Thursdays and Saturdays. Check the Grove Farm website (http://grovefarm.org) for details. When you arrive, ring the big bell behind the chimney and a guide will emerge to show you around.

Hanalei Bridge   LANDMARK
A rather attractive one-lane bridge east of Hanalei town. When it's closed due to flooding or construction, there is no way in or out. Translation: pay the bridge some respect.

🏖 Beaches

★ Black Pot Beach Park
(Hanalei Pier)   BEACH
This small section of Hanalei Bay near the Hanalei River mouth usually offers the calmest surf among the wild North Shore swells. Also known as Hanalei Pier for its unmistakable landmark, the sand is shaded by ironwood trees and is popular mainly with novice surfers. In summer, swimming and snorkeling are decent, as is kayaking and SUP.

Use extreme caution during periods of high surf because dangerous shore breaks and rip currents are common. The sandy-bottomed beach slopes gently, making it safe for beginning surfers. Lessons are typically taught just west of the pier, where you'll find surf schools galore. At the park's eastern end, where the Hanalei River empties onto the beach, is a small boat ramp where kayakers launch for trips upriver.

Facilities include restrooms and outdoor showers, and there are lifeguards.

Hanalei Pavilion Beach Park   BEACH
Toward the middle of Hanalei Bay, you'll find this scenic beach park that possesses a white-sand crescent made for strolling.

Waters are typically not as calm as further east by the pier, but swimming and paddling are possible during the calmest summer months. Facilities include restrooms and outdoor showers. Parking is limited. Street parking is often available.

Middles Beach   BEACH
At Mile 4 on the *makai* (ocean) side of the road is a small, scrubby parking area. Walk along the beach or look out to the ocean to see three surf breaks; from left to right, they are **Waikokos**, **Middles** and **Chicken Wings**.

This beach, in the heart of Waipa (p161), is informally known as Middles because of the break. The highway bridge just past the parking area crosses over Waikoko Stream, so the shoreline from the bridge onward is known as Waikoko Beach.

Wai'oli (Pine Trees) Beach Park   BEACH
Offering respite from the sun, this park is equipped with restrooms, outdoor showers, beach volleyball courts and picnic tables. Winter months bring big swells and locals dominate the surf spot here known as **Pine Trees**. The shore break is harder here than any other spot on Hanalei Bay and swimming is dangerous, except during calm summer surf.

Waikoko Beach   BEACH
Protected by a reef on the western bend of Hanalei Bay, this sandy-bottomed beach with no facilities offers shallower and calmer waters than the middle of the bay. Local surfers call this break Waikokos (literally, 'blood water'); look for them in the water and you'll see where the break is.

Hanalei Beach Park   BEACH
With its sweeping views, this makes a great place for a picnic, sunset or lazy day at the beach. Ideally located, its downside is the parking, which can be a challenge. Park along Weke Rd if you have to, as the public lot gets crowded. Facilities include restrooms and outdoor showers. Camping is allowed only with an advance county permit.

🏃 Activities

Less crowded than the Eastside's Wailua River, Hanalei River offers roughly 6 miles of tranquil scenery, ideal for kayaking or stand up paddle surfing.

Okolehao Trail   HIKING
(Ohiki Rd) This 2.5 mile round-trip trail is steep but the jaw-dropping views are worth the sweaty trek through the forest. Given

Hanalei

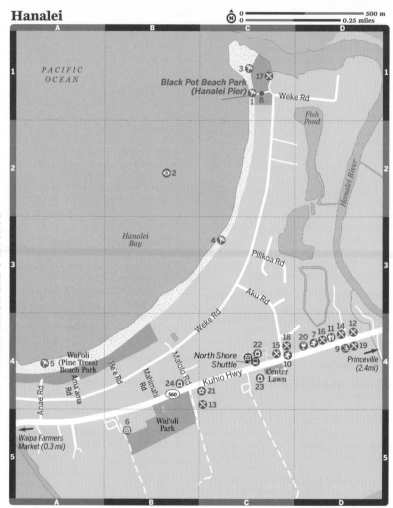

that the first half-mile is particularly tough going (your quads will be burning), there are few other people on the trail and it's a fairly quiet hike. Persevere and you'll be rewarded with stunning scenery that is the start of the Na Pali Coast, Hanalei's taro fields and if you're lucky and it's a clear day, Kilauea Lighthouse. After the initial vista at the power-line tower, the photo opportunities continue as the trail winds gradually upward through silk oak, eucalyptus, koa and wild guava trees. The trail finishes up 1200ft above Hanalei, at a lookout complete with a bench waiting for you to settle in and take in even more panoramic views of the

Pine Trees, Middles, Waikokos and Chicken Wings beaches.

If you're feeling especially keen and wish to go further onto the manta wing twin peaks, you'll require the use of 30 ropes and a lot of dexterity, time and another 1000ft gain in elevation. Note that this extension can be dangerous and is only for advanced hikers. In total it's a full-day, 4.6-mile round-trip.

Coming from Hanalei, veer right immediately before Hanalei Bridge, between the river and the taro fields. Continue down the road for about 0.5 miles to a parking area on the left. You should see the start of the trail across the road. Ensure you take plenty of water.

Hanalei

HANALEI & THE NORTH SHORE HANALEI

Waipa Foundation VOLUNTEERING
(☎808-826-9969; www.waipafoundation.org)
Join the Hanalei community for a hands-on lesson in making poi, a traditional Hawaiian food staple. Call ahead to sign up and to ask about other volunteer opportunities with this nonprofit organization which owns and manages all the land from peak to shore – the traditional extents of a Hawaiian village.

Once all villages' boundaries on the island were similarly drawn, which allowed villagers to maintain their own water source, taro fields, fish ponds and hunting and fishing grounds. Trading between villages wasn't uncommon, but those boundaries were honored island-wide.

Yoga Hanalei YOGA
(☎808-826-9642; www.yogahanalei.com; Hanalei Center, 5-5161e Kuhio Hwy; drop-in class $20) Bhavani Maki leads this Ashtanga-based studio, and if she's not teaching, it will likely be someone she's trained herself. There are four to five classes most days, mostly Vinyasa or Hatha style, except the ropes-wall

class, which is for dangling. For something mellower, come later in the day.

Kayaking & SUP

Kayak Kaua'i
KAYAKING

(☑808-826-9844; www.kayakkauai.com; Kuhio Hwy; Na Pali tour packages from $240, Blue Lagoon Tour $85-95, kayak rental per day with delivery $45-55) This island-wide kayak outfitter with a base on the Wailua River on the Eastside offers extended paddling/camping trips along the Na Pali shore to Kalalau or Miloi'i, and Blue Lagoon paddling and snorkeling day trips around Hanalei. It will also rent and deliver camping and paddling gear island-wide.

Pedal 'n Paddle
ADVENTURE SPORTS

(☑808-826-9069; Ching Young Village, 5-5190 Kuhio Hwy; ⊙9am-6pm) This full-service rental shop is conveniently located and offers some of the best rates in town for renting snorkel sets, boogie boards, SUP sets, kayaks, bicycles and almost all the camping gear you could need for trekking the Na Pali Coast. Daily and weekly rental rates available.

Kauai Island Experience
WATER SPORTS

(☑808-346-3094; www.kauaiexperience.com; 1½hr group/private surfing lesson $80/160, surfboard rental per day $20; ☕) Waterman Mike Rodger's team will teach you to surf, SUP, snorkel, fish, paddle a traditional Hawaiian canoe and more.

Kayak Hanalei
WATER SPORTS

(☑808-826-1881; http://kayakhanalei.com; Ching Young Village, 5-5070a Kuhio Hwy; rental per day surfboard $23, kayak set $35-75, SUP set $55,

2hr surfing or SUP lessons $85-130, kayak tours adult/child 5-12yr $99/89; ⊙8am-4:30pm) This long-standing, family-run outfitter, nicknamed 'Dock Dynasty' rents SUP sets and surfboards at the in-town store and kayaks at the river dock. Eye-roll if you must. Beginners surfing and SUP lessons are available daily except Sunday (reservations advised).

Diving

Kauai Down Under Dive Team
DIVING

(☑808-742-9534, 877-538-3483; http://kauaidownunderscuba.com; 2 tanks $209; ⊙by reservation only May-Sep) If you're already a certified diver, this South Shore–based outfitter is one of two dive shops that feature the Tunnels reef in the calmer summer months. Generally you'll be able to dive the lava tubes both outside and inside the barrier reef just south of Ha'ena Beach Park (p174).

Fathom Five Divers
DIVING

(☑808-742-6991, 800-972-3078; http://fathomfive.com; dives $110-155; ⊙by reservation only May-Sep) The PADI-certified Fathom Five outfit in Koloa also gears up for a North Shore dive at the reef off Makua (Tunnels) Beach during the summer months. Ask about night dives, if you dare.

Surfing

Titus Kinimaka's Hawaiian School of Surfing
SURFING

(☑808-652-1116; www.hawaiianschoolofsurfing.com; 5-5088 Kuhio Hwy; 90min lessons from $65, extreme tow-in classes $250, board rental per hour/day/week $10/30/75; ⊙by appointment only) Call in advance for a lesson with legendary pro big-wave surfer Titus Kinimaka or, more

---

HOMAGE TO KALO

According to Hawaiian cosmology, Papa (earth mother) and Wakea (sky father) gave birth to Haloa, a stillborn brother to man. Haloa was planted in the earth and from his body came *kalo* (taro), a plant that has long sustained the Hawaiian people and been a staple for oceanic cultures around the world.

Kalo is still considered a sacred food, full of tradition and spirituality for Hawaiians. Hanalei is home to the largest taro-producing farm in the state, Ho'opulapula Haraguchi Rice Mill & Taro Farm, where the purple, starchy potato-like plant is grown in *lo'i kalo* (wet taro fields). Rich in nutrients, *kalo* is often boiled and pounded into poi, an earthy, starchy and somewhat sweet and sticky pudding-like food.

Families enjoy poi, defined by some Hawaiians as the 'staff of life,' in different ways. Some prefer it fresh, while others prefer sour poi, or *'awa'awa* (bitter) poi, possibly derived from the method in which poi used to be served – often it sat in a bowl on the table for quite some time.

All traditional Hawaiian households show respect for taro: when the bowl of poi sits on the table, one is expected to refrain from arguing or speaking in anger. That's because any bad energy is *'ino* (evil) – and can spoil the poi.

likely, with one of his minions who line up the boards daily on the beach or at the pier. No more than three students per instructor. Bonus: they'll let you use the boards for a couple of hours after the lesson.

If you're already experienced and confident in heavy surf, you can also arrange private, tow-in classes. You'll have to prove you belong first. The surf shop is also a nice spot to grab board shorts, a rash guard, bikinis or even a GoPro to document your adventure.

Hawaiian Surfing Adventures WATER SPORTS
(☑808-482-0749; www.hawaiiansurfingadventures.com; 5-5134 Kuhio Hwy; 90min group surfing or SUP lesson $65, surfboard/SUP rental per day from $20/50; ☉store 9am-3pm, last lesson starts 2pm) Surfing lessons for novices include 30 minutes on land and one hour in the water. SUP lessons could even get you doing yoga poses atop your board. The company is owned by local Hawaiian surfer Mitch Alepa and his family.

Hanalei Surf Company SURFING
(☑808-826-9000; www.hanaleisurf.com; Hanalei Center, 5-5161 Kuhio Hwy; rental per day snorkel set $5, surfboard $20-25; ☉8am-9pm) Ideal for water-sports rentals, and if you plan to stick around a while, it can arrange surf coaching suited for advanced surfers. Russell Lewis has coached many of the pro surfers coming out of Kaua'i.

Kauai Outrigger Adventures SURFING
(☑808-212-5692; www.kauaioutriggeradventures.com; Hanalei Pier; surfboard/SUP rental per day from $20/40, SUP, outrigger canoe & surfing lessons from $75; ☉usually 8am-4pm) The North Shore's only company for outrigger canoe surfing lessons and tours also offers surf and SUP lessons near the pier, near a Hanalei River put-in.

Hanalei Beach Boys SURFING
(☑808-482-0749; www.hawaiiansurfingadventures.com; 5-5134 Kuhio Hwy; soft tops/epoxy boards per day $20/25, SUP per day $50; ☉9am-3pm) The rental house of the Hawaiian Surfing Adventures family rents soft tops, hard boards and SUP boards too. Weekly rates available.

☞ Tours

★**Na Pali Kayak** KAYAKING
(☑808-826-6900; www.napalikayak.com; 5075 Kuhio Hwy, Hanalei; tours per person $225 plus tax & state park fees) Hiking the Na Pali Coast can be a magnificent experience, but the trail ends at the midway point of the roadless

coastline defined by sheer 4000ft cliffs. Join this full-day tour and you can see it all.

The trip starts with check-in at its shop at 6:30am, launches from Ha'ena Beach Park (p174) and includes a lunch break on the virgin sands of Miloli'i before the final push to Polihale State Park (p231). Along the way, you'll explore sea caves, waterfalls and more. The trip is only offered when the waters are calm, from April to October. If you'd rather paddle either the coast or the river on your own, the shop rents kayaks and camping gear too.

★**Ho'opulapula Haraguchi Rice Mill & Taro Farm Tours** TOURS
(☑808-651-3399; www.haraguchiricemill.org; tours incl lunch adult/child 5-12yr $87/52; ☉tours usually 9:45am Wed, by reservation only) ✐ Learn about cultivating taro on Kaua'i at this sixth-generation family-run nonprofit farm and rice mill (the last remaining in the Hawaiian Islands). On farmer-guided tours, which take you out into the *lo'i kalo* (Hawaiian wet taro fields), you'll get a glimpse of the otherwise inaccessible Hanalei National Wildlife Refuge and learn about Hawaii's immigrant history. Tours gather at the Hanalei Taro & Juice Co (p165) food truck on Kuhio Hwy. A Hawaiian plate lunch is included.

Ride the UFO BOATING
(☑808-826-6114; www.napalitours.com; 4489 Aku Rd; per passenger $193) Board this 32ft catamaran from the beach in Hanalei for four-hour morning or afternoon tours of the Na Pali Coast. Although it also operates in the spring and fall, the tours are best in summer when more placid seas allow guests to explore sea caves and snorkel in pristine lagoons.

Bali Hai Tours BOATING
(☑808-634-2317; www.balihaitours.com; 3½hr cruises adult/child $175/110; 🖮) Explore the Na Pali Coast in a 20ft Zodiac (maximum six passengers) and splash your way to pure nature bliss. Cruise for up to four hours among humpbacks, dolphins and flying fish, and explore sea caves (weather permitting). Departs from Hanalei Pier.

Na Pali Explorer BOATING
(☑808-338-9999; www.napaliexplorer.com; 4½hr tours $99-129; 🖮) Take a coastal snorkeling trip on a rigid-hull inflatable raft, which is hard-bottomed and gives a smoother ride than all-inflatable Zodiacs. The longer 49ft raft,

which carries up to 36 passengers, has a restroom and a canopy for shade. Tours run out of Hanalei Bay. Minimum age for participants is five to eight years, depending on the boat. Tours vary but may include whale-watching, snorkeling and beach landings.

Na Pali Catamaran
BOATING

(☑808-826-6853, 866-255-6853; www.napalicata maran.com; Ching Young Village, 5-5190 Kuhio Hwy; 4hr tours $180-199) This exceptional outfit has been running tours for over 35 years, offering comfy catamaran cruises along the Na Pali Coast from Hanalei Bay. Depending on ocean conditions and the time of year, you might venture into some sea caves. Remember, though, the surf can pound and there's no reprieve from the elements. Minimum age five years.

Captain Sundown
BOATING

(☑808-826-5585; https://captainsundown.com; 6hr tours $195) This outfit is based out of Li-hu'e most of the year, but in the summer it anchors in Hanalei and offers a six-hour, true sailing and snorkeling adventure on the Na Pali Coast. Captain Bob has four decades of experience and many stories. Children under seven years of age are not allowed. Book online.

✴ Festivals & Events

★ Kalo Festival
FOOD, CULTURAL

(http://waipafoundation.org; adult/child $10/1; ⊙Dec; 🖐) ⬭ Each December, Halulu Fish Pond is host to demonstrations on growing taro and pounding poi, traditional Hawaiian games for kids, local food vendors and live music. Waipa is one of the last remaining properties on Kaua'i that extends the traditional reach of a Hawaiian village, from peak to shore. This is a fun way to support and explore it.

Music & Mango Festival
MUSIC, FOOD

(http://waipafoundation.org; adult/child $10/1; ⊙mid-Aug; 🖐) ⬭ A late-summer celebration of locally harvested food and live music happens at the nonprofit Waipa Foundation's farmlands on the outskirts of Hanalei.

Hawaii Sand Festival
ART, MUSIC

(http://hawaiisandcastle.com; ⊙mid-Aug; 🖐) Magnificent sand castles and art sculptures are built on the sands of Hanalei Bay, with free lessons and live music.

Eating

With a captive audience of day-trippers, Hanalei's eateries tend to be overpriced and underwhelming, but there are a few wonderful exceptions to this rule.

Waipa Farmers Market
MARKET $

(☑808-826-9969; www.waipafoundation.org; Kuhio Hwy; ⊙2-4pm Tue; 🖐🖐) ⬭ Set on the Waipa Foundation's old Hawaiian *ahupua'a* (land division), the market is small but ample, with tropical fruit – including centerpiece pineapples – leafy greens, flowers, handicrafts and prepared foods – such as a terrific lasagna, fresh kombucha and fiery salsa – from local chefs and artisans. To tour the community farm on Thursdays, visit the website for details.

Hanalei Bread Company
BAKERY $

(☑808-826-6717; www.restaurantbaracuda.com/hanalei-bread-shop; Hanalei Center, 5-5183 Kuhio Hwy; mains $9-14; ⊙7am-5pm) A new organic bakery and cafe in the old Hanalei Coffee Roasters building owned by the BarAcuda team. Expect fresh-baked crusty breads and baguettes, great coffee, breakfast pizzas with onion, bacon and a soft egg cracked on top, gluten-free crepes, roasted vegetable and goat's cheese sandwiches, and long lines that move fast. Don't sleep on their wonderful pastries!

Harvest Market
MARKET $

(☑808-826-0089; http://harvestmarkethanalei.com; Hanalei Center, 5-5161 Kuhio Hwy; ⊙8am-7pm Mon-Sat, to 6pm Sun; 🖐) ⬭ If wellness is your jam, pick up organic and all-natural snacks and groceries at this local favorite. Put together a beach picnic from the salad bar, smoothie station and weighable bulk-foods section (dried fruit, nuts and such), but beware that prices can sneak up on you.

Bubba's Burgers
BURGERS $

(☑808-826-7839; www.bubbaburger.com/bb-hanalei.html; 5-5161 Kuhio Hwy; burgers $4-10; ⊙10:30am-8pm) There is always a line and if you eat meat, you must at least try Kaua'i's answer to In-N-Out. Even Mark Zuckerberg and his wife did when they were house (ahem, ranch) shopping on the North Shore. The signature Bubba comes with mustard relish and diced onions, the Slopper is served open-faced and smothered with chili. It does teriyaki burgers too, and all the beef is grass fed and Kaua'i grown.

We suggest a double, as the patties are thin. Vegetarians should ask for a taro patty.

Jo Jo's Shave Ice
ICE CREAM $

(☎808-378-4612; www.jojosshaveice.com; Ching Young Village, 5-5190 Kuhio Hwy; shave ice from $6) Hanalei's outpost of the Waimea classic, this humble shave-ice stand in the Ching Young Village mall always has a line. That's because it offers more than 30 flavors of sweet syrupy goodness to drizzle over silky ice shavings. You can choose up to four of them per serving from a menu that includes coconut, *liliko'i* (passion fruit) and piña colada.

Tropical Taco
MEXICAN $

(☎808-827-8226; www.tropicaltaco.com; 5-5088 Kuhio Hwy; mains $13-16; ⊙8am-8pm Mon-Fri, 11am-8pm Sat, 11am-5pm Sun) OK, so the tacos aren't exactly authentic to Mexico, but they are authentic to Kaua'i. Tropical Taco began as Kaua'i's first beloved food-truck operation, and it still offers burritos, tostadas and tacos in thick handmade flour tortillas, piled with local, grass-fed ground beef, locally caught grilled fish or locally grown veggies. Servings are large and will satisfy.

Live Fire
PIZZA $

(☎808-635-0004; www.livefirepizzakauai.com; 5-5100 Kuhio Hwy; pizzas $11-13) A wood-fired pizzeria on wheels earning rave reviews among locals. Pesto and tomato sauces are available, the crust is thin and the 10in pie pan sized for one. Toppings include goat's cheese, anchovies, jalapeños, pepperoni and more.

Turmeric
INDIAN $

(☎808-631-6310; 5100 Kuhio Hwy; mains $7-16; ⊙11:30am-4:30pm Tue-Sat) A saffron-scented Kundalini-themed food truck serving Indian delights such as coconut vegetable and shrimp curries, *chana palak* (a chickpea curry), dahl, fish vindaloo and fresh-baked naan.

Banandi
CAFE $

(www.banandi.com; Chung Young Village, 5-5190 Kuhio Hwy; coffee drinks $3-5, crepes $8-12; ⊙6:30am-7pm; 🐾) The newest coffee joint in Hanalei started as a coffee-and-crepes truck and now also offers its usual menu of savory and sweet crepes in the metallic-edged dining room.

Chicken in a Barrel
BARBECUE $

(☎808-826-1999; www.chickeninabarrel.com; Ching Young Village, 5-5190 Kuhio Hwy; meals $10-17; ⊙11am-8pm Mon-Sat, to 7pm Sun; 🐾) Using a custom-made 50-gallon barrel drum smoker, this island BBQ joint is all about the bird. Grab a heaping plate of chicken or a hoagie sandwich with chili-cheese fries. It does ribs and pulled pork too. Whichever you choose, you won't have to eat again all day. There's a second location in Kapa'a (p128).

Village Snack Shop & Bakery
BAKERY, DELI $

(☎808-826-6841; Ching Young Village, 5-5190 Kuhio Hwy; mains $6-10; ⊙6:30am-4pm Mon-Sat, to 3pm Sun; 🐾) Just your basic mom-and-pop storefront, perfect for stuffing yourself with macnut pancakes before hiking the Na Pali Coast. Show up later in the day for heaping plate lunches and chocolate *haupia* pie.

Pink's Creamery
ICE CREAM, SANDWICHES $

(☎808-824-9134; 4489d Aku Rd; items $4-9; ⊙11am-9pm; 🅿🐾🐾) This side-street ice-cream shop scoops tropical flavors such as banana-macnut brittle, mango and an unreal *haupia* (coconut pudding). It also whips up *liliko'i* and lychee sorbet, tropical fruit popsicles, date shakes and tasty grilled-cheese sandwiches on island-style sweet bread with muenster cheese, *kalua* pig (cooked in the traditional method in an underground pit) and pineapple.

Hanalei Taro & Juice Co
HAWAIIAN $

(☎808-826-1059; www.hanaleitaro.com; 5-5070a Kuhio Hwy; dishes $7-14; ⊙11am-3pm Mon-Sat; 🐾🐾) 🍃 Find this roadside trailer for a taste of poi, the traditional Hawaiian staple food, made right on the family farm in Hanalei Valley. It does tropical taro smoothies, taro hummus, taro burgers, taro *mochi* (Japanese sticky rice cakes) and creative plate lunches too. Those *kalua* pig tacos sound good.

Hanalei Farmers Market
MARKET $

(☎808-826-1011; www.halehalawai.org; Kuhio Hwy; ⊙9:30am-noon Sat; 🐾🐾) 🍃 One of the island's most popular farmers markets happens on the sports fields in front of the community center, Hale Halawai 'Ohana 'O Hanalei. Locals line up before the market opens, then literally run to their favorite farmers' booths. North Shore artisans sell crafts, jewelry and tropical soaps, perfect for gifts or souvenirs.

Pat's Taqueria
MEXICAN, AMERICAN $

(parking lot near Hanalei Pier; items $3-10; ⊙noon-3pm; 🐾) If you're by the pier and heading to the beach, a couple of *kalua* pig tacos or a *mahimahi* burrito with beans and rice on the side won't set you back too much. Kids

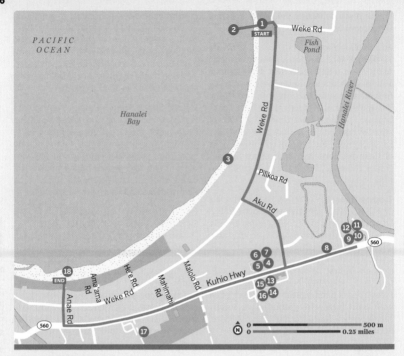

Town Walk
Hanalei Stroll

START BLACK POT BEACH
END WAI'OLI (PINE TREES) BEACH PARK
LENGTH TWO HOURS; 2.3 MILES

Begin the walk at ❶ **Black Pot Beach** (p159), where concrete ❷ **Hanalei Pier** (p159) stretches out to sea and the mocha-tinted Hanelei River empties into the bay. Take off your shoes and walk for a half-mile to ❸ **Hanalei Pavilion Beach Park** (p159), absorbing the beauty that is Hanalei Bay. If the waves are large, you'll see surfers charging the point break way offshore; if seas are calm, take a dip yourself then wash off the salt in the shower before heading south on Weke Rd. Turn left on Aku Rd and arrive at ❹ **Ching Young Village** (p168). Test your uke skills at ❺ **Hanalei Strings** (p169), then begin a long, slow browse of the galleries and shops as you walk the main drag that is Kuhio Hwy back toward the river. If you're into Asian art and design, make sure to hit the wonderful ❻ **On the Road to Hanalei** (p169). Stock up on sweets at ❼ **Chocolat Hanalei** (p172), then shuffle down the road

to ❽ **Barn 808** (p168), our pick as the most stylish fashion boutique in town. At the last shopping center before the bridge, step into ❾ **Black Pearl** (p172), ❿ **I Heart Hanalei** (p172) and ⓫ **Ola's** (p169) for quirky and beautiful gifts, clothing and arts. Then pop into the fish market behind ⓬ **Hanalei Dolphin** for lunch and enjoy it on the picnic tables by the riverside. There isn't always a sidewalk on the highway so be mindful of traffic.

After lunch, cross the street and take the same road back toward ⓭ **Hanalei Center** (p172), where you can visit the museum-like gallery that is ⓮ **Havaiki** (p169) before hunting for vintage gems at ⓯ **Yellowfish Trading Company** (p168). Stop for a coffee at ⓰ **Hanalei Bread Company** (p164), then step to the historic ⓱ **Wai'oli Hui'ia Church** (p158). Ring the bell behind the Mission House chimney and your guide will appear. Afterward, cross the street, hang a right on Anae Rd, lose your shoes and enjoy the rest of the afternoon at ⓲ **Wai'oli (Pine Trees) Beach Park** (p159).

menu (mini burritos, quesadillas etc) available. Cash only.

Big Save
SUPERMARKET $

(☑808-826-6652; www.timessupermarkets.com; Ching Young Village, 5-5172 Kuhio Hwy; ☺7am-10pm; ⚑) For supply runs or immediate snacks, this solid catch-all grocer offers good produce at decent prices, classic rock on the sound system, an enticing selection of fresh fish and a deli called 'The Kitchen' with $6 *poke* bowls.

Fresh Bite
CAFE $

(☑808-652-0744; www.freshbitekauai.com; 5100 Kuhio Hwy; mains $6-14; ☺9am-4pm Thu-Mon) This Hanalei food truck offers breakfasts including egg sandwiches and a sweet potato and steak hash. It does salads and chicken wraps for lunch.

Kalypso
PUB FOOD $$

(☑808-826-9700; www.kalypsokauai.com; 5-5156 Kuhio Hwy; mains $11-19; ☺11am-9pm Mon-Fri, from 8am Sat & Sun) It offers Hawaiian-themed pub grub including crab quesadillas, *poke pupus* (snacks), *huli-huli* chicken, blackened fish entrées and a range of burgers, but its best work is done with *kalua* pig. A Hawaiian specialty, it's a pork shoulder braised for 12 hours. Have it on a sweetbread sandwich with *liliko'i* coleslaw and fried onions or on a quesadilla. It's a great place to watch a ball game and it serves big breakfasts to ravenous families on weekend mornings.

Bouchons
PUB FOOD $$

(☑808-826-9701; www.bouchonshanalei.com; Ching Young Village, 5-5190 Kuhio Hwy; mains $14-24; ☺11:30am-9pm) This here is pub grub with a beachy, Hawaiian twist. There's fish and chips made with fresh, flash-fried *ono* (white-fleshed wahoo), Mexican food, ribs, a range of fresh fish mains, including macadamia-crusted *mahimahi*, and a sushi bar with affordable pricing. The upstairs location in Ching Young Village is appealing too.

Hanalei Bay Pizzeria
PIZZA $$

(☑808-827-8000; www.hanaleibaypizzeria.com; Ching Young Village, 5-5190 Kuhio Hwy; pizzas $10-30; ☺11:30am-8:30pm) A funky dive in Ching Young Village that serves tasty pizzas featuring a terrific crust made with Hawaiian honey and organic extra virgin olive oil (it does a gluten-free version too). Its sausages and *kalua* pig are housemade, there are four sauces to choose from (red, pesto, garlic butter and pineapple BBQ) and it doesn't skimp on the mozzarella.

Hanalei Gourmet
CAFE, DELI $$

(☑808-826-2524; www.hanaleigourmet.com; Hanalei Center, 5-5161 Kuhio Hwy; dinner mains $10-33; ☺8am-10:30pm; ⚑) At this lively sit-down spot, the best bets are huge sandwiches of house-baked bread. Meals – creatively skipping from Asian-style crab cakes to grilled-pork tenderloin – are tasty and unpretentious, even if more mainstream American than local. Twice-weekly musical acts and happy hour (3:30pm to 5:30pm daily) are incentive enough to belly up to this bar. They'll pack picnic lunches for a day out at the beach and the trail.

★ BarAcuda
Tapas & Wine
MEDITERRANEAN $$$

(☑808-826-7081; www.restaurantbaracuda.com; Hanalei Center, 5-5161 Kuhio Hwy; shared plates $7-26; ☺5:30-10pm, kitchen closes at 9:30pm) ✿ This is the most chef-driven spot in Hanalei and its best kitchen. The wine list is expertly curated with a blend of new- and old-world vintners, and the tapas-style plates, featuring local beef, fish, pork and veg, are meant to be shared.

It's not cheap, but when you're delving into spicy bowls of housemade chorizo and clams, nibbling on ahi *poke* cured with tequila, and perfectly seared scallops, you'll understand that this kind of quality is worth the money. The interior is modern and seductive, but grab a table on the deck beneath those dangling lanterns for date-night nirvana. Reservations essential.

Hanalei Dolphin Restaurant
& Sushi Lounge
SEAFOOD, MARKET $$$

(☑808-826-6113; www.hanaleidolphin.com; 5-5016 Kuhio Hwy; mains lunch $12-16, dinner $25-40; ☺restaurant 11:30am-9pm, market 10am-7pm) At one of Hanalei's oldest restaurants, the incisive sushi chefs will play culinary jazz with their daily fresh fish if decision-making is not your forte. Opt for the cooked-food menu if raw fish doesn't grab you. Everything is good here.

The fish market around back sells fish by the pound, assorted sushi rolls, *poke* bowls, a daily fresh-catch sandwich and a chunky seafood chowder. It's a nice spot to grab lunch on the fly.

Postcards Café
FUSION $$$

(☑808-826-1191; http://postcardscafe.com; 5-5075 Kuhio Hwy; mains $24-38; ☺5:30-9pm; ✍) ✿ With innocent charm, this garden cottage with the rusted anchor out front could just as easily be found in the New England countryside. Vegan and seafood dishes often have an appealing world-fusion twist, such as the wasabi-crusted ahi or fennel-crusted lobster tail. A genteel atmosphere will induce nostalgia like a Robert Redford film. Reservations recommended for groups of four or more.

Neide's   BRAZILIAN $$$

(☎808-826-1851; www.facebook.com/Neides-Salsa-and-Samba-149964965035811; Hanalei Center, 5-5161 Kuhio Hwy; mains $15-35; ⊙11:30am-9:30pm) Brazilian and Mexican flavors combine in the rear of the Hanalei Center, with the best seating on the deck out front. It does authentic *muqueca* (seafood stew) with shrimp or fish, seafood enchiladas, fish tacos and sizzling *churrasco* (grilled beef) platters too.

Trucking Delicious   HAWAIIAN

(☎808-482-4101; 5100 Kuhio Hwy; mains $13-14; ⊙11am-4pm Tue-Sat) One of a handful of permanently parked food trucks gathered here, this one serves up local-style plate lunches from a menu that changes weekly. When we came by it served coconut shrimp, chicken and rice, and *kalua* pig and cabbage. It also offered a lobster *poke* bowl and dragonfruit lemonade.

Drinking & Nightlife

Like most of Kaua'i, Hanalei is not a nightlife destination. Most restaurants have bars, but they buzz at happy hour then mellow as the night builds. The noted exception here is a beloved local dive that has managed to become world famous and a tapas bar with a superior wine list.

★Tahiti Nui   BAR

(☎808-826-6277; http://thenui.com; 5-5134 Kuhio Hwy; ⊙11am-10pm Sun-Thu, to midnight Fri & Sat) The legendary Nui (which made a cameo appearance in *The Descendants*) is a tiki dive bar with heart and history, and a rather tasty dinner menu. It's usually crowded from mid-afternoon onward, and can get rollicking nightly with live Hawaiian music. It's especially busy on weekends, when it's the only place open past 10pm.

As far as food goes (mains $18 to $30), we love the seared ahi with wasabi cream and purple sweet potatoes, and the pizzas get rave reviews. On Wednesday nights, the luau (per adult/child $75/45) is a modest all-you-can-eat dinner show. For luau reservations, call ☎808-482-4829.

Iti Wine Bar   WINE BAR

(☎808-826-6277; www.thenui.com/wine-bar; 5-5134 Kuhio Hwy; ⊙11am-10pm) An extension of the laid-back Tahiti Nui vibe, intimate Iti Wine Bar has over 50 wines on the list, and the bites and the mai tais are delicious.

Aloha Juice Bar   JUICE BAR

(Ching Young Village, 5-5190 Kuhio Hwy; drinks from $7; ⊙10am-4pm) Set in the Ching Young Village mall, this inviting juice stall sells local dried fruits and nuts, fist-sized muffins, açai bowls (of course) and chocolate-dipped bananas. But it's best known for fresh veggie and fruit juices, cracked coconuts and delicious shakes.

 ## Entertainment

Hawaiian Slack Key Guitar Concerts   LIVE MUSIC

(☎808-826-1469; www.hawaiianslackkeyguitar.com; Hanalei Community Center, Malolo Rd; adult/13-19yr/6-12 yr $25/20/10; ⊙4pm Fri, 3pm Sun) Slack key guitar and ukulele concerts are performed by long-time musicians Doug and Sandy McMaster year-round in a refreshingly informal atmosphere.

Shopping

Hanalei's handful of boutiques sell everything from tourist kitsch to beach chic to evocative art. Most are at the old-guard **Ching Young Village** (www.chingyoungvillage.com; 5-5190 Kuhio Hwy) and the more upscale Hanalei Center (p172), but there are galleries and boutiques strung along the main drag.

★Yellowfish Trading Company   VINTAGE

(☎808-826-1227; www.yellowfishtradingcompany.com; Hanalei Center, 5-5161 Kuhio Hwy; ⊙10am-8pm) A wonderfully cheery gallery offering a mix of true vintage and vintage-inspired art, handicrafts, books and much more. The vintage stuff is the true gold here: think midcentury glassware, 1950s-era Hawaiian guidebooks, lamps from the same era, guitars and a magnificent collection of dashboard hula girls. It's the Hawaii *Mad Men* episode in treasure-chest form.

Barn 808   CLOTHING

(☎808-320-3555; www.thebarn808.com; 5080 Kuhio Hwy; ⊙10am-7pm) The most stylish boutique on the strip, this rustic wood-floored barn deals in Nick Fouget hats, one-of-a-kind sport coats, soft and cuddly Aviator Nation and Outer Known tees. It has pairs of socks that say 'mother' and 'fucker', and it does

ISLAND INSIGHTS

No doubt being attacked by a *mano* (shark) could be deadly; precautions, such as avoiding swimming in murky waters, especially after a rain, will help you avoid them. But statistically speaking, you're more likely to die from a bee sting than a shark attack and you should be more concerned about contracting leptospirosis or giardiasis in those infamous muddy waters than becoming a midday snack.

Rather than letting any hardwired phobia of large predators get you down, try considering the *mano* from another perspective while in Hawaii: as sacred. For many local families, the *mano* is their *'aumakua* (guardian spirit). *'Aumakua* are family ancestors whose *'uhane* (spirit form) lives on in the body of an animal, watching over members of their living *'ohana* (family and friends). Revered for their ocean skill, *mano* were also considered the *'aumakua* of navigators. Even today, *mano 'aumakua* have been said to guide lost fishermen home, or toward areas of plentiful fish, to make for a bountiful sojourn.

leather bracelets, wallets, John Lennon–style sunglasses, beach bags and aromatherapy votives. If you have kids, don't miss the terrific grom gear.

Hanalei Strings MUSICAL INSTRUMENTS
(☑808-826-9633; www.hanaleistrings.com; Ching Young Village, 5-5190 Kuhio Hwy; ⊙10am-8pm) A long-running and always hospitable shop channeling two passions: music and knitting. It has a wide range of guitars and ukuleles from concert size to tenor and beyond. Quality rises with the price. Its knitting supply flip side features hand-dyed yarns. Free beginner ukulele lessons are offered on Tuesday and Thursday from 6pm to 7pm.

Havaiki ART
(☑808-826-7606; www.havaikiart.com; Hanalei Center, 5-5161 Kuhio Hwy; ⊙10am-5pm) This hidden shop sells traditional, handcrafted Polynesian art handpicked by the owners, from inexpensive tchotchkes to museum-quality artworks. Keep an eye out for more exotic pieces, such as evocative Asmat shields and masks from Papua, ornately carved oars from the Marquesas and wonderful antique tiki, too.

On the Road to Hanalei CLOTHING, GIFTS
(☑808-826-7360; Ching Young Village, 5-5190 Kuhio Hwy; ⊙10am-7pm Mon-Sat, to 6pm Sun) Vibrant batik-print dresses and *pareus* (Tahitian sarongs), handcrafted silver jewelry and Japanese teapots and teacups are just a few of the treasures inside this rustic wooden-floored shop. Easily one of the best in Hanalei.

Ola's ART
(☑808-826-6937; www.dougbrittart.com; 5016 Kuhio Hwy) A joyful gallery filled with the paintings and mixed-media sculptures of owner, artist Doug Britt. The sculptures made from old vintage materials, like binoculars and chess pieces and found sheet metal, are particularly great. It also represents other artists and craftsmen who provide hand-blown glass bowls and platters, as well as some fun metallic rocket and spaceship sculpture.

Art & Soul ART
(☑808-634-0766; 5-5080a Kuhio Hwy; ⊙noon-5pm Mon-Sat) This gallery is owned by water colorist Mercedes Mazda, the resident artist at St Regis for 20 years. It shows his and the work of other local artists, such as Bill Long, Graham Nash's former tour manager, who paints fish on salvaged wood, and Isabel Bryna, who paints portraits of evocative and imagined psychedelic goddesses.

Hanalei Boutique CLOTHING
(☑808-320-3319; www.instagram.com/hanalei_boutique/; Hanalei Center, 5-5161 Kuhio hwy; ⊙10m-5pm Mon-Sat) A small boutique run by a mother-and-daughter team who go on buying trips around the world and have stocked their shop with beach bags crafted from Sri Lankan rice sacks, Mexican serapes, Indonesian sarongs, and clothing designed and made locally. It's tucked away on the 2nd floor and worth finding.

Mark Daniels Gallery ART
(☑807-652-4173; markart@aloha.net; 5-5428 Kuhio Hwy; ⊙noon-5pm most days) An artist-owned gallery offering gorgeous depictions of palms and birds of paradise, water, wind and waves. Mark also stocks wood-block prints and work from his father and mother. Both were also fine artists with very different aesthetics. His mother's work is especially interesting as it depicts mythological moments in Polynesian history.

LAZY DAYS NORTH SHORE & HANALEI BAY

The North Shore of Kaua'i resembles nothing so much as the sort of tropical screen saver you put on your office computer during the dead of winter. A place this beautiful deserves a little extra time; here's how we like to spend it.

BEACH

The smooth, buttery scallop of Hanalei Bay is simply one of the world's great beaches. World-class surfing is the norm, but you want to relax, right? Well, the surf culture that surrounds Hanalei amounts to chill times, seaside picnics and even a few ukelele riffs. Enjoy that sunset.

DINING

Once you get tired of swimming and hiking and swimming some more and hey, let's take another walk, there are few more enjoyable ways of recharging your batteries than going down a North Shore foodie rabbit hole. From fresh sushi, burgers by the beach, shaved ice and vegan pasta, there's a flavor for every palette.

HIKES

The earthly Eden that is Kaua'i's North Shore requires a bit of exploration *au pied*. Indeed, the Na Pali coast hike requires at least two days to complete. A long trek may not be the laziest way of spending your time, but it is a means of utterly disconnecting from the outside world – plus, there are plenty of shorter, more casual walks afoot (pun intended).

1. Delicious take-out burgers
2. Hiking the Na Pali Coast (p138)

MARK BOSTER/GETTY IMAGES ©

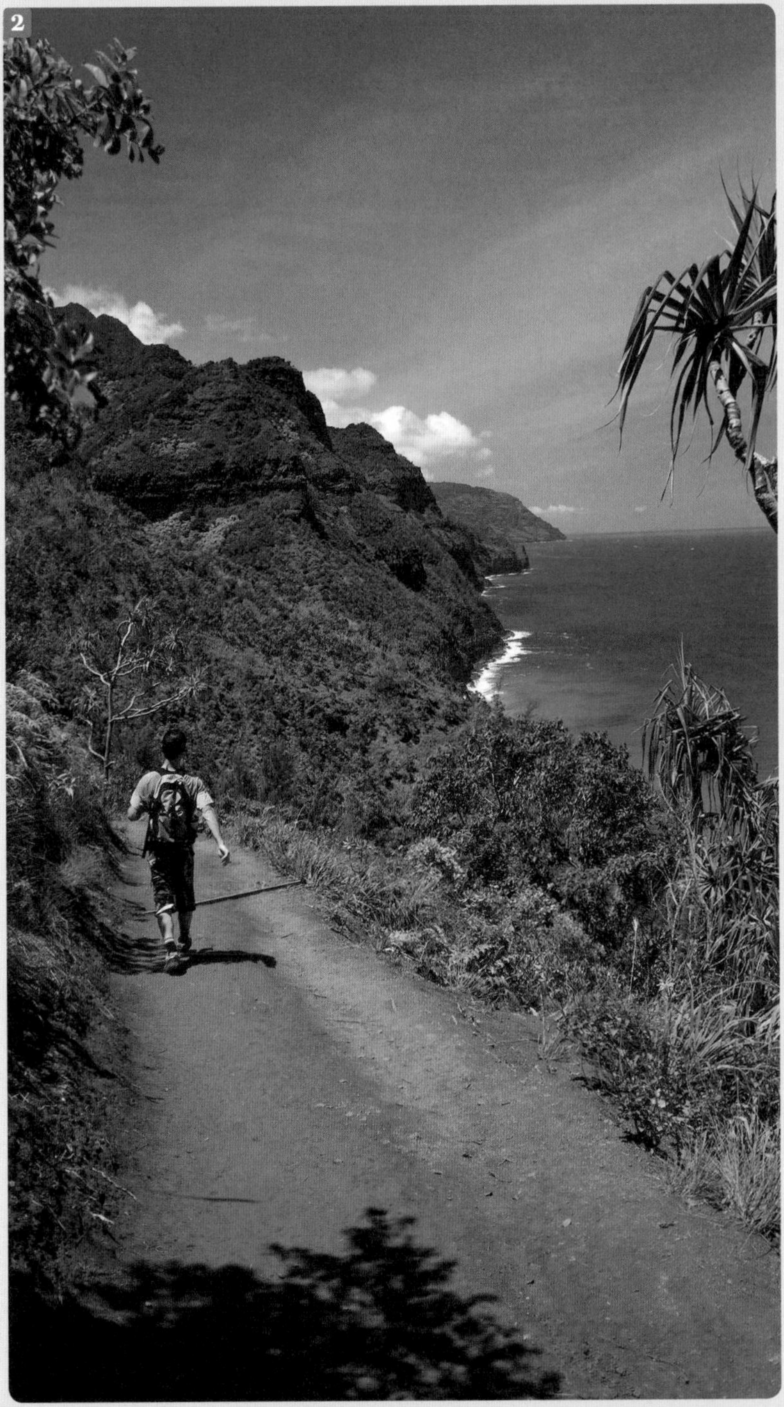

MARJORIE MCBRIDE/ALAMY STOCK PHOTO ©

Surfboard Swap Meet
SURFBOARDS

(Hanalei Center, 5-5161 Kuhio Hwy; ☺9am-1pm 1st Sat of month) Like the name says, this is an old-fashioned surfboard swap meet. It's set out on the lawn out front of the old school building-turned-shopping center. If you plan to stay for a while, it's a good place to pick up a used board, then unload it on your way out of town.

Chocolat Hanalei
CHOCOLATE

(www.chocolathanalei.com; Ching Young Village, 5-5190 Kuhio Hwy; ☺noon-6pm Tue-Sun) The aroma alone will draw you into this compact chocolatier filled with treats. The raw product is grown and made on Oahu, but it makes its own confections – like, say, surfboard-shaped caramels, dark chocolate turtles and macadamia nuts covered in white chocolate and cardamom.

Hanalei Paddler
CLOTHING

(☑808-826-8797; www.facebook.com/Hanalei Paddler; 5-5161 Kuhio Hwy; ☺9am-9pm) A nice blend of beach chic and vital beach and ocean gear like rash guards and paddles, flip-flops and Laird-brand SUPs, backpacks and sun hats, bikinis, T-shirts and sunglasses. It also deals in handbags and barefoot chic dresses perfect for a night out.

Pualani
CLOTHING

(☑808-826-1314; www.pualanihawaii.com; 5-5084 Kuhio Hwy) A bright and happy bikini shop where the name-brand gear is a cut above typical fare and the bikinis come mostly in bright, solid colors. It also offers throws, ball caps, beach bags, dresses and flip-flops.

Mālie
COSMETICS

(☑808-339-3056; www.malie.com/hanalei -boutique; 5-5084 Kuhio Hwy) The Hanalei depot of Kaua'i's long-running, internationally known organic body and beauty brand. Test the seductive body butter and salty scrubs, and sniff triple-milled soaps and spritz perfume, all made from therapeutic and organic natural ingredients.

Black Pearl
JEWELERY

(www.theblackpearl.com; 5-5016 Kuhio Hwy; ☺10am-7pm) A gallery with a blend of high-end jewelery and art. Tahitian pearls are the main product in the jewel case up front, but some of the original canvasses painted by local artists are also quite special.

Sand People
GIFTS & SOUVENIRS

(☑808-826-1008; Hanalei Center, 5-5161 Kuhio Hwy; ☺9:30am-8pm Mon-Sat, from 10am Sun) A bright and fun shop filled with reproduction signage, gift books, beauty products, dishware and a small, chic collection of women's wear from labels like Hard Tail, Johnny Was and Graham and Spencer.

I Heart Hanalei
CLOTHING

(☑808-826-5560; www.shopihearthanalei.com; 5-5106 Kuhio Hwy; ☺11am-9pm) A beachy clothing boutique with more stock than most. You can peruse racks of stylish bikinis, beach cover-ups, sun hats, shorts and yoga wear from labels like Aviator Nation, Project Social and Stone Cold. There's a small collection of men's denim and board shorts too.

Hanalei Center
MALL

(5-5161 Kuhio Hwy) An upscale shopping mall.

Backdoor
CLOTHING, OUTDOOR EQUIPMENT

(☑808-826-1900; www.hanaleisurf.com/back door; Ching Young Village, 5-5190 Kuhio Hwy; ☺8am-9pm) The coolest clothing shop in Ching Young Village offers board shorts, bikinis and rashies for all ages, sundresses, surf and skate boards, sunglasses and a nice stock of Vans too.

Crystals and Gems Gallery
NEW AGE

(☑808-826-9304; www.crystals-gems.com; 4489 Aku Rd; ☺9am-7pm) The whiff of Nag Champa, the jingle of cut-crystal wind chimes, the glint of blue agate pyramids, phallic wedges of smokey quartz, crystal skulls, earrings and bracelets, and some Buddha sculpture too. This is where you can find any manner of crystal and stone, to get that (consumerist) Zen flowing.

Ching Young Store
CLOTHING

(☑808-826-9000; www.hanaleisurf.com; Ching Young Village, 5-5190 Kuhio Hwy; ☺11am-6pm) A clearance space for Backdoor, Hanalei Surf and Hanalei Paddler set in attractive yet bare-bones environs and featuring 50% off bikinis and board shorts, sundresses and denim from last season. It also sells used SUP boards and wire-wrapped jewellery made by resident artists.

Hula Beach Boutique
CLOTHING

(☑808-826-4741; Hanalei Center, 5-5161 Kuhio Hwy; ☺10am-6pm; 🖰) The sarongs are lovely and there are dresses, clutches, handbags and aloha shirts for men too, but the kids stuff is the real draw. Think: cute beach outfits, toys, and aloha shirts for tots. Check the sale rack out front for deals.

Kokonut Kids CHILDREN'S CLOTHING
(☑808-826-0353; www.kokonutkidskauai.com; Ching Young Village, 5-5190 Kuhio Hwy; 🛗) A super-cute kids shop with rash guards, T-shirts, beach hats and aloha wear for groms, along with cuddly stuffed toys and cute horseshoe-shaped pillows for the flight home.

Bikini Hanalei CLOTHING
(☑808-826-7946; 5-5412 Kuhio Hwy; ☻10am-6pm) Associated with Pualani in the center of town, this small shop across from Hanalei school offers cute bikinis and hip beachwear for women.

Root CLOTHING
(☑808-826-2575; www.shoptheroot.net; 4489 Aku Rd; ☻10am-6pm Mon-Sat, from noon Sun) Among the more fashionable boutiques in town, it offers more than beachy threads, including dresses, denim, skirts, blouses and more.

Bikini Room CLOTHING
(☑808-826-9711; www.thebikiniroom.com; 4489 Aku Rd; ☻10am-6pm Mon-Sat, noon-5pm Sun) If you need a wrap, a lovely ball cap with paintings of mountains, flowers or waves, or a new bikini, there's plenty to sort through in this tiny shop with loads of stock.

**Hanalei
Surf Company** CLOTHING, OUTDOOR EQUIPMENT
(www.hanaleisurf.com; Hanalei Center, 5-5161 Kuhio Hwy; ☻8am-9pm) Surf is this outfit's MO. They have all the gear any surfer girl or beach boy might need for riding waves, including boards. Its Backdoor store is across the street.

Aloha From Hanalei GIFTS & SOUVENIRS
(☑808-826-8970; www.divine-planet.com; Ching Young Village, 5-5190 Kuhio Hwy; ☻10am-7pm Mon-Fri, to 6pm Sat & Sun) A kitsch depot of shirts and signage silk screened with such poetry as 'world's okayest surfer' or 'in dog beers I've only had one.' If that kind of thing appeals to you, this is where you can stock up. It also has ball caps, as well as creamy soaps and lotions made with local ingredients.

Next door is its attached gallery under the name Divine Planet. It has a decidedly New Age lean and features jewellery made from the local gem stone calcite.

Hula Moon GIFTS & SOUVENIRS
(☑808-826-9965; Ching Young Village, 5-5190 Kuhio Hwy; ☻10am-6:30pm) A kitschy gift shop with cool aloha coasters, nice coconut-shell and seashell jewelry, and some forgettable

mass-produced handicrafts. Worth a browse on a rainy day.

🛈 Information

Hanalei has no bank, but there are ATMs at the Hanalei Liquor Store and Big Save supermarket.

Hanalei Post Office (☑808-826-1034; www.usps.com; 5-5226 Kuhio Hwy; ☻10am-4pm Mon-Fri, to noon Sat) On the *makai* (seaward) side of the road, just west of Big Save supermarket.

🛈 Getting There & Away

There's one road into and out of Hanalei. During heavy rains (common in winter), the Hanalei Bridge occasionally closes due to flooding and those on either side are stuck until it reopens.

Parking in town can be a headache and absent-minded pedestrians even more so. Everything in Hanalei is walkable. Otherwise, do as the locals do and hop on a bicycle.

If you opted not to rent a car, the **North Shore Shuttle** (p144) links Hanalei to Ke'e with multiple stops in Waniha and Haena along the way.

🛈 Getting Around

Pedal 'n Paddle (☑808-826-9069; Ching Young Village, 5-5105 Kuhio Hwy; ☻9am-6pm) rents cruisers (per day/week $15/60) and hybrid road bikes ($20/80), all including helmets and locks.

Wainiha
☑808 / POP 300

Between Ha'ena and Hanalei rests a little neighborhood steeped in ancient history. The narrow, green recesses of Wainiha Valley were the last hideout of the *menehune,* the legendary 'little people' of the islands. Today the valley remains as it was in the old days: a holdout for Hawaiians, though some vacation rentals have popped up in the area. An unwelcoming vibe is not uncommon. When the locals stare you down, don't take it personally.

◎ Sights

Lumaha'i Beach BEACH
Countless Kaua'i locals consider this their favorite beach on an island blessed with dozens of beauties. It's very cinematic, with thick loamy sand backed by lush mountains and with lava rock outcrops on either end. It's where the 1958 movie *South Pacific* was shot when Mitzi Gaynor wanted to 'wash that man' right out of her hair.

The beach is just over a mile long from one lava rock tabletop to the other and though beautiful, is known on the island as one of the most dangerous. Too many visitors have drowned trying to swim at this beguiling spot, dubbed 'Luma-die' for its rough rip currents and powerful waves. The inlet lacks barrier reefs and breaks, so swimming here is risky, even if the turquoise shallows and deep-blue depths appear inviting. Instead, stay dry and take a stroll (which still requires being water savvy) or go for a run. This is the North Shore's best spot for beach runs.

There are two ways onto Lumaha'i Beach. The first and more scenic is a three-minute walk that begins at the parking area 0.75 miles past Mile 4 on the Kuhio Hwy. The trail slopes to the left at the end of the retaining wall. On the beach, the lava-rock ledges are popular for sunbathing and photo ops, but beware: bystanders have been washed away by high surf and rogue waves.

The other way to access Lumaha'i is along the road at sea level at the western end of the beach, just before crossing the Lumaha'i River Bridge. The beach at this end is lined with ironwood trees.

✖ Eating

★ **Sushigirl Kauai** SUSHI $
(☑ 808-827-8171; www.sushigirlkauai.fish; 5-6607b Kuhio Hwy; mains $12-15; ⊙ 11am-8pm Mon-Sat, noon-4pm Sun) A humble roadside stand that delivers generous and creative *maki* (hand) rolls, mixed *poke* bowls with ahi and *ono* drizzled with *ponzu* (Japanese citrus) sauce, and sushi burritos made with ahi, avocado, beans and organic local veggies. All of the fish served, except for the smoked salmon, is super fresh and locally sourced.

🛍 Shopping

Ohana Shop ART
(5-6607 Kuhio Hwy; ⊙ 11am-5pm) A small shop with spare yet well-curated stock, including elegant shell and Tahitian pearl jewellery, creative children's books, local honey, all-natural lotions, sarongs, beach towels and some fun T-shirts.

Wainiha General Store MARKET
(5-6607 Kuhio Hwy; ⊙ 10am-dusk) If you've left Hanalei and need a few items, don't panic. The 'Last Chance' store sells last-minute beach essentials, including snorkel gear, drinks and snacks. There's an ATM and it rents snorkel gear (per day $9) too.

ⓘ Getting There & Away

Wainiha is a mere blip along the Kuhio Hwy, separated from Hanalei by a series of one-lane bridges. You'll be best suited with a rental car, but **North Shore Shuttle** (p144) serves the area and connects with the **Kaua'i Bus** (p274) in Hanalei. The bike ride from Hanalei is gorgeous and not too hilly, though there are blind curves, so don't ride at night.

Ha'ena

☑ 808 / POP 430

Remote, resplendent and idyllic, this is where the ribbon road ends amid lava-rock pinnacles, lush wet forest and postcard-perfect beaches. In the wet season the cliffs are positively weeping with waterfalls. It's also the site of controversy, as many of the luxury homes on the point were built atop *'iwi kupuna* (ancient Hawaiian burial grounds). No Kaua'i adventure is complete without a drive to the end of road and at least a short hike along the roadless Na Pali Coast.

◉ Sights

★ **Limahuli Garden** GARDENS
(☑ 808-826-1053; http://ntbg.org/gardens/limahuli.php; 5-8291 Kuhio Hwy; self-guided adult/student/child under 18yr $20/10/free; guided tours adult/student & children over 10yr $40/20; ⊙ 9:30am-4pm Tue-Sat, guided tours 10am; 🅿) 🎫 As beautiful as it gets for living education, this garden offers a pleasant overview of endemic botany and ancient Hawai'i's *ahupua'a* (land division) system of management. Self-guided tours take about 1½ hours, allowing you to meditate on the scenery along a 0.75-mile loop trail; in-depth guided tours (minimum age 10 years, reservations required) last 2½ hours.

Volunteer service projects in native ecosystem restoration give ecotourists a glimpse into the entire 985-acre preserve. To get here, turn inland just before the stream that marks the boundary of Ha'ena State Park.

Ha'ena Beach Park BEACH
Not ideal for swimming in winter, because of the regular pounding shore break that creates a strong undertow; this beach is nevertheless good for taking in some sun. During the summer months, the sea is almost always smooth and safe. Ask lifeguards about conditions before going in, especially between October and May.

To the left is **Cannons**, an expert local surf break. Facilities include restrooms, outdoor showers, picnic tables and a pavilion. Overnight camping is allowed. Secure permits in advance.

Maniniholo Dry Cave   CAVE

Maniniholo Dry Cave is deep, broad and rather fun to explore, though the deeper you penetrate the lower the ceiling and the darker your surrounds. A constant seep of water from the cave walls keeps the dark interior dank. As you slowly step toward the rear wall, remember that you are standing below a massive monolith of Jurassic proportions.

You'll not only hear but feel the rumble of thunder and crash of the waves which reverberate all around. And if you believe in that sort of thing and are sensitive to it, you may even feel a palpable *mana* (spiritual essence), especially near the grouping of stones set up around what looks like a fire pit – perhaps a place of counsel or merely shelter in the days long gone. The cave is named after the head fisherman of the *menehune* (the 'little people') who, according to legend, built ponds and other structures here overnight. It sits directly across from Ha'ena Beach Park.

Makua (Tunnels) Beach   BEACH

One of the North Shore's almost-too-beautiful beaches, named for the underwater caverns and lava tubes in and among the near-shore reef. In summer, this is among the best snorkel spots on the island. It's also the North Shore's most popular dive site. In winter, however, the swell picks up and the surf can be heavy.

In the shoulder season, the snorkeling can still be decent, but always use caution and check with locals or lifeguards before heading into the water. Beware especially of a regular current flowing west toward the open ocean. If you can't score a parking spot at one of the two unmarked lots down short dirt roads, park at Ha'ena State Park and walk.

🏃 Activities

Hanalei Day Spa   SPA

(☑808-826-6621; www.hanaleidayspa.com; Hanalei Colony Resort, 5-7130 Kuhio Hwy; massage 50/80min $110/165; ⊙9am-6pm Tue-Sat) If you're tired or need to revitalize, this friendly though modest spa offers some of the island's more competitively priced massages (including Hawaiian *lomilomi*) and body treatments such as an Ayurvedic body wrap.

🍴 Eating

Mediterranean Gourmet   MEDITERRANEAN $$$

(☑808-826-9875; www.kauaimedgourmet.com; Hanalei Colony Resort, 5-7130 Kuhio Hwy; mains $13-29; ⊙noon-8:30pm) A taste of the Mediterranean literally on the Pacific (if the windows weren't there, you'd get salty ocean mist on your face), this fish out of water offers an eclectic range of Euro-inspired dishes such as

HANALEI & THE NORTH SHORE HA'ENA

BACKYARD GRAVEYARDS

Ancient burial sites lie underneath countless homes and hotels throughout Hawaii. Construction workers often dig up *iwi* (bones) and *moepu* (funeral objects), while locals swear by eerie stories of equipment malfunctioning until bones are properly reinterred and prayers given.

In 1990 Congress enacted the Native American Graves Protection and Repatriation Act (www.hawaii.gov/dlnr/hpd/hpburials.htm), which established burial councils on each island to oversee the treatment of remains and preservation of burial sites. Desecration of *iwi* is illegal, and a major affront to Native Hawaiians.

One of Kaua'i's most recent cases involved Ha'ena's **Naue Point**, the site of some 30 confirmed *iwi*. Starting in 2002, and lasting close to nine years, the case went through numerous phases of court hearings, public demonstrations and burial-treatment proposals and ended with the state allowing the landowner to build.

What happens next? Could a landowner lose the right to build? Probably not. Most likely, the state will approve a burial-treatment proposal to remove the *iwi* and reinter them off-site (an outcome that Hawaiians find woefully inadequate).

As well, many hotels and condos were built on land with *iwi* now sitting in storage or still underground. And what happens to those restless spirits? Believe it or not, Po'ipu's Grand Hyatt Resort has a director of Hawaiian and community affairs who does blessings somewhere on resort grounds at least once a month to quell any 'spiritual disturbance.'

rosemary rack of lamb and pistachio-crusted ahi. Food quality and service can be inconsistent, but the menu is unique to the island.

Lunch is served from noon to 3pm. Happy hour blooms in the bar from 3pm to 6pm and features select appetizers. Dinner seating begins at 5pm. It has live music on Saturday and Sunday evenings.

Shopping

Na Pali Art Gallery
ARTS & CRAFTS

(📞808-826-1844; www.napaligallery.com; Hanalei Colony Resort, 5-7130 Kuhio Hwy; ⊘7am-5pm; 📶) Peruse a quality array of local artists' paintings, woodwork, sculptures, ceramics, jewelery and collectibles made from Larimar – a blue volcanic glass sourced from the Dominican Republic. Not everyone loves the coffee served here, but it's the only caffeine in the immediate area.

Getting There & Away

Ha'ena is served by the Kuhio Hwy, with several one-lane bridges between here and Hanalei. If a bridge floods during a storm, you'll be cut off. **North Shore Shuttle** (p144) serves the area and connects with the **Kaua'i Bus** (p274) in Hanalei; still, you'll need your own wheels if you base here.

Ha'ena State Park

Pass the botanical garden, cross a bridge over a gushing river and enter Ha'ena State Park. Sculpted from the narrow lava-rich coastline, it burns with allure, mystique and beauty. Pele (the Hawaiian goddess of fire) is said to have overlooked the area as a home because of the water percolating through its wet and dry caves. Today this 230-acre park remains home to the 1280ft cliff commonly known in the tourism industry as 'Bali Hai,' its name in the film *South Pacific*. Its real name is Makana ('Gift'). Apt, for sure.

Sights

★Ke'e Beach
BEACH

Memorable North Shore sunsets happen at this spiritual spot, where ancient Hawaiians came to practice hula. In summer, the beach offers a refreshing dip to hikers of the nearby Kalalau Trail. But beware that Ke'e Beach may appear calm when it is, in fact, otherwise. Vicious currents have sucked some through a keyhole in the reef out into the open sea.

Never leave small children alone near the waterline. Facilities include outdoor showers and restrooms. Car break-ins are common in the parking lot, so don't leave any valuables behind. If you come for the sunset, and you should, bring mosquito repellent.

Kaulu Paoa Heiau
TEMPLE

🖋 The roaring surf was a teacher to those who first practiced the spiritual art of hula, chanting and testing their skills against nature's decibel levels. Ke'e Beach is the oceanfront site of a cherished heiau (ancient stone temple) dedicated to Laka, the goddess of hula. It's also where the volcano goddess Pele fell in love with Lohiau.

Lei and other sacred offerings found on the ground should be left as is. Enter the

---

DRIVING WITH ALOHA

Lauded as one of the most scenic and breathtaking drives on the island, the drive to the 'end of the road' is impossibly beautiful. However, though you might want to pull over for that must-have photograph, please do so safely as accidents occur when drivers stop suddenly, or in a place with no shoulder, or on a blind curve, to snap a photo. If you're heading to the road's end (Ke'e Beach), take it slowly and enjoy the crossing of each of the seven one-lane bridges, the first of which is in Hanalei.

When crossing these bridges, do as the locals do:

➡ When the bridge is empty and you reach it first, you can go.

➡ If there's a stream of five or fewer cars already crossing as you approach, simply follow them. If you're the sixth car and others are waiting to cross from the other side, yield.

➡ When you see cars approaching from the opposite direction, yield to the entire queue of approaching cars for at least five cars, if not all.

➡ Give the *shaka* sign ('hang loose' hand gesture, with index, middle and ring fingers downturned) as thanks to any drivers who have yielded from the opposite direction.

heiau through its entryway; don't be disrespectful by crossing over the temple walls.

Wet Caves   CAVE

Two wet caves lie within the boundaries of Ha'ena State Park. Formed by the constant pounding of waves many years ago, the massive cavern of **Waikapala'e Wet Cave** is as enchanting as it is spooky. It's on the opposite side and a short walk from the visitor-overflow parking area. **Waikanaloa Wet Cave** is further down on the south side of the highway.

Though some enter the water to experience the sunlight's blue reflection in Waikapala'e's deeper chamber, note the water may be contaminated with leptospira bacteria; the rocks are slippery; and there's nothing to hold onto once you're in the water. But it does make one hell of an Instagram glamour shot. Make sure you have someone watching out for you and shower immediately after.

❶ Getting There & Away

Almost everyone makes day trips here with their own wheels, but Ke'e Beach is served by the **North Shore Shuttle** (p144) every 1¼ hours. First drop-off 7:35am, last pickup 8:05pm.

Na Pali Coast Wilderness State Park

Roadless, pristine and hauntingly beautiful, this 16-mile-long stretch of stark cliffs, white-sand beaches, turquoise coves and gushing waterfalls links the island's northern and western shores. This **state park** (www.hawaiistateparks.org; end of Hwy 560) FREE is arguably Kaua'i's most magnificent natural sight. While fit trekkers tackle the exposed, undulating, slippery trail from Ha'ena to Kalalau Valley, it's also possible to experience the coastline by kayak, raft or catamaran. Kalalau, Honopu, Awa'awapuhi,

Nu'alolo and Miloli'i are the five major valleys along the coast, each seemingly more stunning than the last.

🏃 Activities

Ke'e Beach to Hanakapi'ai Beach   HIKING

Young buck surfers do love to paddle out at Hanakapi'ai, often hiking barefoot with boards under their arm. It shouldn't take you more a few hours to complete this 4-mile (round-trip) trek. Locals suggest that you should never turn your back on the ocean here, especially near the river mouth.

Kaua'i Nature Tours   TOURS

(☑808-742-8305, 888-233-8365; www.kauai naturetours.com; 10hr tours adult/child 7-12yr $150/115; ⊙by reservation only) Geologist Chuck Blay's company guides an excellent 8-mile (round-trip) hike to Hanakapi'ai Falls. All-day tours depart by shuttle van from Po'ipu Beach Park on the South Shore.

❶ Information

Hawaii State Parks (http://hawaiistateparks. org/camping) To secure a legal campsite you must apply at least six months in advance.

❶ Getting There & Away

The parking lot nearest the Kalalau trailhead at Ke'e Beach is quite large, but fills quickly. By midmorning and during the jam-packed summer months, you may find yourself out of luck. Break-ins are rampant; some people advise leaving your car empty and unlocked to prevent damage such as window smashing. Overnight hikers should consider parking at Ha'ena Beach Park (free, but not patrolled) or possibly at private **YMCA Camp Naue** (☑808-826-6419; campnaue@yahoo.com; Kuhio Hwy; tent sites $15) ($5 per night) instead. You can also hop the **North Shore Shuttle** (p144) to Ke'e Beach from Hanalei.

Po'ipu & the South Shore

📞 808

Best Places to Eat

➡ Beach House (p199)

➡ Eating House 1849 (p199)

➡ Makai Sushi (p197)

➡ Koloa Fish Market (p185)

Best Shopping

➡ Art House (p188)

➡ Malie Organics (p202)

➡ Shops at Kukui'ula (p202)

Why Go?

Po'ipu is the nexus of South Shore tourism...and with good reason. This is one of the sunniest spots on the island – with notably less rain (and less green) than other spots to the north. There are amazing sun-kissed brown-baby beaches, plenty of top-end resorts and vacation rental condos, plus some of Kaua'i's best restaurants.

While most vacations here center on the beaches and waterborne activities such as surfing, diving, snorkeling, paddle boarding or just beach bumming, the South Shore also has two world-renowned botanical gardens that showcase beautiful collections of endemic species. The undeveloped Maha'ulepu Coast has lithified sand-dune cliffs and pounding surf that make for an unforgettable walk. And in between, you have the lasting remnants of the sugar-plantation area, with friendly arts galleries, intimate restaurants and interesting historic perspectives in the cozy centers of Koloa and Kalaheo.

When to Go

➡ The weather is generally sunnier here than in other parts of the island, making it a good option for the rainy season months of October to March.

➡ You'll save on hotel costs outside the main seasons and holidays in February to May, or August to October.

➡ Surfing is best here during the summer months (June to August).

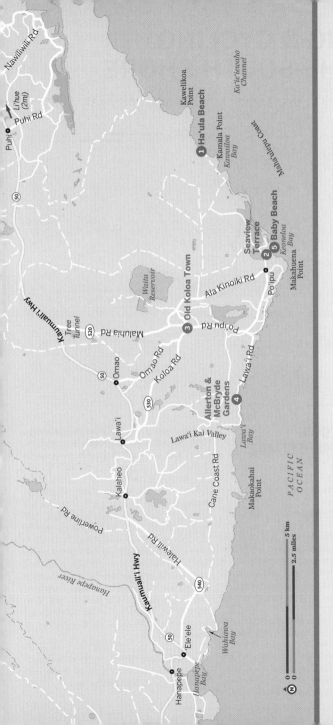

Po'ipu & the South Shore Highlights

1 **Ha'ula Beach** (p193) Indulging your inner Robinson Crusoe at Ha'ula Beach, a wild and secluded cove.

2 **Seaview Terrace** (p202) Marveling at the views from the bar at the Grand Hyatt Kauai Resort, which evokes grandeur among all the cookie-cutter condos of Po'ipu.

3 **Old Koloa Town** (p184) Stepping back in time in Hawaii's first sugar plantation. Established in the 1830s, it forever changed the way of life across the Hawaiian Islands.

4 **Allerton & McBryde Gardens** (p189) Tramping through paradise lost at the National Tropical Botanical Garden where you'll quickly forget Shangri-La.

5 **Baby Beach** (p192) Snorkeling just off Baby Beach – the South Shore offers some of the island's best snorkeling, and you can reach several hot spots right from shore.

HIKING & CYCLING ON THE SOUTH SHORE

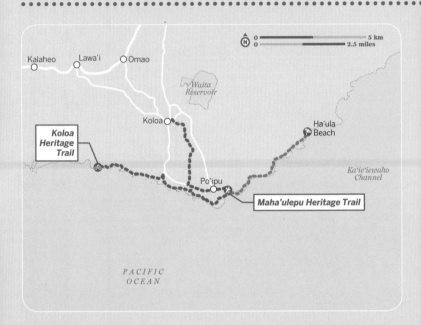

WALKING TOUR: MAHAʻULEPU HERITAGE TRAIL

START SEAVIEW TERRACE
END HAʻULA BEACH
LENGTH THREE TO FIVE HOURS; 4 MILES

One of the best coastal hikes on Kauaʻi, this trail takes you along the coast, past lithified sand dunes and mad-crashing waves to a series of forgotten beaches. You could easily spend all day playing here, or just do a morning walk to take in the glory of the South Coast.

Begin with a light breakfast of croissants and espresso at the Grand Hyatt's **Seaview Terrace** (p202) – you will love the view. Pop down through the lobby and pools to **Shipwreck Beach** (p192). Head eastward, gaining a trail that takes you up and onward toward the edge of **Makawehi Point** (p189).

Now you are on the **Mahaʻulepu Heritage Trail** (Map p186; www.hikemahaulepu.org). Continue past ironwood and kiawe trees on the high-looming cliffs over a geologic formation known as the Paa Dunes, formed some 8000 years ago. As you climb toward the **Poʻipu Bay Golf Course** (p193) you will see limestone and sandstone pinnacles, and find some lava rock tide pools at an ancient site known as Heiau Hoouluia, where offerings were made for good fishing in ancient times. From here, pass through a marked trail on the golf course for a way – keep an eye out for nene birds and flying golf balls – before regaining the trail near Panahoa Point, a hard-rock collection of dunes formed over 300,000 years. You might spot local fishers here.

Rounding the corner, you come to **Makauwahi Cave** (p193), which offers guided tours Wednesday, Thursday, Friday and Saturday, and **Mahaʻulepu Beach** (p193),

The trekking routes that line the South Shore of Kaua'i include primal dramatic coastal vistas that are pretty much guaranteed to elicit a sigh, or jaw drop, or both.

with pretty good snorkeling. You can stay here and picnic.

November through March, keep your eyes on the horizon to spot spouting humpback whales as well as green sea turtles; on land you might see Hawaiian Monk Seals beached here after a good meal.

The trail continues up from here on the cliffs to **Kawailoa Bay** (p193), which houses another virgin beach. Heading up to the cliffs again, past spouting blowholes, you'll arrive at a **Labyrinth** (p191). Take the time to walk the entire track, pondering the vastness of this space, before descending again to the lost beach at **Ha'ula** (p193).

CYCLING TOUR: KOLOA HERITAGE TRAIL

START SPOUTING HORN PARK
END KOLOA
LENGTH FIVE TO SEVEN HOURS; 10 MILES

This unexpected trail takes you past some of the South Coast's most notable historic sites. You can do it by bicycle or foot. Begin at **Spouting Horn Park** (p191), where you can literally stand mesmerized for hours waiting for the biggest spout ever. From there, head along Lawa'i Rd to **Prince Kuhio Park** (p192) and up to the roundabout. Head back down toward the water from the roundabout, going past **Koloa Landing** (p195). Once Kaua'i's largest seaport, this is now a good spot for snorkeling.

Follow the coast past the Sheraton, to the awesome gardens found in the Kiahuna Plantation complex known as the **Moir Pa'u a Laka** (p191). Back on the beach, you'll pass the Kihahouna Heiau, where an ancient temple once stood. You can still see the hala lihilihi'ula trees that marked the perimeter.

Stick to the coast to get to **Po'ipu Beach Park** (p192), a great spot to stop for a swim. From here, get on Ho'owili Rd to Pe'e Rd, dropping down on a small trail if on foot, to **Shipwreck Beach** (p192).

Stop for lunch at the **Grand Hyatt** (Map p190; 1571 Po'ipu Rd) if you need a break, then head back to Po'ipu Rd inland and go west. Head inland on Hapa Rd. With its lava-rock walls, this route has been used since 1200 AD and once had a train line running parallel.

Things get a little more lush as you get closer to the great arts village of Old Koloa Town (p184). Allow a couple of hours to visit the sights, crafts markets and art galleries in town. Start with a tour of the Koloa Jodo Mission, a Buddhist temple that's still used today. From there, head west into the downtown historic area, where you can check out the Sugar Monument, historic buildings and old churches. The Koloa History Center has good exhibits on local history. Finish with a little treat at Koloa Mill Ice Cream and Coffee.

ROAD TRIP > SOUTH SHORE DRIVING TOUR

❶ Living Foods Gourmet Market & Café, Po'ipu

This fun drive takes you to the best the South Shore has to offer. Start with breakfast and maybe picnic-lunch shopping at **Living Foods Gourmet Market & Café** (p198) in Po'ipu.

The Drive > Head westward on the coast, make a quick stop at Spouting Horn Park, then continue up the road to the Allerton and McBryde Gardens.

❷ Allerton & McBryde Gardens

Allerton Garden (p189) has a mandatory guided tour that lasts around 2½ hours. Potter around here, or **McBryde Garden** (Map p186;

☎ 808-742-2623; www.ntbg.org; 4425 Lawa'i Rd; self-guided tours adult/child 6-12yr $30/15; ⏱ visitor center 8:30am-5pm, tours by reservation only; ♿) ✿, where you can self-guide in around 1½ hours – reserve in advance.

The Drive > Drive eastwards back toward Po'ipu, making your way to Po'ipu Beach Park.

❸ Po'ipu Beach Park

Take in the beach scenes at the popular **Po'ipu Beach Park** (p192), where you can play in the waves.

The Drive > Head eastward to Maha'ulepu Beach along Weliweli Rd, which is a rough dirt road.

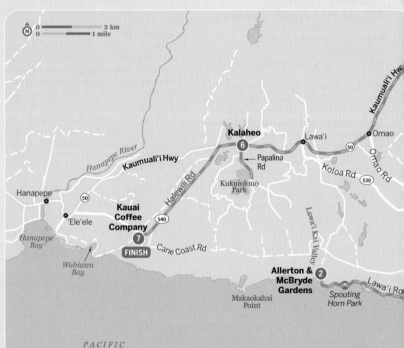

Start Living Foods Gourmet Market & Café, Po'ipu

End Kauai Coffee Company

Length five to seven hours; 18.7 miles

❹ Maha'ulepu Beach

For a wilder beach experience, try the remote **Maha'ulepu Beach** (p193) situated on the windswept Maha'ulepu Coast. The secluded patch of reef offshore boasts excellent snorkeling and even in the summer, there aren't too many people around.

The Drive > Head back the way you came toward Po'ipu then drive north along Ala Kinoiki Rd, driving around three miles to Old Koloa Town.

❺ Old Koloa Town

Koloa has a bunch of spots worth seeing, including an old mill, churches, historic buildings, a Buddhist temple and lots of cool art galleries. If you haven't already organised lunch, grab it to go from the **Koloa Fish Market** (p185).

The Drive > Your GPS will direct you back through town, but head up Maluhia Rd toward Kaumuali'i Hwy instead so you can drive through the Tree Tunnel. Head west on Kaumuali'i Hwy to Kalaheo.

❻ Kalaheo

If you need a break, stop in locally loved **Kalaheo Café & Coffee Co** (p205). Up the road is the main town intersection; head toward the sea from here on Papalina Rd, which takes you to the supercool **Kukuiolono Park** (p204). The park has one of the cheapest golf courses this side of San Francisco, plus a very interesting Japanese Garden that's worth touring. Consider breaking out your lunch here because the sweeping vistas merit just a little more time to really appreciate them.

The Drive > Make your way back into Kalaheo then take Halewili Rd about six miles down to the Kauai Coffee Company.

❼ Kauai Coffee Company

The last tour leaves at 4pm to visit the grounds of the **Kauai Coffee Company** (p212), where you can learn more about coffee cultivation and the roasting process and sample a truly out-of-this-world chocolate and macadamia-nut brew.

❶ Getting There & Away

Most people get here by rental car. You can also get here with **Kaua'i Bus** (p274) or **South Shore Cab** (p279).

❶ Getting Around

You can easily get around the Po'ipu area by foot. To get further afield and between towns, you'll want a rental car. Some roads here are good for cycling.

Koloa

📋 808 / POP 2144

The district of Koloa revolves around a historic sugar-plantation town of quaint painted cottages, now filled with tourist shops, restaurants and galleries. Known today as **Old Koloa Town**, it was founded in 1835 by New England missionaries turned sugarcane entrepreneurs.

Throughout Old Koloa Town, you will find historic placards that tell the story of the town and the rise of sugar. You can dive even more in depth with a visit to the Koloa History Center, the Sugar Monument, the church and the Jodo Mission.

Coming from Lihu'e, take Maluhia Rd (Hwy 520), which leads through the enchanting Tree Tunnel (p185), a mile-long canopy of towering eucalyptus trees. Pineapple baron Walter McBryde planted them as a community project in 1911, using leftover trees from his estate.

History

When William Hooper, an enterprising 24-year-old Bostonian, arrived on Kaua'i in 1835, he took advantage of two historical circumstances: Polynesians' introduction of sugarcane to the islands and Chinese immigrants' knowledge of refinery. With financial backing from Honolulu business people, he leased land in Koloa from the king and paid a stipend to release commoners from their traditional work obligations. He then hired the Hawaiians as wage laborers and Koloa became Hawaii's first plantation town. Visitation led to the establishment of the first hotel in Kaua'i, the Koloa Hotel, which you can still see today. The town withered following the decline of Big Sugar, but like the rest of Kaua'i has made a successful transition to tourism, while retaining its historic facade.

◉ Sights

Koloa History Center　　　　　MUSEUM

(Map p188; www.oldkoloa.com; Koloa Rd; ⊙9am-9pm) FREE This tiny open-air museum traces the town's history through old photos and historic artifacts such as old barber chairs and kerosene dispensers, plows, yolks, saws and sewing machines. In effect, the entire town is part of this museum, as many buildings have placards describing their history.

Koloa Jodo Mission　　　　　TEMPLE

(Map p188; 📞808-742-6735; www.koloajodo.com; 3480 Waikomo Rd; ⊙ services usually 10:30am Sun) Serving the local Japanese community for more than a century, this sect of Buddhism practices a form of chanting meditation. The temple on the left is the original, which dates to 1910, while the larger temple on the right is used for a weekly service followed by a Dharma talk – everyone is welcome. For a guided tour, call ahead. Check the website for the dates of summer Obon festivities, which feature Japanese drumming, folk dancing and more.

Sugar Monument (Old Mill)　　HISTORIC SITE

(Map p188; Koloa Rd) The sugar industry, once Hawaii's largest, began here in 1835. This memorial stands on the site of the first mill. There's little left besides a foundation, an old stone chimney and a bronze sculpture depicting the ethnically diverse laborers of Hawaii's plantation era.

St Raphael's Catholic Church　　CHURCH

(Map p190; 📞808-742-1955; www.st-raphael-kauai.org; 3011 Hapa Rd) Kaua'i's oldest Catholic church is the burial site of some of Hawaii's first Portuguese immigrants. The original 1854 church was made of lava rock and coral mortar with walls 3ft thick – a type of construction visible in the ruins of the adjacent rectory. When the church was enlarged in 1936 it was plastered over, giving it a more typical, whitewashed appearance. Church service hours vary, but you can poke around the old cemetery during daylight.

🏃 Activities

★**Fathom Five Ocean Quest Divers**　DIVING

(Map p188; 📞808-742-6991; http://fathomfive.com; 3450 Po'ipu Rd; dives $95-240) Considered Kaua'i's best dive outfit, Fathom Five offers a full range of options, from Ni'ihau boat dives to certification courses and enticing night dives. Newbies can expect reassuring hand-holding during introductory shore dives. Groups max out at six people, and mixing skill levels is avoided. Scuba and snorkel gear are rented at the full-service shop. Book well in advance.

Boss Frog's Dive, Surf & Bike WATER SPORTS
(Map p188; ☑ 888-700-3764, 808-742-2025; www.bossfrog.com; 3414 Po'ipu Rd; ⊗ 8am-5pm) This outfit rents well-used snorkel gear pretty darn cheaply. You can even return snorkel gear to either its Maui or Big Island shop. Rental bodyboards, surfboards, underwater cameras, beach chairs and umbrellas are also available (but no bikes).

Snorkel Bob's WATER SPORTS
(Map p186; ☑ 808-742-2206; www.snorkelbob.com; 3236 Po'ipu Rd; ⊗ 8am-5pm) The king of snorkel gear rents and sells enough styles and sizes to assure a good fit. Wetsuits, flotation devices and bodyboards are all rented here. You can return snorkel gear to any location on Kaua'i, O'ahu, Maui or the Big Island.

👉 Tours

Koloa Zipline & Kaua'i ATV ADVENTURE
(Map p188; ☑ 808-742-2724; www.koloazipline.com; 3477a Weliweli Rd; zipline $144-165, ATV $252-314; ⊗ tours daily, by reservation only) Take the plunge and zip upside down while enjoying superlative views from the longest (measured in feet, not minutes) zipline tour on the island, and the only one to allow tandem zipping and superman flights. The eight lines take you zooming around the hills by Waita Reservoir. Book at least two weeks ahead, or call the day before for last-minute openings. Minimum age is seven years; maximum weight is 270lbs. The ATV tours take you to lost waterfalls. You can even hire a boat to take you bass fishing on the lake.

Kauai Z Tourz BOATING
(Map p188; ☑ 808-742-7422; http://kauaiztours.com; 3417e Po'ipu Rd; tours adult/child 5-12yr from $80/75) The 'z' is for Zodiac boat, which whisks you off on a snorkeling tour of the South Shore. Options include reefs off Spouting Horn, Prince Kuhio Park and Allerton Garden. You may wish to avoid sites you can reach from the shore yourself. Winter boat trips go out dolphin- and whale-watching (no snorkeling).

DON'T MISS

TREE TUNNEL

If driving from Lihu'e, take Maluhia Rd (Hwy 520) to navigate under the fairytale **Tree Tunnel (Map p186)**, a mile-long canopy of towering swamp mahogany trees (a type of eucalyptus). Pineapple baron Walter McBryde planted the trees as a community project in 1911, when he had leftover trees after landscaping his estate at Kukuiolono.

Koloa Bass Fishing FISHING
(Map p186; ☑ 808-742-2734; www.koloabassfishing.com; Waita Reservoir; per person $150; ⊙) Board a flat-bottomed boat and cruise the Waita Reservoir in search of large mouth bass, tilapia, peacock bass and more.

🎭 Festivals & Events

★ **Koloa Plantation
Days Celebration** CULTURAL, MUSIC
(☑ 808-652-3217; www.koloaplantationdays.com; ⊗ Jul; ⊙) In mid- to late July, the South Shore's biggest annual celebration spans nine days of family-friendly fun with a gamut of attractions (many free), including a parade, *paniolo* (Hawaiian cowboy) rodeo, traditional Hawaiian games, Polynesian dancing, a craft fair, film nights, live music, guided walks and hikes, a beach party and plenty of 'talk story' about the old days.

🍴 Eating

All the eats are found in the town center. There are a couple of really good food trucks that come here often.

★ **Koloa Fish Market** SEAFOOD $
(Map p188; ☑ 808-742-6199; 5482 Koloa Rd; $6-8; ⊗ 10am-6pm Mon-Fri, to 5pm Sat) Line up with those in the know at this hole-in-the-wall. It serves outstanding *poke* in all kinds of flavors (spicy kimchi is the hands-down winner), Japanese-style *bentō* (boxed meals), sushi rolls, seaweed salads and both Hawaiian and local plate lunches grilled to order. Thick-sliced, perfectly seared ahi and rich slabs of homemade *haupia* (coconut) or sweet-potato pie are quite addictive.

Garden Island Grille AMERICAN $
(Map p188; www.gardenislandgrille.com; 5404 Koloa Rd; $10-18; ⊗ 11am-9pm; ⊙⊙) The superfriendly service here brings you closer to the spirit of the island. Food tends toward pub

South Shore

Li'hue (2mi)

Puhi Rd

Kawelikoa Point

Ha'ula Beach

Kamala Point

11 1

6 5 4 12
13 2 Kawailoa Bay

Maha'ulepu
Heritage Trail

9

Maha'ulepu Beach

Maha'ulepu Coast

Ka'ie'iewaho Channel

Kaumali'i Hwy

Waita Reservoir

11

See Koloa
Map (p188)

17

Koloa

14

Po'ipu Bay
Golf Course

Po'ipu

Keoneloa Bay

Makahuena Point

50

520

8

Maluhia Rd

Ala Kinoiki Rd
(Po'ipu-Koloa Bypass)

Kiahuna
Golf Club

Po'ipu Rd

Lawa'i Rd

See Po'ipu Map (p190)

50

Omao

Omao Rd

Koloa Rd

530

Upa Rd

Lawa'i

Lawa'i Kai Valley

5

3

7

15

Lawa'i Bay

Kalaheo

Kukuiolono
Park Golf Course

See Kalaheo Map (p204)

Cane Coast Rd

Powerline Rd

Halewili Rd

540

Hanapepe River

Hanapepe (1mi)

Wahiawa Bay

16 10

Makaokahai Point

PACIFIC
OCEAN

50

South Shore

favorites, with some uniquely Hawaiian ingredients thrown in for good measure. The open garden dining area looks on to the stage, where live music kicks off nightly – shocka!

Koloa Farmers Market   MARKET $

(Map p186; www.kauaigrown.org/koloa-farmers-market; Knudsen Park, Maluhia Rd; ⊙noon-2pm Mon; 🅿) 🍲 Vendors sell mostly flowers and produce, including exotic fruit – try drinking the milk from a whole coconut. Bring small bills and change, and show up on time, as competition is fierce once the whistle blows.

La Spezia   ITALIAN $$

(Map p188; ☎808-742-8824; www.laspeziakauai. com; 5492 Koloa Rd; mains breakfast $8-14, dinner $14-22; ⊙7:30-11am Mon, Tue & Thu-Sat, 8:30-11am Wed, 8am-1pm Sun, 5:30-10pm daily) A step up in sophistication from everywhere else in town, this Italian *ristorante* with polished wooden floors and a wine bar crafts flatbreads, crunchy crostini and housemade sausage and pasta. Surprisingly, it doubles as a creative breakfast spot – turn up for stuffed French toast and Bloody Marys at Sunday brunch.

Pizzetta   ITALIAN, AMERICAN $$

(Map p188; ☎808-742-8881; www.pizzettakauai. com; 5408 Koloa Rd; mains $11-20, pizzas $17-25; ⊙11am-9pm) More than the pasta bowls it's the baked pizzas, with toppings such as *kalua* pig, Hawaiian BBQ chicken or spinach with goat's cheese, that are the draw at this casual spot. Nab a patio table out back.

Food Trucks   STREET FOOD $

(Map p188; ☎808-634-4016; www.chalupas kauai.com; 3477 Weliweli Rd; items $3-10, meals $10-13; ⊙10am-7pm Mon-Fri, 11am-4pm Sat & Sun) Several food trucks work the area around Koloa. One of the best is Chalupa's. Hailing from Veracruz, this Mexican chef and his food truck are worth seeking out behind the shops. Fish tacos and shrimp (garlic, Cajun or spicy *diabla*) plates are what everyone's chowing down on at the picnic tables. BYOB.

Yanagi Sushi   FUSION $

(Map p188; 5371 Koloa Rd; mains $12-15; ⊙11am-3pm Mon-Thu) Look for the 'Dragon Wagon' parked at the old mill site, across the street from the main shopping strip. The enthusiastic, superfriendly Kaua'i-born sushi guru is creative and generous in his plating of fusion rolls. Show up too late and you might find everyone has gone surfing, brah.

Koloa Mill Ice Cream & Coffee   CAFE $

(Map p188; ☎808-742-6544; 5424 Koloa Rd; items from $3; ⊙7am-9pm) Homemade cotton candy, Kaua'i coffee and nothing but the best Maui-made Roselani Tropics ice cream are always served with a smile. If you're indecisive, start with the Kona coffee, macadamia nut or 'Pauwela Sunrise' containing pineapple chunks.

Sueoka Snack Shop   AMERICAN $

(Map p188; ☎808-742-1112; www.sueokastore. com; 5392 Koloa Rd; items $2-5, meals around $7; ⊙9am-5pm or 6pm Tue-Sun) Next door to Sueoka's grocery store, this little yellow takeout window is the smart place to order that picnic lunch, be it teriyaki burgers, fish and chips or mixed plates. For better or worse, all the food tastes home-cooked. It's as inexpensive a meal as you'll find anywhere on Kaua'i. Cash only.

Big Save   SUPERMARKET $

(Map p188; ☎808-742-1614; www.timessuper markets.com; 5516 Koloa Rd; ⊙6am-11pm) Fill up the kitchen of your vacation rental at this local chain supermarket; this is one of its best branches and it stocks some locally

Koloa

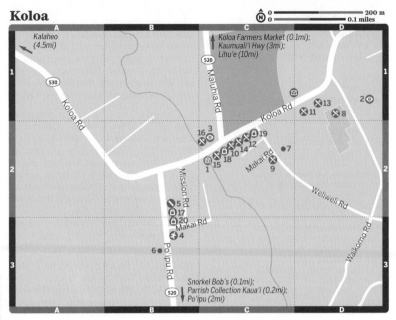

Kalaheo
(4.5mi)

Koloa Farmers Market (0.1mi);
Kaumuali'i Hwy (3mi);
Lihu'e (10mi)

Koloa Rd

Maluhia Rd

Mission Rd

Makai Rd

Weliweli Rd

Waikomo Rd

Po'ipu Rd

Snorkel Bob's (0.1mi);
Parrish Collection Kaua'i (0.2mi);
Po'ipu (2mi)

grown produce. Pick up the value-priced ahi *poke* (cubed raw fish mixed with *shōyu,* sesame oil, salt, chili pepper, *'inamona* or other condiments).

Sueoka Store SUPERMARKET $
(Map p188; ☎808-742-1611; www.sueokastore. com; 5392 Koloa Rd; ☺6:30am-8:30pm Mon-Sat, from 7:30am Sun) On the town's main drag, this small local grocery store holds its own by stocking the basics, plus prepackaged Japanese snacks and Kaua'i-made Taro Ko (p219) chips.

🛍 Shopping

Art House ARTS & CRAFTS
(Map p188; ☎808-742-1400; www.arthouse hawaii.com; 3440 Po'ipu Rd; ☺11am-6pm) Local artists show their plein-air paintings, mixed media and groovy handicrafts such as sweet silver jewelry and art boxes at this brightly lit gallery. Owner Julie Berg's acrylic images shine with infused and energetic color palettes and creative subjects inspired by her travels. Her Lonely Planet guidebook collection is truly epic.

Christian Riso Fine Art
ART

(Map p188; 5400 Koloa Rd; ◷9am-8:30pm) This cute gallery has a fine collection of original oils and plenty of old maps that make for curious and fun souvenirs.

Island Soap & Candle Works
GIFTS & SOUVENIRS

(Map p188; ☑808-742-1945, 888-528-7627; www. kauaisoap.com; 5428 Koloa Rd; ◷9am-9pm) ✎ The aromas wafting out of this shop are enough to turn your head. Wander in and sample the all-natural Hawaii botanical bath and body products, including lip balms, soaps, lotions and tropically scented candles. Some of the products are made on-site at the back of the store, which was established in 1984.

Pohaku T's
CLOTHING

(Map p188; ☑808-742-7500; www.pohaku.com; 3430 Po'ipu Rd; ◷10am-6pm Mon-Sat, to 5pm Sun) Spot the Kaua'i-made clothing hanging out on the lanai (when it's not raining), including unique aloha shirts, and a grab bag of souvenirs indoors. Stonewashed (*pohaku* means stone in Hawaiian) T-shirt designs are printed with Hawaiian themes such as petroglyphs, Polynesian carvings and navigational maps.

ℹ Information

Koloa Post Office (Map p188; ☑808-742-1319; www.usps.com; 5485 Koloa Rd; ◷9am-4pm Mon-Fri, to 11am Sat) Serves both Koloa and Po'ipu.

First Hawaiian Bank (☑808-742-1642; www. fhb.com; 3506 Waikomo Rd; ◷8:30am-4pm Mon-Thu, to 6pm Fri) Has a 24-hour ATM.

ℹ Getting There & Away

Kaua'i Bus (p274) stops in Koloa on its route between Po'ipu and Kalaheo; the latter has onward connections to Lihu'e and the Westside.

Po'ipu

☑808 / POP 979

Often sunnier and drier than the North Shore, Po'ipu (which ironically translates as 'completely overcast' – don't worry, it isn't) is renowned for its beaches, some of which are hidden and so gorgeously wild that they rival the island's best scenery. The quality of Po'ipu sunsets is reflected in the dizzy smiles of awe-drunk tourists, weaving and leaning against one another on the sand.

Po'ipu is a simply pleasant resort area, with condos galore and two sprawling hotels – and the number-one destination on the South Shore. But it's all done in good taste, with no building taller than a palm tree. It's ideal for families – especially those with young children, as several of the beaches are sheltered, with calm waters. Po'ipu has no town center, so most of the tourist activity revolves around two open-air shopping and dining complexes.

There are a few good hikes to be had along the coast here, and the diving, snorkeling, swimming and surfing are nothing short of fantastic.

◉ Sights

Allerton Garden
GARDENS

(Map p186; ☑808-742-2623; www.ntbg.org; 4425 Lawa'i Rd; 2½hr tours adult/child 6-12yr $50/25; sunset $95/45; ◷visitor center 8:30am-5pm, tours by reservation only) An extraordinary tour of this garden, part of the multisite National Tropical Botanical Garden, wanders deep into Lawa'i Valley. Robert Allerton, a wealthy Chicago transplant, spent three decades modifying this beautiful tropical valley, which has its own jungle river and ocean beach, by adding stone walkways, pools, sculptures, waterfalls, gazebos and a tremendous variety of plants. Book ahead for all tours. You can only go here on a guided trip.

Tour guides are knowledgeable and enthusiastic as they leisurely lead groups through the meticulously landscaped grounds. Highlights include otherworldly Moreton Bay fig trees (as seen in *Jurassic Park*), golden bamboo groves, a pristine lagoon and valley walls blanketed with purple bougainvillea during summer. More expensive three-hour sunset tours peek inside Allerton's historic home, where drinks and appetizers are civilly served on the lanai. There's a little cafe and gift shop at the visitor center. From there, you hop on a bus to go out to the gardens.

Makawehi Point
LANDMARK

(Map p190) This gigantic lithified sand dune is east of Shipwreck Beach overlooking Keoneloa Bay. Resist the urge to jump off these cliffs. People have died. To the west is Makahuena Point, the southernmost tip of Kaua'i, a rocky cliff covered with condos that overlooks crashing waves below.

Po'ipu

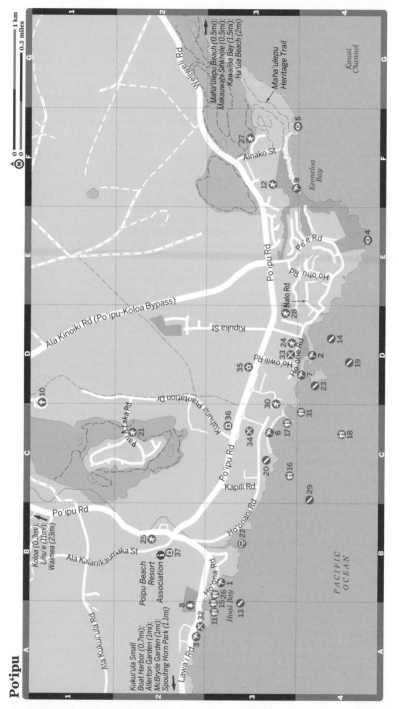

Kukui'ula Small
Boat Harbor (0.7mi);
Allerton Garden (1mi);
McBryde Garden (1mi);
Spouting Horn Park (1.1mi)

Koloa (0.3mi);
Lihu'e (11mi);
Waimea (23mi)

Ala Kukui'ula Rd

Poipu Beach Resort
Association

Ala Kalanikaumaka St

Po'ipu Rd

Lawa'i Rd

Ho'ona Rd

Hoai Bay

PACIFIC
OCEAN

Kapili Rd

Ho'onani Rd

Po'ipu Rd

Kiahuna Plantation Dr

Pau A'aka Rd

Ala Kinoiki Rd (Po'ipu-Koloa Bypass)

Weliweli Rd

Po'ipu Rd

Kiahuna St

Ho'owili Rd

Ho'one Rd

Nalo Rd

Pe'e Rd

Ho'ohu Rd

Po'ipu Rd

Ainako St

Kenneloa
Bay

Maha'ulepu
Heritage Trail

Maha'ulepu Beach (0.5mi);
Makauwahi Sinkhole (0.5mi);
Kawailoa Bay (1.5mi);
Ha'ula Beach (2mi)

Kauai
Channel

1 km
0.5 miles

Po'ipu

Labyrinth at Momilani Kai　　MEMORIAL
(Map p186; Momilani Kai, Maha'ulepu Heritage Trail)
Along the Maha'ulepu Heritage Trail just before Ha'ula Beach on a gorgeous rocky headland, this memorial labyrinth connects you with a mana (spiritual essence) even more powerful than the spectacular blowholes, waves and vistas.

Moir Pa'u a Laka　　GARDENS
(Map p190; ☎808-742-6411; www.outrigger.com; Kiahuna Plantation, 2253 Po'ipu Rd; ⊙sunrise-sunset) FREE On the grounds of Outrigger's Kiahuna Plantation condo complex, this historical cactus and exotic flower garden is a diverting, if modest, collection interspersed with winding paths, a koi pond and colorful

shocks of orchids. Established in the 1930s by Hector Moir, manager of Koloa Sugar Plantation, and his wife Alexandra, the gardens were once far better known than they are today.

Spouting Horn Park　　VIEWPOINT
(Map p186) A concrete walkway and a grassy picnic area sit just above two blowholes in the lava-rock reef where the surf juts through like a minigeyser. The waves can be unpredictable, so you might need to wait for some action. Eruptions are typically less than 30ft and last only seconds, but they can reach twice that height during big surf.To get here, turn right off Po'ipu Rd on to Lawa'i Rd and continue along the coast for less than 2 miles.

Kukui'ula Small Boat Harbor   HARBOR
(Map p186; Lawa'i Rd) With its pavilion and camp tables, Po'ipu's small commercial harbor is not a bad place for a picnic. Walk the jetty, check out the scuba boats and even sunbathe on the small beach by the road.

Prince Kuhio Park   PARK
(Map p190) There is little to see but lava foundations in this memorial park, which contains the ruins of a Hawaiian heiau (ancient stone temple) and fishpond. That said, no one would deny the prince's considerable contributions as the Territory of Hawaii's first delegate to the US Congress.

Makahuena Point   LANDMARK
(Map p190) West of Shipwreck Beach, Makahuena Point is the southernmost tip of Kaua'i.

Beaches

Po'ipu has two different beach areas: the in-town beaches, which front resorts and condos, and the wild beaches along the Maha'ulepu Coast. The former are popular and crowded, the latter unspoiled and surprisingly private.

Po'ipu Beach Park   BEACH
(Map p190; 👶) At the South Shore's most popular beach, there are no monster waves or idyllic solitude, but it's a go-to spot with something for everyone. Patrolled by resident *honu* (sea turtles) in the shallows, the beach is protected by a rocky reef that attracts fish of all kinds.

The beach spills into two separate bays connected by the reef outside and bisected by a sandbar. Add lifeguards, picnic tables, toilets and outdoor showers, and you have one safe, family-friendly beach.

At the end of Ho'owili Rd, there's parking located right across from the beach. There are also three nearby surf breaks and a grassy lawn connecting to Brennecke's Beach (p192) just east.

Po'ipu Beach   BEACH
(Map p190) Although it's nicknamed Sheraton Beach or Kiahuna Beach, this long swath of sand is not private. It merely fronts these hotels and the condo complexes, both of which scored big time with their location here, lying west of Po'ipu Beach Park (p192).

The waters are often too rough for kids, although an offshore reef tames the waves enough for strong ocean swimmers and snorkelers. To get to the beach, drive to the end of Ho'onani Rd.

Experienced surfers and bodyboarders can attempt the breaks near the Sheraton, but those waters are famous for sneaker sets (rogue waves that appear out of nowhere) and the rocky coast makes it difficult to get offshore and back.

Brennecke's Beach   BEACH
(Map p190) With a sandbar bottom and a notch of sand and sea wedged between two lava rock outcrops, this little beach attracts a cadre of bodyboarders, bobbing in the water, waiting for the next set at any time of day or year. No surfboards are allowed near shore, so bodyboarders rule. Tourists sit on the roadside stone wall, gawking at the action. The beach flanks the eastern edge of Po'ipu Beach Park (p192). Check with lifeguards there before venturing out.

Baby Beach   BEACH
(Map p190; 👶) Introduce tots to the ocean at this beach, where the water is barely thigh high. The sandy shore runs behind a row of beach homes on Ho'ona Rd west of Koloa Landing. Access is easy but parking is limited (don't block any driveways). Look for the beach-access sign that marks the path down to the beach. Don't confuse this Baby Beach with the one in Kapa'a on the island's Eastside.

Lawa'i (Beach House) Beach   BEACH
(Map p190) For such a tiny beach, this snorkeling and surfing spot gets lots of attention. Almost adjacent to Lawa'i Rd, just west of the landmark Beach House Restaurant, it's not especially scenic or sandy. But during calm surf, the waters are rich snorkel turf, especially for novices. Expect a crowd of vacationers from nearby timeshares and condos. Restrooms, outdoor showers and a smidgen of public parking are found across the street from the beach.

Shipwreck Beach   BEACH
(Map p190) Unless you're an expert surfer, bodyboarder or bodysurfer, keep your feet dry at 'Shipwrecks'. Instead, come for an invigorating walk along the half-mile crescent of light-gold sand. You'll have some company, as the Grand Hyatt overlooks much of the beach along Keoneloa Bay. Row after row of waves crash close to shore, giving this beach a rugged, untamed feel.

To the east of the bay looms Makawehi Point (p189), a gigantic lithified sand dune. Beware that cliff-jumpers (or those who accidentally fall due to erosion) have been

MAKAUWAHI SINKHOLE

You may well think this enormous sinkhole is a lost world. The only way in is by squeezing through a tiny opening in a rock wall. Suddenly you find yourself in a beautiful, open-air atrium, with palm trees dwarfed by high cliffs and an enormous cave system beneath.

While this is arguably the richest fossil site in the Hawaiian Islands, very few people seem to know about it. Since 1996 it has been excavated by scientists with the help of students, volunteers and visitors, yielding fascinating results. The site has provided evidence for the widespread extinction of species in Hawaii following human settlement. Paleontologist David Burney's well-written book *Back to the Future in the Caves of Kaua'i* tells this cautionary tale.

Makauwahi Cave (Map p186; ☑808-634-0605, 808-212-1710; www.cavereserve.org; ◷ guided tours 10am-2pm Wed, Fri, Sat & Sun or by appointment) ⚑ FREE is located at the western end of Maha'ulepu Beach (p193), but is best approached from above by car, then on foot. Trail guides are usually available in a self-serve box, or downloadable online. The sinkhole is currently open to visitors for free guided tours (no reservations). Check the website for up-to-date tour times and directions.

seriously injured and have even died. To the west is Makahuena Point (p192), the southernmost tip of Kaua'i, a rocky cliff overlooking crashing waves that is covered with condos.

🏝 Maha'ulepu Coast Beaches

The windswept Maha'ulepu Coast resembles no other on Kaua'i: lithified sand-dune cliffs, pounding surf, secluded coves and three outstanding beaches with very few people on them. Swimming can be dicey, even in summer, so use your best judgment.

★ Ha'ula Beach   BEACH

(Map p186) Ha'ula is an isolated bay and pocket beach nestled into the shoreline. You'll feel like Robinson Crusoe here, particularly when swinging in a hammock made from a washed-up fishing net. If you're lucky, you might see a monk seal hauling out on the beach. *Kokua* (please) stay back at least 50yd to avoid disturbing these critically endangered marine mammals. The beach is a 15-minute walk beyond Kawailoa Bay along the coast, past a rugged headland.

★ Maha'ulepu Beach   BEACH

(Gillin's Beach; Map p186; http://malama-mahaulepu.org) You'll feel like you're sitting on the reef in this secluded spot, so it's no surprise that there's excellent snorkeling. To get here, hike the Maha'ulepu Heritage Trail (p180) from Shipwreck Beach or drive 1.5 miles on the dirt road that begins after the Grand Hyatt, turning right where it dead-ends at a gate (open 7:30am to 6pm daily, to 7pm in summer, and strictly enforced). Continue to the parking area, where a trail leads to the

beach. Look out for the sole house on the entire coast, the **Gillin Beach House**, originally built in 1946 by a civil engineer with the Koloa Sugar Plantation.

Kawailoa Bay   BEACH

(Map p186) The beach at Kawailoa Bay has sand dunes at one end and cliffs at the other. The reliable breeze here makes it a popular spot for windsurfing and kitesurfing, while the ironwood trees bordering the beach create an impromptu picnic area. It's also a local fishing spot. Coming from Maha'ulepu Beach, continue down the coastal Maha'ulepu Heritage hiking trail on foot or follow the inland dirt road by car until you run into Kawailoa Bay.

🏃 Activities

Anara Spa   SPA

(Map p190; ☑808-742-1234; www.anaraspa.com; Grand Hyatt Kaua'i Resort & Spa, 1571 Po'ipu Rd; ◷ by appointment only) The Grand Hyatt does everything grandly and this 45,000-sq-ft spa, embellished with tropical gardens and waterfalls, is no exception. Spa treatments inspired by Hawaiian healing arts are given in private garden-view rooms. Don't miss the lava-rock showers. Access to the lap pool and a fitness center offering yoga and wellness classes is complimentary with a minimum 50-minute treatment. Reservations required.

Po'ipu Bay Golf Course   GOLF

(Map p190; ☑808-742-8711, 800-858-6300; www.poipubaygolf.com; 2250 Ainako St; green fees incl cart rental $135-250, club rent $60) Known for its magnificent views of mountains and sea, this 18-hole, par-72 course designed by

THE NATIONAL TROPICAL BOTANICAL GARDEN & MCBRYDE GARDEN TRAILS

The **National Tropical Botanical Garden** (www.ntbg.org) is not a single place, but a nonprofit organization. It is chartered by the US Congress and runs five gardens and three preserves, four of which are on Kaua'i: the **Allerton Garden** (p189) and the **McBryde Garden** (p182) in Po'ipu, and the **Limahuli Garden** (p174) near Ha'ena, on the North Shore. Of the rest, the Kahanu Garden is on Maui, the Awini and Ka'upulehu Preserves are on the Big Island, and the Kampong is on Biscayne Bay in Coconut Grove, Florida. Headquartered in Kalaheo, the organization is focused on research, conservation and education aimed at the preservation and survival of tropical plants. The name can be confusing sometimes, as it is often used to refer to the Allerton and McBryde Gardens, where the organization began.

At McBryde Garden, the self-guided tour allows you to wander in the vast grounds without watching the clock. Advance reservations are required, however. Transport to the park is included in the entrance fee, with buses leaving every hour from park headquarters. There are five interpretative trails on-site.

➡ **Spice of Life Trail** If you're going to do one trail at McBryde, this is it. It's really short, but takes you up a hillside through a tropical forest that feels out of this world.

➡ **Hawaiian Life Canoe Garden** This short loop takes you past plants the first Polynesian voyagers took with them to the islands. There were roughly 30 plant species that these intrepid explorers brought with them to sustain life – and a new civilization – on a new world.

➡ **Biodiversity Trail** This curated trail takes you through 7 billion years of natural history, showing you the plant species that existed or stem from points in time.

➡ **Reading Palms** Trail Palm tree species on parade.

➡ **Native Plant Gardens** Dive into Hawaii's native plants.

Robert Trent Jones Jr hosted the PGA Grand Slam for 13 years. It sports 85 bunkers, multiple water hazards and unpredictable winds. Rates drop dramatically in the afternoons. Club and shoe rentals available.

Skyline Eco-Adventures   ZIPLINE
(Map p190; ☑800-425-9374; www.zipline.com/kauai; 2829 Ala Kalanikaumaka St; zipline $114-158; ☺7am-9pm) Choose from five to eight zips at this chain operation with a canopy platform outside Omao. Reservations are required.

Outfitters Kauai   BICYCLE RENTAL
(Map p190; ☑808-742-9667, 888-742-9887; www.outfitterskauai.com; Po'ipu Plaza, 2827a Po'ipu Rd; bicycle rental per day $25-45; ☺9am-4:30pm) Perhaps because of the lack of bike lanes, cyclists are scarce in Po'ipu. However, you can rent bikes here, including road, mountain and hybrid models. Rates include a helmet and lock. Phone reservations recommended.

Spa at Koa Kea   SPA
(Map p190; ☑808-828-8888; www.koakea.com; Koa Kea Hotel & Resort, 2251 Po'ipu Rd; ☺by appointment only) This boutique spa has just five treatment rooms (including one for couples). It offers a variety of massage styles. Choose from Hawaiian *lomilomi* and *pohaku* (hot stone), as well as body scrubs and treatments using island-sourced ingredients such as *kukui* (candlenut) and coconut oils, Kaua'i coffee and red clay. Book ahead.

Kiahuna Golf Club   GOLF
(Map p190; ☑808-742-9595; www.kiahunagolf.com; 2545 Kiahuna Plantation Dr; 18 holes $85, 9 holes $60, rental clubs $32-52) A relatively inexpensive and forgiving 18-hole, par-70 course designed by Robert Trent Jones Jr, interestingly incorporating some archaeological ruins. The scenery is excellent, with some ocean views, although the course is often windy. Rental clubs available.

Poipu Kai Tennis Club   TENNIS
(Map p190; ☑808-742-8706; www.poipukai.org/tennis.html; 1775 Po'ipu Rd; per person per day $20, racket rental $5; ☺8am-noon & 2-6pm) Rent one of six hard courts or two artificial grass courts with ocean views at this resort racquet club. It has tennis clinics and

round-robin tourneys. You can either make a reservation or just show up.

CJM Country Stables
HORSEBACK RIDING

(Map p186; ☑ 808-742-6096; www.cjmstables.com; off Po'ipu Rd; 2hr group rides $110-140, private rides from $140; ⊘ rides usually 9:30am & 2pm Mon-Sat, 1pm Wed & Fri; ⊕) The Maha'ulepu Coast is a perfect landscape to see by horse. CJM offers two gentle tours of the purely nose-to-tail walking variety suitable for the whole family. More experienced riders may opt for a private ride. Do like the cowboys do and wear long pants.

Diving

The Po'ipu coast offers the majority of the island's best dive sites, including Sheraton Caverns (p195), a series of partially collapsed lava tubes, with shafts of glowing sunlight illuminating their dim, atmospheric interior; General Store (p195), with sharks, octopuses, eels and the remains of an 1892 shipwreck; and Nukumoi Point (p195), a shallow site as well as habitat for green sea turtles. Dive boats and catamaran cruises typically depart from Kukui'ula Small Boat Harbor (p192).

★ Seasport Divers
DIVING

(Map p190; ☑ 800-685-5889, 808-742-9303; www.seasportdivers.com; Po'ipu Plaza, 2827 Po'ipu Rd; shore/boat dives from $90/135; ⊘ 8am-6pm) This leading outfit schedules a variety of dives from shore or by boat, including twice-daily South Shore boat trips and a rare and wonderful three-tank dive to Ni'ihau, available twice-weekly from late spring through early fall. All dives are guided by instructor-level dive masters; any group with noncertified divers includes an additional instructor. Rental equipment available. Book in advance.

Koloa Landing
SNORKELING, DIVING

(Map p190) Koloa Landing, at the mouth of Waikomo Stream, was once Kaua'i's largest port. Nineteenth-century farmers used it to ship Kaua'i-grown sugar, oranges and sweet potatoes from here. It was the third-busiest whaling port among the Hawaiian Islands, surpassed only by Honolulu and Lahaina, Maui.

The landing waned after the road system was built; it was abandoned in the 1920s. Today only a small boat ramp remains. Underwater, it's another story: Koloa Landing is popular for snorkeling and it's also the best shore-diving spot on the South Shore.

Its protected waters reach depths of about 30ft and it's generally calm all year. Underwater tunnels, a variety of coral and fish, sea turtles and monk seals await.

Sheraton Caverns
DIVING

(Map p190) Located 400 meters offshore from the Sheraton, this uberpopular boat dive takes you to partial lava tubes, overhangs and archways. It's sea-turtle heaven.

Beach House
DIVING

(Map p190) In the waters fronting the Beach House, this intermediate and advanced boat dive takes you down 35 to 75 feet. The highlight is an arch where a school of blue-striped grunts live. Also expect turtles and tang.

Brennecke's Ledge
DIVING

(Map p190) This drift dive is best for experienced divers. You'll be rewarded with a ledge that drops to an overhang, and tons of fish. The current moves fast, so you need to be comfortable in the water.

Ice Box
DIVING

(Map p190) This is a good spot for an intermediate diver, with dives to ledges around 60 to 90 feet. You might just see soldierfish, white-tip reef sharks and turtles.

Nukumoi Point
DIVING

(Map p190) A South Shore diving spot and habitat for green sea turtles.

General Store
DIVING

(Map p186) Better for intermediate and advanced divers because of the current, this spot has it all: black coral, butterfly fish, conch and plenty of chances of spotting dolphins. There are some remains of a freighter that sank here.

Kauai Down Under
DIVING

(Map p190; ☑ 808-742-9534; www.kauaidownunderscuba.com; Sheraton Kauai Resort, 2440 Ho'onani Rd; boat dives incl equipment rental from $159; ⊘ by reservation only) With one instructor per four guests, personal attention is guaranteed. This outfit offers introductory noncertified one-tank dives, two-tank scooter dives, and night dives for the truly adventurous. It also has a multitude of classes including the recommended prearrival online academic portion of the certification for those wanting to maximize playtime while on the island. Make reservations in advance.

Turtle Bluffs
DIVING

(Map p186) Located just west of the General Store (p195) dive site, this is a good spot to find turtles, snappers and the occasional reef shark.

Three Fingers
DIVING

(Map p186) A good site for beginners, with little current and shallow dives 25 to 75 feet, this boat dive site outside the harbor features three lava fingers (yep, that's where it gets its name), plus schools of blue-striped grunts and surgeon fish.

Surfing & Stand Up Paddle Surfing

Po'ipu's killer breaks and year-round waves make it a popular spot for surfing lessons and rentals.

★ Kaua'i Surf School
SURFING, SUP

(Map p190; ☑808-651-6032; www.kauaisurf school.com; Ho'onani Rd; 2hr group/private surfing lessons $75/175; ⊙ by reservation only; 🖮) With 90 minutes of teaching, 30 minutes of free practice, and only four students per instructor, you get your money's worth. Ages four and up are welcome in group lessons as long as they can swim; alternatively, book a special one-hour private lesson for kids. Ask about surf clinics, surf camps, private surf coaches and SUP lessons.

Nukumoi Surf Shop
WATER SPORTS

(Map p190; ☑808-742-8019; www.nukumoi. com; 2100 Ho'one Rd; snorkel set & bodyboard/ surfboard/SUP rental per day from $6/30/60; ⊙8am-sunset) For surfboard, snorkel and SUP rentals, this shop is right across from Po'ipu Beach Park. Check your gear carefully before heading out. Great local surf beta.

Hoku Water Sports
SURFING, SUP

(Map p190; ☑808-639-9333; www.hokuwater sports.com; 2251 Po'ipu Rd; 2hr group/private surfing lessons $75/200, 80min SUP lessons $70, outrigger canoe tours $50; ⊙ by reservation only) Group surfing lessons include just one hour with an instructor and an hour of free surfing. For a unique experience, surf the waves while paddling a Hawaiian outrigger canoe.

Po'ipu Surf
SURFING

(Map p190; ☑808-742-8797; www.poipusurf. com; Shops at Kukui'ula, 2829 Ala Kalanikaumaka St; surfboard/SUP rental per day from $20/40; ⊙9am-9pm) Local surf and skate shop renting beginner and performance surfboards and SUP sets at competitive rates. Weekly discounts available.

Kauai Stand-up Paddle & Surf
SURFING, SUP

(☑808-652-9979; www.kauaisurfandsup.com; 2hr group/private surfing lessons $75/120, 2hr SUP lessons $85, surfing & SUP tours $120-150; 🖮) This locally owned, small-group outfitter runs kids' surf camps in summer, offers family discounts and has 30 years of experience to bring to the table. It's also the only one to offer custom SUP tours island-wide.

Waiohai
SURFING

(Map p190) Always breaking by the Marriott. Two to eight feet is good, making it decent for pretty good beginner riders.

PK's
SURFING

(Map p190) Good wave with an easy takeoff outside the Prince Kuhiuo Condos. Good for intermediate riders that at least know how to make it to the lineup.

Cowshead
SURFING

(Map p190) Long right-hander that's nice and hollow. Better at four to 10 feet.

First Break
SURFING

(Map p190) Doesn't break when it's small. Look for eight to 12 feet for solid right rides. It's quite a paddle out – a couple of hundred yards.

Donovans
SURFING

(Learners; Map p190) This is where nearly all of the area's surf lessons happen. Come here if you are just getting going. Rolls all the way into the sand – less worry about rocks.

Centers
SURFING

(Map p190) A bit fickle. It's not quite as reliable as other breaks here. Split-peak on a reef.

Acid Drop
SURFING

(Map p190) A South Shore surfing break. It has lefts and rights. It's a reef break better suited to experts. Best ridden at six to 10 feet.

⏩ Tours

Travel Hawaii
TOURS

(Map p190; ☑808-742-7015; Po'ipu Shoping Village, 2360 Kiahuna Plantation Dr; ⊙8am-8pm) This superfriendly tourist information kiosk from Diamond Resorts can book tours, give you local advice and get you out on adventures large and small.

Outfitters Kauai
KAYAKING

(Map p190; ☑808-742-9667; www.outfitters kauai.com; Po'ipu Plaza, 2827a Po'ipu Rd; zipline $118-158; ⊙7am-5pm) Take a unique kayaking tour of the Na Pali Coast or the Wailua River,

SOUTH SHORE SNORKELING HOT SPOTS

Take the plunge at these top-rated South Shore snorkeling areas with handy beach access:

➡ **Koloa Landing** (p195) Once Kaua'i's largest port, this site is known for the best shore diving, with a quick drop-off to 45ft. The edge is also great for advanced snorkeling. Expect to see large schools of fish, eels and the usual turtles. Avoid the sandy middle ground.

➡ **Lawa'i (Beach House) Beach** (p192) If you don't mind the crowds, you'll find good coral, lots of reef fish and sea turtles, all within a depth of 3–12ft. There are restrooms and outdoor showers on shore.

➡ **Maha'ulepu Beach** (p193) Though often overlooked because of its seclusion, this near-shore reef is perhaps the best of the lot, though you'll need calm wind and water.

➡ **Po'ipu Beach Park** (p192) Ranging from 3 to 12ft, this shallow protected bay is great for families, although experts will enjoy it as well. Snorkeling is best on the left side as you enter. Facilities include lifeguards, outdoor showers and restrooms.

➡ **Prince Kuhio Park** (p192) Directly across the street from this grassy park, ocean waters ranging from 3 to 21ft deep appeal to both beginners and advanced snorkelers. There's a rocky shoreline, but the bay is protected.

---

opt for jungle ziplines, or a Waimea Canyon downhill bike. Really it's the kayaking and ziplining that make this outfitter famous. Tandem, open-cockpit kayaks or sit-on-top, self-bailing kayaks with pedal rudders make it easy for novices, but if you get seasick, think twice. Make tour reservations in advance. No nonswimmers or children under 12 years old. Na Pali tours run May through September.

Captain Andy's Sailing Adventures   BOATING
(Map p186; ☑ 808-335-6833, 800-535-0830; www.napali.com; Kukui'ula Small Boat Harbor; 2hr tours adult/child 2-12yr $79/59; ☺ departs 4pm or 5pm Sat) If you're dreaming of a scenic sunset cruise down the Maha'ulepu Coast by catamaran, Captain Andy is a real pro. Cross your fingers to spot whales between December and April. Tours, which depart only once a week, include appetizers, cocktails and live music. Book at least three days ahead.

Festivals & Events

★ **Prince Kuhio**
Celebration of the Arts   CULTURAL
(http://princekuhio.net; ☺ Mar) The South Shore hosts this two-week celebration in mid- to late March. Events include hula dancing and slack key guitar music, a rodeo, canoe racing, 'talk story' time, an artisan fair, (p125) Hawaiian cultural presentations on *kapa* (bark cloth), lei and poi making, stone and wood carving, and much more.

✗ Eating

In Po'ipu, some top restaurants rely on ocean views and ambience to get you through an average dinner – which you pay heavily for. Budget travelers should look for the few restaurants that are split-level, offering separate menus on each floor that target two different price ranges.

★ **Kaua'i Culinary Market**   MARKET $
(Map p190; ☑ 855-742-9545; http://kukuiula.com; Shops at Kukui'ula, 2829 Ala Kalanikaumaka St; ☺ 3:30-6pm Wed; ☑ ⓐ) ✐ An upscale take on the traditional island farmers market features not only a couple dozen local farmers and food vendors, but also free live music, cooking demonstrations by South Shore chefs and *pau hana* (happy hour) drinks in an outdoor beer and wine garden.

Makai Sushi   SUSHI $
(Map p190; ☑ 808-639-7219; Po'ipu Plaza, 2827 Po'ipu Rd; $13-16; ☺ 11am-7pm Mon-Fri, 11am-5pm Sat & Sun) Inside the Kukui'ula Market, this sushi kiosk keeps it simple with just six choices on the menu. Go with the Gorilla Poke Bowl – ahi, *ono*, salmon, avocado, cucumber and a bunch of other textures and flavors. The rolls are also excellent. There's only a small bar, so consider taking your food to the beach.

Da Crack   MEXICAN, AMERICAN $
(Map p190; ☑ 808-742-9505; www.dacrack.com; Po'ipu Plaza, 2827 Po'ipu Rd; $9-13; ☺ 11am-8pm Mon-Sat, to 4pm Sun; ⓐ) A guilty pleasure, this

PO'IPU ON A BUDGET

McBryde Garden (p182) The self-guided tour (half the price of the **Allerton Garden** (p189) tour) lets you stroll at your own pace amid palms, orchids and rare native species.

Maha'ulepu Heritage Trail (p180) Walk the island's last accessible undeveloped coastline and bear witness to striking limestone cliffs unlike anything else across the Hawaiian Islands.

Shoreline snorkeling If you want to pay the extra money to hire a boat, you can just head out from the shore. Rent equipment from Boss Frog's and explore Po'ipu's eye-catching marine life from just beyond the shore.

Beach House Restaurant lawn (p199) If you can't afford dinner at this fine-dining icon, park yourself on the adjacent grassy knoll and enjoy the free show: lithe local surfers, an unobstructed horizon and blazing sunsets.

Kukuiolono Golf Course (p204) This neighborhood nine-hole course is welcoming, unpretentious – and only $9.

taco shop (literally, it's a hole in the wall) cooks up tacos, burritos and rice-and-beans bowls overstuffed with batter-fried fish, *carnitas* (braised pork), shredded chicken or chipotle shrimp. Expect to wait.

Living Foods Gourmet
Market & Café   MARKET, CAFE $

(Map p190; ☎808-742-2323; http://shopliving foods.com; Shops at Kukui'ula, 2829 Ala Kalanikaumaka St; mains $10-18; ◷7am-9pm; 🖉🐕) 🍴 High-priced even by island standards, the often-organic, gluten-free and/or all-natural products sold here include cheeses, meats and imported wines, along with a selection of local produce and artisanal foodstuffs such as Kaua'i-made juices, nuts, honey, salts, coffee and cookies. The cafe sells *poke* bowls, wood-fired pizza and more.

Papalani Gelato   ICE CREAM $

(Map p190; ☎808-742-2663; www.papalani gelato.com; Po'ipu Shopping Village, 2360 Kiahuna Plantation Dr; scoop $4; ◷11am-9:30pm; 🖉🐕) Deliciously sweet treats are all made on-site. You can't go wrong with classic pistachio, but for local flavor, get a scoop of macadamia-nut butter or coconut gelato, or guava, *liliko'i* or lychee sorbet. Second location at the Anchor Cove Shopping Center (p97) in Lihu'e.

Kukui'ula Market   SUPERMARKET $

(Map p190; ☎808-742-1601; Po'ipu Plaza, 2827 Po'ipu Rd; ◷8am-8:30pm Mon-Fri, to 6:30pm Sat & Sun) Locally owned grocery store stocking almost everything a vegan, vegetarian or gluten-free DIY eater needs. The noteworthy Makai Sushi (p197) is here too. A juice bar at the back makes smoothies and acai bowls until 4pm on weekdays, 3pm on weekends.

Bubba's Burgers   BURGERS $

(Map p190; www.bubbaburger.com; Shops at Kukui'ula, 2829 Ala Kalanikaumaka St; $3.50-9; ◷10:30am-8pm) Bubba's has been serving up burgers since 1936 in Kaua'i. The Po'ipu location maintains the old beach-burger shack feel of the other locations. Burgers are delightfully greasy, with crispy fries and grass-fed Kaua'i beef. Go for the teriyaki burger.

Puka Dog   FAST FOOD $

(Map p190; ☎808-742-6044; www.pukadog.com; Po'ipu Shoping Village, 2360 Kiahuna Plantation Dr; hot dogs $7-8; ◷10am-8pm; 🖉) These specialty hot dogs are more popular with tourists than with locals and come with a toasty Hawaiian sweet bread bun, a choice of Polish sausage or a veggie dog, a 'secret' sauce and tropical fruit relish (mango and pineapple, yum).

The Olympic Cafe   AMERICAN $$

(Map p190; ☎808-742-8717; Po'ipu Shoping Village, 2360 Kiahuna Plantation Dr; $10-28; ◷6am-9pm; 🅿) The ceiling fans move slowly in this friendly tropical diner in the Po'ipu Shopping Village. The menu features a few Hawaiian twists, like the Kalua Pig Burrito, but mostly you will get classic Americana-slash-Mexicana, with a good selection of south-of-the-border favorites. Breakfasts are huge and delicious! Head to the Side Car for drinks later.

Tortilla Republic   MEXICAN $$

(Map p190; ☎808-742-8884; http://tortilla republic.com/hawaii; Shops at Kukui'ula, 2829 Ala Kalanikaumaka St; dinner mains bar $11-21, restaurant $14-32; ◷restaurant 5:30-9pm Sun-Thu, to 10pm Fri & Sat, bar 8am-1pm Mon-Fri, from 9am Sat & Sun) In a plantation-style building with two levels, you'll find a buzzing margarita bar and taqueria downstairs, and a dining room upstairs that's intriguingly decorated with an onyx bar top, metalwork sculpture and carved wooden doors from Guadalajara. While the food is just as artfully designed, with some new takes on old favorites, portions are awfully small for these prices. Save some dollars with the bar menu or starters.

The Dolphin Poipu   HAWAIIAN $$

(Map p190; ☑ 808-742-1414; www.hanaleidolphin. com; Shops at Kukui'ula, 2829 Ala Kalanikaumaka St; $16-38; ⊘ 11:30am-9pm) Brought to you by the same people as Hanalei's famous Dolphin, this second location is not as good... but is still a solid option for a casual meal in Po'ipu. Save some bucks by combining appetizers and an inventive sushi roll – the seafood chowder is outstanding.

Brennecke's Beachfront
Restaurant & Beach Deli   AMERICAN $$

(Map p190; ☑ 808-742-7588; www.brenneckes. com; 2100 Ho'one Rd; deli sandwiches $6-10, restaurant mains lunch $11-20, dinner $14-30; ⊘ deli 7am-9pm, restaurant 11am-10pm, bar 10am-close; 🖬) Part sports bar, part restaurant, this institution across from Po'ipu Beach Park has served up endless plates of ribs, steak, fresh fish, pasta, burgers and tacos for three decades, along with tropical cocktails and cold brewskis. The downstairs deli is the only breakfast burrito or club sandwich within range of your beach towel.

Eating House 1849   HAWAIIAN $$$

(Map p190; www.eatinghouse1849.com; Shops at Kukui'ula, 2829 Ala Kalanikaumaka St; $21-45; ⊘ 5-9:30pm) Roy Yamaguchi is a legendary Hawaiian restaurateur. His latest spot, the Eating House, is near pitch perfect at every plate, at every sizzling beef plate, and every nuanced and flavorful *poke*. Don't hesitate to splurge here – you will be well rewarded. Time your dinner for sunset. This is one of the few spots in the Kukui'ula with good ocean views.

Keoki's Paradise   HAWAII REGIONAL $$$

(Map p190; ☑ 808-742-7534; www.keokispara dise.com; Po'ipu Shopping Village, 2360 Kiahuna Plantation Dr; bar mains $11-20, restaurant dinner mains $22-35; ⊘ restaurant 4:45-9:30pm, bar 11am-10:30pm) Natural woods, tiki torches and water features combine to form a warm jungle-lodge atmosphere. The higher-priced dining room offers grilled meats and seafood, while the Bamboo Bar is all about tropical *pupu* (snacks) and pub grub. Throw in a great selection of draft beers and nightly live music, and Keoki's is a winner.

Merriman's Fish House   HAWAII REGIONAL $$$

(Map p190; ☑ 808-742-8385; www.merrimans hawaii.com; Shops at Kukui'ula, 2829 Ala Kalanikaumaka St; bar mains $11-17, restaurant dinner mains $24-50; ⊘ bar 11:30am-10pm, restaurant 5-9pm)
🌶 Upstairs is a breezy surf-and-turf dining room, where 90% of all menu ingredients are locally caught or grown and the fusion cuisine is designed by a famous chef. Sunset views are excellent from the plantation house's upper lanai, so book ahead. Downstairs is a family-friendly spot for burgers and pizza (happy hour 3:30pm to 5:30pm daily).

Beach House Restaurant   SEAFOOD $$$

(Map p190; ☑ 808-742-1424; www.the-beach -house.com; 5022 Lawa'i Rd; mains lunch $10-19, dinner $20-48; ⊘ 11am-10pm; 🖉) There are many oceanfront restaurants in Po'ipu, but only one iconic spot for sunset dining and special occasions such as weddings, birthdays and anniversaries. The focus of the Pacific Rim cuisine is fresh fish – island fishers are identified by name on the menu – but sauces are heavy. For sunset dining, reserve a 'first seating' weeks in advance. Vegan and gluten-free menus available.

Plantation Gardens
Restaurant & Bar   HAWAIIAN $$$

(Map p190; ☑ 808-742-2121; http://pgrestaurant. com; Kiahuna Plantation, 2253 Po'ipu Rd; mains $24-37; ⊘ restaurant 5:30-9pm, bar from 5pm) Set in a historic plantation house, this long-standing favorite is known more for its ambience than its food. The open-air setting in tropical gardens is lovely, particularly with the tiki-torch illumination. The menu meanders from traditional takes on seafood to more modern fusion additions. The drinks here – like the lavender piña colada – are so good you might forget yourself.

Rum Fire   FUSION $$$

(Map p190; ☑ 808-742-4786; www.rumfirekauai. com; 2440 Hoonani Rd; $20-40; ⊘ 5:30-10pm Tue-Sat) Rum Fire is one of the more elegant beachfront spots on the South Shore. It features a somewhat bold fusion list of seafood and continental cuisine. The large open dining room provides 180-degree views of the Pacific and the cool blue and green lighting design gives the sense of cosmo-chic with little left over for island romance. Enclosed in glass – and with piped-in AC – the place feels less Hawaiian than other joints nearby. Come early to appreciate sunsets.

PO'IPU & THE SOUTH SHORE PO'IPU

CHASE CLAUSEN/SHUTTERSTOCK ©

1. Old sugarcane factory
After finding that Hawaii was ideal for growing sugarcane, foreigners quickly established small plantations across Kaua'i.

2. Baby Beach (p192), Po'ipu
Here the water is barely thigh high – ideal for introducing children to the ocean.

3. St Raphael's Catholic Church (p184)
Kaua'i's oldest Catholic church was built in 1854 out of lava rock and coral mortar.

4. Allerton Garden (p189)
Highlights of this extraordinary garden include a jungle river and ocean beach, stunning fig trees and knowledgeable tour guides.

Red Salt
FUSION $$$

(Map p190; ☑ 808-828-8888; www.koakea.com; Koa Kea Hotel & Resort, 2251 Po'ipu Rd; mains $33-69; ⊙ restaurant 6-10pm, lounge 5:30pm-midnight) At this romantic hideaway, fusion dishes such as pan-seared *opah* (moonfish) with king crab and a sake-spiked coconut broth or vanilla-bean-seared mahimahi elevate the culinary game. Seafood appetizers, sushi and strong cocktails are served in the svelte lounge and there's always that root-beer float with warm macnut cookies or *liliko'i*-ginger crème brûlée for dessert. Valet parking is complimentary.

Whalers General Store
MARKET

(Map p190; Po'ipu Shoping Village, 2360 Kiahuna Plantation Dr; ⊙ 7am-9:30pm) This small market lacks good local foods, but has plenty of liquor and some fun curios.

Drinking & Nightlife

This is the most energetic nightlife on the South Shore. And even that is severely lacking. Head to the restaurants in the malls or one of the resorts for the best nightlife.

★ Seaview Terrace
BAR

(Map p190; ☑ 808-240-6456; http://kauai.hyatt.com; Grand Hyatt Kauai Resort & Spa, 1571 Po'ipu Rd; ⊙ 5:30-11am & 4:30-10pm) Don't miss Po'ipu's grandest and most memorable ocean view. In the morning, this stepped terrace is an espresso and pastry cafe. Later in the day, a torch-lighting ceremony announces sunset, with live music and occasional hula dancing before 9pm. Show up early for a prime viewing table (no reservations). Head directly through the hotel lobby and atrium toward the sea.

Bangkok Happy Bowl
LOUNGE

(Map p190; http://aspenthai.net/kauai-thai-food; Po'ipu Shopping Village, 2360 Kiahuna Plantation Dr; $13-20; ⊙ 11am-10pm Tue-Sun) The sushi and Thai food at this open-air Po'ipu Shopping Village eatery are passable – and quite affordable. This is also one of the few places in the area with regular live music and a somewhat lively bar-lounge scene. It has live acts most nights and karaoke Thursdays are popular with locals and visitors.

☆ Entertainment

'Auli'i Luau
LUAU

(Map p190; ☑ 808-634-1499; http://auliiluau.com; Sheraton Kaua'i Resort, 2440 Ho'onani Rd; adult from $101, child 3-12yr from $49, youth 13-17yr from $74; ⊙ 6pm Mon & Thu Mar-Sep, 5:30pm Mon & Thu Oct-Feb) The Sheraton's luau banks on its oceanfront setting. The Polynesian revue and dinner buffet are both pretty standard. Beware: the joker emcee demands audience participation. When it rains, the luau happens in a hotel ballroom – not fun. Save bucks by sitting on the beach and watching the show with a glass of wine.

Po'ipu Beach Athletic Club
LIVE MUSIC

(Map p190; ☑ 808-742-2111; www.poipuclub.com; 2290 Poipu Rd) This athletic club and pool is also the best concert venue on the South Shore. Salt-N-Pepa, UB40 and other super-fun acts have played at the outside venue.

Havaiki Nui Luau
LUAU

(Map p190; ☑ 808-240-6456; www.hyatt.com/gallery/kauailuau; Grand Hyatt Kaua'i Resort & Spa, 1571 Po'ipu Rd; adult/child/teen $108/72/102; ⊙ 5:15-8pm Thu & Sun) The Havaiki Nui Luau is a well-oiled pan-Polynesian production befitting the Grand Hyatt's beachfront setting. Unfortunately, sometimes they move it indoors to accommodate weddings or bad weather – choose your dates carefully.

🛍 Shopping

Malie Organics Boutique
BEAUTY, GIFTS

(Map p190; ☑ 808-332-6220, 866-767-5727; www.malie.com; Shops at Kukui'ula, 2829 Ala Kalanikaumaka St; ⊙ 10am-9pm) 🍃 *Kukui* nuts, mangoes, coconuts and vanilla are just a few of the island plant 'essences' utilized by this homegrown bath- and body-products company. It stocks Kaua'i's high-end resorts with its sprays, soaps, body creams and candles, but this is its only retail outlet.

Shops at Kukui'ula
MALL

(Map p190; ☑ 808-742-9545; http://kukuiula.com/theshops; 2829 Ala Kalanikaumaka St; ⊙ 10am-9pm) An upscale outdoor shopping mall conveniently located at the Po'ipu roundabout offers more than 30 restaurants and designer shops, including fine-art galleries such as cutting-edge Galerie 103, a few high-end jewelry stores and some only-in-Hawaii fashion boutiques such as Mahina and Blue Ginger.

Palms Gallery   ART
(Map p190; ☑808-320-3866; www.palmsgallery. com; Shops at Kukui'ula, 2829 Ala Kalanikaumaka St; ☉10am-9pm) This large gallery space has a variety of original oils, watercolors and sculptures. Some of it's cheesy...some of it's wonderful and dynamic and colorful.

Allerton Garden Gift Shop   BOOKS, GIFTS
(Map p186; ☑808-742-2623; www.ntbg.org; 4425 Lawa'i Rd; ☉8:30am-5pm) Stocks an excellent array of books (especially nature and Hawaiiana titles), as well as quality nature-themed gifts and souvenirs.

Po'ipu Shopping Village   MALL
(Map p190; ☑808-742-2831; www.poipushop pingvillage.com; Po'ipu Shoping Village, 2360 Kiahuna Plantation Dr; ☉most shops 9am-9pm Mon-Sat, 10am-7pm Sun) A small-scale outdoor mall sports affordable, vacation-centric shops (think aloha-wear, T-shirts, swimwear and souvenirs) such as beachy boutique Sand People and Honolua Surf Co for surf-style fashions; and By the Sea for a huge variety of 'rubbah slippah' (flip-flops). There are a half-dozen restaurants here too.

James Coleman Art Gallery   ART
(Map p190; ☑808-742-8338; www.jamescoleman gallerykauai.com; Po'ipu Shoping Village, 2360 Kiahuna Plantation Dr; ☉10am-9pm Mon-Sat, to 7pm Sun) The gallery owner (a Hollywood original that used to work for Disney) combines island motifs with plenty of Pacific blues in his work. He sometimes paints in the gallery.

❶ Information

The Clinic at Po'ipu (Shops at Kukui'ula, 2829 Ala Kalanikaumaka; ☉8am-5pm Mon-Fri) Basic medical clinic.

Poipu Beach Resort Association (Map p190; ☑808-742-7444, 888-744-0888; www.poipu-beach.org; Shops at Kukui'ula, 2829 Ala Kalanikaumaka St; ☉9:30am-2pm Mon-Fri) Go online for general visitor information about Po'ipu and the entire South Shore, including beaches, activities, accommodations, dining, shopping and events.

❶ Getting There & Away

Navigating is easy, with just two main roads: Po'ipu Rd (along eastern Po'ipu) and Lawa'i Rd (along western Po'ipu). You'll need a car, scooter or bike to go anywhere here besides the beach. It's possible to walk along the roads, but the vibe is more suburbia than surf town.

The **Kaua'i Bus** (p274) runs through Koloa into Po'ipu, stopping along Po'ipu Rd at the turnoff to Po'ipu Beach Park and also by the Hyatt. It's an option for getting here from other towns, but not very useful as transport around the resort area.

Kalaheo

☑808 / POP 4595

Kalaheo is a one-stoplight cluster of eateries and little else. But along the back roads, this neighborly town offers peaceful accommodations away from the tourist crowd, rolling green hills overlooking the scene, and a calm serenity not found on the main tourist trail.

When you pass through town, be sure to stop for a tour of the Kauai Coffee Company and Kukuiolono Park (where you can play golf supercheap). The shrines at the Lawa'i International Center are otherworldly.

If you plan to hike at Waimea Canyon and Koke'e State Parks, but also want easy access to Po'ipu beaches, Kalaheo's central location is ideal. Alas, there are no great beaches right here, making this more of a bedroom community for the South Shore.

◉ Sights

★**Lawa'i International Center**   HISTORIC SITE
(Map p204; ☑tour reservations 808-639-4300; www.lawaicenter.org; 3381 Wawae Rd, Lawa'i; admission by donation; ☉2nd & last Sun of the month, tours depart 10am, noon & 2pm) FREE Spiritual. Stirring. Enchanting. Such words are often used to describe this quiet place. Originally this was the site of a Hawaiian heiau, but in 1904 Japanese immigrants placed 88 miniature Shingon Buddhist shrines, each about 2ft tall and made of wood and stone, along a steep hillside path here to symbolize the famous 88 pilgrimage shrines of Shikoku, Japan. For years, island pilgrims would journey here to meditate upon these shrines.

The site was abandoned by the 1960s and half of the shrines were scattered in shards. In the late 1980s, a crew of volunteers, led by Lynn Muramoto, formed a nonprofit group, acquired the 32-acre property and embarked on a back-breaking project to repair or rebuild the shrines.

PO'IPU & THE SOUTH SHORE KALAHEO

Kalaheo

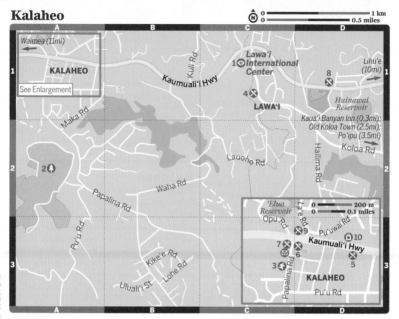

Kalaheo

◎ Top Sights
1 Lawa'i International Center C1

◎ Sights
2 Kukuiolono Park A2

◉ Activities, Courses & Tours
3 Kalaheo Yoga C3
Kukuiolono Golf Course .... (see 2)

◉ Eating
4 Fresh Shave C1
5 Kalaheo Café & Coffee Co D3
6 Kalaheo Farmers Market D3
7 Kauai Kookie Bakery & Kitchen C3
8 Lanakila Kitchen D1
9 The Right Slice D3

◉ Shopping
10 Aloha XCHNG D3
Collection at the Cafe .... (see 5)

Today, all 88 are beautifully restored and there is a wonderful wooden temple, the Hall of Compassion, that has also been built. Leisurely tours include a detailed history and hillside trail walk that amounts to a mini pilgrimage. Everyone is welcome, since the center is a nondenominational sanctuary.

Kukuiolono Park   PARK
(Map p204; 854 Pu'u Rd; ⊙6:30am-6:30pm) Unless you're staying in Kalaheo, you'll probably skip a visit to this little park with its own nine-hole golf course (p204). It's worth a quick stop for a stroll through the **Japanese garden**. Better still is the Hawaiian Rock Garden, a very interesting collection of carved rock artifacts, with some explanatory signs.

Throughout the gardens you will find sweeping views and grassy grounds, perfect for strolling, picnicking or running. Kukuiolono means 'light of Lono,' referring to the torches that Hawaiians once placed on this hill to help guide canoes safely to the shore. To get here, turn left on to Papalina Rd from Kaumuali'i Hwy (heading west).

🏃 Activities

Kukuiolono Golf Course   GOLF
(Map p204; ☑808-332-9151; Kukuiolono Park, 854 Pu'u Rd; green fees $9; ⊙6:30am-6:30pm, last tee time 4:30pm) There are only nine holes, but they come with spectacular ocean and valley views and zero attitude. The course was built in 1927 by Walter McBryde (think McBryde Garden (p182)) and later donated to the public. McBryde clearly loved golf: he's buried by the eighth hole. The driving

range and cart and club rentals are about as cheap as the green fees.

Kalaheo Yoga
YOGA
(Map p204; ☑ 808-652-3216; www.kalaheoyoga.com; 4427 Papalina Rd; per class $18, 3-/4-class pass $48/62) A bright, harmonious yoga space one block from the highway teaches a few classes daily, including gentle, restorative and vinyasa flow. Preregister for classes online.

Eating

Most eateries center on the main town crossroads.

★Fresh Shave
DESSERTS $
(Map p204; www.thefreshshave.com; 3540 Koloa Rd, Lawa'i; shave ice from $6; ⊘ 11am-3pm Wed-Fri, to 5pm Sat; ☑ ☑) ✦ Out of a shiny vintage Aristocrat trailer comes the best shave ice on the island, made using fresh, organic and often local ingredients such as apple bananas and coffee. Opening hours vary, but be forewarned that this roadside pit stop is always mobbed with neighborhood moms and kids after school.

Kalaheo Farmers Market
MARKET $
(Map p204; www.kauai.gov; Kalaheo Neighborhood Center, 4480 Papalina Rd; ⊘ 3-5pm Tue; ☑) ✦ Just a straightforward, small-town produce market. It's one of the countywide Sunshine Markets, so no shopping allowed before the whistle blows.

The Right Slice
PIES $
(Map p204; ☑ 808-212-5798; http://rightslice.com; 2-2459 Kaumualii Hwy; $6-30; ⊘ 11am-6pm Mon-Sat) Homemade pies with local ingredients. Delicious for take out. They'll even pack it up and ship it back to the mainland.

Kauai Kookie Bakery & Kitchen
CAFE, BAKERY $
(Map p204; ☑ 808-332-0821; 2-2436 Kaumuali'i Hwy; mains $5-11, meals $8-13; ⊘ 5:30am-4pm) Stop at this roadside diner for simple but filling breakfasts, *bentō* and Asian and island-style fusion dishes served as plate lunches to an almost exclusively local customer base. It does an authentic oxtail soup too. For a bigger selection of the famous cookies, visit the Hanapepe factory store (p222).

Lanakila Kitchen
HAWAIIAN $
(Map p204; ☑ 808-332-5500; www.lanakilapacific.org/welcome-to-lanakila-kitchen; 2-3687 Kaumuali'i Hwy; meals $8-10; ⊘ 6:30am-2:30pm Mon-Fri) A local's haunt, this tiny cafe with a cause serves a steam table of meat and fish dishes, which you can pick and mix for plate lunches, such as chicken *laulau,* teriyaki fish, tofu stir-fry and more. It also does *ono* fish burgers, ahi *poke* bowls, soups, salads and pies. Proceeds benefit an employment program for people with disabilities.

★Kalaheo Café & Coffee Co
CAFE $$
(Map p204; ☑ 808-332-5858; www.kalaheo.com; 2-2560 Kaumuali'i Hwy; mains breakfast & lunch $5-15, dinner $16-28; ⊘ 6:30am-2:30pm Mon-Sat, to 2pm Sun, 5-8:30pm Tue-Thu, to 9pm Fri & Sat) Adored by locals and visitors alike, this always-busy cafe has a spacious dining room and brews strong coffee. Order egg scrambles with grilled cornbread for breakfast, or a deli sandwich (*kalua* pork with guava BBQ sauce – yum) and a salad of local greens for lunch. Weightier dinner plates include hoisin-glazed fresh catch and salt-rubbed ribs. Expect a long wait at breakfast time. The parking lot gets crowded, so consider parking on the highway shoulder.

🔒 Shopping

Collection at the Cafe
ARTS, GIFTS
(Map p204; ☑ 808-332-5858; 2-2560 Kaumuali'i Hwy; ⊘ 9am-3pm) An airy walk-through gallery displaying ever-changing works by local artists, including oil paintings, watercolors and prints, hand-crafted shell jewelry and more.

Aloha XCHNG
SPORTS & OUTDOORS
(Map p204; www.thealohaexchange.com; 2-2535 Kaumualii Hwy; ⊘ 10am-6pm Mon-Sat) This small-time Kalaheo outdoors shop has all the patagucci clothing you could ever ask for – plus a limited supply of surfboards and camping gear. Service can be inattentive.

ℹ Information

Kalaheo Post Office (Map p204; ☑ 808-332-5800; www.usps.com; 4489 Papalina Rd; ⊘ 9am-3:30pm Mon-Fri, to 11:30am Sat)

ℹ Getting There & Away

Kaua'i Bus (p274) stops at the main intersection in town. But you are better off with a rental car.

Waimea Canyon & the Westside

🎵 808

Best Places to Eat

➡ Japanese Grandma (p221)

➡ G's Juicebar (p226)

➡ Wrangler's Steakhouse (p227)

➡ Bobbie's (p220)

Best Nightlife

➡ Kauai Island Brewery & Grill (p216)

➡ Port Allen Sunset Grill & Bar (p215)

➡ Wrangler's Steakhouse (p227)

➡ Hanapepe Art Night (p219)

➡ Waimea Theater (p227)

Why Go?

This is the edge of the world. And everything from the people to the food to the landscape is somehow more wild, more uncharted than on the rest of the island. You won't find many top-notch resorts or restaurants, but you will get a genuine broad-grinned spirit that is proud, authentic and directly Hawaiian.

With several noteworthy parks, lots of sunshine and access to the world famous Na Pali Coast, this is an adventurer's dream come true. There are deep, riveting red canyons, impossibly steep jungle cliffs, forgotten surf breaks, empty beaches, chart-topping views, waterfalls and a seemingly infinite expanse of ocean.

Kaua'i doesn't get more local than the Westside, where revered traditions and family pride reign. You're more likely to hear fluent Hawaiian, spot a real-life *paniolo* (Hawaiian cowboy) and see fishers sewing their nets here than anywhere else on the island.

When to Go

➡ Many people time their trips to the Westside to include the exciting Friday Art Nights in Hanapepe. You'll love checking out the fun, lyrical and sometimes totally cheeseball creations local artists come up with. Food, drinks and a generally festive environment make it popular with locals and tourists alike.

➡ The weather here is generally drier than the north part of the island, thanks to something called island rain-fade, meaning it's good to go all year round.

➡ A few farmers markets and yearly festivals stand out here. Don't miss October's Eo e Emalani I Alaka'i.

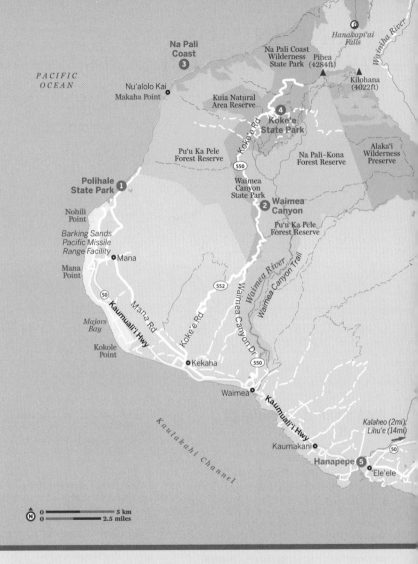

Waimea Canyon & the Westside Highlights

1 Polihale State Park
(p231) Pondering eternity at the edge of the world, which ancient Hawaiians believed to be the jumping-off point for souls leaving for the underworld.

2 Waimea Canyon (p231) Driving jaw-dropping canyon vistas and ocean views so striking you may wonder if this painterly vision is real or not.

3 Na Pali Coast Boat Tour
(p225) Zipping into sea caves, bouncing over waves and snorkeling remote reefs – aah!

4 Koke'e State Park
(p233) Stopping at roadside lookouts to peek over into remote valleys, then lacing up your hiking boots and hitting the trails.

5 Art Night in Hanapepe
(p216) Feeling groovy every Friday, when sleepy Hanapepe's pint-sized main street fills with local artists, food vendors and crowds of visitors for Art Night.

HIKING IN WESTERN KAUA'I

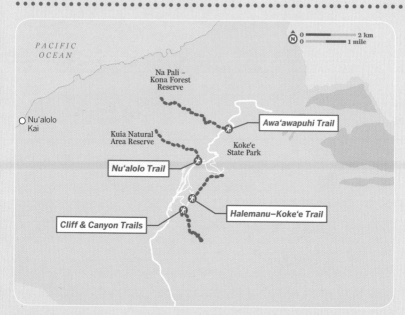

PACIFIC
OCEAN

Na Pali –
Kona Forest
Reserve

Nu'alolo
Kai

Kuia Natural
Area Reserve

Koke'e
State Park

Awa'awapuhi Trail

Nu'alolo Trail

Cliff & Canyon Trails

Halemanu–Koke'e Trail

AWA'AWAPUHI & NU'ALOLO TRAILS

START KOKE'E LODGE
END KOKE'E LODGE
LENGTH EIGHT TO 10 HOURS; 14 MILES

Start at dawn from **Koke'e Lodge** (p236) – it probably won't be open yet, but it's worth a try for a big pancake breakfast. You can get a jump on your day by staying in the park at the Koke'e State Park Cabins or YWCA Camp Sloggett. Otherwise, you'll need to drive in, and leave your car at the **Nu'alolo Trailhead** (Map p214). It's located just a few hundred feet from the lodge.

This is the more difficult of the two trails that head out from here, so it's good to start early. It's a full 3.8 miles out, with pretty good steep sections that take you ultimately to **Lolo Vista Point** (p234), where you'll find absolutely amazing views of the Na Pali Coast.

You might be tempted from here to try the Nu'alolo Cliffs Trail. But it's been closed since 2014, and with good reason. It's eroded and

dangerous as hell. Instead, head back from whence you came. A big burger awaits you for lunch at the Koke'e Lodge, or you can always have a picnic in the pretty grassy area right in front.

After lunch, hop in the car and head up canyon for a mile to the **Awa'awapuhi Trail** (Map p214). At 3.2 miles one way, this is the 'easier' of these two trails. You'll see more people than on the morning trail, and you might have to wait for people to pass (and maybe cling to a tree) to get around the steep sections. Your reward: arriving at **Awa'awapuhi Lookout** (p234) and taking in the cascading views of the cliffs below.

Each trail has elevation gains around 2000ft, making them epic for fit people (and less suitable for youngsters aged under 12). Each has fairly similar flora and fauna and takes you from high-altitude desert-like settings through rain forests thick with birdlife. Make sure you bring enough water and food to keep you properly hydrated, plus a beer for when you get back to the picnic area at the Koke'e Lodge – you earned it!

Graced as it is with the 'Grand Canyon of the Pacific,' it's little surprise the west side of Kaua'i boasts some of the island's most spectacular hiking and trekking opportunities.

CLIFF, CANYON & HALEMANU–KOKE'E TRAILS

START KOKE'E MUSEUM
END YWCA CAMP SLOGGETT
LENGTH FIVE TO SIX HOURS; 4.6 MILES

Combining two favorite trails in Koke'e State Park, this adventure gets you closer to a towering waterfall, amazing views and plenty of feathered friends.

Start this day-long journey early, when the birds are out and the trails are still empty. If you aren't a true crack-of-dawner, stop at the **Koke'e Museum** (p234) before the hike. It has good trail descriptions, plus interesting exhibits on local flora, fauna and natural history.

From there, drive or walk to the **Cliff & Canyon Trails trailhead** (Map p214;). There are remarkable views of Waimea Canyon right from the start. The Cliff Trail itself is just 0.1 miles, a good way to get the old heart started before you begin your descent into the canyon. Rounding the ridge, you will hit the Canyon Trail. It's a knee buster with over 1700ft of up and down. If you have problems with your knees, or it's wet, consider bringing a walking stick to help support you down some of the steeper sections.

The views every step of the descent are truly awesome. You won't see the waterfall along the way, but it really doesn't matter because you'll love spotting soaring seabirds, and possibly even some wild game or feral goats. The trail bottoms out and ascends steeply up the other side of the canyon, where things get a little more lush and tropical.

This part of the canyon is much more brown, red and earthy than the stretches further north. It's about the grand views, sheltering Hawaiian sky and the chance to spot a perfect rainbow encircling the canyon like a warm Technicolor hug.

As you continue down the valley, you'll run into a parking lot, where people with 4WDs can skip much of the hike (why didn't you think of that?). It's a half-mile or so from here to a lookout over the valley that is nothing short of heavenly. Follow signs to **Waipo'o Falls** (Map p214). You won't be able to actually see the falls; rather, you'll find a pool with some small cascades running into it. This is the top of the falls. Stop here for lunch, enjoying the lyrical breeze and sound of falling water.

Follow the trail up to the canyon rim at **Kumuwela Lookout** (p230). From here, you backtrack most of the way – if you're tired, head back to the car. If not, take a side trip on the **Black Pipe Trail** (p235). It's just another 0.5 miles on this trail to get you back to the road. Look carefully for native hibiscus and *iliau* (a plant endemic to Kaua'i's Westside).

Head north along the road for a few hundred feet to reach the start of the **Halemanu–Koke'e Trail** (Map p214;).

This is much more leisurely hiking than the first trail. Along the route, keep your eyes open for koa and ohia trees. These endemic trees make this one of the better birding trails in the park. You might spot *apapane*, *'i'iwi* and *moa*, as well as the occasional feral chicken or lost seabird. If you are lucky, you might even spot a nene (Hawaii's state bird), which can often be seen in the park. Be sure not to disturb their nests. You'll see a lot of banana *poka* plants here. These draping vines have pretty pink flowers, but are one of the most invasive species found in the park. For those that really hate non-natives (plants, not people), consider volunteering your next day with the Koke'e Resource Conservation Program.

The trail is pretty passable, even for youngsters, and ends near **YWCA Camp Sloggett** (Map p214; 808-245-5959; www.campingkauai.com; tent sites $15, cottage, lodge or bunkhouse $120-200). To return to the starting point, you'll either hike back on the same trail, bum a ride, or hoof it on the road (an easier walk though traffic can be burdensome). For real adventurers, consider a night at Camp Sloggett. It's as rough as you get, so bring your own bedding, but waking in the morning to the sound of songbirds in this small corner of Eden is a delightful experience.

Remember to bring plenty of water, food and sun gear. The trails can get downright nasty in rain, though the Canyon Trail tends to be better. For protection from the sun, slather on sunscreen and wear a good hat. You might want to bring along binoculars and perhaps a bird guide.

ROAD TRIP >
WAIMEA CANYON DRIVE

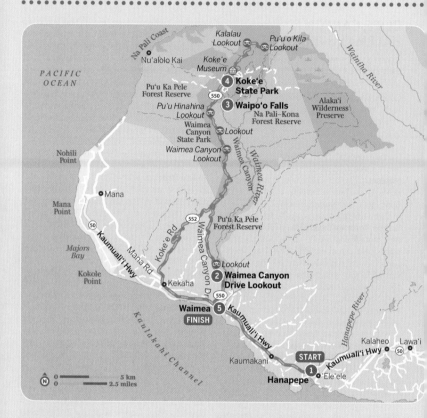

❶ Hanapepe

The most iconic drive in perhaps all of Hawaii, the trip up Waimea Canyon takes you from desert flats, up past a cascading waterfall and on to the edge of the Na Pali Coast wilderness.

Start with breakfast at Bobbie's (p220) or Little Fish Coffee (p220) in the funked-out arts village of **Hanapepe**. Once you've had your fill of granola or loco moco, hop in the car and travel along the Kaumuali'i Hwy to Waimea Canyon Dr (also known as Hwy 550).

The Drive > You'll begin to ascend from the coast here on the windy Waimea Canyon Dr that hovers above the Waimea River up towards the lookout.

❷ Waimea Canyon Drive Lookout

At Mile 4.5, get out of the car to check out the oddly martian waterfalls found at the first **Waimea Canyon Drive Lookout** (p230), then skedaddle up to another impossibly gorgeous **lookout** (p231) at Mile 5.5. This one offers a little bit of hiking and rock scrambling that's fun for the whole family.

The Drive > Just up from here, Waimea Canyon Dr merges with Koke'e Rd, where you'll continue northward towards Waipo'o Falls.

❸ Waipo'o Falls

The entire canyon and its true grandeur comes into more clear focus at the **Waimea Canyon Lookout** (p231) near Mile 10. The next **lookout** (p231), with several spots around Mile 12, is perhaps the most breathtaking, as it includes views of **Waipo'o Falls**, the 800ft cascade that punctuates the far canyon wall.

The Drive > Up another couple of miles between Miles 13 and 14, pull off for views at the Pu'u Hinahina Lookout before continuing on to Koke'e State Park.

❹ Koke'e State Park

Here the landscape fades from rusted red to verdant green as if in an instant. Stop at the **Koke'e Museum** (p234) to get some insights on area hikes, then head up the road to **Kalalau Lookout** (p234) near Mile 18, where you can see clear down to the Na Pali Coast! One last stop at the equally gorgeous **Pu'u o Kila Lookout** (p234) and you are done.

The Drive > Head back along Koke'e Rd, taking the exit down to Waimea.

❺ Waimea

Once you're back in Waimea, take a stroll along the beach at sunset or rustle up dinner at **Wrangler's Steakhouse** (p227).

MARK SEGAL/GETTY IMAGES ©

Kalalau Lookout (p234), Koke'e State Park

❶ Getting There & Away

Kaua'i Bus (p274) has service here. With that said, you are way better off with a rental car. Some car-rental agencies do not allow you to drive the road to Polihale or the backroads inland. Bike tours down Waimea Canyon are ridiculously fun.

Port Allen & Around

The island's next biggest harbor after Lihu'e, Port Allen centers on a mini mall packed with charter companies and wedged into a largely industrial port area. The majority of the island's Na Pali Coast tours leave from Port Allen and, depending on the season, there is a variety of ways to experience the spectacular seascape – from snorkeling in summer to whale-watching in winter. The small Port Allen Airport faces the harbor from across the bay, but is adjacent to Hanapepe, not 'Ele'ele, the town closest to the port.

There is a smallish Glass Beach and overlook just south of town worth checking out before or after your Na Pali tour.

❶ Sights

McBryde Sugar Company Cemetery
CEMETERY

(Map p214; Glass Beach, Port Allen) FREE This cemetery above Glass Beach has a pretty amazing view, and the Chinese and Japanese engraved headstones are ornate and beautiful. During the sugarcane boom at the end of the 19th century, worker camps encircled the area. Lots of people died in the tough conditions and were buried here by Buddhist priests. To get here, take Aka'ula St (the last left before entering the Port Allen wharf) past the fuel storage tanks, then curve to the right down a bumpy dirt road.

★Kauai Coffee Company
FARM

(Map p186; 📞808-335-0813, 800-545-8605; http://kauaicoffee.com; 870 Halewili Rd; ⊗9am-5:30pm Jun-Aug, to 5pm Sep-May; guided tours usually 10am, noon, 2pm & 4pm daily) 🅿 FREE A short drive east of town on Hwy 540, the island's biggest coffee estate is planted with more than 4 million trees, producing about 60% of the state's entire crop. Around the back of the plantation store and visitor center you can glimpse the roasting process, peruse historical photographs and sample estate-grown coffees including a robust peaberry and flavored chocolate macadamia nut.

Afterward, take a quick self-guided walking tour of the farm, or join a free guided tour. The rolling seaside plantation, where coffee berries are cooled by trade winds, is 100% powered by renewable energy. Dive further into the brewing process with an in-depth tour and tasting, available Tuesday and Thursday at 8:30am ($20).

Glass Beach
BEACH

(Map p214) Trash as art – many a visitor has pored through the colorful well-worn remnants of glass spread along the shoreline here. Glass 'pebbles,' along with abandoned metals (some with newfound patina, some not so much), are washed up from an old dumpsite nearby.

To get to the little cove, take Aka'ula St (the last left before entering the Port Allen wharf) past the fuel storage tanks, then curve to the right down a bumpy dirt road about 100yd to the beach. Preserve this unique location by leaving the ocean glass behind.

Glass Beach Overlook
VIEWPOINT

(Map p214; Glass Beach) About 110yd past Glass Beach, stop here for some gorgeous ocean views.

❸ Tours

A number of companies offer very similar Na Pali Coast snorkeling, sunset and dinner tours. Book ahead online for discounts. Beware that motion sickness is common, especially on the Zodiac rafts, which offer little respite from the waves and sun. The journey may be less rough departing from Waimea's small boat harbor instead.

★Captain Andy's Sailing Adventures
BOATING

(Map p218; 📞808-335-6833, 800-535-0830; www.napali.com; Port Allen Marina Center, 4353 Waialo Rd; tours adult/child 2-12yr $119/89) This outfit offers a high-end sailing experience aboard the *Southern Star* – its 65ft flagship luxury catamaran – and a more rugged, adrenaline-addled Zodiac raft tour of the sea caves and secluded beaches of the Na Pali Coast. Six-hour raft trips include a beach landing at Nu'alolo Kai (weather permitting, April to October only), along with snorkeling and easy hiking. Sunset dinner cruises add an awesome sky to the coast's

WAIMEA CANYON & THE WESTSIDE IN...

Two Days

Follow Rte 550 through **Waimea Canyon State Park** (p230) all the way to **Pu'u o Kila** (p234) in **Koke'e State Park** (p233), stopping at the many stunning lookouts along the way. Make sure you pause at the **Koke'e Museum** (p234) (where you can also plan a hike for day three).

Make your way to Hanapepe and try lunch at **Japanese Grandma** (p221). In **Historic Hanapepe** (p216), stroll the main street for souvenirs, objets d'art and a few shots of the 'Old West,' ideally during Friday Art Night.

The morning of day two brings the chance to see the great Na Pali from the sea with a **Na Pali Coast Raft Trip** (p226) – a very different experience than by land.

In Waimea, check out the **Historical Sites** (p224). Where else can you visit a Russian fort, Captain Cook's statue and an ancient Hawaiian aqueduct, all in an hour? There's not a great deal to see at any one stop, but the overall impact feels a bit like you're wandering through a historical tag sale.

Be sure to stop by the **West Kaua'i Technology & Visitor Center** (p223) first to pick up the Kaua'i Historical Society's publication, *Touring Waimea*.

Five Days

On day three, choose a few trails to hike in **Koke'e State Park** (p233) , or maybe just one, and spend the day enjoying one of nature's great works of art. If you're in good shape, take on two hikes in a day.

Day four provides some well-deserved reflection time. Contemplate eternity with a **picnic** beneath the cliffs at Polihale Beach (**Map p214**). No answers? Have a few more deli eats from your **Ishihara Market** take-out meal (p226).

Dine at **Wrangler's Steakhouse** (p227) because after a few days of Westside adventures, you deserve a thick steak, not to mention a saloon.

The sunset at **Kekaha Beach Park** (p230) is as good as the ol' yellow orb gets on the Westside, with great views to Ni'ihau, its satellite isle, and Lehua, so don't miss it.

If the kids need a break from the action, spend day five at **Salt Pond Beach Park** (p217), a mellow, family-style beach replete with lifeguards and facilities. Make sure you pack a snorkel and, if you're really ambitious, a BBQ picnic.

Consider a sunset trip to **Glass Beach** (p212), with drinks to follow at the **Kauai Island Brewery & Grill** (p216).

bewitching cliffs, as well as a chef-prepared meal washed down with a 'sneaky tiki.'

Blue Dolphin Charters BOATING
(Map p218; ☎808-335-5553; http://bluedolphinkauai.com; Port Allen Marina Center, 4353 Waialo Rd; tours adult/child 5-11yr/youth 12-17yr from $119/90/106) Sailing 65ft catamarans, this outfit offers a standard array of tours, including a seven-hour Na Pali and Ni'ihau snorkel trip and a four-hour sunset dinner cruise. Uniquely, it'll take you on a one-tank dive – even if it's your first time scuba diving – and the Zodiac rafts are equipped with hydrophones for listening underwater to whales in winter. Inquire about sportfishing charters.

Kaua'i Sea Tours BOATING
(Map p218; ☎800-733-7997, 808-826-7254; www.kauaiseatours.com; Port Allen Marina Center,

4353 Waialo Rd; tours adult/child under 13yr/youth 13-17yr from $115/75/105) Take a seat on the 60ft catamaran *Lucky Lady* for a snorkel or sunset dinner cruise, or clamber aboard a rigid-hull inflatable raft for a more adventurous Na Pali trip. Six-hour raft tours add a beach landing and a guided walking tour of Nu'alolo Kai (weather permitting, between April and October only), along with sea-cave and waterfall explorations.

Holo Holo Charters BOATING
(Map p218; ☎800-848-6130; www.holoholocharters.com; Port Allen Marina Center, 4353 Waialo Rd; tours adult/child 5-12yr from $115/99) Holo Holo's 50ft sailing catamaran and rigid-hull inflatable rafts happily do Na Pali snorkeling tours and sunset sails that include food and drinks. The power cat

Westside

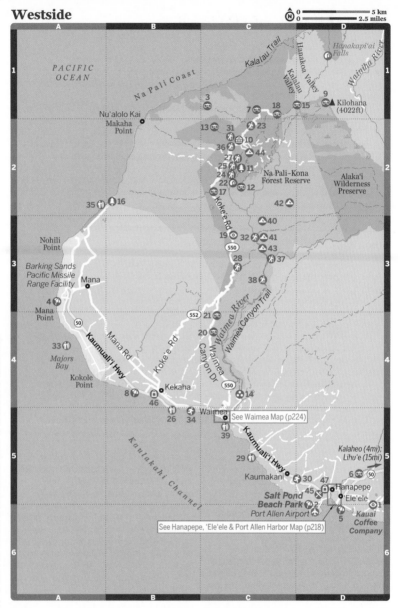

Map legend showing numbered locations across the Westside of Kaua'i including Na Pali Coast, Pacific Ocean, Nu'alolo Kai, Makaha Point, Kalalau Trail, Hanakapi'ai Falls, Waintha River, Kilohana (4022ft), Na Pali-Kona Forest Reserve, Alaka'i Wilderness Preserve, Nohili Point, Barking Sands Pacific Missile Range Facility, Mana, Mana Point, Majors Bay, Kokole Point, Kekaha, Koke'e Rd, Waimea River, Waimea Canyon Dr, Waimea Canyon Trail, Kaumuali'i Hwy, Waimea, Kaumakani, Salt Pond Beach Park, Port Allen Airport, Hanapepe, 'Ele'ele, Kauai Coffee Company, Kaulakahi Channel.

See Waimea Map (p224)

See Hanapepe, 'Ele'ele & Port Allen Harbor Map (p218)

Kalaheo (4mi); Lihu'e (15mi)

takes you on a longer, 3½-hour sunset tour serving substantial appetizers and cocktails, or the marathon seven-hour Ni'ihau and Na Pali Coast snorkeling combo that includes continental breakfast and a buffet lunch.

Catamaran Kahanu
BOATING

(Map p218; ☏808-645-6176; www.catamaran kahanu.com; Port Allen Marina Center, 4353 Waialo Rd; tours adult/child from $79/60) This small-group catamaran affords a personal experience, whether you take a Na Pali

Westside

snorkel trip or a sunset dinner or winter whale-watching cruise. The super-friendly captain and his crew talk story about Hawaiian culture and marine traditions on your way out to sea. Big discounts for online bookings.

Eating

All the eats can be found in the central commercial district.

Kauai Ramen　　　ASIAN, FUSION **$**
(Map p218; ☑808-335-9888; 'Ele'ele Shopping Center, 4469 Waialo Rd; mains $7-11; ⊙11am-10pm; ⊕) A hot bowl of spicy seafood ramen with grilled *gyoza* (pork dumplings) and fried rice on the side might just be what your tummy needs after being rollicked by the waves on a Na Pali Coast boat tour. The bargain-priced menu is nominally Japanese, but with Chinese and local island -style dishes rolled in.

Grinds Café　　　DINER **$$**
(Map p218; ☑808-335-6027; www.grindscafe. net; 'Ele'ele Shopping Center, 4469 Waialo Rd; mains $8-20; ⊙5:30am-9pm Mon & Fri-Sun, 6am-3pm Tue-Thu) This family restaurant in a barnlike building is good for a hearty meal with the locals. It's strong on sandwiches, salads and specialty pizzas; big breakfasts are served all day. Dinners aren't particularly cheap, however.

☗ Drinking & Nightlife

Port Allen Sunset Grill & Bar　　　BAR
(Map p218; ☑808-335-3188; http://portallensun setgrillandbar.com; Port Allen Marina Center, 4353 Waialo Rd; ⊙11am-10pm) Because of the patio, this is the place to hang out while you are waiting for your tour to start or if you want to grab a bite afterwards. Located at the water end of the Port Allen Marina Center, it has a small bar and covered

NU'ALOLO KAI: A LAST PARADISE?

On the remote, rugged Na Pali Coast and accessible only from the sea, Nu'alolo Kai is perhaps the ultimate end-of-the-earth location. Its beach is trapped between two soaring cliffs, framing an empty ocean that goes on for thousands of miles. The site is blessed by a fringing reef that is teeming with fish and shellfish.

Nu'alolo Kai was once linked by a precarious cliffside path to Nu'alolo 'Aina, a terraced valley whose fertile soil was planted with taro and whose walls held burial caves. This isolated paradise was inhabited by about 100 people for 600 years, until 1919. They lived in thatched pole houses, commuting between reef and fields, completely self-sufficient. Men did most of the fishing, while women and children harvested seaweed and shellfish. They weren't entirely cut off from the rest of the island, however. There was once a trail here from Koke'e (now washed away) and their beach was the safest stop for Hawaiians canoeing between Hanalei and Waimea.

Today all that is left are the stone foundations of various structures, but it's enough to get you thinking. To help preserve Nu'alolo Kai, just three companies currently have landing rights: **Kaua'i Sea Tours** (p213) and **Captain Andy's Sailing Adventures** (p212) provide guided tours of the archaeological site, while Waimea-based **Na Pali Explorer** (p225) only lands on the beach. Weather usually restricts boat landings to between mid-April and late October only.

outdoor seating area. Popular bar-food picks (mains $13 to $15) include the macnut-crusted calamari steak.

Kauai Island Brewery & Grill   BREWERY
(Map p218; ☑ 808-335-0006; www.kauaiisland brewing.com; 4350 Waialo Rd; ☉ 11am-9:30pm) The founder of the once beloved, now defunct brewery in Waimea is still brewing in Port Allen. Sample the hoppy, high-alcohol IPAs, the lauded Pakala Porter, South Pacific Brown or light *liliko'i*-infused ale. Drinks and decent pub grub (mains $13 to $15) are discounted during happy hour (3:30pm to 5:30pm daily). While we wish there were a patio, it's still a great bet after your Na Pali tour.

🛍 Shopping

Kauai Chocolate Company   FOOD
(Map p218; ☑ 808-335-0448; www.kauaichoc olate.us; Port Allen Marina Center, 4341 Waialo Rd; ☉ 10am-6pm Mon-Fri, 11am-5pm Sat, noon-3pm Sun) Sample the fudge and truffles with creamy ganaches, mousses and delicate creams of papaya, *liliko'i*, coconut, guava, Kaua'i coffee or sugarcane. The chocolate *'opihi* (limpet) is the biggest seller, followed by handmade chocolate bars chock full of macnuts.

Original Red Dirt Shirt   CLOTHING
(Map p218; ☑ 800-717-3478; www.dirtshirt.com; 4350 Waialo Rd; ☉ 8am-6pm) With punny sayings such as 'Older than Dirt' and 'Life's

Short, Play Dirty,' these shamefully touristy T-shirts can be useful if you're planning on hiking, since most of Kaua'i's dirt wants to destroy your clothing and dye your shoes permanently red.

Port Allen Marina Center   MALL
(Map p218) Down by the harbor. You'll find tour-boat and activity operators here.

'Ele'ele Shopping Center   MALL
(Map p218) A shopping plaza next to the Kuhio Hwy.

ℹ Information

'Ele'ele Post Office (Map p218; ☑ 808-335-5338; www.usps.com; 4485 Waialo Rd; ☉ 9am-noon & 1-4pm Mon-Fri)

ℹ Getting There & Away

Port Allen is about 30 minutes (20 miles) from Li'hue. **Kaua'i Bus** (p274) stops here.

Hanapepe

☑ 808 / POP 2638

Sleepy Hanapepe is a historic farming and port town that prospered during Hawaii's sugar plantation days. Although taro, a touch of cane and other crops are still grown in this wide, red-earth valley accessed by a sinuous riverside road and hemmed in by craggy cliffs on both sides, downtown has been the domain of art galleries for decades. More recently, groovy young entrepreneurs have moved in and in their hands Kaua'i's 'biggest little town' may soon become the island's hippest, most creative place. It's a town where quirk is cool and where young, brainy locals who have trouble identifying with the island-dominant surf culture can feel at home. Most visitors turn up on Friday's Art Night (p219), which is absolutely the best time to see Hanapepe.

History

Hanapepe was not a plantation town, but was built by entrepreneurial immigrants, largely from Asia. The architectural style of false fronts and porches came from them, as it did in the Old West. Many who retired from the sugar plantations or disliked their working conditions came here to begin small farms or businesses. This included labor union organizers in the early 1900s who were not allowed to reside at plantation camps. In 1924 a pitched battle between Filipino strikers and police, known as the Hanapepe Massacre, left 20 dead.

Hanapepe was the island's commercial center until overtaken by Lihu'e in the 1930s. It then morphed into a military R&R town. After a period of decline, artists began settling in and the town reinvented itself once again, propelled by an activist spirit that seems to be rooted in the local soil.

Hanapepe also has its own cinematic history: it doubled as the Australian outback in the TV miniseries *The Thorn Birds* (1983), the Filipino Olongapo City in the movie *Flight of the Intruder* (1991) and as a model for the Hawaiian town in Disney's animated movie *Lilo and Stitch* (2002).

⊙ Sights

The best sights in Hanapepe are the galleries, although their owners would undoubtedly prefer that you think of them as stores. For Kaua'i, this is a unique concentration of artists, so if you're looking to purchase some art, this is the place to do it.

★ **Salt Pond Beach Park**   BEACH
(Map p214; 🚺) Named for its saltwater flats, where seawater is still drained and harvested for reddish-pink sodium crystals, this crescent-shaped beach is great for lounging. With a shallow (but not too shallow) swimming area accessible from the sand and sheltered by a rock reef, it's popular with local families. Full facilities

include BBQ grills, outdoor showers, restrooms, lifeguards and camping.

Turn *makai* (seaward) onto Lele Rd, off the Kuhio Hwy just west of Hanapepe, then hang a right on Lokokai Rd. Stronger swimmers and snorkelers may venture through the narrow keyhole in the reef and swim further west where the water clarifies and fish gather along a rugged coast defined by jagged lava cliffs. But beware of ocean conditions, because currents and tides can shift in a blink. Check with the lifeguards before venturing out.

Swinging Bridge   LANDMARK
(Map p218) Built in 1911 and rebuilt after the 1992 hurricane, this narrow wood and cable suspension bridge spans the Hanapepe River just before it snakes inland between stark red-earth cliffs. It does swing and moan a bit in the wind. It's tucked behind the Aloha Spice Company. No diving!

**Angela Headley Fine Art
& Island Art Gallery**   GALLERY
(Map p218; ☑808-335-0591; www.islandart kauai.com; 3876 Hanapepe Rd; ⊙11am-5pm Mon-Sat, plus 6-9pm Fri) Make this your first stop in Hanapepe for contemporary Hawaiian art: reverse acrylic paintings and giclée prints on wood and metal that are luminous blends of color. It's a somewhat more adventurous gallery than the rest, but it also sells a few baubles, bracelets and foodstuffs.

Bright Side Gallery   GALLERY
(Map p218; ☑808-634-8671; www.thebrightside gallery.com; 3890 Hanapepe Rd; ⊙11am-4pm Mon-Fri, plus 6-9pm Fri) Representing both island and US mainland artists, this fun, whimsical space never takes itself too seriously. Surf themes show up in many of the oils, acrylics and giclées, though it's the wood carvings that really steal the show.

**Art of Marbling & Robert
Bader Wood Sculpture**   GALLERY
(Map p218; ☑808-335-3553; 3890 Hanapepe Rd; ⊙10am-5pm Sat-Thu, to 9pm Fri) Becky J Wold's original marbled silk scarves and sarongs hang from bamboo poles alongside her husband's wooden bowls and sculpture, making this a unique gallery experience.

Hanapepe Valley Lookout   VIEWPOINT
(Map p214) Popping up shortly after Mile 14, this lookout offers a view deep into Hanapepe

WAIMEA CANYON & THE WESTSIDE HANAPEPE

Hanapepe, 'Ele'ele & Port Allen Harbor

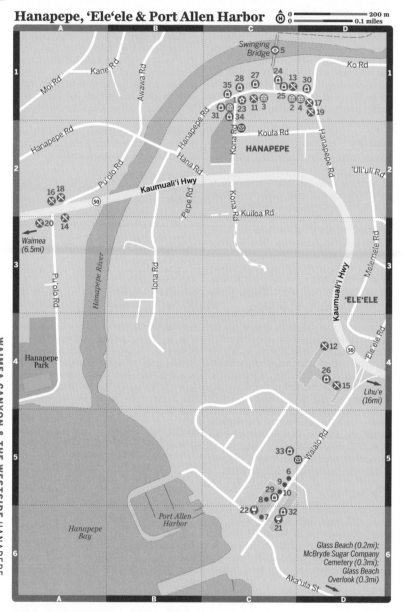

Valley, where the red-clay cliffs are topped by wild green sugarcane. This sight is but a teaser for the dramatic vistas awaiting at Waimea Canyon.

While the sugar business has faded, Hanapepe Valley remains an agriculture stronghold with grazing cattle and local farmers growing taro. Look *makai* (seaward) across the highway and you'll see the region's cash crop: coffee.

Arius Hopman Gallery GALLERY
(Map p218; ☎808-335-0227; www.hopmanart.com; 3840c Hanapepe Rd; ☺10am-2pm Mon-Fri,

Hanapepe, 'Ele'ele & Port Allen Harbor

plus 6-9pm Fri) Art photography and plein-air watercolors spotlight Kaua'i's tropical landscapes, flora and fauna, from mango and banana trees to sunrise breaking over the Na Pali Coast. Ask about digital photography classes.

Dawn Traina Gallery GALLERY
(Map p218; ☑808-335-3993; 3840b Hanapepe Rd; ⊙6-9pm Fri or by appointment) Traditional Hawaiian themes come to life in many different media, including oil paintings, limited-edition giclées and scratchboards (hard-panel carving reminiscent of scrimshaw).

Amy-Lauren's Gallery GALLERY
(Map p218; ☑808-335-2827; www.amylaurens gallery.com; 4545 Kona Rd; ⊙11am-5pm Mon-Thu, to 9pm Fri, noon-5pm Sat) Here's a chance to buy (or at least gaze upon) an original instead of a giclée print. This boutique gallery invites passersby inside with vibrantly colored oil paintings, photography and mixed media.

⚝ Festivals & Events

★ Art Night ART, FOOD
(www.hanapepe.org; ⊙6-9pm Fri) On any given Friday night, Hanapepe comes to life and gives everyone an extended peek into its art world. Galleries stay open later and

the town's main drag is transformed by musicians and street vendors. Visitors and locals come to stroll, browse and snack streetside on everything from barbecue to hot, sugary *malasadas* (Portuguese fried dough, served warm and sugar-coated).

During this weekly event, galleries hold open houses and artists often make themselves available. On egalitarian display are island-inspired originals, Hawaiiana vintage, pure kitsch and the works of Sunday dabblers to fine-art photography, watercolors and a sampling of Asian art. The action centers on Hanapepe Road.

**Kaua'i Chocolate
& Coffee Festival** FOOD & DRINK
(www.hawaiichocolatefestival.com; Hanapepe Rd; ⊙late Oct) A spin-off from a popular festival in Honolulu, this local caffeine-fest has tastings, demonstrations, live entertainment and farm tours.

✕ Eating

Most of the eateries center on the main road. They close really early.

★ Taro Ko Chips Factory HAWAIIAN $
(Map p218; ☑808-335-5586; 3940 Hanapepe Rd; per small bag $4-5; ⊙8am-5pm) Thinly sliced *kalo* (taro) that's been seasoned with garlic

THE HANAPEPE MASSACRE?

On September 9, 1924, a surprisingly little-known chapter in Hawaiian (and American) history unfolded in Hanapepe.

That year a sugar workers' strike spread to Kaua'i. Strikers were demanding a decent minimum wage, an eight-hour workday and equal pay between men and women. Filipino workers had their own particular grievances. They were the last group of laborers to arrive in Hawaii and were generally given the worst housing and lowest-paying jobs. More than half weren't even considered residents.

On Kaua'i, 575 Filipino workers joined the strike and set up a headquarters in Hanapepe. After six weeks of little progress, the frustrated strikers seized two Filipinos who had not joined the strike and held them in a schoolhouse. Kaua'i deputy sheriff William Crowell arrived with 40 troops, including many trained sharpshooters, whom he positioned on a nearby hill. Crowell went in with three deputies and demanded that the strikers turn over their captives, which they did. But a crowd also followed Crowell from the schoolhouse, waving their cane knives in the air. It is not clear what happened next – whether Crowell and his men were attacked, or whether the sharpshooters opened fire prematurely – but in the ensuring melee, 16 strikers were gunned down and four deputies were stabbed to death. Crowell was injured, but survived. There was little public outcry and the Hanapepe Massacre disappeared into the history books. Today no one knows where the strikers are buried.

salt, slathered with oil and tortured in a deep wok makes for some crispy, slightly sweet but mostly salty crunching. The farmer who grows the taro is also the chef, so show aloha.

Hanapepe Farmers Market
MARKET $
(Map p214; Hanapepe Town Park; ☺3-5pm Thu) 🍴 One of the countywide Sunshine Markets. Small-scale farmers truck in the goods themselves and locals line up before the whistle blows just to score the best produce.

Paco's Tacos
MEXICAN $
(Map p218; ☎808-335-0454; 4505 Pu'olo Rd; dishes $8-15; ☺10am-8pm Mon-Sat) Grab takeout or sit at picnic tables outside this Baja-style roadside shack offering all the usual suspects, including *carne asada* (grilled meat) tacos, shrimp burritos and enchilada platters. Mexican food never tasted so Hawaiian.

Lappert's Hawaii
ICE CREAM $
(Map p218; ☎808-335-6121; www.lapperts hawaii.com; 1-3555 Kaumuali'i Hwy; scoops from $4; ☺10am-6pm) The famed ice-cream chain started operations right here along the highway in 1983 at this quaint little roadside shop and factory. The business is way too big for Hanapepe-based production now, but this humble shop still scoops the goodness of tropical flavors such as 'Kauai Pie' (Kona coffee ice cream, chocolate fudge, macadamia nuts, coconut flakes and vanilla-cake crunch).

Bobbie's
HAWAIIAN $
(Map p218; ☎808-334-5152; 3824 Hanapepe Rd; meals $9-12; ☺10am-3pm & 5-8pm Mon-Wed, 10am-2:30pm Thu-Sat, plus 5-8:30pm Fri) In a small storefront, this humble lunch counter makes huge plate lunches of local faves such as *loco moco* and chicken katsu (deep-fried fillets), as well as BBQ chicken and ribs on Friday nights. It's not good-for-you food, but it certainly tastes darn good.

Little Fish Coffee
CAFE $
(Map p218; ☎808-335-5000; www.facebook. com/LittleFishCoffee; 3900 Hanapepe Rd; items $3-11; ☺6:30am-5pm Mon-Thu & Sat, to 9pm Fri; 🛜) The colorful chalkboard menu at this cute coffee shop lures you with espresso drinks, fruit smoothies, granola bowls, homemade soups, garden salads and bagel and panini sandwiches. Sit inside amid the retro artwork and music, or on the back patio splashed with both sun and shade.

Kaua'i Pupu Factory
HAWAIIAN $
(Map p218; ☎808-335-0084; 1-3566 Kaumuali'i Hwy; mains $7-10; ☺9am-5:30pm Mon-Fri, to 3pm Sat) A down-home-style deli is your source for fresh *poke* – try a scoop of *tako* (octopus) or ahi with *limu* (seaweed) – and Hawaiian plate lunches with bundles of *laulau* and *lomilomi* salmon. If you've got a big group, get enough for everyone, pack a cooler and head to the beach.

Wong's Restaurant & Omoide Bakery
CHINESE, HAWAIIAN $

(Map p218; ☑ 808-335-5066; www.wongso moide.com; 1-3543 Kaumuali'i Hwy; mains $8-12; ⊙ 8am-9pm Tue-Sun) A popular diner that serves up local plantation-style fare, such as saimin (local-style noodle soup) with pork or a whole roasted duck. But the real reason to stop by is the *liliko'i* (passion fruit) chiffon pie.

★ Japanese Grandma
SUSHI $$

(Map p218; ☑ 808-855-5016; www.japanese grandma.com; 3871 Hanapepe Rd; sushi $9-20; ⊙ 11am-3pm & 5:30-9pm Thu-Mon, 11am-3pm Tue-Wed) The whole island was excited when Japanese Grandma opened its doors in 2016. While it has to work on some details (like the lighting and service), the sushi is outstanding. The smallish eatery with open kitchen and attached crafts market delivers the best sushi on this side of the island. Choose from any number of inventive rolls, sushi and *nigiri* (oblong-shaped sushi).

☆ Entertainment

Aside from Friday Art Nights, there's little nightlife to speak of here.

Storybook Theatre of Hawaii
THEATER

(Map p218; ☑ 808-335-0712; www.storybook.org; 3814 Hanapepe Rd; 90min walking tour per individual/couple/family $18/25/30; ⊙ tours depart 9:30am Tue & Thu; 🔊) The Storybook Theatre, which tours Hawaii with puppets who 'talk story' (chat), has been around for 15 years. Schedules vary, but it's worth a peek on Art Night (p219), when it sometimes hosts kids' activities. Book ahead to join one of its historical walking tours of Hanapepe (no puppets, sorry!), which finishes with a relaxing Chinese herbal tea served in the garden.

 ## Shopping

Talk Story Bookstore
BOOKS, MUSIC

(Map p218; ☑ 808-335-6469; www.talkstory bookstore.com; 3785 Hanapepe Rd; ⊙ 10am-5pm Sat-Thu, to 9:30pm Fri) The USA's westernmost bookstore is a funky indie bookseller's paradise, the kind that may even fill e-reader enthusiasts with musty page-turning nostalgia. New books by local authors are stocked up front, but it's mostly used fare here, with more than 100,000 books (organized by both genre and, curiously, author gender), vintage Hawaiian sheet music and vinyl records.

Banana Patch Studio
ARTS & CRAFTS

(Map p218; ☑ 800-914-5944, 808-335-5944; www.bananapatchstudio.com; 3865 Hanapepe Rd; ⊙ 10am-4:30pm Mon-Thu, to 9pm Fri, to 4pm Sat) This studio puts out functional crafts rather than fine art – koi watercolors, wooden tiki bar signs, pottery with tropical flowers, souvenir ceramic tiles and coasters – but there's plenty to behold in this crowded little space, which is usually packed with shoppers. There is also a branch in Kilauea (p150) on the North Shore.

Kauai Fine Arts
ART

(Map p218; ☑ 808-335-3778; 3751 Hanapepe Rd; ⊙ 9:30am-4:30pm Mon-Thu & Sat, to 9pm Fri) If you want to get your hands on a unique piece of memorabilia, step inside to peruse fossilized shark teeth, antique and newer tiki carvings, prints of old Pan Am ads, oldworld maps and vintage botanical prints.

Salty Wahine
FOOD

(Map p214; ☑ 808-378-4089; http://saltywahine. com; 1-3529 Kaumuali'i Hwy; ⊙ 9am-5pm) Beside the highway on the outskirts of town, this factory shop is a smorgasbord of salt and spice blends with island flavors from herbs to fruit.

A SOILED SHIRT

The well-known dirt shirt originated on Kaua'i back in the 1990s, after Hurricane 'Iniki covered the island with its trademark red soil. As the legend goes, a stack of white tees was stained in the process...and the dirt shirt was born. The rich red color is essentially rusted volcanic rock, with the redness coming from iron oxide. Among the Hawaiian Islands, only Kaua'i features such plentiful red dirt, thanks to five million years of erosion.

Minds differ on who actually discovered the dirt shirt, but more importantly (for the shopper) there is now only one factory outlet on the island. The **Original Red Dirt Shirt** (p216) has an unmissable red store in 'Ele'ele. It has also expanded to other islands and to the US mainland, cleverly using the red dirt of Arizona and Utah.

When it's new, be sure to wash your dirt shirt separately, at least the first few times. Manufacturers now claim that the dye holds fast, but in the past one dirt shirt thrown in the laundry had the surprising ability to replicate.

KAUA'I EDUCATION ASSOCIATION FOR SCIENCE & ASTRONOMY

Minimal light pollution makes Kaua'i's Westside ideal for taking in the night sky. To this end, the **Kaua'i Education Association for Science & Astronomy** (KEASA; Map p214; ☑ 808-332-7827; www.keasa.org) holds free monthly 'starwatches' on Saturdays closest to the new moon. Educators share both their gear and insights with the public, beginning at sunset. Bring a light jacket, a lawn chair, insect repellent and a small flashlight preferably covered with red cellophane.

Follow Hwy 50 west past Hanapepe. After Mile 18, turn right at the fork to Kaumakani School. Follow the signs to the sports field and remember to turn off your headlights when approaching. Prepare to have your mind blown. Space: it goes on forever.

'Black Lava' and *kiawe* (Hawaiian mesquite) sea salt, coconut-infused cane sugar and *li hing mui* margarita salt are bestsellers.

Aloha Spice Company
FOOD
(Map p218; ☑ 800-915-5944, 808-335-5960; www.alohaspice.com; 3857 Hanapepe Rd; ⊙ 10am-4:30pm Mon-Thu, to 9pm Fri, to 4pm Sat) You can smell the savory, smoky goodness as soon as the bells on the swinging front door announce your presence. In addition to local spices, this place also sells sauces and jams, lotions and oils, nuts and chocolate, teas and Kaua'i-made tropical-fruit popsicles.

Jacqueline on Kaua'i
CLOTHING
(Map p218; ☑ 808-335-5797; 3837 Hanapepe Rd; custom shirts $60-200; ⊙ 9am-6pm Mon-Thu, Sat & Sun, to 9pm Fri) Friendly Jacqueline makes her mark with aloha shirts custom-made while you wait (usually one to two hours). She also does children's sizes, and with coconut buttons no less. You choose the fabric and she does the rest. Place an order at the beginning of Art Night (p219) and you're good to go by the end.

Puahina
CLOTHING
(Map p218; ☑ 808-335-9771; 4141 Kona Rd; ⊙ 11am-4pm Mon-Thu, 11am-4pm & 6-8:30pm Fri, Sat & Sun by appointment) Bold designs set this small boutique apart. You'll find wearable keepsakes that fuse traditional motifs with contemporary styles. Look for original-design shirts, skirts and tops adorned by native ferns, as well as unusual shell jewelry. The shop also carries Maui-made Hana Lima Soap Co bath and body products with alluring tropical scents.

Kauai Kookie Company
FOOD
(Map p214; ☑ 808-335-5003; www.kauaikookie.com; 1-3529 Kaumuali'i Hwy; ⊙ 8am-5pm Mon-Fri, from 10am Sat & Sun) Though some say it's more novelty than delicious, Kauai Kookie has a local following rivaling that of Girl Scout cookies. Classic tastes sold at the factory warehouse shop include Kona coffee and chocolate chip–macadamia nut.

Machinemachine
CLOTHING
(Map p218; www.machinemachineapparel.com; 3800 Hanapepe Rd; ⊙ 5:30-9pm Fri) Shannon Hiramoto, a fifth-generation Kaua'i-born designer, scours flea markets and thrift stores for aloha wear and other tossed-out fashions, which she upcycles into funky, elegant dresses, skirts and cloth-covered journals. She has a devoted cult following and does most of the sewing in her Hanapepe workshop.

JJ Ohana
GIFTS & SOUVENIRS
(Map p218; ☑ 808-335-0366; www.jjohana.com; 3805b Hanapepe Rd; ⊙ 8am-6pm Mon-Thu, to 9pm Fri, to 5pm Sat & Sun) There aren't many places where you can find both $2.50 comfort food and a $7000 necklace. This family-run spot offers affordable daily food specials (such as chili and rice) and high-quality, Hawaii-made crafts and souvenirs, such as koa wood bowls, coral and abalone-shell jewelry, and Ni'ihau shell lei.

ⓘ Information

Hanapepe Post Office (Map p218; ☑ 808-335-5433; www.usps.com; 3817 Kona Rd; ⊙ 9am-1:30pm & 2-4pm Mon-Fri)
American Savings Bank (☑ 808-335-3118; www.asbhawaii.com; 4548 Kona Rd; ⊙ 8am-5pm Mon-Thu, to 6pm Fri) Has a 24-hour ATM.
Bank of Hawaii (☑ 808-335-5021; www.boh.com; 3764 Hanapepe Rd; ⊙ 8:30am-4pm Mon-Thu, to 6pm Fri) Has a 24-hour ATM.

ⓘ Getting There & Away

Veer *mauka* (inland) onto Hanapepe Rd, the main drag, at the 'Kaua'i's Biggest Little Town' sign on the Kuhio Hwy. **Kaua'i Bus** (p274) will drop you near the main drag.

Waimea

808 / POP 1855

One of several Waimeas in Hawaii, this is not O'ahu's legendary surf spot nor is it the Big Island's upscale cowboy town. But in some ways, Kaua'i's Waimea is equally intriguing. Part Hawaiian hamlet, part big-dollar agriculture stronghold, it's the original landing spot of Captain Cook and the jumping-off point for visiting spectacular Waimea Canyon and Koke'e State Parks.

Waimea means 'reddish-brown water,' which refers to the river that picks up salt from the canyon and colors the ocean red. Sugar plantations played a role in the town's development and the skeleton of the old mill can still be seen amid the tech centers that house both defense contractors working at the nearby Pacific Missile Range Facility and an even more controversial presence: multinational chemical companies that develop genetically modified seeds for worldwide crop cultivation.

While many itineraries skip the town, there's enough history here, plus a decent beach for walking, to make it a fun afternoon adventure.

◉ Sights

★ West Kaua'i Technology & Visitor Center
MUSEUM

(Map p224; 808-338-1332; www.westkauaivisitorcenter.org; 9565 Kaumuali'i Hwy; ⊙10am-4pm Mon-Fri; 🖰) 🎯 FREE Orient yourself historically to the Westside with modest exhibits on Hawaiian culture, Captain Cook, sugar plantations and the US military. The gift shop sells locally made artisan crafts, including rare Ni'ihau shell lei. This complex doubles as a visitor center and offers a free, three-hour historic Waimea walking tour at 8:30am Mondays (call to register by noon on the previous Friday).

Waimea Hawaiian Church
CHURCH

(Map p224; 4491 Halepule Rd; ⊙services 9am Sun) This simple low-slung replica of an original missionary church hosts a Sunday Hawaiian-language mass that can be a fun and interesting way to connect with local culture. History buffs will be interested to know that the first Christian missionaries came to Waimea in 1820. The original church was built here by the Reverend George Rowell in 1865 after a theological dispute with his missionary partner.

Russian Fort Elizabeth State Historical Park
HISTORIC SITE

(Map p224; http://dlnr.hawaii.gov/dsp/parks/kauai; off Kaumuali'i Hwy; ⊙dawn-dusk) FREE A Russian fort in Hawaii? Yes, it's true. Constructed in 1817 and named after the Empress of Russia, Fort Elizabeth commanded the entrance to Waimea River. The octagonal design ranges from 350ft to 450ft across. In addition to a cannon, it once harbored a Russian Orthodox chapel. Apart from impressive walls, some 20ft high, there is little else to see nowadays. There's a pretty beach here. It's by the riverfront so it isn't great for swimming, but it makes for a pleasant afternoon stroll.

Lucy Wright Park
PARK

(Map p224) At this small municipal park next to the Waimea River, you'll find picnic tables, restrooms and outdoor showers. Camping is permitted on the flat grassy area, but the site doesn't hold much appeal. A plaque commemorating the landing sites of Captain Cook has gone missing.

Hofgaard Park
PARK

(Map p224) In the Westside town of Waimea, this little shady corner park is home to the Captain Cook statue. There are a few handy historic plaques that explain the history of the area.

Menehune Ditch
ARCHAEOLOGICAL SITE

(Kikiaola; Map p214; Menehune Rd) 🎯 Not much remains to be seen of this unique and still functional aqueduct, yet its archaeological significance is immeasurable. It's the only example of pre-contact cut and dressed stonework in Hawaii, said to be the work of the *menehune* (the 'little people'), who allegedly completed it within one night for *ali'i* (royalty). To get here, follow Menehune Rd inland from Kaumuali'i Hwy nearly 1.5 miles to the bridge along the Waimea River. Look for the interpretive signboard opposite.

Captain Cook Monument
MONUMENT

(Map p224; Hofgaard Park, cnr Waimea Rd & Kaumuali'i Hwy) Captain James Cook changed the course of Hawaii history when he sailed into Waimea Harbor with his ships *Resolution* and *Discovery* in January 1778. Partly obscured by trees, Cook's likeness is a replica of the original statue by Sir John Tweed in Whitby, England.

WAIMEA CANYON & THE WESTSIDE WAIMEA

Waimea

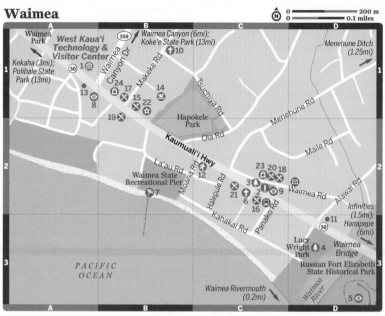

Waimea

Waimea Town Center   ARCHITECTURE
(Map p224) Surprisingly, Waimea offers some interesting architecture, including the neoclassical First Hawaiian Bank (p227) (1929), the art-deco Waimea Theater (p227) (1938), and a historic church, the crushed coral-covered Waimea United Church of Christ (p224), first built during the early mission-ary era and faithfully reconstructed after Hurricane 'Iniki.

Waimea United Church of Christ   CHURCH
(Map p224; Makeke Rd) A historic church, the crushed coral-covered Waimea United Church of Christ was first built during the early missionary era and faithfully reconstructed after Hurricane 'Iniki.

Waimea State Recreational Pier
BEACH

(Map p224; www.hawaiistateparks.org; La'au Rd) This wide black beach, flecked with microscopic green crystals called olivine, stretches between two scenic rock outcroppings and is bisected by the namesake fishing pier. It's especially beautiful at sunset. Facilities include restrooms, picnic areas and drinking water.

Rare Hawaiian Honey Company
FARM STORE

(☑808-775-1000, 888-663-6639; www.rarehawaiianhoney.com; 66-1250 Lalamilo Farm Rd; ☺9am-4pm Mon-Fri) ⌀ This sales and tasting room specializes in locally produced 'white honey,' which resembles a pearlescent butter. It's not cheap (an 8oz jar costs $15 to $21), but it's tasty and genuinely rare: this bee butter comes from a small forest of kiawe trees in Puako. The thriving family-run business is the brainchild of former lawyer Richard Spiegel, who in the mid-1970s began collaborating with bees and the sweet nectar of kiawe flowers.

Waimea Sugar Mill
FACTORY

(Map p224; 9852 Kaumuali'i Hwy) FREE The evocative skeleton of the old Waimea Sugar Mill still stands over town. Originally built in the 1830s, this mill pumped out sugar from the Westside, fueling Kaua'i's economy until 1945. Over the years, new waves of immigrants, from Germany, England, China, Norway and beyond toiled in the mills. Today it's a good spot for a picnic and a cool backdrop to the Menehune Products Fair.

🏃 Activities

Na Pali Explorer
BOATING

(Map p224; ☑303-338-9999; www.napaliexplorer.com; 9814 Kaumuali'i Hwy; raft tour adult/child $139/119, tour with beach landing $149/129) This Westside shop does it right, with small raft tours. You can choose to beach and hike up to a little village, or go for the rip-roaring experience aboard a rigid-hull inflatable boat. The larger raft has a canopy. Bring a towel to dry off after snorkeling.

Waimea Rivermouth
SURFING

(Map p214) This river break takes you both right and left. Southern swells work best here. Expect it to be crowded. And being a river break, expect the water to be dirty.

Na Pali Sportfishing
FISHING

(Map p214; ☑808-635-9424; Kikiaola Small Boat Harbor, Kekaha; 4-/6-/8hr trips per person $145/180/245) If there is anything to upend a deep-sea fishing trip, it's hanging green over the side. This outfit has lessened that risk with a 34ft catamaran, which makes for a much steadier platform. Standard catch includes yellowfin, skipjack, marlin, mahimahi and wahoo. All gear supplied.

Infinities
SURFING

(Map p214) This is an exposed point break between Hanapepe and Waimea. It cranks all year round, but can be busy.

Waimea Swimming Pool
SWIMMING

(Map p224; 9691 Kaumuali'i Hwy; ☺7:30am-2:45pm Tue & Thu, 10am-4:30pm Wed, Fri & Sat, noon-4:30pm Sun) A county-run public pool located in the back of the Waimea Theater.

RUSSIAN FORT ELIZABETH

So how did the Russians end up with a fort (p223) in Kaua'i? In the early 19th century, the Russian American Company in Sitka, Alaska, wished to open trade with Hawaii to access food for its settlements. They sent several ships, one of which was wrecked in Waimea in 1815. Another, led by the wily Georg Anton Schäffer, was sent to recover the cargo and to set up a permanent trading post. Schäffer signed an agreement with King Kaumuali'i of Kaua'i giving the Russians certain trading rights. After failing to win assistance from King Kamehameha on the Big Island, Schäffer tried to get the already rebellious Kaumuali'i to turn against Kamehameha in favor of Russian protection.

Construction of three forts followed, two in Hanalei and one in Waimea, which commanded the river. Named after the Russian empress, Fort Elizabeth was the largest, with cannon, barracks, a trading house, gardens, homes for 30 families and a Russian Orthodox chapel. The fort was not yet complete, however, when allegiances shifted decisively against the high-handed Schäffer. Acting on King Kamehameha's request, King Kaumuali'i expelled the entire Russian contingent. Today Fort Elizabeth remains the most impressive reminder of Russian efforts to gain influence in Hawaii.

☞ Tours

Taking Na Pali Coast tours that start from Kekaha's Kikiaola Small Boat Harbor (instead of Port Allen near Hanapepe) means the journey isn't as rough.

Big Island Bike Tours CYCLING
(☑ 800-331-0159; www.bigislandbiketours.com; tours from $160; ⊕) Established by an experienced pro cyclist, this company offers various group rides, including two in the Honoka'a area. Both start in Waimea, where the company is based; one goes to the Waipi'o Valley Lookout, while the other ascends into Pa'auilo and the Hawaiian Vanilla Company.

Na Pali Riders BOATING
(Map p224; ☑ 808-742-6331; www.napaliriders. com; 9600 Kaumuali'i Hwy; 4hr tour adult/child 5-12yr $159/119) Get a first-hand peek at sea caves (weather permitting) with Captain Chris Turner, who likes to think of his Zodiac raft tour as being 'National Geographic' in style (read: he likes to travel fast, blare Led Zeppelin and talk story). Warning: the no-shade, bumpy ride isn't for the faint of heart. Morning and afternoon departures available. Cash discounts.

Liko Kaua'i Cruises BOATING
(Map p224; ☑ 888-732-5456; http://liko-kauai. com; 4516 Alawai Rd; 4hr cruise adult/child 4-12yr $140/95) Run by a Kaua'i-born-and-raised Hawaiian, whose ancestors hailed from Ni'ihau, this outfit sails to the Na Pali Coast in its 49ft power catamaran with a shade canopy and forward-facing padded seats. Tours go as far as Ke'e Beach during summer. Snorkel gear provided.

✲ Festivals & Events

★ **Waimea Town Celebration** CULTURAL
(www.waimeatowncelebration.com; ⊕ mid-Feb; ⊕) ⏺ FREE Free fun includes a *paniolo* (Hawaiian cowboy) rodeo; storytelling; canoe, SUP and surf-skiing races; local food vendors; carnival games; an arts-and-crafts fair; and lei-making and ukulele-playing contests.

✕ Eating

This is probably the best culinary selection on the Westside. Places close early.

★ **Ishihara Market** SUPERMARKET, DELI $
(Map p224; ☑ 808-338-1751; 9894 Kaumuali'i Hwy; ⊕ 6am-7:30pm Mon-Thu, to 8pm Fri & Sat, to 7pm

Sun) It's an ad-hoc lesson in local cuisine shopping at this historic market (c 1934) with deli. Trusty take-out meals (get here before the lunch rush) include sushi, spicy ahi *poke* and smoked marlin. Daily specials and marinated ready-to-go meats are available for those wanting to barbecue. The parking lot is often full – it's that popular.

G's Juicebar HEALTH FOOD $
(Map p224; ☑ 808-634-4112; 9691 Kaumuali'i Hwy; snacks from $7; ⊕ 7am-6pm Mon-Fri, 9am-5pm Sat) You quest for Kaua'i's top acai bowl might reach the finish line inside this Rastafarian stronghold. A Marley bowl comes with kale and bee pollen; the Kauai Bowl is with mango juice and shaved coconut. Fresh tropical juice smoothies and yerba mate tea will quench your thirst.

Super Duper Two ICE CREAM $
(Map p224; ☑ 808-338-1590; 9889 Waimea Rd; snacks from $3; ⊕ noon-9pm Mon-Thu, to 10pm Fri & Sat) Across the street from Captain Cook's statue, this place lives up to its moniker. Stop in for tropically flavored shakes, sundaes, floats or old-fashioned scoops of Roselani ice cream (made on Maui) in crispy handmade waffle cones.

Yumi's DINER $
(Map p224; ☑ 808-338-1731; 9691 Kaumuali'i Hwy; mains $5-10; ⊕ 7:30am-2:30pm Tue-Thu, 7am-1pm & 6-8pm Fri, 8am-1pm Sat) 'Friendly, filling and reasonably priced' sums up this local institution, where you can get a plate lunch with some chicken katsu or teriyaki beef, a burger, a mini *loco moco* or a special bowl of saimin. Be sure to order a slice of coconut pie or the pumpkin crunch for dessert.

**Jo-Jo's Anuenue Shave Ice
& Treats** DESSERTS $
(Map p224; 9899 Waimea Rd; snacks from $3; ⊕ 10am-5:30pm; ⊕) This shack delivers icy flavor: all syrups are homemade without additives and won't knock you out with sweetness. The superstar item is the *halo halo* (Filipino-style mixed fruit) with coconut.

Island Taco MEXICAN $
(Map p224; ☑ 808-338-9895; www.islandfish-taco.com; 9643 Kaumuali'i Hwy; mains $6-13; ⊕ 11am-5pm) At this island-fusion taquería, tortillas are stuffed with wasabi-coated or Cajun-dusted seared ahi, fresh cabbage and rice. Have the same trick done with mahimahi, tofu, shrimp with papaya seeds or *kalua* pork with spinach instead. Wet burritos and

taco salads round out the menu. It's a local chain, but still feels pretty boutique in its approach.

Shrimp Station
SEAFOOD $

(Map p224; ☑ 808-338-1242; 9652 Kaumuali'i Hwy; mains $8-13; ⊙ 11am-5pm; 🛱) Want shrimp? Whether sautéed scampi-style, coconut- or beer-battered, in taco form or ground up into a 'shrimp burger,' crustaceans is what this roadside chow hut is all about. Look for the flamingo-pink sign out front.

Wrangler's Steakhouse
STEAK $$

(Map p224; ☑ 808-338-1218; www.innwaimea. com/wranglers.html; 9852 Kaumuali'i Hwy; lunch meals around $10, dinner mains $18-30; ⊙ 11am-8:30pm Mon-Thu, 4-9pm Fri & Sat, 4-8:30pm Sun; 🛱) Yes, it's touristy, but this Western-style saloon dishes up plantation lunches in authentic *kaukau* (food) tins full of shrimp and vegetable tempura, teriyaki steak, rice and kimchi. Sizzling dinner steaks are decent; the seafood and soup-and-salad bar less so. Save room for peach cobbler. There's atmospheric seating on the front lanai or back porch.

☆ Entertainment

Hit up the restaurants or take in a movie – this is a city that sleeps.

Waimea Theater
CINEMA

(Map p224; ☑ 808-338-0282; www.waimea theater.com; 9691 Kaumuali'i Hwy; adult/child 5-10yr $8/6) This art-deco movie theater is the place for a rainy day or for an early-evening reprieve from sun and sea. Kaua'i is a little behind with new releases and schedules are erratic, but since this is one of only two functioning cinemas on the island (the other is in Lihu'e), no one's complaining.

🛍 Shopping

Kaua'i Granola
FOOD

(Map p224; ☑ 808-338-0121; 9633 Kaumuali'i Hwy; ⊙ 10am-5pm Mon-Sat) Before you head up to Waimea Canyon and Koke'e State Parks, drop by this island bakery for snacks such as trail mix, macadamia-nut cookies, chocolate-dipped coconut macaroons and tropically flavored granola.

Aunty Lilikoi
Passion Fruit Products
FOOD, GIFTS

(Map p224; ☑ 808-338-1296, 866-545-4564; www. auntylilikoi.com; 9875 Waimea Rd; ⊙ 10am-6pm)

Find something for almost any occasion: award-winning passion fruit–wasabi mustard, passion-fruit syrup (great for banana pancakes), massage oil (the choice for honeymooners) and a tasty lip balm (ideal for après surf), all made with at least a kiss of, you guessed it, *liliko'i*.

Menehune Product Fair
ARTS & CRAFTS

(Map p224; http://menehuneproductsfair.x10host. com/; 9852 Kaumuali'i Hwy; ⊙ 9am-4pm Wed-Sun) Peruse through crafts stalls, sample BBQ chicken or just talk story at this home-spun fair. Some days you won't find many vendors around, but it's a fun stop and a good chance to see craftsmen and women at work.

ℹ Information

Division of Forestry & Wildlife (Map p94; ☑ 808-274-3433; http://dlnr.hawaii.gov/ dofaw/; 3060 Eiwa St, Room 306, Lihu'e; ⊙ 8am-3:30pm Mon-Fri) For remote backcountry camping on the Westside, the Division of Forestry & Wildlife issues permits for four campgrounds in Waimea Canyon, three campgrounds (Sugi Grove, Kawaikoi and Waikoali) in and around Koke'e State Park, and the Wai'alae Cabin campground near the Alaka'i Wilderness Preserve.

Division of State Parks (Map p94; ☑ 808-274-3444; www.hawaiistateparks.org; 3060 Eiwa St, Room 306, Lihu'e; ⊙ 8am-3:30pm Mon-Fri) Office issues camping and hiking permits for Na Pali Coast Wilderness State Park and camping permits for Koke'e State Park and Polihale State Park.

Waimea Public Library (☑ 808-338-6848; 9750 Kaumuali'i Hwy; ⊙ noon-8pm Mon & Wed, 9am-5pm Tue, Thu & Fri; 🛜) Free wi-fi; online computer terminals available with temporary nonresident library card ($10).

First Hawaiian Bank (☑ 808-338-1611; www. fhb.com; 4525 Panako Rd; ⊙ 8:30am-4pm Mon-Thu, to 6pm Fri) Has a 24-hour ATM.

West Kauai Medical Center (☑ 808-338-9431; www.kvmh.hhsc.org; 4643 Waimea Canyon Dr) Basic 24-hour emergency services.

West Kaua'i Technology & Visitor Center (☑ 808-338-1332; www.westkauaivisitorcenter.org; 9565 Kaumuali'i Hwy; ⊙ 12:30-4pm Mon, 9:30am-4pm Tue & Wed, 9:30am-12:30pm Fri) Free internet computer access.

ℹ Getting There & Away

Waimea is easily reached by rental car. **Kaua'i Bus** (p274) also services the village.

LAZY DAYS WAIMEA CANYON & THE WESTSIDE

The South Side of Kaua'i extends into its western extreme, a dry, sunny land of red dirt hills and long, lingering sunsets. Out here, a combination of magnificent landscapes and welcoming small towns makes for a destination that's hard to rip yourself away from.

WALKS

From the red dirt trails that wind through Waimea Canyon – 'the Grand Canyon of the Pacific' – to an art walk in the charming town of Hanapepe, there are tons of ways of accessing the beauty and gifts of the Westside on foot. While there are intense hikes in Waimea Canyon, a few casual strolls also skirt that feature's natural wonders.

SHOPPING

Over the years, Hanapepe has grown into what must be the westernmost bohemian artist enclave in the USA. As a result, this tiny town is packed with art galleries that throw their doors open on Friday evenings. You can also find various artisans, jewelers and craftspeople trading their wares any day of the week.

PICNIC

Head to Hanapepe or the town of Waimea, stock up on some grubs (you can never go wrong with *poke*, but don't forget to bring a cooler) and head to Salt Pond Beach Park, Waimea Canyon or to the western shore of the island. Consume delicious food, wash it down with fresh fruit juice and watch the sun dip into the Pacific. Bliss.

1. Hanapepe stores (p221)
2. Salt Pond Beach Park (p217), Hanapepe

2

Kekaha

808 / POP 3537

Kekaha is an old working-class sugar town and today it's home to many military families. There's no town center here and no services to speak of, but Kekaha Beach Park offers one of the most beautiful sunsets on the island. If you're looking for a scenic beach near the base of Waimea Canyon, staying here is an option. There are literally dozens of beautiful homes and condos available for short- and long-term rentals – many with ocean views. Most visitors will find it too remote, however.

Sights

Kekaha Beach Park   BEACH
(Map p214) Kaua'i's Westside is known for its unrelenting sun and vast beaches. Just west of Kekaha town, this long stretch of sand is best for beachcombing and catching sunsets. Before jumping in, find a lifeguard and make sure it's OK to swim, since the beach lacks reef protection. In high surf, the currents are extremely dangerous. Under the right conditions, however, it's good for surfing and bodyboarding. Facilities include outdoor showers, restrooms and picnic tables.

Barking Sands Beach   BEACH
(Map p214) Between Kekaha Beach Park and Polihale State Park, the Westside's biggest beach stretches for around 15 miles. Much of it is taken up by the US Navy's **Barking Sands Pacific Missile Range Facility**, which is closed to the public.

Activities

Davidson Point   SURFING
(Map p214) This exposed reef break works all year round. It gets going with offshore winds from the northeast. It's best suited for strong intermediate and advanced riders. Be careful of rips.

Major's Bay   SURFING
(Map p214) Steep point break with a nearby beach break that offers mostly rights. Make sure you don't intrude on the military base.

Shopping

Kekaha Farmers Market   MARKET
(Map p214; Kekaha Neighborhood Center, 8130 Elepaio Rd; 9-11am Sat) A handful of local farmers and flower growers gather every Saturday morning just off the Kaumuali'i Hwy.

 Getting There & Away

The Kaumuali'i Hwy borders the coastline. Kekaha Rd, the town's main drag, lies parallel and a few blocks inland. All you'll find in town are a post office and a couple of stores. Further east toward Waimea, Kekaha Rd and Kaumuali'i Hwy meet near the Kikiaola Small Boat Harbor. **Kaua'i Bus** (p274) services the town.

Waimea Canyon State Park

Of all Kaua'i's unique wonders, none can touch Waimea Canyon for grandeur. Few would expect to find a gargantuan chasm of ancient lava rock, 10 miles long and over 3500ft deep. It's so spectacular that it has been popularly nicknamed 'the Grand Canyon of the Pacific.' Flowing through the canyon is Waimea River, Kaua'i's longest, fed by tributaries that bring reddish-brown waters from Alaka'i Swamp's mountaintop.

Waimea Canyon was formed when Kaua'i's original shield volcano, Wai'ale'ale, slumped along an ancient fault line. The horizontal striations along the canyon walls represent successive volcanic eruptions. The red colors indicate where water has seeped through the rocks, creating mineral rust from the iron ore inside.

Drives here on a clear day are phenomenal. Don't be disappointed by rain, as that's what makes the waterfalls gush. Sunny days following rain are ideal for prime views, though slick mud makes hiking challenging at these times.

Sights

Waimea Canyon Drive
Lookout 1   LOOKOUT
(Map p214; Waimea Canyon Dr, Mile 4.5) FREE
This lookout at Mile 4.5 on Waimea Canyon Dr gives a good intro view to the canyon to the east. Hop over the road (carefully) to check out a little red-earth waterfall route to the west.

Kumuwela Lookout   VIEWPOINT
(Map p214) Located at the end of the Canyon Trail in Koke'e State Park. Enjoy epic canyon and waterfall views from the picnic table, where you can rest.

POLIHALE STATE PARK

A massive expanse of beach – the end of one of the longest (15 miles) and widest (300ft) in the state – Polihale is as mystical as it is enchanting. Translated as 'home of the underworld,' traditional Hawaiian belief holds Polihale as the place where souls depart for the afterlife. The cliffs at the end of the beach are home to ancient Hawaiian ruins constructed over the ocean as the jumping-off place for spirits.

A journey to **Polihale State Park** (Map p214; https://hawaiistateparks.org/kauai;) along a rutted 4.8-mile dirt road takes you to the edge of eternity. The wide virgin beach curls into dunes that climb into bluffs. Families come here to camp and picnic, surf and watch sunsets. Just to the north, you can catch the first glimpse of the Na Pali cliffs.

The beach is only accessible by the rough dirt road from Mana village off the Kaumuali'i Hwy. It's generally passable – even by car – if you go slow, but many car-rental companies prohibit you from driving on it, especially without a 4WD. The park has restrooms, outdoors showers and a picnic area, but no lifeguards – exercise caution if you go swimming and only enter the water during calm conditions.

Polihale has some good beach breaks that tend to shift with the winds. Be warned: currents can be strong. On the south end, look for a reef break at Queen's Pond. On the north, hit up the beach peaks or go to Echo's, just at the start of the Na Pali cliffs (advanced riders only). Skilled boogie boarders will have fun here.

Want to spend the night? The rustic campsites are perfect for weekends at the edge of the world. Advance reservations are required (online) to **camp** (Map p214; https://camping.ehawaii.gov/camping; per tent site $18 up to 6 people) at the primitive sites. What you will get are beautiful sunset views, late afternoons and early mornings without a soul in sight, and mind-blowing views of Ni'ihua and the Na Pali Coast. There are showers and toilets here, but note that campfires are not allowed.

Waipo'o Falls Lookout   WATERFALL
This 800ft waterscape can be seen from a couple of small unmarked lookouts before Mile 12 and then from a lookout opposite the picnic area shortly before Mile 13. The picnic area has restrooms and drinking water.

Waimea Canyon Drive   SCENIC DRIVE
(Map p214) In addition to jaw-dropping canyon vistas and ocean views, you can also see several fine specimens of native trees, including koa and ohia, as well as invasive species such as kiawe. The valuable hardwood koa proliferates at the **hunter's check station**. Look for the trees with narrow, crescent-shaped leaves. Take the time for stops at Waimea Canyon Drive Lookout 1 (p230) and 2 (p231).

Waimea Canyon Drive Lookout 2   LOOKOUT
(Map p214; Waimea Canyon Dr, Mile 5.5) Hike to the east for amazing verdant views of the canyon below.

Pu'u Hinahina Lookout   VIEWPOINT
(Map p214) A majestic canyon lookout (elevation 3640ft) showing the river glistening in the distance and giving panoramic views down to the ocean. There are two lookouts near the parking lot at a marked turnoff between Miles 13 and 14.

Waimea Canyon Lookout   VIEWPOINT
(Map p214; Hwy 550 Mile 10.3) This breathtaking vista is about 0.3 miles north of Mile 10, at an elevation of 3400ft. The canyon running in an easterly direction off Waimea Canyon is Koai'e Canyon, an area accessible to backcountry hikers.

🏃 Activities

For experienced hikers, several rugged trails lead deep into Waimea Canyon. Keep in mind these trails are shared with pig hunters and are busiest on weekends and holidays. Trail maps are available at the Koke'e Museum (p234) in Koke'e State Park.

Hiking poles or a sturdy walking stick will ease the steep descent into the canyon. Note the time of sunset and plan to return well before dark, as daylight will fade inside the canyon long before sunset. Beware of rain, which creates hazardous conditions in the canyon: red-dirt trails quickly become slick and river fords rise to impassable levels.

WAIMEA CANYON & THE WESTSIDE WAIMEA CANYON STATE PARK

MORE HAWAIIAN ISLANDS

If you're staring out to sea thinking that Kaua'i and its neighbor, Ni'ihau, mark the end of the Hawaiian Islands, think again – there's more! The Northwestern Hawaiian Islands begin more than 150 miles northwest of Kaua'i and stretch for another 1200 miles. They represent an enormous area of some 140,000 sq miles of ocean known as Papahānaumokuākea Marine National Monument (www.papahanaumokuakea.gov), the largest protected marine area in the world.

This 'other Hawaii' is grouped into 10 clusters, containing both atolls and single-rock islands. From east to west, the clusters are Nihoa Island, Mokumanamana (Necker Island), French Frigate Shoals, Gardner Pinnacles, Maro Reef, Laysan Island, Lisianski Island, Pearl and Hermes Atoll, Midway Atoll and Kure Atoll. The total land mass is less than 6 sq miles, however, which is why they remain incognito. Managed by the **US Fish & Wildlife Service** (FWS; www.fws.gov/refuge/Midway_Atoll/), Midway Atoll is normally the only island open to visitors.

Interestingly, Nihoa and Necker islands, the two closest to Kaua'i, were inhabited by Native Hawaiians from around AD 1000 to 1700. More than 135 archaeological sites have been identified there. As many as 175 people lived on Nihoa, while Necker was used for religious ceremonies. The fact that anyone at all could live on these rocks is remarkable. Nihoa juts from the sea like a broken tooth, with 900ft sea cliffs, and is only 1 sq km in size. Necker is one-sixth that. What some people will do for a bit of sun.

While packing light is recommended, take enough water for your entire trip, especially the uphill return journey. Do not drink freshwater found along the trails without treating it. Cell phones will not work here. If possible, hike with a companion or at least tell someone your expected return time. Wear brightly colored clothing to alert hunters of your presence.

Koai'e Canyon Trail   HIKING

(Map p214; http://hawaiitrails.ehawaii.gov) After traversing roughly half a mile up the canyon along the Waimea Canyon Trail, you'll intersect the Koai'e Canyon Trail, a moderate 3-mile (one way) trek that takes you down the south side of the canyon to some swimming holes (avoid them during rainy weather due to the possibility of hazardous flash floods).

This route offers three camps. After the first, **Kaluaha'ulu Camp** (Map p214; www.hawaiistateparks.org/camping; ☺ per night $18), stay on the eastern bank of the river – do not cross it. Later you'll come upon the trailhead for the Koai'e Canyon Trail (marked by a brown-and-yellow Na Ala Hele sign). Watch for greenery and soil that conceal drop-offs alongside the path.

Next up is **Hipalau Camp** (Map p214; www.hawaiistateparks.org/camping; per night $18). Following this, the trail is hard to find. Keep heading north. Do not veer toward the river, but continue ascending at approximately

the same point midway between the canyon walls and the river.

Growing steeper, the trail then enters Koai'e Canyon, recognizable by the red-rock walls rising to the left. The last camp is **Lonomea Camp** (Map p214; www.hawaiistateparks.org/camping; per night $18). Soak up the best views at the emergency helipad before retracing your steps.

Kukui Trail   HIKING

(Map p214; http://hawaiitrails.ehawaii.gov; off Waimea Canyon Dr) This narrow switchbacking trail drops 2000ft in elevation over 2.5 miles without offering much in the way of sweeping views, though there's a river at the bottom. The climb back out of the canyon is for seriously fit and agile hikers only. Another option is to only hike about a mile down, where there's a bench with an astonishing view.

To get to the trail, first find the Iliau Nature Loop trailhead just before Mile 9 on Hwy 550. Keep your eyes peeled for a small sign directing hikers to turn left and hike down the steep slope, with the hill at your back. When you hear the sound of water, you're near the picnic shelter and **Wiliwili Camp** (Map p214; www.hawaiistateparks.org/camping; per night $18) area, where overnight camping is allowed with an advance permit. Mostly it's hunters who camp here. Depending on weather, the sun can be unrelenting, so bring a hat and sunblock.

Pu'u Ki-Wai'alae Trail   HIKING

(Map p214; https://hawaiitrails.org) This 11-mile one-way trail is accessed from the Waimea Canyon Trail. The trail breaks east from there, continuing to the Wailalae Cabin, where you can camp by permit.

Iliau Nature Loop   HIKING

(Map p214; https://hawaiitrails.ehawaii.gov; off Waimea Canyon Dr) This easy, mostly flat 0.3-mile nature loop is a good leg-stretcher for those itching to get out of the car but who are ill-equipped for a big trek. *Iliau*, a plant endemic to Kaua'i's Westside, grows along the route and produces stalks up to 10ft high. The marked trailhead comes up shortly before Mile 9 on Hwy 550. For a top-notch panorama of Waimea Canyon and its waterfalls, you only have to walk for about three minutes past the bench on your left.

Waimea Canyon Trail   HIKING

(Map p214; http://hawaiitrails.ehawaii.gov) The relatively flat, 11.5-mile (one-way) Waimea Canyon Trail fords the Waimea River several times. You can pick it up at the bottom of Waimea Canyon at the end of Kukui Trail, then follow it out to Waimea town, or hike upstream in reverse. An entry permit is required (available at self-service trailhead registration boxes). Bring mosquito repellent. You might see locals carrying inner tubes on the upstream hike, so they can float home the easy way.

Cycling

Mountain bikers can take 4WD hunting-area roads off Waimea Canyon Dr, even when the yellow gates are closed on non-hunting days. The exception is Papa'alai Rd, which is closed to non-hunters.

Outfitters Kauai   CYCLING

(☑ 808-742-9667, 888-742-9887; www.outfitters kauai.com; Po'ipu Plaza, 2827a Po'ipu Rd, Po'ipu; 4½hr tours adult/child 12-14yr $108/98; ☺ tour check-in usually 6am & 2:30pm daily, by reservation only) For lazy two-wheeled sightseeing, it's hard to beat this 13-mile downhill glide along Waimea Canyon Dr. The experience is much better than looking out a car window, as you cruise along with a comfy, wide saddle and high-rise handlebars. Morning tours avoid the setting sun's glare. Tours include snacks and drinks. Reservations required.

❶ Getting There & Away

The southern boundary of Waimea Canyon State Park is about 6 miles uphill from Waimea. You can reach the park by two roads: more scenic Waimea Canyon Dr (Hwy 550), which starts in Waimea just past Mile 23, or Koke'e Rd (Hwy 552), starting in Kekaha off Mana Rd. The two routes merge between Miles 6 and 7.

Koke'e State Park

Expansive Koke'e (ko-*keh*-eh) State Park is a playground for ecotourism. It's home to inspirational views, as well as some of the island's most precious ecosystems. Botanists will revel in the variety of endemic species, while birders will have their binoculars full. Hikers enjoy some reprieve from the sun as they tackle a variety of trails for all skill levels.

The rainy season lasts from October through May, although you might need a waterproof layer at any time of year. The park's elevation (2000 to 4000ft above sea level) necessitates some light insulation – bring a fleece jacket, or a heavier one if you are camping in winter, when temperatures can dip below 40ºF (4ºC). Although one of the park's charms are its bumpy 4WD roads, the state has paved the main road from beginning to end.

⊙ Sights

Koke'e State Park   PARK

(Map p214; https://hawaiistateparks.org/kauai; ♿) FREE The sprawling Koke'e State Park is the starting point for almost 50 miles of outstanding hiking trails. Here, you'll see terrain unlike that found anywhere else on the island, including the largest concentration of extant native bird species in Hawaii.

Remote Alaka'i Swamp (p235) in particular gives a unique view of Kaua'i's native ecosystem; not only is the swamp inhospitable to exotic species but, due to its high elevation, it is one of the few places across Hawaii where mosquitoes, which transmit avian diseases, do not flourish. Ancient Hawaiians never established a permanent village in these chilly highlands and came mainly to collect feathers from forest birds and to cut koa trees for canoes. But an extraordinarily steep ancient Hawaiian trail once ran down the cliffs from Koke'e to Kalalau Valley on the Na Pali Coast. Today the park's only paved road will take you to the Kalalau Lookout (p234), a coastal overlook among the most breathtaking across the Hawaiian islands.

Awa'awapuhi Lookout
VIEWPOINT

(Map p214) The end of the Awa'awapuhi Trail in Koke'e State Park affords incredible, hard-earned views from atop the island's famous Na Pali cliffs.

Pu'u o Kila Lookout
VIEWPOINT

(Map p214) The paved park road (subject to periodic closures) heads a mile beyond the Kalalau Lookout before it dead-ends at a parking lot. The views of Kalalau Valley are similarly spectacular to those at Kalalau Lookout, but usually less crowded. Pu'u o Kila is also the trailhead for the Pihea Trail.

Kalalau Lookout
VIEWPOINT

(Map p214) At Mile 18, the Kalalau Lookout stands up to the ocean, sun and winds with brave, severe beauty. Hope for a clear day for views of Kalalau Valley, but know that even on a rainy day, the clouds could quickly blow away to reveal gushing waterfalls and, of course, rainbows.

Though it might be hard to imagine due to the extremity of the terrain, as late as the 1920s Kalalau Valley was home to many residents who farmed rice. The only way into the valley nowadays is via the North Shore's Kalalau Trail or by sea kayaking.

Koke'e Museum
MUSEUM

(Map p214; ☑ 808-335-9975; www.kokee.org; donation $3; ⊙ 9am-4:30pm; ▣) ✔ Inside this two-room museum you'll find detailed topographical maps, exhibits on flora and fauna, and local historical photographs. It also has botanical sketches of endemic plants and taxidermic representations of some of the wildlife that calls Koke'e home. The gift shop sells a handy fold-out map of the park and its hiking trails, as well as a self-guiding brochure for the short nature trail out back. There is a nice flat picnic area outside and the shop operators are always good for some hiking tips.

Lolo Vista Point
VIEWPOINT

(Map p214) Amazing viewpoint at the end of the Nu'alolo Trail.

Pihea Lookout
VIEWPOINT

(Map p214) A mile along the Pihea Trail from the Pu'u o Kila Lookout, this high-arching lookout provides great views down across the valleys. It sits at 4284ft. Because it's so close to the road, the trail can get crowded; continue on for better views and less people.

Kilohana Lookout
VIEWPOINT

(Map p214) Peer over the cliffs down onto the Na Pali Coast from this lookout deep inside Koke'e State Park. The viewpoint is accessed near the top of Kilohana at 4030ft at the end of the Alaka'i Swamp Trail.

Activities

Koke'e Resource Conservation Program
VOLUNTEERING

(☑ 808-335-0045; www.krcp.org) ✔ If you are so taken with Koke'e's spectacular beauty that you want to contribute your time and energy into keeping it beautiful, get into the backcountry with this ecological restoration organization to eradicate invasive species and restore the island's native habitat.

In exchange for work, you get transport to and from the airport, plus a unique way of learning about native flora and fauna. It's backbreaking work, but think of it as a hike with some weed-whacking in between.

Hiking

Koke'e's sheer size can make it tough to nail down where to start. The 4WD roads that access many trailheads complicate things more. Be prepared for wet, cold weather anytime. For trail information, stop at the Koke'e Museum (p234) and consult the Na Ala Hele (p272) website.

In total, Koke'e State Park boasts 45 miles of trails that range from swampy bogs to wet forest to red-dirt canyon rim with clifftop views that can cause vertigo even in wannabe mountain goats. Hiking here offers chances to spy endemic species of animals and plants, including Kaua'i's rare, endangered forest birds.

Halemanu Rd, just north of Mile 14 on Koke'e Rd, is the starting point for several scenic hikes. Whether or not the road is passable in a non-4WD vehicle depends on recent rainfall. Note that many car-rental agreements forbid any off-road driving.

★ Hike Kaua'i Adventures
HIKING

(☑ 808-639-9709; www.hikekauaiadventures.com; half-/full day up to 4 people $200/320) Longtime resident Jeffrey Courson leads guests on bespoke hiking adventures all over the island. He's hiked every trail on Kaua'i and will tailor an ideal hiking itinerary to meet your needs. He leads with knowledge of the flora and fauna and the island's deep history, and he includes door-to-door service too. You'll have a blast with Jeffrey.

ALAKA'I SWAMP

Nothing provides an out-of-the-ordinary hiking experience the way Alaka'i Swamp does. Designated a wilderness preserve in 1964, this soggy paradise has a hiking trail that is almost completely lined with wooden planks, mainly to discourage off-trail trekking. The state started laying these planks around 1989; and it was a time-consuming process that was delayed when Hurricane 'Iniki hit in 1992. There are still ambitions to cover part of the Pihea Trail, but the Alaka'i Swamp Trail already has some planks missing.

Nevertheless, you'll traverse truly fantastic terrain on this hike, including misty bogs with knee-high trees and tiny, carnivorous plants. On a clear day, you'll get outstanding views of the Wainiha Valley and the distant ocean from Kilohana Lookout. If it's raining, don't fret: search for rainbows and soak up the eerie atmosphere. Queen Emma was said to have been so moved by tales from this spiritual place that she sojourned here while chanting in reverence.

The swamp has its own unique biological rhythms and there are far more endemic birds than introduced species here – elsewhere in Hawaii the opposite is true. Many of these avian species are endangered, some with fewer than 100 birds remaining today.

Pihea Trail to Alaka'i Swamp Trail   HIKING
(Map p214) This rugged, strenuous 7.5-mile round-trip trek begins off Koke'e Rd at Pu'u o Kila Lookout (p234). A mere mile in, Pihea Lookout (p234) appears. After a short scramble downhill, the boardwalk begins. About 1.8 miles later, you'll come to a crossing with the **Alaka'i Swamp Trail**. Taking a left at this crossing puts you on the trail toward Kilohana Lookout (p234).

Continuing straight on the Pihea Trail will take you to Kawaikoi Campground instead. Most hikers begin this trip at Pu'u o Kila Lookout because it's accessible via the paved road.

Both of these trails may be muddy and not recently maintained. The stretch between Alaka'i Crossing and Kilohana Lookout includes hundreds of steps, which can be hell on your knees. Expect to take all day to finish the hike.

Black Pipe Trail   HIKING
(Map p214) An alternative start or end to the popular Canyon Trail, this half-mile trail is a good spot to see native hibiscus and *iliau* (a plant endemic to Kaua'i's Westside).

Pu'u Ka Ohelo Berry Flat Trail   HIKING
(Map p214) This trail is 2 miles long one way. It takes you past redwood, sugi pine and koa, and sports a high-canopy alive with native birds. There's a lot of little rough hunting trails through here. Make sure you know your way before leaving the main trail. The trail starts at the beginning of the Mohini Rd.

Po'omau Canyon Ditch Trail   HIKING
(Map p214) Accessed from the Berry Flat Trail, this strenuous 4-mile round-trip hike takes you along an irrigation ditch, past verdant forests and meadows, and gives good overlooks of two waterfalls.

Kawaikoi Stream Trail   HIKING
(Map p214) This easy, 1.8-mile loop trail initially follows Kawaikoi Stream through a grove of Japanese cedar and California redwood trees, rises up on a bluff, then loops back down to the stream before returning to where you started. Find the trailhead upstream from Sugi Grove Campground on Camp 10–Mohihi Rd (4WD only).

To get to the trailhead from the Koke'e Museum, turn left onto Hwy 550, then left again at the first dirt road (Mohihi). You'll reach a picnic area after 3.7 miles. Park there, and ford the stream before you continue up to Sugi Grove Campground.

⛯ Festivals & Events

★ **Eo e Emalani I Alaka'i**   DANCE, MUSIC
(www.kokee.org; Koke'e Museum; ⊘ Oct) A one-day outdoor dance festival at the Koke'e Museum in early October, commemorating Queen Emma's 1871 journey to Alaka'i Swamp. The festival includes a royal procession, hula dancing, live music and more.

Banana Poka Round-Up   ART, MUSIC
(www.kokee.org; Koke'e Museum; ⊘ late May; ⛾) This unique festival strips Koke'e of an invasive pest from South America, the banana poka vine, then weaves baskets from it. Come for live music, a rooster-crow-

ing contest and the 'Pedal to the Meadow' bicycle race.

Eating

Koke'e Lodge
AMERICAN **$**

(Map p214; ☑808-335-6061; Koke'e Rd; mains $5-9; ☺cafe 9am-2:30pm, takeout until 3pm; ⓓ) This summer camp-style restaurant's strong point is convenience. And that goes a long way in Koke'e, where you're a 30-minute drive from any other dining options. Pancakes, salads, sandwiches, burgers and booze are served here. The gift shop, which stays open until 3:30pm or 4pm daily, sells sundries, souvenirs, snacks and drinks.

❶ Information

Koke'e Museum (☑808-335-9975; www.kokee.org; Koke'e Rd) Sells inexpensive trail maps and provides basic information on trail conditions. You can call for real-time mountain weather reports.

❶ Getting There & Away

The park's southern boundary lies beyond Pu'u Hinahina Lookout on Koke'e Rd. After Mile 15, you'll pass the park's cabins, restaurant, museum and campground. The nearest place for provisions and gas is Waimea, 15 miles away.

Understand Kaua'i

Kaua'i Today

Kaua'i strives to balance progress with preservation, isolation with integration. On one hand you have community and local interests that aim to protect local culture and the environment and build a brighter future for the island's children. On the other hand, mandates, social trends and politics infiltrate their way from mainland USA. As far as current trends indicate, Kaua'i continues to find balance in an unbalanced world.

Best on Film

The Descendants (2011) Contemporary island life, with all of its heartaches and blessings.
From Here to Eternity (1953) Classic WWII-era drama leading up to the Pearl Harbor attack.
The North Shore (1987) Glorious cheesy and highly quotable, this movie is bitchin! 'Yeah right barney, bitchin!'
50 First Dates (2004) Silly rom-com shot on gorgeous Windward O'ahu beaches.
Blue Hawaii (1961) Romp poolside with a ukulele-playing Elvis during Hawaii's tiki-tacky tourism boom.

Best in Print

Kaua'i Tales (Frederick B Wichman; 1985) Recounts 18 legends of Kaua'i.
Kaua'i: The Separate Kingdom (Edward Joesting; 1988) Strong historic storytelling.
The Story of Koloa (Donald Donohugh; 2001) Localized account of plantation life in Koloa.
Shark Dialogues (Kiana Davenport; 1994) Multigenerational family saga, stretching from ancient times to the plantation era.
Wild Meat and the Bully Burgers (Lois-Ann Yamanaka; 1996) Novel about growing up local and speaking Hawaiian pidgin.
Hotel Honolulu (Paul Theroux; 2001) Satirical tale about a washed-up writer managing a Waikiki hotel.

Economy, Politics & Community

The island has a love-hate relationship with tourism. About a third of the island's economic output comes from visitation and around a quarter of the population works in the industry. On any given day, the island's 71,000-odd residents work, play and jostle for position with over 24,000 visitors.

More tourism means more crowded roads and less affordable housing. It means greater energy usage and strains on land use. More tourism also means jobs and money for better schools, community programs and land protection initiatives.

There are several large construction works moving forward to make room for more visitors, including most notably the Timbers Resort redevelopment of the former Kaua'i Lagoons site and redevelopment of the Coco Palms in Wailua.

Many locals say the rise in tourist housing has made it harder and harder to afford to live here. Homelessness on Kaua'i and across the Hawaiian Islands has grown substantially in recent years, with around 400 homeless people on Kaua'i, a 30% jump from the year before.

The 2014 study 'Climate Change Impacts on Hawaii' commissioned by the Hawaii Tourism Authority suggested that sea-level rise could cost the state an estimated $661 million per year in lost hotel revenue, with a yearly price tag topping $2 billion.

A lack of high-performing schools, some chronic recidivism related to methamphetamine (ice) use, environmental issues, beach shutdowns, historic preservation, traffic jams, military drills at Barking Sands, who's-seeing-who and today's surf report round out the menu of talking points for most 'talk story' sessions at the local coffee shop or bentō joint.

In the end, Kaua'i is so far away – and so purposefully removed – that it tends to transcend politics. Life is about enjoying the sunrise and sunset, catching good waves and being with family. Life is good.

Sustaining Good Communities

Community is what almost all island residents care most about. Under the leadership of Mayor Bernard Carvalho Jr, Kaua'i County is working toward achieving the ambitious goals set by the 'Holo Holo 2020' program, which aims to 'grow Kaua'i responsibly.'

Tangibly, the high-flying improvement agenda involves more than three dozen separate community projects, ranging from the mundane, but very necessary – repaving roads, expanding bus service, upgrading local parks etc – to the forward-thinking and inspiring (for example, working to increase Native Hawaiian stewardship of the island's important cultural sites and building the county's first 'green' affordable housing).

Another global trend that has found its way to Kaua'i's shores is the sustainability movement. Perhaps it would be more accurate to say that Kaua'i has rediscovered its sustainable roots, as ancient Hawaiians were inherently green.

The first area of interest here is sustainable agriculture. There is a major movement on Kaua'i toward becoming self-sufficient in food production. And why not? We are talking about an island with hundreds of thousands of acres of fertile fields and relatively few people. Consequently, imported food is increasingly viewed like fossil fuels – necessary at the present moment, but definitely to be avoided in the future.

Genetic engineering of crops and pesticide use are hot-button issues. A 2013 Kaua'i ordinance approved by local voters created buffer zones and pesticide notifications for agriculture, while on the Big Island and Maui genetically engineered tests were banned. The issue went up to the US Court of Appeals in November 2016, with the court striking down the local bans. Organizers may appeal or seek legislative action to reinstate the county-led initiatives.

Agriculture, homeless populations, climate change and other factors are also affecting the quality of Hawaii's signature resource: its waters. In 2016 Maha'ulepu Beach access was closed by state officials because of high bacteria levels. The beach area has now reopened, but watch for signs here and elsewhere on the island.

Another key area of interest is renewable energy. In the past Kaua'i has had a surprising deficit in this area, as evidenced by the many gas-guzzling pickups prowling island highways. Spurred by the statewide Hawaii Clean Energy Initiative, Kaua'i has become a leader in solar power and is making progress with hydropower, the latter targeting island rivers. The goal is to reduce energy use by 30% and fossil-fuel use by 50% by 2023. It's a bold goal, but with numerous solar and hydro plants coming on line, it may be achievable.

POPULATION: **71,735**

AREA: **552 SQ MILE**

INFLATION: **2.8%**

UNEMPLOYMENT: **4.6%**

if Kaua'i were 100 people

31 would be Asian
30 would be White
20 would be mixed
9 would be Native Hawaiian
9 would be Latino/Latina
1 would be African American

belief systems
(% of population)

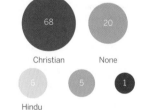

Christian 68 — None 20 — Hindu or Buddhist 6 — Mormon 5 — Jewish 1

population per sq mile

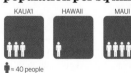

KAUA'I — HAWAII — MAUI

= 40 people

History

As with most islands, the history of Kaua'i is charted by arrivals. The arrival of plants and animals, the arrival of humans, the arrival of European explorers, the arrival of disease, the arrival of missionaries, the arrival of sugar, the arrival of the tourist horde.

Surfing was falling out of favor in the 20th century in Hawaii, but was resurrected when Jack London wrote about it in 1907 in an article titled 'A Royal Sport.'

Like other Hawaiian Islands, Kaua'i grew up in relative isolation. That is, until Captain Cook first landed in Waimea on the island's Westside in 1778. This transformational point in the island's history brought disease, new commerce, new technology, new religions and new ways of doing things. And while the broad strokes of Kaua'i's history connects with that of the other islands, it has a fiercely independent streak that goes back to the days of the Hawaiian kings. In some ways this independence remains a common denominator for life on the island today. Under the leadership of *mo'i* (island king) Kaumuali'i, Kaua'i and Ni'ihau were the last of the Hawaiian Islands to join Kamehameha I's kingdom in 1810. Unlike the other islands, they did so peacefully, more than 15 years after the rest of the islands were bloodily conquered.

But Kaua'i was slow to grow. It remained a sugar-plantation island into the 20th century – with notable migrations of Chinese, Japanese and Filipino workers. It only became iconic as a tropical paradise after WWII, when Hollywood glamorized Lumaha'i Beach in Mitzi Gaynor's *South Pacific* (1958) and the long-gone Coco Palms Resort in Elvis Presley's *Blue Hawaii* (1961). In 1982 Kaua'i was hit by Hurricane 'Iwa. Just 10 years later, it was again devastated by Hurricane 'Iniki, the most powerful hurricane to ever strike Hawaii; it left six people dead, thousands of people homeless and caused $1.8 billion dollars of damage statewide.

Walk the Koloa, Waimea and Maha'ulepu Heritage Trails to connect with Kaua'i's history.

First Beginnings

Around six to 10 million years ago, volcanoes formed the islands of Kaua'i and O'ahu, the oldest of the Hawaiian Islands in geological time – the surrounding islands popped above the Pacific Ocean just 500,000 years ago. From this remarkable birth, the air, wind and currents transformed the land from volcanic rock to the tropical paradise you see today.

TIMELINE	30 million BC	AD 1000–1200	AD 1200–1400
	The first Hawaiian island, Kure, rises from the sea, appearing where the Big Island is today. Borne by wind, wing and wave, plants, insects and birds colonize the new land.	Polynesian colonists traveling thousands of miles across open seas in double-hulled canoes arrive in Hawai'i.	The Tahitian Long Voyages bring new gods to the islands.

The beginnings were slow. Seeds borne on currents, in logs or on bird feathers found their way to the island. Each new introduced species changed the islands' ecology forever. And it happened way less frequently than you would imagine. Given the isolation of the archipelago, many experts postulate that successful introductions of species only occurred once every 20,000 or 30,000 years.

The First Settlers

Exactly how and when Kaua'i was first settled remains a controversy. Most archaeologists agree that the first humans migrated to the Hawaiian Islands from the Marquesas Islands. This settlement marked the end of a 2000-year period of migration by ancient seafarers, originally from Southeast Asia, that populated Polynesia.

Most original scholarship places the date of the first Hawaiian settlers around 500AD. More recent radiocarbon dating, combined with tracking of linguists, culture and other factors, places the date closer to 1000 to 1200 AD. The last migrations likely started from Tahiti. Known as the Long Voyages, they lasted from 1000 to 1400AD and were likely voyages of discovery and not settlement.

The Tahitians also brought with them new gods, like Kāne, lord of creation and his opposing force Kanaloa; Lono, the god of peace, and Ku, the god of war.

These new dates offer an almost revolutionary perspective to Hawaiian history. What was considered a thousands-year-old culture may have developed in a much shorter time. Some point out that the original settlers could have been subdued by more powerful later migrations, thus justifying the mythology of the *menehune* ('little people' who were forced to live in the mountains).

The original settlers made their journeys in double-hulled canoes 60ft long and 14ft wide, without any modern navigational tools. Instead they relied on the 'star compass,' a celestial map based on keen observation (and perfect memory) of star paths. They had no idea what, if anything, they would find thousands of miles across open ocean, though many scholars now indicate that they brought with them the tools and resources they would need to populate a new world (seeds, women and children, plants and animals, gods and mythology). Amazingly, experts estimate that Hawai'i's discoverers sailed for four months straight without stops to restock food and water.

By and large, the consensus is that Kaua'i was the first island to be settled in the archipelago. These first settlers likely lived in caves, later building more substantial structures and small villages.

Historical Sites

Nu'alolo Kai (p216; Na Pali Coast)

Grove Farm Homestead (p86; Lihu'e)

Makauwahi Sinkhole (p193; Po'ipu)

Kilauea Lighthouse (p144: Kilauea)

Russian Fort Elizabeth State Historical Park (p223: Waimea)

HISTORY THE FIRST SETTLERS

One Kamehameha attack on Kaua'i was thwarted when a case of plague wiped out a number of his warriors and chiefs.

1300	1778	1810	1815–17
Na Pali Coast settled at Nu'alolo Kai. Settlement survives 600 years.	Captain James Cook lands at Waimea; Hawai'i will never be the same again.	Kamehameha I unites the major Hawaiian Islands under one kingdom, called Hawai'i after his home island.	Georg Scheffer fails to conquer Hawai'i for Russia; he departs before finishing Fort Elizabeth on the southwest coast.

The Ancient Way of Life

Ancient Hawaiians had a hierarchical class system. At the top were the *ali'i nui* (high chiefs, descended from the gods), who each ruled one of the four major islands (including Kaua'i). One's rank as an *ali'i* was determined by one's mother's family lineage, making Hawaii a matrilineal society.

The second class comprised *ali'i 'ai moku* (district chiefs) who ruled island districts and *ali'i 'ai ahupua'a* (lower chiefs) who ruled *ahupua'a,* pie-shaped subdistricts extending from the mountains to the ocean. Also ranked second were the kahuna (priest, healer or sorceror), experts in important skills such as canoe building, religious practices, healing arts and navigation.

The third, and largest, class were the *maka'ainana* (commoners), who were not chattel of the *ali'i* and could live wherever they pleased but were obligated to support the *ali'i* through taxes paid in kind with food, goods and labor.

The final *kaua* (outcast) class was shunned and did not mix with the other classes, except as slaves. No class resented their position, for people accepted the 'natural order' and based their identity on the group rather than on their individuality.

Although the hierarchy sounds feudal, Hawaiian society was quite different because *ali'i* did not 'own' land. It was inconceivable to the Hawaiian mind to own land or anything in nature. Rather, the *ali'i* were stewards of the land – and they had a sacred duty to care for it on behalf of the gods. Further, the ancients had no monetary system or concept of trade for profit. They instead exchanged goods and services through customary, reciprocal gift giving (as well as through obligations to superiors).

Strict religious laws, known as the kapu (taboo) system, governed what people ate, whom they married, when they fished or harvested crops, and practically all other aspects of human behavior. Women could not dine with men or eat bananas, coconuts, pork and certain types of fish.

Surfing in Hawaii goes back to the beginning, when early Polynesian settlers brought the practice of bodyboarding to the islands. It was on Hawaii that the practice of standing on boards really took hold and surfing held a central part in local culture with surf competitions, prized breaks that only the royalty could ride (and plenty of leftovers for the commoners), and intricate cultural traditions that guided the selection, creation and storage of surfboards made from koa, *wiliwili* and breadfruit wood.

Check out *Paradise of the Pacific* by Susanna Moore for interesting storytelling on ancient Hawaii.

Captain Cook took extreme measures to protect the islanders from his dirty sailors and VD, but women would often dress as men to sneak onboard – and men would exchange everything from nails to shark meat for the company.

1819	1820	1835	1848
King Kamehameha I dies and the Hawaiian religious system is cast aside.	Samuel and Mercy Partridge Whitney establish a mission at Waimea. Without the kapu system, Hawaiians prove ready to convert.	First successful commercial milling of sugar in Hawaii begins in Koloa.	Under the influence of Westerners, the first system of private land ownership is introduced.

From Hawaiian Kingdom to US Territory

Captain Cook

When esteemed British naval captain James Cook inadvertently sighted the uncharted island of Oʻahu on January 18, 1778, the ancient Hawaiians' 500 years of isolation were forever lost. This new arrival transformed Hawaii in ways inconceivable at the time.

Strong winds on that fateful day pushed Cook away from Oʻahu and toward Kauaʻi, where he made landfall on January 20 at Waimea Bay. Cook promptly named the islands the Sandwich Islands, after his patron, the Earl of Sandwich.

Cook and his men were enthralled with Kauaʻi and its inhabitants, considering them to be robust and handsome in physical appearance, and friendly and generous in trade dealings. Meanwhile the Hawaiians, living in a closed society for hundreds of years, found the strange white men to be astounding. Most historians believe that they regarded Cook as the earthly manifestation of the great god Lono.

After two weeks, Cook continued to the Pacific Northwest for another crack at finding the elusive Northwest Passage across North America.

PROMISED LAND

Ancient Hawaiians had no concept of land ownership. The gods owned the land and people were stewards. In practical terms, the king controlled the land and foreigners had no means to own any.

In the 1840s, Americans sought to secure long-term property rights. In 1848, they convinced the Hawaiian government to enact the Great Mahele, a revolutionary land reform act that redistributed all kingdom lands into three parts: crown lands, chief lands and government lands (for the benefit of the general public).

Two years later the government went further and allowed foreign residents to buy land. Sugar growers and land speculators bought huge parcels for minimal sums from chiefs lured by quick money and from commoners ignorant of deeds, taxes and other legal requirements for fee-simple land ownership.

Native Hawaiians lost much of their land and struggled with ensuing economic problems. In 1920, Kauaʻi's native son Prince Kuhio (congressional delegate for the Territory of Hawaii) convinced the US Congress to pass the Hawaiian Homes Commission Act, which set aside almost 200,000 acres of government land for Native Hawaiians to lease for $1 per year. It sounds terrific, but there are problems. Much of this land is remote and lacks basic infrastructure, such as roads and access to water and electricity. Lessees must build their own homes, which many applicants cannot afford. And applicants end up waiting for years, even decades. Today there are over 19,000 residential applicants waiting across the state. Only about 8300 leases have been granted since 1920.

1864	1890	1893	1900
Sugar baron-to-be George Norton Wilcox takes over the lease for Grove Farm in Lihuʻe.	Lihuʻe Hotel opens with emphasis on sunbathers; it's the first fully fledged tourist hotel in Kauaʻi.	The Hawaiian monarchy, under Queen Liliʻuokalani, is overthrown, ending 83 years of rule.	Hawaii becomes a US territory.

Searching in vain for eight months, he returned south to winter in the Hawaiian Islands.

In November 1778, Cook sighted Maui for the first time, but did not land, choosing instead to head further south to explore the nearby island of Hawai'i with its towering volcanic mountains. After landing in picturesque Kealakekua Bay in January 1779, Cook's luck ran out. An escalating series of conflicts ensued. When one of his ship's boats was stolen, Cook attempted to kidnap the local chief as ransom and was driven back to the beach. A battle ensued, killing Cook, four of his men and 17 Hawaiians.

The Hawaiian Kingdom

Among the Hawaiian warriors that felled Captain Cook was a robust young man named Paiea. Between 1790 and 1810, this charismatic leader, who became known as Kamehameha the Great, managed to conquer the islands of Hawai'i, Maui, Moloka'i and O'ahu.

To make his domain complete, Kamehameha tried to conquer Kaua'i, too, but was thwarted by the formidable chief Kaumuali'i. Kamehameha did, however, negotiate a diplomatic agreement with the chief, which put the island under Kamehameha's new kingdom, but gave Kaumuali'i the right to rule the island somewhat independently.

Kamehameha is credited with unifying all of the islands, establishing a peaceful and solidified kingdom. He was widely acknowledged as being a benevolent and just ruler, much loved by his people until his death in 1819.

Enter the Missionaries

When Kamehameha died, his 23-year-old son Liholiho (Kamehameha II) became *mo'i* (king) and his wife, Queen Ka'ahumanu, became *kuhina nui* (regent) and co-ruler. Both of them were greatly influenced by Westerners and eager to renounce the kapu system. In a shocking blow to tradition, the two broke a strict taboo against men and women eating together and later ordered many heiau (ancient stone temples) and *ki'i* (idols) destroyed. Hawaiian society fell into chaos. Thus when the first missionaries to Hawai'i arrived in April 1820, it was a fortuitous moment for them. The Hawaiian people were in great social and political upheaval and many, particularly the *ali'i* (chiefs), found the Protestant faith an appealing replacement.

The Hawaiians had no written language, so the missionaries established a Hawaiian alphabet using Roman letters and taught them how to read and write. This fostered a high literacy rate and publication of 100 Hawaiian-language newspapers. Eventually, however, missionaries sought to separate the Hawaiians from their 'hedonistic' cultural roots. They prohibited hula dancing because of its 'lewd and suggestive

---

Of Hawai'i's eight ruling monarchs, only King Kamehameha I had children, who eventually inherited the throne. His dynasty ended less than a century after it began with the death of Kamehameha V in 1872.

In *Blue Latitudes: Boldly Going Where Captain Cook Has Gone Before,* Tony Horwitz examines the controversial legacy of Captain Cook's South Seas voyages, weaving amusing real-life adventure tales together with bittersweet oral history.

1924	1925	1934	1941
Hanapepe Massacre leaves 20 dead as Filipino strikers confront police.	The first air flight between the mainland and Hawaii is made. Eleven years later, Pan American launches the first commercial mainland–Hawaii flights.	First movie, *White Heat,* shot on Kaua'i.	Japanese attack Pearl Harbor; Japanese sugar workers are spared internment camp.

movements,' denounced the traditional Hawaiian chants and songs that honored 'heathen' gods, taught women to sew Western-style clothing, abolished polygamy and even banned the language they had taught them to write.

Many missionaries became influential advisors to the monarch and received large tracts of land in return, prompting them to leave the church altogether and turn their land into sugar plantations.

Big Sugar

Foreigners quickly saw that Hawaii was ideal for growing sugarcane and established small plantations using Hawaiian labor. But by then the native population had severely declined, thanks to introduced diseases. To fill the shortage, workers were imported from overseas starting in the 1860s, first from China, and soon after from Japan and the Portuguese islands of Madeira and the Azores.

The influx of imported foreign labor and the rise of the sugar industry had a major impact on the islands' social structure. Caucasian plantation owners and sugar agents rose to become the elite upper economic and political class, while the Hawaiians and foreign laborers became the lower class, without much of a middle class in between. Labor relations became contentious, eventually resulting in the formation of unions and strike action.

The plantation era provides the best artifacts of Kaua'i's short history. You can see old mills, plantation-era houses and other artifacts in places like Koloa (p184), Waimea (p225) and the Kaua'i Museum (p88) in Lihu'e, while the McBryde and Allerton Gardens (p189) preserve some of the pomp and circumstance of the era.

Overthrow of the Monarchy

In 1887 the members of the Hawaiian League, a secret antimonarchy organization run by sugar interests, wrote a new constitution and by threat of violence forced King David Kalakaua to sign it. This constitution, which became known as the 'Bayonet Constitution,' limited voting rights and stripped the monarch's powers, effectively making King Kalakaua a figurehead.

When Kalakaua, Hawai'i's last king, died in 1891, his sister and heir, Princess Lili'uokalani, ascended the throne. She tried to restore the monarchy, but on January 17, 1893, the leaders of the Hawaiian League, supported by both John L Stevens (the US Department of State Minister to Hawaii) and a 150-man contingent of US marines and sailors, forcibly arrested Queen Lili'uokalani and took over 'Iolani Palace in Honolulu – a tense but bloodless coup d'état. The Kingdom of Hawai'i was now the Republic of Hawai'i.

To keep in touch with contemporary issues that are important to the Hawaiian community, both in the islands and in the global diaspora, browse the independent news and culture magazine *Mana* (www.welive mana.com).

For a history of Hawaii you can finish on the flight over, *A Concise History of the Hawaiian Islands* by Phil Barnes captures a surprising amount of nuance in fewer than 90 pages.

1946	1958	1959	1975
Tsunami generated off Alaska strikes Hawaiian Islands – 45ft wave hits North Shore, killing 14 and knocking out bridges.	Mitzi Gaynor's *South Pacific* becomes an international hit. The movie was shot on Kaua'i's North Shore.	Hawaii becomes the 50th US state.	A Micronesian navigator and Hawaiian crew sails the voyaging canoe *Hokule'a* from Hawaii to Tahiti (2400 miles) without any modern means of navigation.

Annexation, War & Statehood

American interests pushed hard for annexation, while Hawaiians fought to prevent this final acquisition. In 1897 more than 21,000 people (almost half the population of Hawaii) signed an anti-annexation petition and sent it to Washington. In 1898 President William McKinley nevertheless approved the annexation, perhaps influenced by the concurrent Spanish-American War, which highlighted Pearl Harbor's strategic military location.

Statehood was a tough sell to the US Congress, but a series of significant historical events paved the way. In 1936 Pan American Airways launched the first commercial flights from the US mainland to Hawaii, thus launching the trans-Pacific air age and the beginning of mass tourism. A wireless telegraph (and later telephone) service between Hawaii and the mainland alleviated doubts about long-distance communication. Most importantly, WWII proved both the strategic military role of Pearl Harbor and the loyalty and heroism of Japanese immigrants.

During WWII the Japanese were initially banned from joining the armed forces, due to great suspicion about their loyalty. In 1943 the US government yielded to political pressure and formed an all-Japanese combat unit, the 100th Infantry Battalion. While only 3000 men were needed for this unit, more than 10,000 men volunteered.

By the war's end, another all-Japanese unit, the 442nd Regimental Combat Team, composed of 3800 men from Hawaii and the mainland, had received more commendations and medals than any other unit. The 100th Infantry also received special recognition for rescuing the so-called 'Lost Battalion,' stranded behind enemy lines in France.

While still a controversial candidate, the islands were finally admitted as the 50th US state in 1959.

> In the 19th century, New England missionaries needed six months to sail from Boston around Cape Horn to Hawai'i. Early-20th-century Matson steamships embarking from San Francisco took just five days to reach Honolulu.

The Hawaiian Renaissance

After WWII, Hawaii became America's tropical fantasyland. The tiki craze, surfer movies, aloha shirts and Waikiki were all Westernized, commercial images, but they made Hawaii iconic to the masses. Simultaneously, Hawaiians were increasingly marginalized by Western social, political and economic influences. The Hawaiian language had nearly died out, land was impossible for most Hawaiians to buy, and many of the traditional ways of life that had supported an independent people for over 1000 years were disintegrating. Without these, Hawaiians lost much of their own identity and even felt a sense of shame.

The 1970s introduced a cultural awakening, due largely to two events: in 1974 a small group called the Polynesian Voyaging Society (http://pvs.kcc.hawaii.edu/) committed themselves to building and sailing a replica of an ancient Hawaiian voyaging canoe, to prove that the first Polynesian settlers were capable of navigating the Pacific without the use of Western

> The rise of consumerism presented by the introduction of money and Western goods was a substantial factor in the demise of the kapu system.

1976	1982	1983	1992
The grassroots organization Protect Kaho'olawe 'Ohana files a lawsuit in the Federal District Court to halt the US Navy's use of Kaho'olawe island as a practice bombing site.	Hurricane 'Iwa strikes Kaua'i – 1900 homes damaged or destroyed, 44 boats sunk, resorts wrecked.	Kilauea Volcano on Hawai'i starts its latest eruption. The longest eruption in recorded history, it engulfed roads and even the entire village of Kalapana.	Hawaii's most powerful hurricane ever, 'Iniki, destroys 1420 houses; four people are killed. Kaua'i declared a disaster area.

EYE OF THE STORM

Almost two decades after Hurricane 'Iniki blasted Kaua'i, residents can still give blow-by-blow accounts of their survival on September 11, 1992. 'Iniki blew in with sustained winds of 145mph and gusts of 165mph or more (a weather-station meter in mountainous Koke'e broke off at 227mph). It snapped trees by the thousands and totally demolished 1420 homes (and swept over 60 out to sea). Another 5000 homes were severely damaged while over 7000 sustained minor damage. Most of the island lacked electricity for over a month, and some areas lacked power for up to three months. Thirty-foot waves washed away entire wings of beachfront hotels, particularly those in Po'ipu and Princeville.

During the immediate aftermath, residents were remarkably calm and law-abiding despite the lack of power, radio or TV. Communities held parties to share and consume perishable food. Looting was minor and when grocers allowed affected residents to take what they needed, they insisted on paying.

Miraculously, only four people died, but the total value of the damage to the island was $1.8 billion. While locals notice the changed landscape, newcomers would never realize the havoc wreaked 15 years ago.

technology such as sextants and compasses. When the *Hokule'a* made its maiden 4800-mile round-trip voyage to Tahiti in 1976, it instantly became a symbol of rebirth for Hawaiians, prompting a cultural revival unparalleled in Hawaiian history.

The same year, a small grassroots group, the Protect Kaho'olawe 'Ohana (PKO), began protesting against the treatment of Kaho'olawe, an island the US military had used as a training and bombing site since WWII. The PKO's political actions, including the island's illegal occupation, spurred new interest in reclaiming not only Kaho'olawe (which the navy relinquished in 2003) and other military-held lands, but also Hawaiian cultural practices, from hula to *lomilomi* massage.

Public schools started teaching Hawaiian language and culture classes, while Hawaiian immersion charter schools proliferated. Hawaiian music topped the charts, turning island-born musicians into now-legendary superstars. Small but vocal contingents began pushing for Hawaiian sovereignty, from complete secession from the USA to a nation-within-a-nation model.

The community website www.hawaiihistory.org offers an interactive timeline of Hawaii's history and essays delving into every aspect of ancient Hawaiian culture, with evocative images and links.

1994	2006	2007	2009
The Po'ipu Bay Golf Course hosts the annual PGA Grand Slam of Golf from 1994 to 2006. Tiger Woods takes first place for five consecutive years, from 1998 to 2002, and then two more in 2005 and 2006.	Torrential rainstorms for over 40 days in February and March cause Kaloko Dam on the North Shore to break, causing a flash flood of 300 million gallons of water into the ocean. Seven people are swept away to their deaths.	Protesters prevent Super Ferry from entering Nawiliwili Harbor on its inaugural voyage, ending service to Kaua'i.	Age of sugar ends on Kaua'i with closure of Gay & Robinson mill in Kaumakani.

People of Kaua'i

The people of Kaua'i are diverse in many ways, but most share a few common characteristics. Sure, they know how to spread the love, but being a small island, they also know how to mind their own business. One of the central concepts here is *aloha 'aina* (love of the land). Head out to a community market or local beach and you will probably also witness a love for the sea, a love for family and tranquility, a love for community, a love for isolation and a love for spirit. Residents may be native Hawaiian, descendants of early setters and immigrants, *kama'aina* (born here), end-of-the-road escapists, hippies, farmers, doctors and businesspeople, snowbirds or transplants. In some ways, these disparate groups manage to coexist. The saying 'small island big inferno' definitely comes to mind.

Above Hula dancers, Lihu'e (p253)

Kaua'i Identity

Local Versus Transplant

Born-and-raised Kauaians tend to be easygoing and low-key for the most part, preferring the unpretentious small-town life. Multigenerational locals take pride in their roots and enjoy knowing and being known within their community – which is a good thing since anonymity is a short-lived state, thanks to the 'coconut wireless'. Stereotypes of an unwelcoming local contingent do exist and there is some justification for that – after all, the infamous Wolfpak Surf Gang got its start on the North Shore.

Resistance has been one of Kaua'i's strong suits throughout its history and the way that this still manifests itself today is in an insider-outsider mentality that can linger beneath the surface of everyday interactions. However, we find that if you give aloha, you get aloha.

Island life is different and its pace of life is a few gearshifts down from that of the modern get-it-done-yesterday world. For most island-folk, tradition trumps change. Locals can be resentful of the influx of mainland transplants and their progressive ideals diluting traditional communities, especially on the North Shore. Yet other transplants seem to quickly find their feet: befriending neighbors, immersing themselves in the culture and simply slowing down and respecting local ways. As the saying goes, 'Kaua'i will either suck you in or spit you out.'

Typical transplants include post-college wanderers, surfer dudes, wealthy retirees or middle-aged career switchers seeking idyllic seclusion.

Regional Differences

Despite the island's compact size, each geographical location has its own distinct vibe. Lihu'e, the county seat, is a functional town where people go to work, not to play. Wailua's upcountry remains a favorite residential area while coastal Kapa'a has taken on a burgeoning hippie front. Hanalei is a surf town, dominated by suntanned blonds and affordable only to multimillionaires. Po'ipu's sun-splashed beaches serve as a perennial summer camp for retirees, and the Westside – more so than any other region – has retained an audible echo of its multiethnic plantation-history traditions.

WHAT'S IN A NAME?

Haole White person (except local Portuguese). Translates as 'shallow breather.' Often further defined as 'mainland haole' or 'local haole.'

Hapa Person of mixed ancestry, most commonly referring to *hapa haole,* who are part-white and part-Asian.

Hawaiian Person of Native Hawaiian ancestry. It's a faux pas to call any Hawaii resident 'Hawaiian' (as you would a Californian or Texan), thus ignoring the existence of an indigenous people.

Kama'aina Literally defined as 'child of the land,' refers to a person who is native to a particular place. In the retail context, '*kama'aina* discounts' apply to any resident of Hawaii (ie anyone with a Hawaii drivers license).

Local Person who grew up in Hawaii. Locals who move away retain their local 'cred,' at least in part. But longtime transplants never become local. It is an inherited, elite status. To call a transplant 'almost local' is a welcome compliment, despite its emphasis on the insider-outsider mentality.

Neighbor Islander Person who lives on any Hawaiian Island other than O'ahu.

Transplant Person who moves to the islands as an adult.

Lifestyle

Most residents focus on the outdoors. With the ocean as the primary playground, surfing is the sport of choice, along with fishing, free diving, hunting and 'cruisin' as popular pastimes. The workday starts and ends early and most find a comfortable work/home balance.

The vast majority of residents work in fields somehow related to tourism or the service industry. There are smaller groups of farmers and fishers, craftspeople and, of course, like anywhere else, there are doctors and lawyers and time-share salespeople.

Head to the beach at sunset and you'll see the balance at work. Locals, visitors, businesspeople all stop to take a last sunset surf session or just watch the sun dip below the horizon.

Not surprisingly, many Kaua'i locals follow traditional lifestyle patterns. They often marry early and stick to traditional male and female domestic roles. The easy lifestyle, especially in surf towns like Hanalei, seems to squelch ambitions to travel the world or attend mainland universities.

Locals and transplants tend to diverge in their careers and ambitions. Locals tend toward more conventional, 'American dream' lives, meaning marriage, kids, a modest home, stable work and free nights and weekends. Mainland transplants are here for other reasons: retirement, a dream B&B or organic farm, waves, art, or youthful shenanigans. All are free to be unconventional on Kaua'i.

In many ways you still see the remnants of ancient Hawaiian faiths both at home and in the church. It's not a hugely religious society, but you will find people of all faiths, with a strong Christian contingency and notable populations focusing on Eastern philosophies.

Multiculturalism

The overwhelming majority of Kaua'i's current immigrants are white, so the island's diversity is based on historic minorities: Native Hawaiians and plantation immigrants (predominantly Filipino and Japanese).

During plantation days, whites were wealthy plantation owners and their legendary surnames remain household words (eg Wilcox Memorial Hospital and Rice St). Their ingrained privilege is one reason why some resentment toward haole lingers. As time passes and the plantation era fades, the traditional stereotypes, hierarchies and alliances have softened.

That said, no ethnic group in Hawaii ever remained exclusive; instead, they freely adopted and shared cultural customs, from food to festivals to language. Folks of all backgrounds dance hula, craft hardwood bowls, play the ukulele and study the Hawaiian language.

Hawaiian Words

aloha – love, hello, welcome, goodbye

hale – house

kane – man

kapu – taboo, restricted

mahalo – thank you

makai – a direction, toward the sea

mauka – a direction, toward the mountains (inland)

pau – finished, completed

pono – goodness, justice, responsibility

wahine – woman

ISLAND ETIQUETTE

➡ Practice acquiescence, be courteous and 'no make waves' (don't make a scene).

➡ Try to use basic Hawaiian words.

➡ Treat ancient Hawaiian sites and artifacts with respect.

➡ Dress casually as the locals do.

➡ Remove your shoes before entering homes and B&Bs.

➡ Give a thank-you *shaka* ('hang loose' hand gesture, with index, middle and ring fingers downturned) if a driver lets you merge or stops before a one-lane bridge.

➡ Don't assume being called a haole is an insult (but don't assume it's not either).

➡ Tread lightly with locals when surfing; otherwise it can quickly become unpleasant.

➡ If you give aloha, you'll get aloha.

Koke'e Museum (p234), Koke'e State Park

Today there is no ethnic majority in the Hawaiian Islands. Due to this multiculturalism, you will find a blend of cultural influences and names. Many local Hawaiians have Caucasian or Asian surnames, for example.

Generally, locals feel bonded with other locals. While tourists and transplants are usually welcomed with open arms, they must earn the trust and respect of the locals. It is unacceptable for an outsider to assume an air of superiority and try to 'fix' local ways. Such people will inevitably fall into the category of 'loudmouth haole.'

The Hawaiian language is not widely spoken, though with the rise of immersion schools and renewed interest in 'everything Hawaiian' you'll probably hear it more today than 50 years ago. What you get instead is an island patois that combines surfer lingo, Hawaiian words and plenty of colorful metaphors.

Social Issues

Among social issues on Kaua'i, two stand out: education and substance abuse. With only three public high schools on the island, education remains a weak point. North Shore students, for example, can average three hours a day commuting to and from school. And with an 'us versus them' mentality often present between the student body and the faculty, public school can end up being more of a containment facility than an institution of learning. Parents, especially if they're mainland transplants, often try to get their kids into private schools.

Crystal methamphetamine, or 'ice' as it's referred to locally, is an issue that's growing at an alarming rate. With Hawaii's considerable reliance on importing goods, ice has been able to make its way onto the islands with ease. As there is no inpatient rehab facility on the island and there's a lack of funding from any direction, progress is some-

LOCAL PHRASEOLOGY

brah – shortened form of *braddah* (brother)

chicken skin – goose bumps from cold, fear, thrill

coconut wireless – the 'grapevine'; local gossip channels

da kine – whatchamacallit; used whenever you can't think of the appropriate word

cruisin' – refers to going with the flow, dating, roaming about, driving around, sitting still in one place, and many other active or passive activities or states of being

fo' real? – Really? Are you kidding me?

high makamaka – stuck-up, snooty, pretentious; literally high 'eyes,' meaning head in the air

howzit? – Hey, how's it going? As in 'Eh, howzit brah?'

rubbah slippahs – literally 'rubber slippers'; flip-flops

talk story – chitchat or any casual conversation

to da max – used as an adjective or adverb to add emphasis, as in 'da waves was big to da max!'

thing residents can only hope for with fingers crossed. And with the extremely addictive nature of the drug, crimes like theft (including gas siphoning) and even fatalities are inevitably one or two paces behind. Yet even with all of these stern facts clearly visible, this issue seems to remain half-swept under the collective social carpet of denial – perhaps an example of the darker (and sadder) repercussions of a remote and rural community's exposure to the outside world.

Arts & Crafts

E komo mai (welcome) to these unique Polynesian islands, where storytelling and slack key guitar are among the sounds of everyday life. Contemporary Hawaii is a vibrant mix of multicultural traditions and underneath it all beats a Hawaiian heart, pounding with an ongoing revival of Hawaii's indigenous language, artisanal crafts, music and the hula.

Hula

In ancient Hawai'i, hula sometimes was a solemn ritual, in which *mele* (songs, chants) were an offering to the gods or celebrated the accomplishments of *ali'i* (chiefs). At other times hula was lighthearted entertainment, in which chief and *kama'aina* (commoner) danced together, including at annual festivals such as the makahiki held during harvest

Above Polynesian mask

season. Most importantly, hula embodied the community – telling stories of and celebrating itself.

Hula still thrives today, with competitions and expositions thriving across the islands.

Island Music

Hawaiian music is rooted in ancient chants. Foreign missionaries and sugar-plantation workers introduced new melodies and instruments, which were incorporated and adapted to create a unique local musical style. *Leo ki'eki'e* (falsetto, or 'high voice') vocals, sometimes just referred to as soprano for women, employs a signature *ha'i* (vocal break, or split-note) style, with a singer moving abruptly from one register to another. Contemporary Hawaiian musical instruments include the steel guitar, slack key guitar and ukulele.

But if you tune your rental-car radio to today's island radio stations, you'll hear everything from US mainland hip-hop beats, country-and-western tunes and Asian pop hits to reggae-inspired 'Jawaiian' grooves. A few Hawaii-born singer-songwriters, most famously Jack Johnson, have achieved international stardom. To discover new hit-makers, check out this year's winners of the Na Hoku Hanohano Awards (www.nahokuhanohano.org), Hawaii's version of the Grammies.

Ukulele

Heard all across the islands is the ukulele, derived from the *braguinha*, a Portuguese stringed instrument introduced to Hawaii in 1879. Ukulele means 'jumping flea' in Hawaiian, referring to the way players' deft fingers swiftly move around the strings. The ukulele is enjoying a revival as a young generation of virtuosos emerges, including Nick Acosta, who plays with just one hand, and genre-bending rockers led by Jake Shimabukuro, whose album *Peace Love Ukulele* (2011) reached number one on Billboard's world music chart.

Both the ukulele and the steel guitar contributed to the lighthearted *hapa haole* (Hawaiian music with predominantly English lyrics) popularized in the islands after the 1930s, of which *My Little Grass Shack* and *Lovely Hula Hands* are classic examples. For better or for worse, *hapa haole* songs became instantly recognizable as 'Hawaiian' thanks to Hollywood movies and the classic *Hawaii Calls* radio show, which broadcast worldwide from the banyan-tree courtyard of Waikiki's Moana hotel from 1935 until 1975.

Can't resist the rhythms of the hula? Look for low-cost (or even free) introductory dance lessons at resort hotels, shopping malls and local community centers and colleges. No grass skirt required!

Cowboy Heritage

Spanish and Mexican cowboys introduced the guitar to Hawaiians in the 1830s. Fifty years later, O'ahu-born high-school student Joseph Kekuku started experimenting with playing a guitar flat on his lap while sliding a pocket knife or comb across the strings. His invention, the Hawaiian steel guitar *(kika kila)*, lifts the strings off the fretboard using a movable steel slide, creating a signature smooth sound.

In the early 20th century, Kekuku and others introduced the islands' steel guitar sounds to the world. The steel guitar later inspired the creation of resonator guitars such as the Dobro, now integral to bluegrass, blues and other genres, and country-and-western music's lap and pedal steel guitars. Today Hawaii's most influential steel guitarists include Henry Kaleialoha Allen, Alan Akaka, Bobby Ingano and Greg Sardinha.

Slack Key Guitar

Since the mid-20th century, the Hawaiian steel guitar has usually been played with slack key *(ki ho'alu)* tunings, in which the thumb plays the bass and rhythm chords, while the fingers play the melody and improvisations, in a picked style. Traditionally, slack key tunings were closely guarded secrets among *'ohana* (extended family and friends).

The legendary guitarist Gabby Pahinui launched the modern slack key guitar era with his first recording of 'Hi'ilawe' in 1946. In the 1960s, Gabby and his band the Sons of Hawaii embraced the traditional Hawaiian sound. Along with other influential slack key guitarists such as Sonny Chillingworth, they spurred a renaissance in Hawaiian music that continues to this day. The list of contemporary slack key masters is long

KAUA'I ON SCREEN

Kaua'i has an extraordinary cinematic history; when Hollywood wants paradise, this is their first stop. Below are some of the most popular movies filmed on the island. For a free map of all films and locations, stop by the Kaua'i Visitors Bureau in Lihu'e.

Jurassic World (2015)

Pirates of the Caribbean 4 (2011)

Just Go with It (2011)

The Descendants (2011)

Soul Surfer (2011)

Avatar (2010)

High School Reunion Season 5 (2008)

Perfect Getaway (2008)

Tropic Thunder (2008)

Jurassic Park 3 (2001)

Manhunt (2001)

The Time Machine (2001)

Mighty Joe Young (1998)

George of the Jungle (1997)

The Lost World: Jurassic Park (1997)

Outbreak (1995)

Jurassic Park (1993)

Honeymoon in Vegas (1992)

Hook (1991)

Lord of the Flies (1990)

Throw Momma from the Train (1987)

The Thorn Birds (1983)

Raiders of the Lost Ark (1983)

Seven (1980)

Fantasy Island (1977)

Islands in the Stream (1977)

King Kong (1976)

Gilligan's Island (1964)

Blue Hawaii (1961)

South Pacific (1958)

Pagan Love Song (1950)

White Heat (1934)

Hula dancer, Kaua'i

and ever growing, including Keola Beamer, Ledward Ka'apana, Martin and Cyril Pahinui, Ozzie Kotani and George Kuo.

Traditional Crafts

In the 1970s, the Hawaiian renaissance sparked interest in artisan crafts. The most beloved traditional craft is lei-making, stringing garlands of flowers, leaves, berries, nuts or shells. More lasting souvenirs include wood carvings, woven baskets and hats, and Hawaiian quilts. All of these have become so popular with tourists that cheap imitation imports from across the Pacific have flooded into Hawaii, so shop carefully and always buy local.

Fabric Arts

Lauhala weaving and the making of *kapa* (pounded-bark cloth) for clothing and artworks are two ancient Hawaiian crafts.

Traditionally lauhala served as floor mats, canoe sails, protective capes and more. Weaving the lau (leaves) of the hala (pandanus) tree is the easier part, while preparing the leaves, which have razor-sharp spines, is messy work. Today the most common lauhala items are hats, placemats and baskets. Most are mass-produced, but you can find handmade beauties at specialty stores.

Making *kapa* (called tapa elsewhere in Polynesia) is no less laborious. First, seashells are used to scrape away the rough outer bark of the wauke (paper mulberry) tree. Strips of softer inner bark are cut (traditionally with shark's teeth), pounded with mallets until thin and pliable, and further softened by being soaked in water to let them ferment between beatings. Softened bark strips are then layered atop one another and pounded together in a process called felting. Large sheets of finished *kapa* are colorfully dyed with plant materials and stamped or painted by hand with geometric patterns before being scented with flowers or oils.

In ancient times, *kapa* was worn as everyday clothing by both sexes and used as blankets for everything from swaddling newborns to burying the dead. Today authentic handmade Hawaiian *kapa* cloth is rarely seen outside of museums, fine-art galleries and private collections.

Kaua'i's Contemporary Art Scene

Most artwork by Kaua'i artists is highly commercial: colorful, representational works that appeal to the tourist eye. Unique pieces (usually less marketable) that go beyond the stereotypes do exist, but they're harder to find and are displayed mainly in Honolulu museums and galleries. On Kaua'i, try the Kaua'i Society of Artists (p88) and the cluster of galleries in Hanapepe.

Notable fine artists (to name only a few) include the following:

Carol Bennett Meditative paintings of underwater movement.

A Kimberlin Blackburn (www.akimberlinblackburn.com) Uninhibitedly colorful, stylized sculptures and paintings.

Liedeke Bulder (www.liedekebulderart.com) Classic botanical paintings and skyscape watercolors.

Margaret Ezekiel Pastel drawings of cloudscapes or the human figure.

Mac James (www.macjamesonkauai.com) Nature paintings and drawings with contemporary environmental themes.

Bruna Stude (www.brunastude.com) Elegant B&W underwater photography.

Island Writings

For traditional myths and legends of Kaua'i, you can't go wrong with master storyteller Frederick B Wichman's anthologies, including *Touring the Legends of Koke'e* and *Touring the Legends of the North Shore,* both published by the Kaua'i Historical Society (www.kauaihistoricalsociety1914. com). Talk Story (p221) in Hanapepe is the best bookstore on the island.

Hawaii has been the home of many modern painters, and scores of visiting artists have drawn inspiration from the islands' rich cultural heritage and landscapes. *Encounters with Paradise: Views of Hawaii and Its People, 1778–1941,* by David Forbes, is a vivid art-history tour.

Lei

Greetings. Love. Honor. Respect. Peace. Celebration. Spirituality. Good luck. Farewell. A Hawaiian lei – a handcrafted garland of fresh tropical flowers – can signify all of these meanings and many more. Lei-making may be Hawaii's most sensuous and transitory art form. Fragrant and ephemeral, lei embody the beauty of nature and the embrace of *'ohana* (extended family and friends) and the community, freely given and freely shared.

The Art of the Lei

In choosing their materials, lei makers express emotions and tell a story, since flowers and other plants may embody Hawaiian places and myths. Traditional lei makers may use feathers, nuts, shells, seeds, seaweed, vines, leaves and fruit, in addition to more familiar fragrant flowers. The most common methods of making lei are by knotting, braiding, winding, stringing or sewing the raw natural materials together.

Worn daily, lei were integral to ancient Hawaiian society. In the islands' Polynesian past, they were part of sacred hula dances and given as special gifts to loved ones, as healing medicine to the sick and as offerings to the gods, all practices that continue today. So powerful a symbol were they that on ancient Hawaii's battlefields, a lei could bring peace to warring armies.

Today, locals wear lei for special events, such as weddings, birthdays, anniversaries and graduations. It's no longer common to make one's own lei, unless you belong to a hula *halau* (school). For ceremonial hula, performers are often required to make their own lei, even gathering raw materials by hand.

Modern Celebrations

For visitors to Hawaii, the tradition of giving and receiving lei dates back to 19th-century steamships that brought the first tourists to the islands. Later, disembarking cruise-ship passengers were greeted by vendors who would toss garlands around the necks of *malihini* (newcomers).

In 1927, the poet Don Blanding and Honolulu journalist Grace Tower Warren called for making May 1 a holiday to honor lei. Every year, Lei Day is still celebrated across the islands with Hawaiian music, hula dancing, parades, and lei-making workshops and contests.

The tradition of giving a kiss with a lei began during WWII, allegedly when a hula dancer at a USO club was dared by her friends to give a military serviceman a peck on the cheek when offering him a flower lei.

Lei Etiquette

➡ Do not wear a lei hanging directly down around your neck. Instead, drape a closed (circular) lei over your shoulders, making sure equal lengths are hanging over your front and back.

➡ When presenting a lei, bow your head slightly and raise the lei above your heart. Do not drape it with your own hands over the head of the recipient because this isn't respectful; let them do it themselves.

➡ Don't give a closed lei to a pregnant woman for it may bring bad luck; choose an open (untied) lei or *haku* (head) lei instead.

➡ Resist the temptation to wear a lei intended for someone else. That's bad luck. Never refuse a lei, and do not take one off in the presence of the giver.

➡ When you stop wearing your lei, don't throw it away. Untie the string, remove the bow and return the lei's natural elements to the earth (eg scatter flowers in the ocean, bury seeds or nuts).

LEI MODERN CELEBRATIONS

You can find lei across the island. Keep a lookout for eye-catching Ni'ihau shell lei.

On the 'Garden Island,' leathery, anise-scented mokihana berries are often woven with strands of glossy, green maile vines. Mokihana trees thrive on the rain-soaked western slopes of Mt Wai'ale'ale.

Landscapes & Wildlife

The Hawaiian Islands are the most isolated land masses on earth. Born of barren lava flows, they were originally populated only by plants and animals that could traverse the Pacific – for example, seeds clinging to a bird's feather or fern spores that drifted thousands of miles through the air. Most flora and fauna that landed here didn't survive. Scientists estimate that new species became established maybe once every 20,000 years – and these included no amphibians, no browsing animals, no mosquitoes and only two mammals: a bat and a seal.

Above Hawaiian monk seal

The wildlife that did make it here found a rich, ecologically diverse land to colonize. Developed in isolation, many of these species became endemic to the islands, meaning that they're found nowhere else in the world. Unfortunately, Hawaii has the highest rate of extinction in the nation and nearly 25% of all federally listed threatened and endangered species in the US are endemic Hawaiian flora and fauna. Only time will tell how climate change will affect the island's unique species.

Animals

For wildlife enthusiasts, the island's main attractions are both resident and migratory birds, as well as myriad ocean creatures.

Ocean Life

Up to 10,000 migrating North Pacific humpback whales come to Hawaiian waters for calving each winter, and whale-watching can be excellent off Kaua'i's South Shore. Pods of spinner dolphins, with their acrobatic spiraling leaps, regularly approach boats cruising in Kaua'i's waters and can also be seen from the shoreline off Kilauea Point.

Threatened *honu* (green sea turtles) are traditionally revered by Hawaiians as an *'aumakua* (protective deity). Snorkelers often see *honu* feeding on seaweed along rocky coastlines or in shallow lagoons. Endangered Hawaiian monk seals also occasionally haul up on shore, which is a thrill for beachgoers who by law must observe turtles and seals from a distance.

Birds

Kaua'i is a birder's dream, with copious creatures soaring over its peaks and down its valleys. Lowland wetlands feature four endangered waterbirds that are cousins of mainland species: the Hawaiian duck, Hawaiian coot, Hawaiian moorhen and Hawaiian stilt. The best place to view all four species is the North Shore's Hanalei National Wildlife Refuge. Although public access to the refuge is strictly limited, an overlook opposite Princeville Center provides a great view of the birds' habitat, with a serene river, shallow ponds and cultivated taro fields.

The endangered nene, Hawaii's state bird, is a long-lost cousin of the Canada goose. Nene once numbered as many as 25,000 on all the islands, but by the 1950s only 50 were left. Intensive breeding programs have raised their numbers to around 2500 on three main islands: Maui, Kaua'i and Hawai'i (Big Island). You might see them in Hanalei wetlands,

SWIMMING WITH DOLPHINS

Hawaiian spinner dolphins are some of the most amazing, intuitive and curious creatures on earth. A highlight of many a trip is the chance to see these cetaceans up close. The dolphins are facing increased pressure from humans, however, according to the National Oceanic and Atmospheric Administration (NOAA), meaning you should think carefully about how you engage with dolphins while visiting.

There are a number of factors to consider. The number of dolphin-focused tours has grown across the islands, from about 10 in 2006 to over 70 today. Furthermore, dolphins hunt at night and then come in to the shallows during the day to rest. NOAA argues that swimming with them during these resting periods affects their natural life cycles. In 2016, NOAA proposed a rule to clarify the Marine Mammal Protection Act and prohibit swimming with and approaching Hawaiian spinner dolphins within 50yd. The proposed rule was a sticking point for many people on Kaua'i and as of press time, it remains unclear what actions will be taken.

There are a few noteworthy exceptions to the rule. Persons who inadvertently come within 50yd, or who are approached by dolphins would be exempt. Vessels that are underway and approached, but make no effort to change course to intercept dolphins would also be exempt from the rule. This logic is designed to stop the practice of leap-frogging (less common on Kaua'i than the other islands), where boats take turns intercepting dolphin pods.

There are no dolphin encounters with caged dolphins on Kaua'i.

Flowers of the *'ohi'a lehua* tree

around golf courses and open fields, and at Kilauea Point National Wildlife Refuge.

Native forest birds are more challenging to observe, but the keen-eyed may spy eight endemic species remaining at Koke'e State Park, especially in the Alaka'i Wilderness Preserve. The *'apapane*, a type of honeycreeper, is the most abundant: a bright-red bird the same color as the lehua flowers from which it takes nectar.

Today, two-thirds of all endemic Hawaiian birds are extinct, the victims of aggressive, introduced birds and infectious diseases. In 1992, Hurricane 'Iniki also contributed to this catastrophic decline: it was the last time three species were seen on Kaua'i. To learn more about Kaua'i's birds, Birds of Kaua'i (www.kauaibirds.com) is a good starting point and SoundsHawaiian (www.soundshawaiian.com) is a real treat for the ears, offering crisp recordings of island birdsong.

Plants

Ancient Hawaiians would scarcely recognize Kaua'i, having never encountered the tropical flowers, fruit trees and lush landscape that today epitomize the island. Mangoes came from Asia, macadamia nuts from Australia and coffee from Africa. Today many botanists and farmers advocate biodiversity, so alien species aren't necessarily bad. But, of Hawaii's 1300 endemic plant species, over 100 are already extinct and 273 are endangered.

Native Forest Trees

Over 90% of Hawaii's 1000-plus plant species are endemic to the islands. To see native forest trees, visit Koke'e State Park and the 10,000-acre Alaka'i Swamp Wilderness Preserve. Along the Pihea and Alaka'i

Kaua'i waterfalls

Swamp Trails, you'll see the most abundant rainforest tree, 'ohi'a lehua, a hardwood with bright-red or orange pompom-like flowers that provide nectar for forest birds. Another dominant forest tree (or shrub) is lapalapa, with long-stemmed leaves that flutter in the slightest breeze. Among the best-known tree species is koa, an endemic hardwood that is Hawaii's most commercially valuable tree for its fine woodworking qualities, rich color and swirling grain. You can identify koa trees by their distinctive crescent-shaped leaves.

Coastal Plants

Despite the rampant development along some parts of Kaua'i's coast, the shoreline is also a good place to find endemic plants. The harsh environment – windblown, salt-sprayed, often arid land with nutrient-poor, sandy soil – requires plants to adapt to survive, for example, by growing flat along the ground, becoming succulent or developing waxy leaf coatings to retain moisture. You can also see many endemic coastal plants at Kilauea Point National Wildlife Refuge on the North Shore.

National, State & County Parks

About 30% of Kaua'i is protected as state parks and nature reserves. For hiking, don't miss Waimea Canyon State Park and Koke'e State Park, with their spectacular elevated views and numerous trails and campsites. On the Eastside, Nounou Mountain, with three steep but scenic hiking trails, is well-maintained forest-reserve land.

Ha'ena State Park is another favorite, as it has Ke'e Beach, a fantastic snorkeling spot, and the nearby Kalalau Trail leading into Na Pali Coast Wilderness State Park. The miles of sandy beach at Polihale State Park offer an escape from crowds, but beware two potential threats:

hazardous ocean conditions and the bone-rattlingly rough 5-mile un-paved road to get there.

Most of Kaua'i's best easy-access beaches are designated as county parks, such as sunny Po'ipu Beach Park (South Shore), serene 'Anini Beach Park (North Shore), calm Salt Pond Beach Park (Westside) and family-friendly Lydgate Beach Park (Eastside).

There are no national parks on the island, but there are three federal refuges, including the accessible Kilauea Point National Wildlife Refuge, which has spectacular wildlife watching, including migratory whales in winter and the only diverse seabird colony on the main Hawaiian Islands.

The Land

Kaua'i is the oldest and fourth largest of the major inhabited Hawaiian Islands, with volcanic rocks dating back over five million years and most of the island boasting the tropical trifecta of ocean, beach and mountain. Unlike the shiny black terrain seen on much of the lava-spewing Big Island (a baby at less than 500,000 years old), Kaua'i displays the effects of time and erosion, with weathered summits, mountaintop bogs and rainforests, deeply cut valleys and rivers, extensive sandy beaches, coral and algal reefs, and rust-colored soil indelible from both memory and your white sneakers.

Volcanic Origins

Because its volcanic origins lie hidden under a carpet of forests, ferns and shrubland, Kaua'i's landscape, particularly along the North Shore, is overwhelmingly lush and strikes many as the ultimate tropical

KAUA'I'S TOP PARKS & PROTECTED AREAS

NATURE AREA	FEATURES	ACTIVITIES
Alaka'i Wilderness Preserve	rainforest, bogs, forest birds	boardwalk hiking, bird-watching
'Anini Beach Park	sandy beach, calm waters	swimming, windsurfing, picnicking
Ha'ena State Park	sandy beach, historic Hawaiian sites, marine life	swimming, snorkeling
Hanalei Bay	scenic circular bay, sandy beaches, winter waves	surfing, swimming
Hanalei National Wildlife Refuge	scenic views, taro fields, endangered waterbirds	bird-watching (limited access)
Hule'ia National Wildlife Refuge	river, endangered waterbirds	bird-watching (limited access)
Kilauea Point National Wildlife Refuge	seabirds, coastal plants, nene (native Hawaiian geese), historic lighthouse	bird-watching, whale-watching
Koke'e State Park	trails, waterfalls, forest birds & plants, interpretive center	hiking, camping, bird-watching
Maha'ulepu Coast*	lithified sand-dune cliffs, sandy beaches, heiau (ancient stone temples)	walking, windsurfing, surfing
Na Pali Coast State Park	challenging trails, coastal flora, seabirds, archaeological sites	hiking, camping
Polihale State Park	coastal dunes, state's longest beach (dangerous currents)	walking, sunset watching, camping
Waimea Canyon State Park	colossal gorge, forestland	hiking, camping

*Private property not under governmental protection

Top Spouting Horn (p191)
Bottom The nene, Hawaii's state bird

CHRISTIAN WEBER/SHUTTERSTOCK ©

beauty – which partly explains the frequency of visitors showing up for a week or two and staying a lifetime. Many folks' lives have shifted as a result of just driving down the hill from Princeville to Hanalei.

Perhaps duped by its round shape, scientists for decades believed that a single volcano formed Kaua'i. But on the basis of evidence collected since the 1980s, scientists now think that Kaua'i's entire eastern side 'slumped' along an ancient fault line, leaving a steep *pali* (cliff) along Waimea Canyon's western edge. Then, lava from another shield volcano flowed westward to the *pali* and pounded against the cliffs. The black and red horizontal striations along the canyon walls represent successive volcanic eruptions; the red color shows where water seeped through the rocks, oxidizing the iron inside.

Highs & Lows

Now shrunken by age, Kaua'i is also slowly subsiding into the ocean floor. Don't worry, the rate is less than an inch per century. Still, over eons those inches have cost the island 3000ft in elevation, making today's high point the 5243ft Kawaikini. Among the most visually spectacular valleys is Kalalau, with its curtain-like folds and knife-edge ridges, topping out just above 4000ft at lookouts where the road ends in Koke'e State Park. Views of the Na Pali sea cliffs are spectacular but can be seen only from the deck of a boat, the windows of a helicopter – or, for the fit and eco-conscious, from the Nu'alolo or Awa'awapuhi Trails in Koke'e State Park or the grueling 11-mile Kalalau Trail in Na Pali Coast Wilderness State Park.

Survival
Guide

Directory A–Z

Climate

Lihu'e

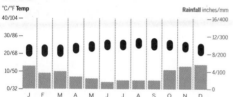

Princeville

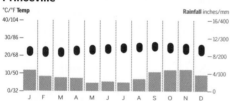

Koke'e State Park

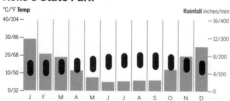

fruits and plants, in order to prevent entry of invasive species. The rabies-free state enforces strict pet quarantine laws, though you can slice the time to five days if you meet specific requirements. For complete details, contact the **Hawaiian Department of Agriculture** (http://hdoa.hawaii.gov).

Electricity

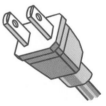

**Type A
120V/60Hz**

Customs Regulations

Non-US citizens and permanent residents may import the following duty free:

➡ 1L of liquor (if over 21 years)

➡ 200 cigarettes or 50 non-Cuban cigars (if over 21 years)

➡ $100 worth of gifts Hawaii has strict restrictions against bringing in any fresh

Type B
120V/60Hz

Food & Drink

Dining in Kaua'i tends to be quite casual – even when it is elegant. Top tourist restaurants require reservations (sometimes several days in advance).

Fish markets Taking a *bentō* box, *poke* or sushi roll to go is a local tradition and most towns have a worthwhile fish market – and rotating farmers markets – worth checking out.

Joints Be they taco stands, noodle spots, hamburger places or juice bars, the small-time joints of the island are the lifeblood of island cuisine. Look for lines out the door at lunchtime to pick a top spot.

Restaurants There are plenty of fancy tourist restaurants, often with live entertainment.

Health

➡ For emergency medical assistance anywhere in Hawaii, call 911 or go directly to the emergency room (ER) of the nearest hospital.

➡ For nonemergencies, consider an urgent-care center or walk-in medical clinic.

➡ Some insurance policies require you to get preauthorization for medical treatment from a call center before seeking help. Keep all medical receipts and documentation for claims reimbursement later.

Health Insurance

Kaua'i is a long way from everywhere. Having a good travel health-insurance plan if you are not on a US policy would be helpful. US policies work here, but you may find you are out of network for much of your needs.

Availability & Cost of Health Care

➡ Health care costs are the same or slightly higher than mainland US. This means it's expensive.

➡ The best hospital is in Lihu'e at the **Wilcox Memorial Hospital.** (☎808-245-1100; www.wilcoxhealth.org; 3-3420 Kuhio Hwy)

➡ There is currently no hyperbaric chamber on Kaua'i. But there are plans to launch one in 2017.

Infectious Diseases

The best ways to prevent the spread of infectious diseases is to wear a condom and avoid being bitten by mosquitoes.

DENGUE FEVER

➡ There was a small outbreak of dengue fever on the Big Island in 2015–16, with no known cases in Kaua'i. (http://health.hawaii.gov).

➡ Dengue is transmitted by aedes mosquitoes, which bite preferentially during the daytime and breed primarily in artificial water containers.

➡ Dengue usually causes flu-like symptoms, including fever, muscle aches, joint pains, severe headaches, nausea and vomiting, often followed by a rash.

➡ If you suspect you've been infected, do not take aspirin or NSAIDs (eg ibuprofen), which can cause hemorrhaging. See a doctor as soon as possible for diagnosis and monitoring; severe cases may require hospitalization.

GIARDIASIS

➡ Symptoms of this parasitic infection of the small intestine include nausea, bloating, cramps and diarrhea and may last for weeks.

➡ To protect yourself, don't drink from untreated water sources (eg waterfalls, ponds, streams, rivers), which may be contaminated by animal or human feces.

➡ Giardiasis is diagnosed by a stool test and treated with antibiotics.

HEPATITIS A

There was an outbreak of Hepatitis A on Kaua'i and O'ahu in 2016. The outbreak was related to scallops being served at a sushi restaurant.

HIV & AIDS

➡ Out of 1.4 million, there were a total of 2430 reported cases of HIV on the Hawaiian Islands in 2013.

➡ HIV is primarily spread in the US through sex and shared needles.

LEPTOSPIROSIS

➡ Leptospirosis is acquired by exposure to untreated water or soil contaminated by the urine of infected animals, especially rodents.

EATING PRICE RANGES

The following price ranges refer to a main course.

$ less than $12

$$ $12–30

$$$ more than $30

➡ Outbreaks often occur after flooding, when overflow contaminates water sources downstream from livestock or wild animal habitats.

➡ Initial symptoms, which resemble a flu, usually subside uneventfully in a few days, but a minority of cases involve potentially fatal complications.

➡ Diagnosis is through urine and/or blood tests and treatment is with antibiotics.

➡ Minimize your risk by staying out of bodies of freshwater (eg pools, streams, waterfalls); avoid these entirely if you have open cuts or sores.

➡ On hiking trails, take warning signs about leptospirosis seriously. If you're camping, water purification and good hygiene are essential.

STAPHYLOCOCCUS

➡ Hawaii leads the nation in antibiotic-resistant staphylococcus infections. Staph infections are caused by bacteria, which often

enter the body through an open wound.

➡ To prevent infection, practice good hygiene (eg wash your hands thoroughly and frequently; shower or bathe daily; wear clean clothing). Apply antibiotic ointment (eg Neosporin) to any open cuts or sores and keep them out of recreational water; if cuts or sores are on your feet, don't go barefoot, even on sand.

➡ If a wound becomes painful, looks red, inflamed or swollen, leaks pus or causes a rash or blisters, seek medical help immediately.

ZIKA

➡ Hawaii had no locally acquired Zika cases and no mosquitoes transmitting the disease within the state as of 2016.

➡ There were a total of 10 cases of Zika imported to the state in 2016, with two coming to Kaua'i.

➡ Zika is spread mostly by the bite of an infected aedes

mosquito. These mosquitoes bite during the day and night.

➡ Zika can be passed from a pregnant woman to her fetus. Infection during pregnancy can cause certain birth defects.

➡ Zika can be passed through sex from a person who has Zika.

➡ There is no vaccine or medicine for Zika. Learn more at www.cdc.gov/zika.

Environmental Hazards

BITES & STINGS

➡ Any animal bite or scratch – including from unknown dogs, feral pigs etc – should be promptly and thoroughly cleansed with soap and water, followed by application of an antiseptic (eg iodine, alcohol) to prevent wounds from becoming infected.

➡ Hawaii is currently rabies-free. The state has no established wild snake population, but snakes are occasionally seen, especially in sugarcane fields.

INSECTS

➡ The most effective protections against insect bites are common-sense behavior and clothing: wear long sleeves and pants, a hat and shoes.

➡ Where mosquitoes are active, apply a good insect repellent, preferably one containing DEET (but not for children under two years old).

➡ Some spider bites (eg from black widows or brown recluses) contain toxic venom, which children are more vulnerable to; for anyone who is bitten, apply ice or cool water to the affected area, then seek medical help.

➡ Centipedes also give painful bites; they can infiltrate buildings, so it's best to check sheets and shoes.

➡ Leeches found in humid rainforest areas do not transmit any disease but their bites can be intensely itchy, even for weeks afterward.

MARINE ANIMALS

➡ Marine spikes, such as those found on sea urchins, scorpionfish and lionfish, can cause severe localized pain. If this occurs, immediately immerse the affected area in hot water (as hot as can be tolerated). Keep topping up with hot water until the pain subsides and medical care can be reached. Do the same for cone-shell stings.

➡ Stings from jellyfish and Portuguese man-of-war (aka bluebottles) also occur in Hawaii's tropical waters. Even touching a bluebottle hours after it's washed up onshore can result in burning stings. Jellyfish are often seen eight to 10 days after a full moon, when they float into Hawaii's nearshore waters, often on the islands' leeward shores.

If you are stung, douse the affected area in vinegar, or carefully peel off the tentacles with gloved hands, then rinse the area well in sea water (not freshwater or urine), followed by rapid transfer to a hospital; antivenoms are available.

VOG

➡ Vog, a visible haze or smog caused by volcanic emissions from the Big Island, is often (but not always) dispersed by trade winds before it reaches other islands. On the Big Island, vog can make sunny skies hazy in West Hawai'i, especially in the afternoons around Kailua-Kona.

➡ Short-term exposure to vog is not generally hazardous; however, high sulfur-dioxide levels can create breathing problems for sensitive groups (eg anyone with respiratory or heart conditions, pregnant women, young children and infants). Avoid vigorous physical exertion outdoors on voggy days.

TAP WATER

The tap water in Kaua'i is drinkable, though in some places it might not taste that great. One good tip is to fill a large bottle with tap water and let it sit in the fridge overnight.

Insurance

Worldwide travel insurance is available at www.lonelyplanet.com/travel-insurance. You can buy, extend and claim online anytime – even if you're already on the road.

Internet Access

Wi-fi is available at many accommodations. Smaller accommodations (eg B&Bs) typically provide free wi-fi; larger hotels will often charge $12 to $15 per day for in-room access, but that can often be negotiated out of the bill. Make sure to handle that ahead of time, or simply use the lobby wi-fi.

Most towns have at least one cafe with wi-fi. It's free at Starbucks (Lihu'e and Waipouli).

Laundry

Most condos, B&Bs, inns and vacation-rental homes include free or inexpensive use of washers and dryers; hotels typically offer coin-operated laundry facilities.

Legal Matters

➡ You are entitled to an attorney from the moment that you are arrested. The **Hawaii**

State Bar Association (☏808-537-9140; http://hawaiilawyerreferral.com; Suite 1000, 1100 Alakea St, Honolulu; ⌚8:30am-4:30pm Mon-Fri) is one starting point to find an attorney. If you can't afford one, the state is obligated to provide one for free.

➡ Driving with a blood alcohol level of 0.08% or higher constitutes driving under the influence (DUI).

➡ Possessing marijuana and narcotics is illegal, although smoking a joint rarely leads to arrest unless other crimes are involved. Still, better not to get spotted doing so.

➡ Hitchhiking and public nudity (eg at nude beaches) are illegal but the laws are rarely enforced.

➡ Smoking cigarettes is prohibited in all public spaces, including airports, bars, restaurants and businesses, and, as of 2015, state parks and beaches.

➡ While the Department of Commerce & Consumer Affairs (www.cca.hawaii.gov) deals primarily with residents' issues, visitors who want to lodge a complaint against a business should contact the Department's Office of Consumer Protection.

LGBTIQ Travelers

Sexual preference on Kaua'i is basically a non-issue. The island culture here is very welcoming and diverse. Hawaii has strong legislation which protects minority groups, and there is also a constitutional guarantee of privacy regarding sexual behavior between consenting adults. That said, there's neither a gay scene nor any public displays of affection on the island, as locals tend to keep their private lives to themselves.

Maps

Franko's Maps (www.frankos maps.com) Outstanding full-color, fold-up, waterproof maps ($7 to $11) that pinpoint snorkeling, diving, surfing and kayaking spots, and also identify tropical fish.

Kaua'i Island Atlas & Maps (www.envdhawaii.com) Like a land version of the Franko map ($10), with all sorts of info on climate, geology and culture, along with town insets. Available at Koke'e Natural History Museum.

Kaua'i: Island of Discovery Nice fold-out tourist freebie available from Kaua'i Visitors Bureau, Lihu'e. Identifies all locations used in feature films.

Na Ala Hele (Map p94; http://hawaiitrails.ehawaii.gov) Detailed topographical trail maps ($5 in person, $6 by mail) for hikers, from the Division of Forestry & Wildlife. The interactive website is also a tremendous resource.

TopoZone (www.topozone.com) If you're a geographer, backcountry explorer or map fiend, TopoZone has general topographical maps.

Money

ATMs are available in all major towns. Visa and MasterCard are widely accepted. American Express and Discover hit or miss.

ATMs & Eftpos

ATMs are available 24/7 at banks, supermarkets, convenience stores, shopping centers and gas stations. Expect a surcharge of about $2 per transaction, plus any fees charged by your home bank.

Credit & Debit Cards

Major credit cards are widely accepted at larger businesses, and they're necessary to rent a car, order tickets by phone and book a hotel room. But smaller businesses such as B&Bs may not accept credit cards. In those cases, a Paypal or Venmo account may suffice if you'd rather not deal in cash.

Tipping

Leaving no tip is rare and requires real cause.

Hotel bellhops $1 to $2 per bag.

Housekeeping staff $2 to $4 daily.

Parking valets At least $2 when handed back your car keys.

Restaurants Tip 15% to 20%, unless gratuity is included.

Taxi drivers Tip 10% to 15% of metered fare.

Opening Hours

Standard opening hours year-round are as follows:

Banks 8:30am–4pm Monday to Friday, some to 6pm Friday, and 9am–noon or 1pm Saturday

Bars & Clubs to midnight daily, some to 2am Thurday to Saturday

Businesses 8:30am–4:30pm Monday to Friday, some post offices 9am–noon Saturday

Restaurants breakfast 6–10am, lunch 11:30am–2:30pm, dinner 5–9:30pm

Shops 9am–5pm Monday to Saturday, some also noon-5pm Sunday

Post

➡ The US Postal Service (www.usps.com) delivers mail to and from Kaua'i. Service is reliable but slower than within continental USA. First-class airmail between Kaua'i and the mainland takes up to four days.

➡ First-class letters up to 1oz (about 28g) cost 49¢ within the USA, $1.15 internationally.

➡ You can receive mail c/o General Delivery at most post offices on Kaua'i, but you must first complete an application in person. Bring two forms of ID and your temporary local address. The accepted application is valid for 30 days; mail is held for up to 15 days. Many accommodations will also hold mail for incoming guests.

Public Holidays

New Year's Day January 1

Martin Luther King Jr Day Third Monday in January

Presidents' Day Third Monday in February

Kuhio Day March 26

Good Friday Friday before Easter Sunday

Memorial Day Last Monday in May

King Kamehameha Day June 11

MINIMUM LEGAL AGE TO...

ACTIVITY	AGE
Drink alcohol	21
Buy tobacco	18
Vote in an election	18
Drive a car	16

Independence Day
July 4

Statehood Day
Third Friday in August

Labor Day
First Monday in September

Election Day
Second Tuesday in November

Veterans Day
November 11

Thanksgiving
Fourth Thursday in November

Christmas Day
December 25

Safe Travel

Kaua'i can be a safe and easy-to-navigate destination for seasoned travelers, but however beautiful, nature can pose a threat.

➡ Drownings happen in high surf and in sheltered coves. Always be aware of currents, swell and tides, and when in doubt, don't go out.

➡ Roads can be dark at night, which can be disorienting and intimidating for big-city drivers.

➡ Keep valuables out of sight when parked at beaches and trailheads.

Hiking & Swimming

The major risks on Kaua'i lie here. In 2016, 11 people drowned on Kaua'i, nearly one every month. Most who drown here are tourists.

The climate, while idyllic in one sense, can bite back if you venture onto trails without ample food, water or bad weather gear. Rivers can rise fast too. Make sure you are prepared for the elements and your level of activity before you venture out.

Theft & Violence

Kaua'i is a pretty quiet place and there's virtually no nightlife. Populated areas, such as towns and major sights, are relatively safe. Having said that, the island has its issues, like everywhere else.

➡ There's a drug problem, generally involving ice (crystal methamphetamine) or *pakalolo* (marijuana), which fuels petty crime. Be on guard at deserted beaches and parks (eg Nawiliwili Beach Park, Keahua Arboretum) after dark.

➡ Car break-ins occur mainly in remote areas, including roadside parks, campgrounds and parking lots, but not always.

➡ There's a deep insider/outsider mentality, with racial overtones. Certain beaches, surf spots, swimming holes and rural neighborhoods are unofficially considered locals only. In these places haole (white) tourists might encounter resentment or worse. The key is to avoid confrontation. Be careful in places where that bright new aloha shirt makes you stand out. Be aware when driving that this is not downtown Manhattan. When in doubt, drive slow, and don't use that horn.

Trespassing

➡ Heed *kapu* (no trespassing) signs on private property.

➡ Like the rest of the US, Hawaii does not have the open-access laws found in certain European countries.

Tsunami

During the 20th century, Kaua'i was hit by two major tsunamis. Both ravaged the North Shore, causing 14 deaths in 1946, and demolishing 75 homes and washing out six essential bridges in 1957. Today, new homes built in tsunami-prone areas (flood zones) must be built high off the ground.

➡ If you're at the coast when a tsunami occurs, immediately head inland.

➡ The front section of local telephone books has maps of areas susceptible to tsunamis and safety evacuation zones.

➡ Kaua'i has four civil defense sirens that can be used to issue a tsunami warning.

Telephone

Cell Phones

Cell reception is good except in remote locations. Only tri- or quad-band models work in the USA.

Network Coverage

Verizon has the best cellular network across the state, but AT&T and Sprint have decent coverage. While coverage on Kaua'i is good in major towns, it's spotty or nonexistent in rural areas.

Further Information

You need a multiband GSM phone to make calls in the USA. If your phone doesn't work, pop in a US prepaid rechargeable SIM card (with an unlocked multiband phone) or buy an inexpensive prepaid phone.

Phone Codes

➡ Domestic long-distance calls must be preceded by 1.

➡ Toll-free numbers (area codes ☏800, ☏866, ☏877 or ☏888) must be preceded by 1.

➡ For all Kaua'i calls from a local landline, dial only the seven-digit number. For interisland calls, dial 1-808 and then the seven-digit number; long-distance charges apply.

➡ For Kaua'i, Hawaii and all out-of-state calls from a cell phone, dial the 10-digit number beginning with the ☏808 area code.

➜ For direct international calls, dial ✆011 plus the country code, area code and local number. An exception is Canada, where you dial ✆1 plus the area code and local number, but international rates still apply.

➜ If you are calling from abroad, the US country code is ✆1.

Pay Phones & Phonecards

➜ Prepaid phonecards are sold at convenience stores, supermarkets and other locations.

Time

➜ Hawaii has its own time zone and does not observe daylight saving time.

➜ During standard time (winter), Hawaii time differs from Los Angeles by two hours, from New York by five hours, from London by 10 hours and from Tokyo by 19 hours. During daylight saving time (summer), the difference is one hour more for countries that observe it.

➜ In midwinter, the sun rises around 7am and sets around 6pm. In midsummer, it rises before 6am and sets after 7pm.

➜ Upon arrival, set your internal clock to 'Hawaiian time,' meaning slow down!

Tourist Information

Tourist information kiosks aren't really a thing on Kaua'i, but the local tourist board,

Kaua'i Visitors Bureau (Map p94; ✆808-245-3971; www.gohawaii.com/kauai; 4334 Rice St, Suite 101; ⊗8am-4:30pm Mon-Fri), does have a useful website.

Travelers with Disabilities

Accommodations Major hotels are equipped with elevators, phones with telecommunications device for the deaf (TDD) and wheelchair-accessible rooms (which must be reserved in advance). These services are unlikely in B&Bs and small hotels.

General Information Kaua'i County can be a resource, though its website (www.kauai.gov/visitors) is clunky. If you have specific questions about traveling with a disability on Kaua'i, call the American Disability Act (ADA) Coordinator at the Office of the Mayor (808-241-4921). The **Disability and Communication Access Board** (✆808-586-8121; http://health.hawaii.gov/dcab/) also provides a tip sheet specifically for Kaua'i at www.health.hawaii.gov/dcab/files/2015/12/Traveler-Tips-Kauai.pdf.

Mobility There are currently no car-rental agencies with lift-equipped vehicles. Gammie HomeCare (www.gammie.com) rents portable ramps, wheelchairs, hospital beds, walking aids and other medical equipment. **Wheelchair Getaways of Hawaii** (✆800-638-1912; www.wheelchairgetaways.com) rents wheelchair-accessible vans. Kaua'i County provides a Landeez all-terrain wheelchair

at lifeguard stations at Po'ipu, Lydgate and Salt Pond Beach Parks. All **Kaua'i county buses** (Map p88; ✆808-246-8110; www.kauai.gov/Bus; 3220 Ho'olako St, Lihu'e; one-way fare adult/senior & child 7-18yr $2/1) are wheelchair lift equipped.

Seeing-Eye & Guide Dogs These dogs are not subject to the general quarantine rules for pets if they meet the Department of Agriculture's minimum requirements; see http://hawaii.gov/hdoa/ai/aqs/guide-service-dogs-entering-hawai-i for more details. All animals must enter the state via Honolulu International Airport.

Resources

Download Lonely Planet's free Accessible Travel guide from http://lptravel.to/AccessibleTravel.

Visas

Visitor Extensions

To remain in the US longer than the date stamped on your passport, you must go to the Honolulu office of the **US Citizenship & Immigration Service** (www.uscis.gov; 500 Ala Moana Blvd, Bldg 2, Room 400, Kaka'ako) before the stamped date to apply for an extension.

Further Information

Upon arriving in the US, all foreign visitors must have their two index fingers scanned and a digital photo taken, a process that takes under a minute. For more information, see the Travel Security section of the US Department of Homeland Security (https://www.dhs.gov/how-do-i/for-travelers) site.

Volunteering

Although paid work on Kaua'i can be hard to find, volunteers are often welcome, especially in the botanic gardens and state parks.

Hui O Laka (☑808-335-9975; www.kokee.org) Work to eradicate invasive species, plant endemic species and participate in a bird count.

Kaua'i Habitat for Humanity (☑808-335-0296; http://kauaihabitat.org/volunteer/) ✎ Join a team of volunteers to build affordable homes for families in need.

Malama Kaua'i (☑808-828-0685; www.malamakauai.org) Volunteers needed for half-day shifts at Kilauea's community gardens.

National Tropical Botanical Garden (NTBG; ☑North Shore 808-826-1668 ext. 3, South Shore 808-332-7324 ext 232; www.ntbg.org/donate/volunteer.php) Apply in advance to work in two of the most astonishingly beautiful botanical gardens in the world.

Sierra Club (www.hi.sierraclub.org/kauai) Apply to be a volunteer with the island chapter of the age-old environmental group founded by the legendary John Muir.

Surfrider Foundation (☑808-635-2593; http://kauai.surfrider.org) Join a beach cleanup and help mitigate marine plastic pollution.

Work

➡ US citizens can legally work in Hawaii, but considering the high unemployment rate, opportunities are limited. Short-term employment will probably mean entry-level jobs in the service industry. Specific outdoor skills (eg scuba diving) might land you a job with an activity outfit.

➡ Check the listings in newspaper classifieds and also the Big Island Craigslist (http://honolulu.craigslist.org/big) website.

Transportation

GETTING THERE & AWAY

Getting here is easy, especially from the mainland USA and Canada, with numerous flights daily. Often, flights will get here with layovers in Honolulu. There are no ferry services here.

Flights, cars and tours can be booked online at lonelyplanet.com/bookings.

Air

Roughly 99% of visitors to Hawaii arrive by air. Hawaii's major interisland carrier – reliable Hawaiian Airlines – offers frequent interisland flights in jet planes, as well as turboprop service through its new subsidiary brand, 'Ohana by Hawaiian. Island Air provides scheduled service daily in turboprop planes with six daily round-trip flights between Lihu'e and Honolulu.

Smaller turboprop planes fly so low that their flights almost double as sightseeing excursions – fun! The only drawback to turboprop planes is that carry-on baggage are usually much more strict, so you may end up paying extra to check all of your luggage.

Expect further schedule changes and possible shake-ups in the interisland flight biz. Interisland airfares vary wildly, from $50 to $190 one way. Round-trip fares are typically double the price without any discounts. Usually, you'll find that the earlier you book, the cheaper the fare.

While it's often possible to walk up and get on a flight among the four biggest islands (particularly to/from Honolulu), advance reservations are recommended, especially at peak times.

Airline regulations concerning surfboards, bicycles and other oversized baggage vary and can be restrictive, not to mention expensive – ask before booking.

Airports & Airlines

The vast majority of incoming flights from overseas and the US mainland arrive at **Honolulu International Airport** (HNL; ☑808-836-6411; http://hawaii.gov/hnl; 300 Rodgers Blvd; ☎), where travelers can then catch an interisland flight to Kaua'i. In Honolulu, you will pass through customs. Airlines flying directly to **Lihu'e Airport** (LIH; Map p88; ☑808-274-3800; http://hawaii.gov/lih; 3901 Mokulele Loop) from the US mainland and Canada include Alaska Airlines, American Airlines, Hawaiian Airlines, United Airlines and WestJet.

Note that you will pass through agricultural inspection on departure from Kaua'i.

CLIMATE CHANGE & TRAVEL

Every form of transport that relies on carbon-based fuel generates CO_2, the main cause of human-induced climate change. Modern travel is dependent on airplanes, which might use less fuel per kilometer per person than most cars but travel much greater distances. The altitude at which aircraft emit gases (including CO_2) and particles also contributes to their climate change impact. Many websites offer 'carbon calculators' that allow people to estimate the carbon emissions generated by their journey and, for those who wish to do so, to offset the impact of the greenhouse gases emitted with contributions to portfolios of climate-friendly initiatives throughout the world. Lonely Planet offsets the carbon footprint of all staff and author travel.

ROAD DISTANCES & TIMES

Average driving distances and times from Lihu'e are as follows. Allow more time during morning and afternoon rush hours and on weekends.

DESTINATION	MILES	TIME
Anahola	14	25min
Hanalei	31	55min
Hanapepe	18	30min
Kapa'a	11	20min
Ke'e Beach	39	1¼hr
Kilauea Lighthouse	25	40min
Koke'e State Park	42	1½hr
Po'ipu	14	25min
Port Allen	17	30min
Princeville	30	50min
Waimea	23	40min
Waimea Canyon	37	1¼hr

TRANSPORT OPTIONS

Book ahead for rental cars. Major car-rental agencies have booths outside Lihu'e Airport's baggage-claim area, with complimentary shuttles to off-airport parking lots. Taxis wait curbside, or you can use an airport courtesy phone to call one. Average fares from Lihu'e airport include Kapa'a ($25), Lihu'e ($10) and Po'ipu ($40 to $50). For families or groups, it may be more economical to book an airport shuttle with **Speedi Shuttle** (☑877-242-5777; www.speedishuttle.com).

TICKETS

Hawaii is a competitive market for US domestic and international airfares, which vary tremendously by season, day of the week and demand. Competition is highest among airlines flying to Honolulu from major US mainland cities, especially between Hawaiian Airlines and Alaska Airlines, while Allegiant Air serves smaller US regional airports.

The 'lowest fare' fluctuates constantly. In general, return fares from the US mainland to Hawaii cost from $400 (in low season from the West Coast) to $800 or more (in high season from the East Coast).

Departure tax is included in the price of a ticket.

Sea

The only commercial passenger vessels docking at Nawiliwili Harbor in Lihu'e are cruise ships, mainly **Norwegian Cruise Line** (NCL; ☑855-577-9489; www.ncl.com) and **Princess Cruises** (☑800-774-6237; www.princess.com).

GETTING AROUND

Car & Motorcycle

Major international car-rental companies have booths at Lihu'e Airport, with free shuttle buses running to off-airport parking lots nearby. Locally owned rental agencies **Kauai Car & Scooter Rental** (☑808-245-7177; www.kauaimopedrentals.com; 3148 Oihana St; ⏰8am-5pm) and **Kaua'i Harley-Davidson** (☑808-212-9495; www.kauaiharley.com; 3-1878 Kaumuali'i Hwy; ⏰8am-5pm) are located in Lihu'e, while **Rent a Car Kauai** (☑808-822-9272; www.rentacarkauai.com; 4-1101 Kuhio Hwy), based in Kapa'a on the Eastside, offers free airport pickups and drop-offs. Note that arriving on the island without reservations usually subjects you to higher rates and limited availability. Rental cars may be entirely sold out during peak travel times, so it's best to book ahead. Mix it up by renting a VW Westfalia Camper through **Kauai Camper Rental** (☑808-346-0957; www.kauaicamperrental.com).

If you have the money, definitely go for a 4WD (Jeep Wranglers being the most popular version on the island). Cars are sometimes prohibited by contract from traveling on dirt roads and will limit your exploration opportunities. That said, most roads are passable by regular car, as long as you go slow.

Kaua'i has a belt road running three-quarters of the way around the island, from Ke'e Beach in the north to near Polihale State Park in the west.

Driving Licenses

➡ An International Driving Permit (IDP), which must be obtained before you leave home, is necessary only if your country of origin is a non-English-speaking one.

➡ You need a valid motorcycle license to rent one, but a standard driving license will suffice for mopeds. The minimum age for renting a car is generally 25, though some agencies make exceptions; motorcycle is 21; for a moped, it's 18.

Insurance

➡ With the exception of remote areas such as Waimea Canyon Rd and the North Shore beyond Princeville, fuel is available everywhere, but expect to pay 20% more than on the mainland. Towing is also expensive and should be avoided at all costs. Fees start at around $65, plus $6.50 per mile.

Road Conditions, Hazards & Rules

➡ Kaua'i remains very rural, with only one coastal highway connecting all major destinations. It's hard to get lost for long.

➡ Highway congestion has been lessened by road-widening, but there is still rush-hour traffic, especially between Lihu'e and Kapa'a. To help combat this, a 'contra-flow' lane is created from 5am to 10:30am weekdays on Kuhio Hwy (Hwy 56) in the Wailua area; this turns a northbound lane into a southbound lane by reversing the flow of traffic.

➡ Stay alert for one-lane-bridge crossings. Whenever there's no sign on one-lane stretches, downhill traffic must yield to uphill traffic.

➡ While drivers do tend to speed on highways, in-town driving is courteous and rather leisurely. Locals don't honk (unless a crash is imminent), they don't tailgate and they let faster cars pass. Do the same.

➡ State law prohibits more than one rider per moped, as well as requiring that they be driven in single file at a maximum of 30mph. Also, mopeds are not to be driven on sidewalks or freeways, but rather on roads with lower speed limits or on the highway shoulder.

DIRECTIONS

Makai means 'toward the ocean'; *mauka* means 'toward the mountain.' Refer to highways by common name, not by number.

➡ The state requires helmets only for motorcycle or moped/scooter riders under the age of 18. Rental agencies provide free helmets for all riders: it's safer to use them.

Hitchhiking & Ride-Sharing

Hitchhiking is technically illegal statewide and hitch-hiking anywhere is not without risks. Lonely Planet does not recommend it. Hitchers should size up each situation carefully before getting in cars and women should be wary of hitching alone. People who do choose to hitchhike will be safer if they travel in pairs and let someone know where they are planning to go.

HIGHWAY NICKNAMES

Locals call highways by nickname rather than by number.

HIGHWAY	NICKNAME
Hwy 50	Kaumuali'i Hwy
Hwy 51	Kapule Hwy
Hwy 56	Kuhio Hwy
Hwy 58	Nawiliwili Rd
Hwy 520	Maluhia Rd (Tunnel of Trees)
Hwy 530	Koloa Rd
Hwy 540	Halewili Rd
Hwy 550	Waimea Canyon Dr & Koke'e Rd
Hwy 560	Kuhio Hwy (continuation of Hwy 56)
Hwy 570	Ahukini Rd
Hwy 580	Kuamo'o Rd
Hwy 581	Kamalu Rd & Olohena Rd
Hwy 583	Ma'alo Rd

Hitchhiking is not a common practice among locals. You're most likely to find a ride along the North Shore.

Taxi

The standard flag-fall fee is $3, plus 30¢ per additional 0.1 miles or up to 45 seconds of waiting; surcharges may apply for luggage, surfboards, wheelchairs and bicycles. Cabs line up at the airport during business hours, but they don't run all night or cruise for passengers. Elsewhere, you'll need to call ahead in advance. Most taxi companies operate islandwide, but it's usually faster to call one that's closer to your location.

➡ **Akiko's Taxi** (☎808-822-7588; www.akikostaxikauai. net; ⊙5am-10pm) Based in Lihu'e.

➡ **Kauai Taxi Company** (☎808-246-9554; http:// kauaitaxico.com) Based in Lihu'e.

➡ **North Shore Cab** (☎808-639-7829; www. northshorecab.com) Based in Kilauea.

➡ **Pono Taxi** (☎800-258-6880; www.ponotaxi.com) Based in Lihu'e.

➡ **South Shore Cab** (☎808-742-1525) Based in Po'ipu.

Behind the Scenes

SEND US YOUR FEEDBACK

We love to hear from travelers – your comments keep us on our toes and help make our books better. Our well-traveled team reads every word on what you loved or loathed about this book. Although we cannot reply individually to your submissions, we always guarantee that your feedback goes straight to the appropriate authors, in time for the next edition. Each person who sends us information is thanked in the next edition – the most useful submissions are rewarded with a selection of digital PDF chapters.

Visit **lonelyplanet.com/contact** to submit your updates and suggestions or to ask for help. Our award-winning website also features inspirational travel stories, news and discussions.

Note: We may edit, reproduce and incorporate your comments in Lonely Planet products such as guidebooks, websites and digital products, so let us know if you don't want your comments reproduced or your name acknowledged. For a copy of our privacy policy visit lonelyplanet.com/privacy.

WRITER THANKS

Greg Benchwick

Thanks the most to my darling daughter Violeta and sister Cara for accompanying me on this research trip. My intern Sylvia was a great help in finding the local scoop and diving into island life. And of course, my editor Alex and cowriter Adam are all-stars any day and everyday.

Adam Skolnick

Much aloha and *mahalo* to Taj Jure and Marc-Andre Gagnon, Jeffrey Courson, Susan Dierker, Camille Page and her whole lovely family, Derek Pellin, Gary Hooser, Andrea Brower, Michelle Marsh, Josh Meneley, John Moore and Jacklynn Evans. Thanks also to Alexander Howard, Greg Benchwick and the entire Lonely Planet team for the collaboration. And many *mahalos* to the Garden Island itself. You are home.

ACKNOWLEDGEMENTS

Climate map data adapted from Peel MC, Finlayson BL & McMahon TA (2007) 'Updated World Map of the Köppen-Geiger Climate Classification', Hydrology and Earth System Sciences, 11, 163344.

Cover photograph: Na Pali Coast, Brandon Verdoorn/500px ©

THIS BOOK

This 3rd edition of Lonely Planet's *Kaua'i* guidebook was researched and written by Greg Benchwick and Adam Skolnick and curated by Adam Karlin. The previous two Lonely Planet guides to Kaua'i were written by Sara Benson, Paul Stiles and E Clark Carroll. This guidebook was produced by the following:

Destination Editor
Alexander Howard

Product Editors
Rachel Rawling, Tracy Whitmey

Senior Cartographer
Corey Hutchison

Book Designer
Nicholas Colicchia

Assisting Editors
Imogen Bannister, Melanie Dankel, Kellie Langdon, Lou McGregor, Kristin Odijk, Maja Vatrić

Assisting Book Designers
Ania Bartoszek, Gwen Cotter

Cover Researcher
Naomi Parker

Thanks to
Kate Chapman, Joel Cotterell, Brendan Dempsey-Spencer, Kate Mathews, Clara Monitto, Wayne Murphy, Claire Naylor, Karyn Noble, Darren O'Connell, Lauren O'Connell, Martine Power, Kirsten Rawlings, Victoria Smith, Luna Soo, Angela Tinson, Tony Wheeler

Index

Map Legend

Sights

- Beach
- Bird Sanctuary
- Buddhist
- Castle/Palace
- Christian
- Confucian
- Hindu
- Islamic
- Jain
- Jewish
- Monument
- Museum/Gallery/Historic Building
- Ruin
- Shinto
- Sikh
- Taoist
- Winery/Vineyard
- Zoo/Wildlife Sanctuary
- Other Sight

Activities, Courses & Tours

- Bodysurfing
- Diving
- Canoeing/Kayaking
- Course/Tour
- Sento Hot Baths/Onsen
- Skiing
- Snorkeling
- Surfing
- Swimming/Pool
- Walking
- Windsurfing
- Other Activity

Sleeping

- Sleeping
- Camping

Eating

- Eating

Drinking & Nightlife

- Drinking & Nightlife
- Cafe

Entertainment

- Entertainment

Shopping

- Shopping

Information

- Bank
- Embassy/Consulate
- Hospital/Medical
- Internet
- Police
- Post Office
- Telephone
- Toilet
- Tourist Information
- Other Information

Geographic

- Beach
- Gate
- Hut/Shelter
- Lighthouse
- Lookout
- Mountain/Volcano
- Oasis
- Park
- Pass
- Picnic Area
- Waterfall

Population

- Capital (National)
- Capital (State/Province)
- City/Large Town
- Town/Village

Transport

- Airport
- BART station
- Border crossing
- Boston T station
- Bus
- Cable car/Funicular
- Cycling
- Ferry
- Metro/Muni station
- Monorail
- Parking
- Petrol station
- Subway/SkyTrain station
- Taxi
- Train station/Railway
- Tram
- Underground station
- Other Transport

Note: Not all symbols displayed above appear on the maps in this book

Routes

- Tollway
- Freeway
- Primary
- Secondary
- Tertiary
- Lane
- Unsealed road
- Road under construction
- Plaza/Mall
- Steps
- Tunnel
- Pedestrian overpass
- Walking Tour
- Walking Tour detour
- Path/Walking Trail

Boundaries

- International
- State/Province
- Disputed
- Regional/Suburb
- Marine Park
- Cliff
- Wall

Hydrography

- River, Creek
- Intermittent River
- Canal
- Water
- Dry/Salt/Intermittent Lake
- Reef

Areas

- Airport/Runway
- Beach/Desert
- Cemetery (Christian)
- Cemetery (Other)
- Glacier
- Mudflat
- Park/Forest
- Sight (Building)
- Sportsground
- Swamp/Mangrove

OUR STORY

A beat-up old car, a few dollars in the pocket and a sense of adventure. In 1972 that's all Tony and Maureen Wheeler needed for the trip of a lifetime – across Europe and Asia overland to Australia. It took several months, and at the end – broke but inspired – they sat at their kitchen table writing and stapling together their first travel guide, *Across Asia on the Cheap*. Within a week they'd sold 1500 copies. Lonely Planet was born.

Today, Lonely Planet has offices in Franklin, London, Melbourne, Oakland, Dublin, Beijing and Delhi, with more than 600 staff and writers. We share Tony's belief that 'a great guidebook should do three things: inform, educate and amuse'.

OUR WRITERS

Adam Karlin

Curator I am a Lonely Planet author based out of where I am. Born in Washington DC and raised in the rural Maryland tidewater, I've been exploring the world and writing about it since I was 17. It's a blessedly interesting way to live one's life. Also, it's good fun.

Greg Benchwick

Lihu'e, Po'ipu & the South Shore, Waimea Canyon & the Westside A long-time Lonely Planet travel writer, Greg has rumbled in the jungles of Bolivia, trekked across Spain on the Camino de Santiago, interviewed presidents and grammy-award winners, dodged flying salmon in Alaska and climbed mountains (big and small) in between. Greg's Lonely Planet work includes guides to Mexico, Yucatán, Cancún, Chile, Alaska, Colorado, Puerto Vallarta & Pacific Mexico, Honduras, Bolivia, Nicaragua, Ecuador, Peru, Malaysia, Kaua'i, USA, Southwest USA Trips, Central America on a Shoestring and South America on a Shoestring. He has also worked on Lonely Planet's reference books, including *Bluelist*, *USA Book* and *Great Adventures*.

Adam Skolnick

Kapa'a & the Eastside, Hanalei Bay & the North Shore Adam's travel obsession bloomed while working as an environmental activist in the mid '90s. These days he's an award-winning journalist and travel writer who writes about travel, culture, human rights, sports and the environment for a variety of publications, including the *New York Times*, *Playboy*, *Outside*, BBC.com, *Wired*, ESPN.com, and *Men's Health*, and he's authored or co-authored over 35 Lonely Planet guidebooks. An avid open-water swimmer and diver, he's also the author of the critically acclaimed narrative nonfiction book, *One Breath: Freediving, Death and the Quest to Shatter Human Limits*. He lives in Malibu, California.

Published by Lonely Planet Global Limited
CRN 554153
3rd edition – September 2017
ISBN 978 1 78657 706 1
© Lonely Planet 2017   Photographs © as indicated 2017
10 9 8 7 6 5 4 3 2 1
Printed in China